JOURNAL OF A ROUTE

JOURNAL OF A ROUTE

Across India, Through EGYPT,

TO

ENGLAND,

BY

LIEUTENANT-COLONEL FITZCLARENCE

GYAN

Published by

GYAN

Gyan Publishing House
5, Ansari Road
Daryaganj, New Delhi-110002
Phone: 011-47034999, 9811692060
E-mail: books@gyanbooks.com

Distribution Network
gyanbooks.com
India, USA, Canada, UK, Australia, France

ISBN : 978-81-212-1181-9 (PB)
First Published, 1819

2nd Impression 2021

Printed at: Gyan Press, Delhi.

Journal of A Route
Author: Lieutenant-Colonel Fitzclarence

JOURNAL

OF

A ROUTE

ACROSS INDIA, THROUGH EGYPT,

TO

ENGLAND,

IN THE

LATTER END OF THE YEAR 1817, AND THE BEGINNING OF 1818.

BY

LIEUTENANT-COLONEL FITZCLARENCE.

LONDON:

JOHN MURRAY, ALBEMARLE-STREET.

1819.

G Fitz Clarence del.

Engraved by R. Havell & Son.

PETTAH THE CITADEL & PETTAH OF DOWLUTABAD.

A Fortress belonging to the Nizam, near Aurungabad.

London Published April 1819, by John Murray, Albemarle Street.

DEDICATED, BY PERMISSION,

TO

His Royal Highness

THE PRINCE REGENT,

AS A

HUMBLE TOKEN

OF THE

GRATITUDE AND ATTACHMENT

OF

THE AUTHOR.

IT has been the object of the author of this work to convey to the public some information regarding the historical events of the late important contest in India, together with such reflections on our political and military relations in that quarter as occurred to his mind. In his personal narrative it has been his aim to add amusement to instruction; but the reader who wishes only to become acquainted with the more material incidents can easily separate them, by casting his eye on the contents of the different chapters. In describing customs and manners, he is sensible he may have incurred the imputation of prolixity; but in perusing works of this kind himself, he has, as he conceives, found that the various features and shades of character, whether of individuals or communities, were best depicted by a narrative of actual incidents, though in themselves of little or no general interest.

The author has to regret that the rapidity of his progress (unavoidable by the nature of his duty) should have prevented him from gratifying to the full his desire of research. He has no merit to claim but that of fidelity, and some share of industry, the matter being extracted from daily notes which he kept, and which the leisure of a long confinement from a severe accident, soon after his arrival in England, enabled him to arrange, and reduce to a shape which he now submits to the candid and indulgent reader.

London, April 12, 1819.

CONTENTS.

CHAPTER I.

THE SITUATION, MILITARY AND POLITICAL, OF INDIA AT THE OPENING OF THE CAMPAIGN.

CHAPTER II.

THE SITUATION, MILITARY AND POLITICAL, OF INDIA AT THE OPENING OF THE CAMPAIGN.

CHAPTER III.

THE SITUATION, MILITARY AND POLITICAL, OF INDIA AT THE OPENING OF THE CAMPAIGN.

CHAPTER IV.

INDIA—PERSONAL NARRATIVE.

CHAPTER V.

INDIA—PERSONAL NARRATIVE.

CHAPTER VI.

INDIA—PERSONAL NARRATIVE.

CHAPTER VII.

INDIA—PERSONAL NARRATIVE.

CHAPTER VIII.

INDIA—NARRATIVE OF EVENTS AT NAGPOOR.

CHAPTER IX.

INDIA—PERSONAL NARRATIVE.

CHAPTER X.

INDIA—PERSONAL NARRATIVE.

CHAPTER XI.

INDIA—PERSONAL NARRATIVE.

CHAPTER XII.

INDIA—PERSONAL NARRATIVE.

CHAPTER XIII.

INDIA—NARRATIVE OF THE OPERATIONS OF THE ARMY OF THE DEKHUN.

CHAPTER XIV.

INDIA—PERSONAL NARRATIVE.

CHAPTER XV.

INDIA—PERSONAL NARRATIVE.

CHAPTER XVI.

INDIA—PERSONAL NARRATIVE.

CHAPTER XVII.

INDIA—PERSONAL NARRATIVE.

CHAPTER XVIII.

INDIA—PERSONAL NARRATIVE.

CHAPTER XIX.

INDIA—PERSONAL NARRATIVE.

CHAPTER XX.

INDIA—NARRATIVE OF EVENTS AT POONAH.

CHAPTER XXI.

INDIA—NARRATIVE OF EVENTS AT POONAH.

CHAPTER XXII.

INDIA—PERSONAL NARRATIVE.

CHAPTER XXIII.

INDIA—PERSONAL NARRATIVE.

CHAPTER XXIV.

ON BOARD THE HONOURABLE COMPANY'S CRUISER MERCURY.

CHAPTER XXV.

ON BOARD THE HONOURABLE COMPANY'S CRUISER MERCURY.

CHAPTER XXVI.

EGYPT—PERSONAL NARRATIVE.

CHAPTER XXVII.

EGYPT—PERSONAL NARRATIVE.

CHAPTER XXVIII.

EGYPT—PERSONAL NARRATIVE.

CHAPTER XXIX.

EGYPT—PERSONAL NARRATIVE.

CHAPTER XXX.

EGYPT—PERSONAL NARRATIVE.

CHAPTER XXXI.

EGYPT—PERSONAL NARRATIVE.

CHAPTER XXXII.

EGYPT—PERSONAL NARRATIVE.

CHAPTER XXXIII.

EGYPT—PERSONAL NARRATIVE.

CHAPTER XXXIV.

MEDITERRANEAN—ACCOUNT OF THE INTERIOR OF AFRICA.

JOURNAL

OF

A ROUTE

ACROSS INDIA, THROUGH EGYPT, TO ENGLAND,

IN THE

LATTER END OF THE YEAR 1817, AND THE BEGINNING OF 1818.

CHAPTER I.

Predatory system in India—The invasion of the Company's territory by the Pindarries—Their atrocities—Severe loss to the revenue—Political effect on India—The British government bound by treaties to destroy them—Their origin and history—Etymology of the name Pindarry—Rise—Mentioned as early as 1689—Assist at the battle of Paniput, 1761—Their increase—Numbers in 1804—Numbers in 1809—Numbers in 1811—Formerly divided into great tribes—Scindiah Shaee—Holkar Shaee—Lately divided into three durrahs—those of Chetoo, of Wussul Mehumed, and Kureem Khan—Possessions of the first, of the second, of the last—Form in truth an inferior state, with an immense military population—Cruelties—Natives destroy themselves in preference to enduring their barbarities—Plunder, marches, and arms—Rights of the chiefs—They draw on them the displeasure of the British government—Painful reflections on the conduct of the Native governments to their subjects—Determination of the British government to extirpate them—Governor-general quits Calcutta for the upper provinces—Advantages of his presence in the field—The whole British Army in India take the field—Reasons for that measure—Wretched policy of the Mharattas—Contrast between the British and Native governments—The Governor-general arrives at Khanpoor.

THE horrid predatory system which has so long desolated India with the ravages of an active banditti, formed of the refuse of all countries and religions, and presenting the uncommon spectacle of a community of robbers (exceeding in numbers any of which history furnishes an example), yet permitted to exist in the neighbourhood of states which made no attempt to eradicate them, was an anomaly in the political world. It early drew the attention of the Governor-general, as being an increasing evil subversive of all order; and the necessity of crushing it was more forcibly evinced by the repeated ravages of our territory within these last three years. This became the more urgent as the confederation annually gained strength, and it was highly requisite to prevent their rising into a great power, not only positively, by the increase of their numbers, but relatively, by our becoming weaker in common with our allies, through the damage sustained in our revenue and resources by their various incursions and spoliations. Examples are not wanting of a similar association becoming a powerful state: that of the Mharattas is in point. Their great founder Sevajee, from being only a landholder, opposed the whole power of Aurungzebe, and secured his estates and conquests by predatory inroads into those of his neighbours. In time the Pindarries would have settled in the countries, which they had previously contented themselves with plundering; and we should have had fresh dynasties and governments arise, like those of the Bhoonslah, Scindiah, Holkar, and the Gwykwar. The Pindarries had in 1812, 1816, and 1817, "rushed like a torrent" upon the provinces of Mirzapoor, Guntoor, and Gangam, all in our possession, and with the barbarity so common, I may almost say so universal among them, had committed the most cruel and wanton excesses on our subjects. Their atrocities were so great, that although their principal object was plunder, yet in a society so depraved, and "respecting neither the laws of God nor man," pillage was often the least unjustifiable act which they perpetrated.

It must be recollected, and duly felt, that the natives of our provinces in India are equally the subjects of the King of Great Britain, with those of Canada or the West Indies; and that the official persons on the spot, who hold his delegated authority, are bound to protect those who look up to them for the security of themselves and property. It was therefore our most sacred duty to shield them as much as possible from further ravages and misery; and this desirable and highly necessary object was only to be attained by extirpating in their very haunts the growing hordes, which had so far advanced towards becoming an integral state, that their rising strength could not be repressed by any native power, and it was only under our strong arm that the peaceful agriculturists could hope for protection from their incursions. They had for many years levied at pleasure the resources of our allies, by plundering their ryots*; and the consequent loss of revenue was even greater than what they actually destroyed or carried off, as the peasants, for many miles on each side of their devastated track (which can only be compared to that of a flight of locusts, leaving all behind them a dreary waste), excused themselves from paying their arrears to government, under the pretence of having suffered by the invasion. It was impossible to learn the real extent or limits of the mischief, since it was so much the interest of the farmer to exaggerate it. Even had these desperate robbers not crossed our frontier, still so vitiated a state of society must soon have affected the population of our dominions; and we must, earlier or later, have felt the disorganization arising from so corrupt a system, which would in time have poisoned all India, and had even already shaken all regular government and established order: an effect produced not more by these spoliations, than by the convulsions they occasioned and fostered, in offering an asylum to criminals and offenders of every description.

But putting aside all these weighty reasons, we were bound by the several offensive and defensive treaties we had formed with the various states of India, to secure their territories, in common with our own, from all violent aggressions; and so severely had the state

* Subjects, and throughout India more generally used for agriculturists.

of Nagpoor suffered from these depredators, that they were distinctly mentioned and introduced by name into the subsidiary treaty* of the 27th of May, 1816, by which we guaranteed the security of his dominions to the Rajah from all nations, including the Pindarries.

Before proceeding, it may be convenient to give as distinct an account as possible of these freebooters, whose very name was unknown a few years since in England, and whose rapid rise to importance must have surprised all, but more especially those, who not having read Indian history, or made themselves masters of Eastern politics, and judging of both on European data, would almost doubt the possible existence of so perverted a state of society. They may be compared to the bands led by the Condottieri of Italy in the middle ages; and had it been customary to have rewarded these with grants of land, as is done in India by jaghires†, it is possible, that by gaining territorial possession and establishing themselves as organised robbers, they might have become as formidable to Europe as the Pindarries have to the governments of India.

The history of this army of freebooters affords a curious instance of a settlement of outlaws, growing into a real power; and in all probability an example of what, in an early stage of society, was the germ of many a state; and every reader will naturally apply it to the embryo age of Rome. Several etymologies of Pindarry have been suggested, but the most probable is that which traces it from Pind, *plunder*, in the ancient Hindee. Their origin, like that of most nations, is in great measure wrapt in obscurity. They are said to be mentioned by Ferishta as early as 1689, at the siege of Bejapoor. We find that in 1722 the province of Malwa was overrun with banditti, and it was deemed necessary to employ an officer of rank to clear it, particularly the districts of Chanderi. And we further learn that about the same period, Nuzzur Alli Khan, who was on

* Laid before parliament.

† Landed estates.

his way to take possession of the government of Khandeish, on arriving at Seronj, was obliged to send to Aurungabad for a guard to escort him through certain difficult passes, rendered dangerous by these freebooters. From these two circumstances, particularly the latter, which describes the Pindarry country, as it existed in 1817 (the route of this chief to Aurungabad, across the Nerbuddah, either by Hindiah, or Choolee Mehissur, lying directly through the difficult and strong country below the Ghauts), it would appear that some lawless community was settled here at that early period. They do not, however, make any considerable figure in history till 1761, when they assisted on the unsuccessful side at the battle of Paniput, so fatal to the Mharattas; and the only distinct account of a prior date is that of the head of one of the present durrahs (a Hindee word, meaning a collective body), who traces his ancestry back to a chief named Ghauzee-ou-Deen-Khan, the commander of a body of horse, who accompanied and served under Bajerow, the first usurping Peishwah, on an expedition into Hindostan, A. D. 1735. This chief received as a reward for his assistance a jaghire, or grant of land on the Nerbuddah, at Canonga. On the death of Ghauzee-ou-Deen-Khan, the leaders of his durrah are supposed to have set up for themselves, and their numbers are stated to have been considerable. A son of Ghauzee-ou-Deen-Khan was killed in the service of Runojee Scindiah in Hindostan, and was succeeded in his command of horse by two sons, upon whom Madojee Scindiah bestowed for their services the jaghire of Sutwas, near the Nerbuddah, but at present it appears to have passed from the family. These again left two sons, Dost Mehumed, and Wussul Mehumed; the former is lately dead, and is succeeded by his son, a minor, under the guardianship of his uncle, who has charge of the durrah. In 1794 a large community of Pindarries was settled on the Nerbuddah. After the battle of Kurdlah, in 1795, taking advantage of the weakness and wars of the neighbouring states, they rose greatly in power, and since 1803 have made very rapid strides towards independence. In 1804, when General Malcolm was at Scindiah's head-quarters, he estimated the Pindarries in camp at about 10,000 men, which was by no means their whole force: out of this number about 6000 were admirably mounted. In 1809 they were estimated at 24,500 men, of whom about 14,000 were good cavalry; in 1811 they were about 26,000, with a like proportion of valuable horses, and of late years they have continued to increase considerably in numbers. Previous to the beginning of this century, they looked up to Scindiah and Holkar as their superior chiefs, and were divided into two great tribes, one called the Scindiah Shaee, and the other the Holkar Shaee. The exact meaning of the word shaee is not known, but the body guard of the kings of Delhi were called Allah Shaees and Valla Shaees; the latter of whom were musqueteers. Each Shaee had distinct standards. The Scindiah Shaee had the Bhugwah-colour, the same as that used by the Mharattas, between red and orange, with a white snake in the middle. This Shaee had also 100 hircarrahs or scouts, with sticks mounted with snakes' heads in silver. The Holkar Shaee had for its standards stripes alternately of black, white, and blue; and each leader in both tribes had small flags called Lugges. They have, however, of late years, separated into three principal durrahs, those of Chetoo, or Setoo, Wussul Mehumed, and Kureem Khan. Setoo is said to be the son of a Jhat, and is represented as being very hostile towards Kureem. Kureem Khan is a Mahometan, and of Wussul Mehumed we have already spoken. Setoo held very considerable jaghires from Scindiah, and had in 1811 established a foundery of cannon. He had in his pay a large number of hircarrahs, to procure intelligence; but the valour of this durrah was never so much respected as that of Kureem. Setoo had also several elephants. The towns and adjacent lands occupied by his durrah were Sutwas, Tuleyn, Nemawur, Rajore, Hurringaon, Chippanier, Gopalpoor, Kantifoor, Oochonda,

Sudellpoor, Tomree, and Kumnas; and the principal station was at Nemawur. This chief could muster about 10,000 horse. The durrah of Wussul Mehumed consisted of about 8000 horse, 800 infantry, and some guns, and held the following places and adjoining lands—Bagrode, Damnode, Tunde, Russulpoor, Packrone, Serwasse, Karewye, Oodipoor, and Gunge Bassouda. Kureem Khan is a chief of considerable ability, and some years ago organized a small independent territory, and held Seharangpoor, Koshalpoor, and several other possessions. His name and character have done much to recruit his durrah. He had above 10,000 horse and 1000 infantry, and held the Punj Mehals, consisting of Ashta, Techore, Doraha, Deviporah, and Sehore, besides Koraud, Kuganir, and Burseah. In addition to these, there are several inferior chiefs. Thus these freebooters, from many causes and by degrees, had accumulated a force of perhaps 40,000 horse, and differed from other associations of plunderers, in having a small territory, which had been granted to their chiefs by several of the princes in the neighbourhood and by former leaders of the Mharatta armies, as a reward for their services, so that, in reality, they formed an inferior state, with an immense military population, daily and rapidly increasing. The irregular soldiery of India, having looked upon war as their profession for so many years, did not find employment during the long peace since 1803, 4, and 5, but despising an agricultural life, hastened to swell the ranks of these marauders; and from the enfeebled state of the Mharatta powers, in consequence of their defeats in 1803, and subsequently in 1805, they have not had the means to check this new confederacy, which had become to these states a dangerous neighbour, though, in the event of a rupture with us, an acceptable reinforcement. The collective territory of the Pindarries was situated to the north of the river Nerbuddah, extending from the west of the possessions of the ruler of Sorger, along its banks, to the north of what little country remained to the Newab of Bopaul. Its utmost length was a hundred miles, and its breadth, including the Punj Mehals, in some places forty miles. The Punj Mehals were nominally held in jaghire by the Vinchoor-Kur of his highness the Peishwah. These lawless wretches consisted of almost every sect of Hindoos and Mahometans in India, and from their vicious feelings and habits, they received with open arms any disbanded soldier, disaffected subject, needy adventurer, or criminal flying from justice, who directly became Pindarries. The history of the world cannot, I suppose, produce a more diabolical association: they fattened on the miseries of others, and laid whole kingdoms under contribution. As soon as the river Nerbuddah became fordable, generally in November (which river alone presented a barrier to them from June to October), and the khereef, or autumn harvest, was off the ground, they sallied forth to rob both friends and foes, and their ravages extended many hundred miles from their homes, where they left their wives and families guarded by their infantry. But previous to 1812 it had only been the country of our allies which suffered from their depredations. In that year they plundered part of the province of Mirzapoor, and threatened the town of the same name, one of the greatest commercial marts in our dominions, which, situated on the Ganges, receives from the south the merchandize of the European market and of Bengal, and from the north the produce of Cashmeer, the Punjab, and Hindoostan; and supplies these to our own provinces, the provinces of the Newab Vizier, and of the Mharattas, through Bogulcund. In 1816 they fell upon the province of Guntoor, and their atrocities cannot be better expressed than in the words of an official paper laid before parliament: "Their spoliations are marked with the most savage barbarity; every village which they have pillaged contains victims of their fury, and a few hamlets only have escaped their destructive rage." The state of wretchedness in which the sufferers were left, from the destruction of their property, and the inhuman cruelty of the invaders, is said "to have exhibited a picture of the most consummate misery that ever was witnessed." This incursion being above six hundred miles from their settlements, proves how much more extensive and enterprising their luhbers became from continual success, and it is difficult to say where they would have stopped, had not their devastations drawn on them our strong and retributive arm. Luhber, it may be observed, is the term they use for one of these expeditions, and the chief who commands it is designated a Luhberee; a Thokdar is the name they give to a chief who commands from above 500 horse to 1000; a leader who commands above 100 to 500, is a Muhaldar; and an inferior to these, a Foyjewallah. The surprising velocity with which they moved, certainly quicker than any other cavalry in the world, enabled them generally to evade pursuit. Having no tents or baggage, they would, at a moderate calculation, march one hundred miles in two days, three hundred in a week, and five hundred in a fortnight; but when pushed for time or by circumstances, they moved inconceivably faster. From the horrid scenes of human misery which they continually contemplated, and in which they were actors, they became cruel and sanguinary in the highest degree; and, hardened to all commiseration, they never scrupled as to the means by which they procured money. When they sacked a village, they put the inhabitants to various tortures, to force them to discover their little hoards, and, giving loose to their sensual appetites, ravished the women, often punishing with death those who offered any resistance: the Hindoo women, too, from an idea of contamination and shame, frequently drowned themselves in wells after being violated. They had even so far extinguished the feelings of men, as on some occasions with a demoniac fury to cut off the womens' breasts; and it was not an unusual practice to cut off the hands of children, as the shortest way of procuring the bracelets from their arms.

Each man furnished himself and horse with provisions during the expedition, trusting much of course to what might be found;

and what they did not consume in a village, they generally destroyed, and not uncommonly burned the houses: indeed many of their excesses appear to have been without any other motive than a malignant spirit of destruction. But to give at once an idea of the dread which their approach inspired, it will only be necessary to state a single example. At the time of their invasion of Guntoor the inhabitants of a village called Ainavole, rather than encounter their well known cruelties and persecutions, and submit to the violation of their wives and daughters, unanimously resolved, with a firmness and resolution not unusual amongst the Hindoos, to sacrifice themselves and their families; and when their resistance was proved to be unavailing, they performed the *joar*, by setting fire to their habitations, and perishing themselves with their wives and children in the flames, in one common funeral pile. This noble and exalted instance of honourable sentiment must interest British feelings for the future security and domestic happiness of the kinsmen of these victims, and loudly called on us to annihilate with an avenging sword the detested cause of so high-minded a sacrifice.

To carry off their plunder, the Pindarries had sometimes relays of ponies and bullocks, but the most valuable part they secured about their persons. If they were closely pursued they dispersed, and thus escaped; but if not pressed they did not march above thirty or forty miles a day. They shod their horses before they set out; and to make them undergo the greater fatigue, supported them with opium and spices. They generally halted in the middle of the day, and rested half the night. During the rains they never went from their homes, looking upon that season as a time of repose; and but seldom crossed the Nerbuddah after May, for fear of its rising, and cutting off their retreat*. The ruin they spread on all sides could not be more strongly marked than by the increase of their numbers during

* The early Mharatta armies, in their plundering excursions to the southward, paid a like deference to the river Kishna.

these expeditions; for the inhabitants whom they had plundered, seeing no future security for the property of which they might again be possessed, were driven by want and despair to join the robbers, and in their turn attempt to repair their losses by plundering their neighbours*.

The Pindarries were generally armed with a spear, twelve feet long, and, like all the Indian cavalry, very dexterous in its use. Matchlocks were not common amongst them, and it is supposed, that out of every five men, two were fighting men, two others mere plunderers, mounted on inferior horses, and the remaining one on a pony, armed with a sword or spear. They obey and look up to their chiefs, who have household troops or men in whom they can confide in their own pay, and mounted on their own horses. All elephants, palanqueens, and umbrellas which fell into their hands, were claimed by these chiefs; but it is not known how they divided the rest of their plunder†. It was difficult to obtain correct intelligence respecting the direction of their march; and it was but seldom they were heard of, till the scattered villagers, wounded and abused, brought the first information of the conflagration of their houses, and the loss of their all. At times, however, they have had the misfortune to fall in with our cavalry, who were annually in the field to intercept them, and have suffered very severely; but this did not deter them from continuing their flagitious practices.

But at length their crimes drew on them the notice of a government which felt for those under its charge, and possessed the inclination and the means to rid the earth of such a curse; and happy was it for India that such a power existed, as it would never have

* Dow gives us an instance of this: when Chusero, son of Jehan Ghuir, rebelled and burnt the suburb of Delhi in 1606, many, to retrieve their affairs, joined him to make reprisals on the world for the loss which they had sustained.

† During the time of the Mahometan conquests, all elephants taken in war belonged to the King of Delhi.

entered into the mind of a native prince to have undertaken a war solely from motives of benevolence and protection to his subjects, without the prospect of increase of dominion or accumulation of wealth; neither of which could accrue on this occasion. It would indeed be a novel era in native politics for the resources derived from the subjects to be turned to their advantage by their rulers; for, in general, the means furnished by the people to the prince or governor only tend by an increase of wealth to nourish ambition, the generator of war and of desolation to the country of the unhappy ryot; and it has been experienced that whenever a short period of tranquillity ensued, the accumulation of revenue was invariably the forerunner of internal or foreign commotions, and of renewed misery.

Our government, having seen in this point of view the unsettled state of central India, determined to carry into execution plans for the permanent establishment of order; and with this upright and humane intention the governor-general deemed his presence necessary in the upper provinces of the Bengal presidency, in order to be in the vicinity of the troops who were to take possession of the Pindarry country; to approximate in person the independent states of central and western India, and overawe their turbulent durbars during the operations in the ensuing cold weather; and finally to compel them to take active measures in co-operation with ourselves against this scourge. In so extensive a country, unless all the states were of one mind and feeling, it was not in our power to accomplish the object in view, since, by shifting from one country to another, and joining for the time the cavalry of a native prince (who are not distinguished by any uniform), the Pindarries would elude pursuit, and it would be impossible to avoid identifying them with the troops of these sovereigns, as in India the native sirdars of 500 or 1000 horse keep only half that number in full pay, and from a fellow-feeling would screen them from our just vengeance.

The Marquis of Hastings, with his suite, quitted Calcutta on the

8th of July, 1817, on board his boats, and proceeded up the Ganges. By his being immediately near the scene of operations, in the double capacity of governor-general and commander-in-chief, he carried with him in his own person the general controlling power over the vast collective strength and energy of our Indian empire. In the first of these high stations (in addition to other advantages) he prevented references to Calcutta on political questions, so likely to produce those dangerous delays often brought about by the native powers, it being their policy to protract negotiations till the short period for active operations should be passed, and thus save themselves during one year from the probable consequences. If there was any chance of indecision, or fear of responsibility in inferior agents, this was equally done away by the governor-general, in his controlling character, moving from a distant to a central and commanding situation. His lordship, in his comprehensive military capacity, superintended the necessary warlike preparations and combinations which went hand in hand with the political arrangements. His presence in the field also added vigour to all departments, and the equipments of the army being formed under his own eye, it entered on service in that efficient state, in which it ought ever to be in a country where the ascendancy of a government can only be sustained by the relative superiority of its troops over those of the neighbouring powers. The plan of operations, and the organization of the movements, perhaps on as extensive a scale as in any former scene of action, had been concerted with the presidencies of Madras and Bombay: and the military force of both was ordered into the field. His lordship had instructed Lieutenant-General Sir Thomas Hislop, commander of the forces at Madras, to take the command of the general military and political dispositions and negotiations in the Dekhun, and Sir John Malcolm had been appointed the governor-general's political agent, with Major Agnew as his assistant, in his (Sir Thomas's) camp. It may appear at first almost inexplicable, that it should require the whole force of the three presidencies to be drawn forth for the subversion of a band of robbers. But on consideration it will appear necessary, when the very uncertain state of politics in India is recollected, and the extreme want of faith of the native courts, added to the possibility of the Mharattas (by a most ruinous policy) looking upon the Pindarries as a disposable force, ever ready to enter into their service on regular pay; so that without being at any expense till absolutely wanted, they might have a body of cavalry ready to recruit and complete their armies. It is probable that this feeling may even have made them anxious that these hordes should not be exterminated, though at times suffering dreadfully from their incursions. These reasons, together with a knowledge of the naturally jealous feeling towards our extensive possessions and influence on the part of the native sovereigns, and of the turbulent spirits in their courts, ever wishing for innovations, rendered it expedient that our troops should be early in the field in order to prevent or meet any hostility, and at the same time to cover our provinces and those of our allies from the violent and desperate acts of these tribes in their flight from our light pursuing detachments.

In contemplating these incidents one cannot help cherishing some pride on comparing, or rather contrasting, the principles and practice of the British government with those of the native princes. We behold the latter exercising the powers of dominion as if the sole object of government were to extort whatever they could by oppressive imposts, and to employ men and money merely as instruments for promoting their ambition, personal aggrandizement, luxury, and ostentation; not disdaining even to encourage these savage freebooters to promote their ends. Such is the general picture of the governments of India since the Mogul empire fell to pieces. On the other hand, we observe the British government never losing sight of what is the rational end of all government, protection. The ignorant and captious in England hold a very different opinion; but from what I have heard and seen on the spot, our rulers have never neglected those sacred duties of moderation and protection which are due from the governing to the governed, nor forgot that justice, honour, and good faith, are equally matter of good policy as of humanity; inasmuch as it is by these qualities only that the confidence, respect, and affection of our native subjects can be secured, and a permanent ascendancy in India maintained. Acting in conformity with these principles, the British government could not, like the native powers, regard with indifference the enormities of these congregated hordes in the commission of acts incompatible with the existence of society; and to have employed them even against an enemy would have been abhorrent to every sentiment of a civilized nation. It was therefore decided to coerce and put them down, at whatever cost.

The governor-general continued his voyage up the Ganges as high as Khanpoor, where he arrived on the 13th of September.

I shall now be obliged to enter upon an undertaking to which I feel diffident of being able to do due justice: it is to depict the state of India before the opening of the campaign. I should hope, however, to convey to the mind of my reader its true situation in a general point of view, without entering into minute detail, and carefully avoiding all political discussions and opinions except such as must arise out of the matters of fact which I have to relate. I shall therefore commence by briefly enumerating the several powers composing the vast community of India. Though distrusting my own abilities, yet having resided three years in the country, where I hope I have not been an idle observer; and having been upon the spot during the late operations, I will not shrink from the task; begging it may at the same time be understood that what I advance is founded solely on my own feelings, opinions, or belief.

CHAPTER II.

State of India in October and November 1817—Long peace in India—British government left by the war of 1805 the most powerful in India, after the defeat of the Mharattas—British army stands higher than ever in the opinion of the natives since the Nepaul war—Improvements—Rajah of Nagpoor receives a subsidiary force—Fall of the fort of Hattrass—The Peishwah's conduct—Trimbukjee—The Shastry, the Gwykwar's minister—Scindiah—The Peishwah—Holkar—Rajah of Nagpoor, Gwykwar—Rajahpootana Biecaneer—Jesselmeer—Jeypoor—Joudpoor—Oodipoor—Other powers of inferior importance—The Nizam—Mysore—Smaller states—Probability of the destruction of the Pindarries at the commencement of the cold weather—Satisfactory language of the native courts.

INDIA had enjoyed since 1805 a comparative state of peace (the contest with the Gorkahs being at a distance from any of the other native powers, between whom and the seat of war the whole width of our territory interposed), which it had little known for near one hundred years, that is, from the death of Aurungzebe in 1707; and it was hoped that by our reduction of the predatory system, the security and tranquillity of the empire would not only be improved, but placed beyond the chance of being disturbed.

Thus were these operations commenced on a principle, which it would have been happy for the world to have recognised at all times as the sole motive for war, that of pure philanthropy, and ultimate good towards the whole of India, and not the desire of conquest, or lust of power. This war had no object but that of exterminating the enemies of all mankind, who, by their villanies, had placed themselves out of the pale of society; and our exertions, on this occasion, ought to stand recorded in the page of our history, with the expedition to Algiers, as a memorable instance of noble and generous feeling, to which it would be difficult to find another parallel.

The wars of 1803 and 1805 had left the British power paramount

C. Fitz-Clarence del.   Engraved by R. Havell & Son

GORKAH SOLDIER.

London, Published April 1819 by John Murray, Albemarle Street.

in India, yet the policy of the latter period had induced us to give up many of the advantages we had gained, and the long subsequent peace had in some measure weakened us. Before the period of the Nepaul war, the native powers, having forgot the first smart of their disastrous conflicts with us, had begun to hold very high language. The very forbearing hand and pacific policy of the preceding government had not been viewed by them in a proper light, but rather inspired the hope that what had really originated in our mildness and moderation might have been caused by weakness or timidity.

The British army, from a long continuance of peace, in a relaxing and enervating climate, and the misfortunes at the beginning of the Nepaul war, felt the necessity of exertion, after long inactivity; and the advantage of the fresh impetus received from the commander in chief was speedily demonstrated in the happy termination of that war; and in the autumn of 1817 the Bengal army was, perhaps, in as efficient a state as could be desired. The Madras and Bombay armies were equally prepared for service. The success which crowned the Nepaul campaign raised the British forces higher than ever in the opinion of the natives, for all the Mahometan invaders had been invariably defeated in their attempts to penetrate the hills, as much from the difficulty of the country as the hardy character of these eastern highlanders; and the native princes again saw enforced the vigorous policy so requisite in India, of never allowing an insult or encroachment to be passed over unpunished. The authority and power of our government being thus proved, and the high and commanding condition of our army displayed before all India; within the following sixteen months, three most important improvements took place in our political situation. The rajah of Nagpoor died in 1816. He had been our enemy in 1803, and was defeated by us, but did not receive a subsidiary force, and consequently this state remained an independent sovereignty; but on his death his successor received, in May the same year, a subsidiary force, so that he had become, in a certain degree, dependant on us. The circumstances connected with the fall of Hattrass, and the causes which led to the indispensable expulsion of Diah-Ram, though in themselves of small importance, made a deep impression; and the means employed against the fort constituted a new epoch in the military world in India. By the complete success attendant on the bombardment of this place, the hitherto formidable character of the native forts was reduced to a very low standard, and the effects were felt over the whole of our empire, as the native powers, who have not of late years succeeded in making or using shells (with the exception of Nepaul, and, I believe, more as an experiment than any thing else), hold them in the utmost dread; and any hope they might have entertained of a successful defence against us from their fortifications, after failing in the field, must have disappeared;—thus, in the short space of fifteen hours, vanished the phantom which had held its ground so many years in India.

The last of these improvements to which we have alluded was occasioned by the Peishwah's inconsiderate, unjustifiable, and depraved conduct in supporting his former favourite and minister Trimbukjee Dinglia, by which he brought on himself the displeasure of the British government, which could not overlook his want of good faith.

This favourite was the murderer of the Shastry (the Gwykwar's vaqueel), and had been imprisoned by us at Tannah for that crime, whence he had subsequently effected his escape. His highness's conduct in this instance more than ever confirmed a suspicion, which had not been formed without good reason, of his participation in the crime, as it was conceived he connived at the escape of the criminal. But subsequent to this we had accepted his assurances as evidence of his not being concerned in the latter; and cordiality seemed to prevail between him and the British govern-

G. Fitz Clarence del.

Engraved by R. Havell & Son

HATTRASS.

The Fort of Diah Ram, 1817

London, Published April 1819, by John Murray, Albemarle Street.

ment. We had in consequence given him some marks of the utmost confidence respecting our intentions for the reduction of the Pindarries, and the negotiations pending with Dowlut Rao Scindiah on that subject; and there was no measure or proceeding of the British government either in contemplation or progress, which could have tended, in the remotest degree, to alarm or irritate his highness's mind*. But with this appearance of tranquillity it was early discovered from the recruiting of the Peishwah's army, even in the city of Poonah itself; from the rising of a mock insurrection headed by Trimbukjee, within fifty miles of the capital, without any attempt on the part of the Peishwah to check it; from all the supplies taken from the country being regularly paid for, which was totally inconsistent with the conduct of rebels; and from the common belief through his dominions that his highness was concerned, that it was his intention to commence hostilities against us with the immediate object of compelling us, by intimidation or force, to admit the restoration of Trimbukjee to power, and, probably, with yet more extensive views. All these facts could not escape the observation of our resident, and our government being thus certain of his inimical intentions, took means, by surrounding Poonah, his capital, to bring his highness to reason, and force him to sign a treaty in June†, which reduced his strength by valuable cessions of territory, and other important points. After this it was hoped, if any faith could be placed in solemn treaties, that the Mharatta confederation was dissolved, an object the most to be desired in Indian politics. From all these acquisitions to our eastern empire, and our pecuniary resources being most abundant, it will not be thought too much to assert, that never did the British in India stand in a situation of more decided superiority than in the autumn of 1817.

The most simple manner of stating the reciprocal connexion,

* See papers laid before parliament.

† Laid before parliament.

feeling, and position of our government with regard to the native powers, and their relative situation to each other, will be to describe the condition and resources of each state; commencing with the most powerful and independent, and descending to those whose very existence depends on our moderation and justice.

The first, and most prominent, not only for his military strength, but for character, stood Dowlut Rao Scindiah, who, though he had been unsuccessful against us in a former war, had not been induced, like several others of the Mharatta powers, to receive in the heart of his country a subsidiary force; and so far from having any part of his military strength at our disposal, he had a very considerable army disciplined after our manner, totally independent of us, and could boast a large train of artillery. His army, it might be supposed from inactivity and loss of European officers, none of whom were permitted by the treaty to remain in his service, would have become undisciplined and disorganized; but he had in his service a half cast French officer, and some Armenians, and his troops, having been engaged in several intestine disturbances and partial affairs, had kept up their military appearances and feeling. Scindiah held very large possessions in Malwa, Khandeish, Mewyar, and Agimeer; and although the revenue was not very productive, from faults of government and collection, he was supposed to be individually very rich. He was from these causes, and above all from his independent character, looked up to as their only rallying point by all those who were discontented and jealous of the high situation of the British government; but the feeling towards him cannot be more aptly illustrated than by mentioning that a chief of one of the small independent states of Bundelcund, who had been taken under our protection from that of the Peishwah, sent to Scindiah to know how he was to act. Scindiah had for several years established his headquarters in tents under the walls of Gualior, one of the forts we delivered up to him in 1805, within one hundred miles of our frontier; and at this place had under his own command 5000 horse, and 3000 infantry; besides 1500 horse and 3000 infantry with the Soubidar of the province. The rest of his army was posted as follows: Colonel Baptiste, the French half cast, had the largest command under the Maha Rajah himself; his head-quarters were established at Behadur Ghur near Runnode; his force was not collected, being scattered over a considerable tract of country. It consisted of eleven battalions, of which four were Telingas (troops, armed, clothed, and disciplined like our Sepoys), the rest Allygoles and Nejeebs (irregulars); the highest average of these battalions might be 500 men each, in all 5500; and he had also 1000 horse. Bapojee Scindiah was posted at Agimeer. His troops consisted of 3000 horse and 2000 foot. Jeswunt Row Bhow was at Jawud with 1500 horse and 2000 infantry. Ambajee Punt was posted at Budrawar or Budnawar to the west of Oojein, not far from Dhar, in command of 1500 horse and 2000 infantry. Anna Buckshee was posted at Shahjehanpoor with about 1000 horse and 1000 infantry. There is reason to believe, therefore, that the force of this Prince did not exceed 16,000 horse and 18,000 infantry. Four field pieces were attached to each battalion, but sometimes five; and in all he had not less than one hundred and thirty-seven field guns, and the Goulandauze attached to them were very efficient artillerymen. He might have increased his army to a higher amount, with irregular infantry and cavalry, by giving out that he required them to oppose us, for in this country men are always to be had for money.

By a reference to the map it will be seen that much time would have been required to collect the scattered divisions of his troops; and up to the period of the arrival of the governor-general at Khanpoor, no movement had taken place among them. It was believed that Scindiah felt his true situation, and the impossibility of coping with us with any chance of success; and that however he might dread to lose his military character, or the high opinion he held in the estimation of all Hindostan, by subscribing to our wishes, yet it was most sanguinely expected he would find it necessary to fall into our views. But there could be no doubt that his feelings and pride would be much hurt at the very serious and important points he would have to concede on his part; and when the state of his court, which was a military camp, was considered, it was impossible to judge how he might be obliged to act. The movement of the governor-general into Hindostan must have satisfied Scindiah, however, of our determination to carry into effect what had been stated to him by our resident; and by his remaining at Gualior every hope was entertained of his acquiescence. He was nevertheless currently reported to be carrying on a correspondence of more than a suspicious nature with the other powers, yet no open acts, nor even preparations, appeared to evince an intention of breaking with us, and his assurances were of the most satisfactory kind. His real feelings, congenial with those of nearly all the other states, could not, from the peculiarity of our situation in India, but be well known, and it was only the overpowering weight of our army which it was hoped would restrain them. This prince belonged to the Mharatta empire, and by the constitution of it looked up to the Peishwah as his chief. The resident at his court was Captain Close, in whom the utmost reliance could be placed, and every success expected from his negotiations; yet the extreme uncertainty of Mharatta politics, which can never be divined from any known system, rendered it impossible that we could, except from time alone, become acquainted with the real intentions of this chief.

His highness the Peishwah was the next in point of power, from his great command of money and his former station as the head of the Mharatta empire. From its constitution the several rulers comprised in that league, the rajah of Nagpoor, the Gwykwar, Scindiah, and Holkar, were obliged to join and act with him if he declared war; though it had been our anxious wish to put an end to this acknowledgment of his supremacy, and abolish the confederation.

By the treaty* of June, 1817, in the fourth article, his highness solemnly recognized the dissolution of the Mharatta empire, and promised never to have a vaqueel at, or to receive one from any native court in India; yet the states above-mentioned still felt attached to their ancient customs. The Gwykwar, in his own person, was an exception, many disputes having existed for years past between the courts of Baroda and Poonah.

The good understanding which had prevailed between us since 1803 had become very faint since the horrid transaction which had disgraced his highness's court in 1815,—the treacherous murder, as we have already stated, of the Shastry, the minister of the Gwykwar, by Trimbukjee Dinglia, and not without very strong presumption of his highness's privacy and approval: hence the irritation towards our government for the last three years had been of an alarming nature. Gunga Dhur Shastry, who was the principal instrument employed by Colonel Walker for effecting the salvation of the government of the Gwykwar from impending ruin, and the great and important reform which ultimately fixed it in a condition of stability and prosperity, and who had consequently established the highest title to the favour and protection of the British government, was regularly accredited, in concert with our government and under our guarantee, as ambassador plenipotentiary on the part of the Gwykwar, for the purpose of adjusting by negotiation the differences and claims of the two courts, which we were eventually bound to arbitrate. It therefore became our duty to mark our abhorrence of the base assassination by punishing the criminal, and the strongest proofs having established the fact of this favourite's guilt, he was demanded to be delivered up to us, and was placed in con-

* Laid before parliament.

finement. From this he escaped (as before mentioned) and was abetted by the Peishwah, though in arms at the head of a body of cavalry. Our proceedings in vindication of our own dignity, and for security against a prince whom we could no longer trust, naturally increased his disgust, which was farther inflamed by bad advisers. His professions, however, being of the most friendly kind at the commencement of the cold weather, were accepted. He had collected large bodies of troops under the semblance of assisting in the common cause, that of the destruction of the Pindarries, and for the defence of his own territories. By the treaty of 1803 his highness had received a subsidiary force from us, and had also a large body of 12,000 Arab infantry in his pay, supposed to be good troops; and the force of cavalry he could collect, including the southern jagheerdars, who alone could bring 12,000 horse into the field, was very great, perhaps 25,000. In addition to these, he was by the treaty of the preceding June to maintain a force of 5,000 horse, to which a few British officers were to be appointed; thus providing for part of the present redundant warlike generation,—a system which was acted upon throughout India. The arsenal of Poonah contained a large train of artillery. It was, further, impossible to guess how many men he might bring into the field, when his great pecuniary resources were considered. The country under his rule, above the Ghauts, and in the lower Concan, was most productive, and the number of forts, several of them almost inaccessible, scattered over his dominions, very great. By the treaty of June 1817 he had delivered into our hands three strong hill forts in the neighbourhood of Poonah, as guarantees for the execution of the conditions: these were Poorunder, Rye Ghur, and Sone Ghur; but before the cold weather set in, they had been returned into his hands. The Hon. M. S. Elphinstone was our resident at this court, of whose abilities and judgment there never was but one opinion, and whose conduct in the preceding June had met with the governor-general's highest approbation.

A minor, the son of our old enemy Holkar, under the guardianship of the Baie, his mother, was the prince who stood next in influence; but his army was supposed to be only the wreck of what it once was, as it was conjectured after the war of 1805 that this chief was reduced to little better than a freebooter. The only good troops belonging to this state were believed to be under the command of a Mahometan chief, named Ameer Khan, who held large jaghires from Holkar's family, had for some years kept aloof from the court, and was more than bordering on independence. The head-quarters of Holkar, previous to December, cannot be stated with certainty, though there is reason to believe they were in the neighbourhood of Sewassa. Those of Ameer Khan had been for the last year in Dhoondar, where he was carrying on a fruitless siege against Jeypoor; but at the period of the commencement of the cold weather they were established near Maharajporah. Holkar, though unsuccessful against us, had never received a subsidiary force, or had even a resident at his court, and, after Scindiah, was the most independent prince of India. His territories, much intermixed with those of Scindiah, extended over part of Kandeish, Malwa, Marwar, and the rest of Rajahpootana; but they returned little into the treasury, the energies of the government being almost totally decayed, and the troops greatly in arrears, so that little annoyance could be expected from him. These troops were known to consist of some regular battalions, disciplined after our manner, some thousands of horse, and a considerable quantity of artillery. The horse artillery was equipped in a manner similar to our own. It has been before mentioned that this government was one of the ancient Mharatta confederation, but it was hoped that it would, without difficulty, agree to what we might propose.

The rajah of Nagpoor was the next prince in point of power

after those mentioned, and the state had remained till 1816 without a subsidiary force; but the succession becoming disputed on the death of the late rajah, at that period our influence secured the throne to the present prince, who received from us a subsidiary force, and thus weakened the confederation of the Mharatta states, which it was hoped had received its death-blow in June the following year by the solemn acquiescence of the Peishwah. The rajah was a very weak young man, but had some dangerous persons around him, and it was reported kept up, contrary to treaty, a correspondence with the Peishwah, perhaps from attachment to the old constitution. The possessions of this prince extended over great part of the ancient Hindoo province of Gondwannah, and a fine province to the north of the Nerbuddah, the whole of the fine valley south of that river as far as Hosseinabad, and reached as far south as the territory of the Nizam and the northern Circars, and from the banks of the river Wurdah to some small states on the frontiers of Bengal. His revenue consisted of about fifty lacks of rupees, but he had not more than three or four places of strength. In addition to our subsidiary force, he was bound to have ready at the call of our resident, and under his inspection, 3000 cavalry, and 2000 infantry, and as many more under his own orders as he could afford. As the result of this last agreement, and on a similar plea to that of the Peishwah, he had collected in the beginning of the cold weather, in the vicinity of his capital, 8000 infantry, of which 3000 were Arabs, and about 12,000 horse; and his artillery consisted of more than 70 pieces of cannon. He stood affected towards us like all the other states, and he was by relationship attached to the rajah of Sattarah, the former nominal head of the Mharatta empire. Still, our connexion with this state was of the most intimate kind, and the assurances from the durbar * most satisfactory. Mr. Jenkins, our

* The sovereign, his ministers, and military chiefs assembled in full court.

resident to his highness's court, is a gentleman of well known and tried ability.

The only consolidated Mharatta state that remains to be mentioned is that of the Gwykwar, who governs the greatest part of Guzeraut, and who had, by our interference in 1802, been relieved from an overbearing Arab aristocracy, and as early as that period received from us a subsidiary force. By our careful management the government had since recovered from the most pressing pecuniary distresses. Many and long disputes had taken place between this durbar and that of the Peishwah, and the feeling of the former was far less favourable to his highness than any of the other Mharatta states. By the treaty, in June 1817, with the Peishwah, this power had gained all it required, and the differences being settled by us, in a manner much to its advantage, the Gwykwar was bound to us by gratitude and interest, yet there were a number of disaffected persons at Baroda, the capital, who would have been too happy to find our influence destroyed, and an opening made for discord and rupture. His highness was also bound to keep up some cavalry and infantry besides the troops subsidized. An officer of the name of Carnac was resident at his court. There were other small states which had once formed component parts of the Mharatta empire, but they are not of that importance to render it necessary to mention them here.

To the north and to the west of the dominion of Holkar, Scindiah, and the Gwykwar, is a large tract of country, called Rajahpootana, the greater part governed by five principal chiefs, who boast the true Hindoo blood, and trace their ancestors back to the Hindoo kings of Delhi, before the conquest by the Mahometans. These states had for a long period defended themselves against the several sovereigns and sirdars of the Mahometan faith, and were generally rather conciliated than conquered by them, though at times they have suffered severely from the arms of the house of Timour. Their intestine disturbances have occasioned them to call in the Mharattas, under whose iron hand they have of late years sunk, and have been little better than a certain field for booty, when others failed. The two states on the deserts of Biccaneer and Jesslemere have been reduced more by weak and bad princes than by any other cause, though the latter has lost many of its provinces through the invasion of its neighbours; but as these have not come in immediate contact with the Mharattas, they have not suffered from them. The three other states, Oodipoor, Joudpoor, and Jeypoor, from their frontiers extending along the northward and westward of Malwa, had been the great sufferers from the far-spreading incursions of the Mharattas. The first of these traces its existence as a powerful state to the second century of our era, and the noble defence of their country by the inhabitants, against the Mahometans, deserves to be recorded. They, however, in the beginning of the last century, introduced the Mharatta influence, which has nearly ruined the country. In 1762, a civil contention caused Holkar and Scindiah to be called in on one side, and the Seiks on the other; and the Rana did not free his country from them till he had paid fifty lacs of rupees, and given up territory equal to twelve lacs a year, till thirty more were paid. It has since at several periods been forced to the unhappy policy of requiring these foreign arbitrators, and several districts have fallen a prey to them; and the tract called Godware, equal to seven lacs annually, has been in the hands of a corps of cavalry, which the Rana, some years ago, took into his pay. The whole country is in the greatest misery, and by the 4th article of the treaty with Scindiah, in 1805, we were bound not to enter into any alliance with the Rana, who was stated to be a tributary of the Maharajah. Joudpoor was, after a long period of independence, conquered by Aurungzebe, but became again free on his death; the two sons of Abhee Sing, who reigned in

1739, quarrelled on their father's death, and not contented with tearing their country to pieces by their animosities, adopted the ruinous system of introducing the Mharattas, who devastated the country, and all Ajimeer was given up to Scindiah: in 1790, the whole country was overrun, and reduced to slavery. Since this period, another violent commotion had carried Ameer Khan into the country, and the whole fell under this chief's government. All commerce is at a stand, the people oppressed, and, as in Oodipoor, the most deep and general distress prevails. Without infringing the same article of the treaty of 1805, by which we are restrained from interfering with the Rana of Oodipoor, we could not enter into negotiation with the sovereign of this unhappy district. Jeypoor or Dhoondar has, like the other Rajahpoot states, fallen under the influence of the Mharattas, but the capital still remains in the hands of the rajah. After having held out to this state the friendly shield of our protection, and drawn on it the jealousy and dislike of the Mharattas, we had by the policy of 1805 broke from our engagements, and left it at the mercy of every adventurer who could collect a band of robbers. Our government in 1816 made some overtures to the rajah, of which he did not take advantage, so that the negotiation having failed, Ameer Khan has since ravaged the country to the very gates of the capital. There are two other small Rajahpoot states, Banswarrah and Dongerpoor, of no great importance, and the latter is now in the hands of Holkar.

The other powers of India which still remain to be mentioned are either insignificant in their pretensions, or so totally under our guidance and supervision, that little could be feared from them, and they hardly require more notice than a bare mention of their names; yet his highness the Nizam calls for more remarks than the others. The territory of this prince is situated between the countries of the Peishwah and the rajah of Nagpoor, and is very extensive; but the system of government very feeble and inefficient. Being a Mahometan state, it has no feeling of attachment to the Mharattas, who are all Hindoos; and the claim of the Peishwah for the arrears of choute, of which we were arbitrators, rendered them far from cordial to each other. The Mahometans are even more jealous of us than the Hindoos, as our paramount influence and commanding power have superseded theirs; and the lucrative and honourable appointments which once fell to their share are now often filled by our countrymen in the provinces under our government, so that the number of candidates for employment, of the old respectable families of their faith, crowded round the native princes, are beyond all conception more numerous than the situations that can be found for them, which must naturally make them discontented and desirous of a change. His highness, like the rest of the native sovereigns, was jealous of our power, and would rejoice at any reverse we might sustain. The only effective part of the Nizam's army was under our control. Besides some miserable battalions without British officers, the force alluded to is as follows:—

Infantry.

4 Berar battalions under Major Pittman .	4 battalions.
Captain Hare's brigade . .	2 battalions.
Mehummed Salabat Khan's regular infantry	2 battalions.

Cavalry.

Reformed horse under Captain Davis .	4000
Jaghierdar horse of Salabat Khan . .	2000

These troops were employed by us and the chief above named: Salabat Khan holds a large tract of country from the Nizam on military tenure, and is more attached to us than to his sovereign.

The rajah of Mysore, who falls next to be mentioned, was under our influence, subsidized by us, and furnished the same number of cavalry as the Nizam. The pecuniary resources of the Mysore are in the most prosperous state.

The newab of Oude, the king of Tanjore, and other smaller states, are subservient to us in will and deed. The inferior chieftains to the west of the Jumna, of Bhurtpoor, Gohud, the Jagheirdars near Delhi, the Seik chiefs to the north of that city, were as friendly as we could desire, particularly the rajah of Bhurtpoor, who had since the fall of Hatrass become most attentive to our wishes; and the trust he reposed in his fortresses, if not totally done away, was at least much abated. The small states of Kerowlley, Kottah, and Boondie, on the north bank of the Chumbul, had been left by the treaty of 1805 to the mercy of Scindiah, and were most anxious to partake of our protection:—that of Boondie deserved well of us, from the feeling it evinced towards our troops, when retreating under Colonel Monson. The state of Bopal, to which we owed much, for its friendly aid to our division when moving across India under General Goddard, had made most noble struggles for independence, though surrounded by enemies. The capital held out against a siege of ten years, and they were by our interference saved from absolute ruin; but it is almost a miracle how it has continued to be a separate and independent state. The Nepaulese were not much to be dreaded, though report stated that strong suspicions were entertained of their sincerity. Runjeet Sing was not only quiet, but even friendly.

Mr. Metcalf, under the denomination of resident to the court of the king of Delhi, was the governor-general's political agent for all the states and chiefs of the north-western part of India. From his ability and extensive knowledge of this part of the country, and from his residence in the neighbourhood, he was particularly qualified to manage all the political concerns in that quarter.

It will be seen by this hasty sketch, that at the beginning of the cold weather there was every prospect of the total destruction of the Pindarries; for in consequence of the very satisfactory language held by the native courts whose co-operation we required, not so much by military succour as by denying these common enemies all shelter and countenance, we had a right to expect that no difficulty would arise, and that they would continue on the amicable footing we desired and expected.

CHAPTER III.

Military arrangements—Appointment of Brigadiers to the Bengal army—Reserve—Right division—Centre division—Left division Bengal army—General Hardyman's corps of observation—General Toone's corps of observation—Army of the Dekhun—Appointment of brigadiers to the army of the Dekhun—First division—Second division—Third division—Fourth division—Fifth division—Bombay force—Orders for officers against the Pindarries—Line occupied by the Pindarries in the beginning of October—Active operations to give force to the negotiations with Scindiah—Governor-general takes the field—Bridge of boats across the Jumna—March of the centre division—Treaty with Scindiah signed—Ameer Khan throws himself on the protection of the British government—The Baie, mother of Holkar, sends an assurance of attachment to the British government—Reserve—Right division—Fifth division of the army of the Dekhun—Left division Bengal army—Other divisions of the army of the Dekhun—Flight of the Pindarries—Movement of the centre division of the Bengal army, to overawe Scindiah—Hostility of the Peishwah and Holkar.

IT will now be necessary to give an account of the military arrangements. These were to have for their object the covering of our provinces and those of our allies, the forming of corps to act offensively against the Pindarries, and of others to be in reserve in the event of any native power threatening hostilities.

General Marshall, who commanded in the field at Khanpoor, before the arrival of the commander-in-chief, had been directed to prepare the commissariat, and form the artillery and engineer parks for the army under the Bengal presidency. Two months grain was collected for the army, half of which was to accompany it into the field.

His lordship had appointed the following officers brigadiers for the Bengal army, during the particular service:

Colonel Hardyman,
Watson,

Colonel W. Toone,
D'Auvergne,
Frith,
Arnold, C. B.

The reserve, under the command of Major General Sir David Ochterlony, G. C. B., was to assemble at Rewarree, at the end of October, consisting of

Artillery,
1 Reg. native cavalry,
2 Corps of Skinner's horse,
1 European and 5 native battalions,
Simoor battalion,

with a proportion of field-pieces, and a small battering train.

This force was to act upon all the western states, and to give weight to any negotiations that might be carried on with any of the powers in that quarter; and in the event of Scindiah not entering into our terms, it was to proceed against the troops of that prince in Ajimeer, and interposing between them and Ameer Khan, paralyse both at the same time: should Holkar become disaffected, and his sirdars continue faithful to him, it was to move on Ameer Khan's troops.

The next corps to the southward, along the frontier, was under the command of Major General Donkin, being the right division of the army from Bengal. It was ordered to assemble at Dhoolpoor, on the left bank of the Chumbul, in the middle of October. It consisted of

Horse artillery,
1 Reg. dragoons,
Gardner's horse,
1 European battalion,
3 Native battalions,
Pioneers, and a proportion of field-guns.

G. Fitz Clarence del.t Engraved by R. Havell & Son

ROCKET CORPS AND DROMEDARY CORPS.

Bengal Army, 1817.

London, Published April 1819 by John Murray, Albemarle Street.

This force was to command both banks of the river Chumbul, and to move down upon Gualior, should Scindiah oblige us to use coercive measures. In the event of the Pindarries flying to the north-west, detachments from this division were to attempt to cut them off; and by its vicinity to Kerrowlley, Kottah, and Boondie, it was ready to cover these states, should they come under our protection.

The centre division, under the command of Major General Brown, was to be formed on the 20th of October, on the left bank of the Jumna, and consisted of

The Rocket corps,
3 Troops horse artillery,
1 Reg. of dragoons,
2 Reg. native cavalry,
Dromedary corps,
2 Batt. Europeans,
6 Native battalions,
Miners,

with a proportion of field-guns, and a considerable battering-train, including mortars.

This division was accompanied into the field by the commander-in-chief, and was intended, from its magnitude and weight, in case of war with Scindiah, to move down in conjunction with the division from Dhoolpoor on the headquarters of that Prince, and light detachments were to be formed from it, in pursuit of the Pindarries. It was also, should Scindiah sign the treaty, to maintain a commanding position to prevent his swerving from the execution of it.

Another division, the left of the Bengal army, under the orders of Major General Marshall, was directed to assemble at Callinger, in Bundelcund, on the 10th of October, and was to consist of

Horse artillery,
1 Regiment native cavalry,

2 Corps of Rohilla horse,

5 Battalions native infantry,

with a proportion of field-guns, and a small battering train.

This division was to co-operate with the divisions of the army of the Dekhun in the expulsion of the Pindarries from their country, and should a war with Scindiah ensue, would, in concert with those divisions, turn all his positions and threaten his flank and rear.

A corps of observation, to cover our territory from the incursions of the Pindarries, and to be otherwise disposable, was ordered to be formed under Brigadier General Hardyman in the Rewah country, consisting of

1 Regiment native cavalry,

1 European and 1 native battalion,

with a proportion of field-pieces.

Another corps for a similar purpose was assembled under Brigadier General Toone, covering the city of Patna and adjacent country. It was pushed forward along the river Soane to the south of Rotas Ghur. This corps consisted of one European and one native battalion, with a proportion of field guns.

Many small posts, along the whole line of our frontier, from Lhoudianah, on the Sutledge, to the river Nerbuddah, and some advanced beyond it, strengthened the line against the incursions of the Pindarries, but not being on the seat of war need not be enumerated.

In front of General Hardyman, between Callinger and Hosseinabad, some detachments, consisting of five companies at Lohargong, seven at Jubbulpoor, and ten at Gurrawara, were posted to communicate with General Marshall's advancing corps, and with Nagpoor and Hosseinabad.

To the south of Brigadier General Toone's corps, Colonel Rutledge, with his regiment of infantry (the Ramghur Hill corps), and some Rohilla horse, covered Bengal, being posted in the Ramghur hills, and in advance of them.

Having thus stated the several divisions of the Bengal army brought into the field, I shall now proceed to the army of the Dekhun.

The governor-general had directed the following officers of this army to have the local rank of brigadiers.

Colonel S. A. Floyer,
Smith,.
Doveton,
Sir J. Malcolm.

Sir Thomas Hislop had divided the army of the Dekhun into five divisions, and the original arrangements for the cold weather were as follows. The first division, under his own orders, was to consist of

Rocket troop,
1 Squadron 22nd dragoons,
2 Regiments native cavalry,

horse and foot artillery, one European and six native battalions of infantry, a proportion of field-guns, and a battering train.

This division was to penetrate the country of the Pindarries from the south of the Nerbuddah, seize their territory, and expel them. It was also to act upon Scindiah and Holkar, should either of these chiefs engage in the war against us, and from its position would immediately fall upon their possessions in Malwa, and their respective capitals Oojeen and Indoor.

The second division, under the orders of General Doveton, was a reserve posted in the Nizam's dominions, to move on any point in the Dekhun, and at the same time to cover his highness's territories along the frontier of Berar, and was to consist of

1 regiment and a half of native cavalry,
1 regiment of European infantry,

and five battalions of native infantry, a proportion of field-guns, and a battering train.

The third division was to be under the orders of Brigadier General Malcolm, and to consist of Captain Hare's brigade of the Nizam's infantry,

2 battalions native infantry,
A brigade of horse artillery,
2000 Salabat Khan's horse,
4000 Mysore horse,
And six troops of regular cavalry.

This corps was to move against the Pindarries across the Nerbuddah, in conjunction with the first, and other divisions, and was particularly adapted for that service from the troops of which it was formed.

The fourth division, under the command of Brigadier General Smith, was to cover the north frontier of the Peishwah's dominions, and was at the same time disposable for any contingency. It was posted to the north of the Godavery, at Bysapoor, and was to consist of

1 regiment of native cavalry,*
1 regiment of European infantry,
5 battalions of native infantry,

some artillery and pioneers, with a proportion of field-guns.

The fifth division of the army of the Dekhun was under the orders of Colonel Adams, and composed of the Bengal troops which formed the Nagpore subsidiary force. It was posted at Hosseinabad on the Nerbuddah, consisting, as near as I can judge, of

2 regiments of cavalry,
Detachment of foot artillery,
Native light infantry battalion,

* This regiment did not join the general till after the Peishwah's flight from Poonah.

Four or five battalions native infantry,
And one corps of Rohilla horse,
with a proportion of field and a few battering guns.

Three troops of cavalry were detached from this force to Nagpoor. This division was to enter the Pindarry country across the Nerbuddah, communicating with General Marshall, and was directed to advance to the east of Bopal. In addition to these troops brought actually into the field, two battalions of the Madras army were, according to treaty, posted at Nagpoor, being in the neighbourhood of the rajah's person; a detachment from these, and the contingent of 3000 horse and 2000 infantry belonging to his highness, by treaty under the orders of the resident, were to cover his country and the Ghauts, towards the valley of the Nerbuddah.

For the defence of the Nizam's country there were, besides General Doveton's force, four of his own battalions under Major Pitman, and 4000 reformed horse.

Five thousand of the Poonah auxiliary horse and 3000 infantry were to secure the territories of the Peishwah, while a battalion of European infantry and three battalions of native infantry were posted at his highness's capital Poonah. The fortress of Ahmednugger and the cantonments of Seroor were also strong posts of communication from Poonah to the Nizam's frontier. A force was also collected as a reserve, to cover our provinces at Culburga, under the orders of Colonel Pritzler, consisting of two squadrons of dragoons,

1 Reg. native cavalry,
1 European flank battalion,
4 Companies of the rifle corps,
And some regular native infantry.

A body of the Nizam's irregular horse was at the same time to be posted so as to cover Guntoor. A small force was employed under Colonel Munro, who was engaged in the ceded territories of Darwar and Kousgul, to the south of the Peishwah's territory.

The Bombay force, under the orders of Major-General Sir William Keir, was to advance in the beginning of November from Baroda, in Guzeraut, upon Oojeen, and the major-general was to place himself, when acting on the same service, under the orders of Sir Thomas Hislop. This force consisted of

1 Regiment dragoons,
1 European and 4 native battalions,

with a proportion of field-pieces, and a battering train.

It was to be joined by a body of his highness the Gwykwar's horse, and was to cut off the retreat of the Pindarries to the north-west; and should Scindiah or Holkar commence hostilities, it was to seize their dominions in Guzeraut. The remainder of the Bombay army was to attend to the safety of the Gwykwar's frontier.

The different corps of the army from Madras suffered most severely during the rains while moving up towards the Nerbuddah. Much sickness prevailed throughout the Dekhun, and the commander of the forces was, on his way from Madras, extremely ill at Hyderabad, but the strength of his constitution carried him through after he had been given over by his physicians, and he continued his route as soon as he was capable of travelling towards Hindiah on the Nerbuddah.

On his excellency leaving the capital of the Nizam to assume the command of the army, an instrument, in the form of a letter, was obtained, under the seal and signature of that prince, investing his excellency with full powers over the civil and military officers of the government, notifying to them the authority vested in Sir Thomas Hislop, directing them to obey his orders, and even encouraging them, by the promise of reward, to take efficient means to obtain accurate accounts of the approach or movements of the Pindarries.

Sir Thomas ordered depôts of grain to be formed at Mulkapoor, Omrauttee, Nandain, Aurungabad, Ajuntee, Akola, Bassain, and

Jaulna; and the viceroy of Berar made every possible exertion for their completion.

The orders given to officers who were to move against the Pindarries, enemies who were to be considered in the light of public robbers, were as follows:—individuals were to be punished capitally if fully proved to belong to these wretches, whether they were found in our territories, or those of our allies; and of course, if Holkar and Scindiah entered into the governor-general's views, this system was to be acted upon in their countries. In the event of these states taking them into their service, which would necessarily be accompanied by a rupture with us, the same treatment was generally directed, though peculiar circumstances might cause some difference, and this was left to the discretion of the commanding officers. It was ordered that a trial should first take place, and if conviction followed, the punishment should be summary; but commanders were desired to be particularly careful not to destroy the cultivators of the soil in the countries under the rule of the Pindarries. No distinction was to be made between the lowest of them and their chiefs, and every exertion was to be used to seize their families.

The line occupied by the Pindarries at the beginning of October was distant from the Nerbuddah, extending from Ghyarispoor in Bilsah to the vicinity of the Kalee-Scind, about eighty or one hundred miles; but they were still possessed of the country below the Ghauts. This country was strong from jungles and ravines; but they had no forts, and being aware of the storm about to burst on them, were attempting to procure by negotiation with the states in their vicinity a place of strength, in which their families might seek refuge. In this they were uniformly unsuccessful.

They had a retreat to the north-west open to them, which was to be intercepted if possible by detachments from the Bombay army, and the right and centre divisions of the Bengal army; and officers were directed to be very careful that they did not pass them and get into their rear. In fine, being viewed, as has just been stated, as public robbers, their extirpation was aimed at, and not their defeat as an enemy entitled to the rights of war.

The narrative being now brought down to the commencement of the cold weather, and all the military arrangements having been made, it will be necessary to give an account of the active operations tending to the desirable conclusion of the negotiations with Scindiah.

On the 20th of October the governor-general entered the camp of Secundra, on the banks of the Jumna, and after reviewing the centre division, crossed that river by a bridge of boats on the 26th.

I must here stop to describe the bridge formed for the passage of the army. The bridges of boats made by the natives of India have at all times been celebrated; but on this occasion, with the addition of the science and ability of the officers of engineers and pioneers, the work was perhaps the most complete and most efficient for its purpose that had ever been constructed. Unlike the bridges of boats or pontoons in Europe, there was no interval left between them, as they are, on this river, made with a very great swell in the ribs, and, therefore, though the sides touched, there was space sufficient for the water to pass. They were overlaid with long beams crossed by others, and the interstices filled up with boughs of trees and bundles of straw, the whole covered with earth. There was even a railway to secure the passengers from danger. The whole was about 350 yards long and 16 feet wide, and not only allowed the passage of the heaviest artillery, but even of elephants, and it was curious to remark the characteristic sagacity of those animals. From the difficulty which their bulk causes in recovering themselves when falling, they are extremely timid, and very careful where they tread; and the generality of them displayed great alarm till convinced by their mehout, or driver, that there was no danger. After the first step they advanced with confidence, and though the boats sunk near a foot from the increase of the weight, and disturbed the water around, yet they showed no further symptoms of trepidation. The bridge was completed by a tete-de-pont, and garrisoned with five companies.

The division halted on the 27th and 28th to allow the many followers and equipages of the army to cross, and marched on the 29th to Loharee. The following day it moved to Jalaon, halted the 31st of October and 1st of November, and on the 2d entered the camp marked out at Donawara; on the 3d marched to Secunderpoor, and on the 4th halted. The division marched on the 5th to Gidowsah, near Nuddyagong, on the frontier of Scindiah's country, where his lordship received on the 6th the treaty * signed by Scindiah the preceding day, a proof at once of his inferiority, and a discouragemant to the hopes of the disaffected throughout India, who beheld the only power combining independence and great military strength subscribing to terms dictated by our government, and the very troops they hoped to have seen opposed to us become, if not our allies, at least neutralized, and incapable of acting as enemies. This treaty, which has been made public, bound his highness in conjunction with ourselves to root out the Pindarries, and prevent their ever re-assembling; and contains an engagement that the troops of the contracting powers should never cease to prosecute their destruction until it should be accomplished.

The 5000 horse his highness undertook to furnish were to be posted between the eastern frontier of Kottah and the fort of Gualior, to cover the country, and prevent the Pindarries from crossing the Chumbul, so as to complete the cordon formed by the troops of Kottah and Boondie, supported by the division under General Donkin.

On the morning after the receipt of the treaty the governor-

* Laid before parliament.

general moved his camp to the southward to Mehawa, in order to be more distant from Scindiah's frontier, that the army might not any longer hold a threatening position, and to show that we placed confidence in his highness's fidelity.

In addition to the success of this important negotiation, a settlement conformable to the wishes of the governor-general was agreed to on the 9th of November, at Delhi, by the minister of Ameer Khan, now feeling himself absolutely independent of Holkar, and throwing himself upon the generosity of the British government.

The newab, Ameer Khan, by this agreement obtained the guarantee of our government for all the lands he had at any time received under grants from Holkar, and was doubtless happy to have the excuse of our requiring it, for disbanding his army, and delivering up to us his military equipments, including about 150 pieces of cannon.

About the same time Mr. Metcalf received a letter from the Baie, the mother of Holkar, absolutely casting herself upon the mercy of the British government; and nothing occurred which did not tend to confirm the belief expressed in the commander-in-chief's orders on the receipt of the treaty with Scindiah, that every desirable point would be carried by equity and moderation, "and that this was the proudest triumph for the British character."

On the 10th of November his lordship moved his camp to Terrait, on the 13th to Talgong, and on the 15th to Salia; when the Pindarries having shewn an intention of moving to plunder the country on the right bank of the Scind, his lordship despatched Colonel Philpot, with the 24th dragoons, and some squadrons of native cavalry, to Burra Sorger, in order to secure that country.

A very serious distemper, an epidemic cholera morbus, at this time ravaged the camp of the centre division; and it was not until the army crossed the river Betwah at Erij, on the 19th, that it ceased.

Within ten days six European officers and 200 soldiers, with 300 sepoys, and several thousand of the followers of the army, were buried. In the same period, from deaths, or desertion caused by the dread of the epidemic, the camp diminished in number 20,000 souls. From the time of Scindiah's signing the treaty all had remained quiet in his camp, and there appeared no reason to doubt his professions. Every thing around had a most happy aspect, when intelligence was received of hostilities having broken out at Poonah, by the Peishwah having attacked our troops stationed at that city.

The centre division remained encamped upon the same ground in the neighbourhood, till the 5th of December, about the period that accounts were also received of the defection of Holkar.

Sir David Ochterlony, who had been posted with the reserve at Rewarry, as soon as permitted by the signature of the treaty with Scindiah, moved on to Jeypoor, where it is believed he arrived about the first week in December. Sir David had several interviews with Ameer Khan, with whom he was perfectly satisfied.

General Donkin, who had been posted at Dhoolpoor on the Chumbul, being joined by 1200 horse from the rajah of Bhurtpoor, withdrew from that position also in consequence of the treaty with Scindiah, which covered from the Pindarries the country between the Scind, Jumna, and Chumbul.

The rajah of Kottah had expressed his wish to co-operate with us, and had marched his troops to his frontier to join in the common cause. Upon General Donkin's moving from Dhoolpoor, a battalion with two guns was ordered down from the garrison of Agra to take post at that town. General Donkin having been obliged, by the difficulty of the country, to proceed by the north of Hulain and Kosial Ghur, arrived on the 4th of December at Ramporah, and was to move on the 5th in the direction of Oneree. General Marshall had advanced from Calinger by Adji Ghur, Lohar Ghong, to Huttah, west of Sorger, and on the 4th of November continued his route in the direction of the latter place, in the vicinity of which he halted, being in readiness to act in concert with the divisions of the army of the Dekhun, when they crossed the Nerbuddah to expel the Pindarries. General Hardyman was posted in Rewah, and the small detachments in his front continued as before stated.

The 5th division of the army of the Dekhun, posted at Hossienabad, was ready to act when Sir Thomas Hislop advanced. A detachment from this force, consisting of three troops of cavalry, and a battalion of infantry, was ordered to hold itself in readiness to move to Nagpoor if it should be necessary; for though every thing was quiet at that court, yet the contingent had not been furnished according to treaty. The first and third divisions of the army of the Dekhun at Hurdah, near the Nerbuddah, were preparing to cross that river, having been joined about the 10th of November by Sir Thomas Hislop. The various and unpleasant despatches from Poonah made the commander of the forces uneasy with respect to the Dekhun; and on the 14th receiving accounts of the treaty having been signed by Scindiah, and on the 16th of the daring act of hostility which had taken place at Poonah, his excellency determined to send only a division capable of offensive operations across the river, for the expulsion of the Pindarries. This corps his excellency entrusted to the command of Sir John Malcolm. On the 14th of November, Colonel Adams, commanding the force at Hosseinabad, commenced crossing the river Nerbuddah, and General Malcolm followed on the 16th. The first mentioned of these officers was on the 21st near Rasseen, and the latter on the 23d at Ashta. General Marshall was on the 21st at Sorger, and the Pindarries were drawing off, much encumbered with their wives, families, and property. These three divisions pushed on through the Pindarry country in the latter end of November. General Marshall on the 30th arrived at Seronj, a place belonging to Ameer Khan. We were well received by the governor of the fort, who had previously refused an asylum to the families of the Pindarries; and these freebooters now began to feel the consequences of having provoked the wrath of the British government.

The two durrahs of Wussul Mehummud and Kureem Khan retired to the northward to Kolarus, passing without opposition close to Behauder Ghur, the principal station of the troops belonging to Colonel Baptiste, who fled singly or slightly attended towards the Chumbul, terrified as it is supposed at the approach of these lawless bands, plundering the whole country as they proceeded.

The durrah of Cheeto was more to the westward, and Colonel Adams was moving nearly parallel to General Marshall by Burseah on Raj Ghur, with Sir John Malcolm on his left.

The largest portion of the Pindarries having taken their route by Kolarus, in the direction of Gualior, and being in very considerable force, it was impossible to say what effect their proximity might have on Scindiah and his troops, who were far from being pleased with the treaty; and to prevent any violent change in consequence of this accession of strength, if he should avail himself of it, the governor-general determined to leave his position at Erij, and place himself with the centre division near Scindiah's camp. With this view his lordship moved his head-quarters on the 6th of December to Emrokee, on the 7th to Sajapoor, and on the 8th to the west of Simpter, continuing his march to the banks of the Scind, within fifty miles of Gualior. This change of position had become more necessary from a change of the head-quarters of Holkar, who had put his troops in motion, and was marching for his capital, Indoor. This brought the Mharatta chief and his army so nearly in contact with Sir John Malcolm, that the latter had found it expedient in the first week of December to halt his division. The durbar of Holkar, forgetting the friendly message and voluntary assurances of the Baie to Mr. Metcalf when she was in want of money, and being without doubt instigated by the Peishwah, on the plea of belonging to the Mharatta confederacy, and assisted by large sums of money from the same quarter, had assumed the most offensive language in open durbar, reviled Scindiah for his submission to us and desertion of the Peishwah, and announced publicly the intention to assist the head of the Mharatta empire, and join him in the Dekhun.

CHAPTER IV.

Causes of the author's leaving head-quarters—Ordered home over-land with the despatches of Scindiah's treaty—Difficulties of crossing the Peninsula—Various routes proposed—Route to the southward determined upon—To pass through Egypt—Tranquil state of that country—Remarks on the routes to England—Difficulties in crossing the Peninsula increased by the Peishwah's hostility—Route to the Nerbuddah—Obstacles—Defeat of the Peishwah—Holkar's defection—Doubts of the conduct of the Rajah of Nagpoor—General Hardyman moves to his frontier—The author determines to join him—Increasing appearance of disaffection throughout India—Enemy collecting troops at Jubbulpoor—The author quits the camp on the morning of the 8th December, 1817—Movements of the Pindarries—Reflections—Account of the pestilence which had visited the camp—Erij—Mahometan tombs—Palanquin-bearers—Bamoory—Kyrooker—Forts—Koochaicher—Keitah—Mahobah—Unexpected assistance—Tank—Ruins—Gorar—Purswah—Adjighur—Joar—Punnah—Kukkeritte—Arrival at Lohargong—Want of security out of the Company's territory—Disagreeable intelligence from Jubbulpoor—Large collection of troops at that place—Our forces there fall back—Symptoms of approaching hostility—Seapoys under European officers in the native services similar to our own—Decided marks of hostility—Arrangements for proceeding to the southward to join General Hardyman—Position of Lohargong—Strength of the post—Account of an action at Nagpoor—Heavy loss on our side—Reinforcement—Rajah reported to have asked for a suspension of hostilities—Russollah of irregular horse—Various reports.

PRIVATE JOURNAL.

Camp, Sajapoor, 7th December, 1817.

THE various points gained by the treaty with Scindiah being of the utmost consequence, and considered as the most decided proof, by the admission of the greatest independent military chief in India, of our being the predominant power in Hindostan; and being also the first and most important step to the completion of the governor-general's extensive views for the final settlement of this vast empire, it was determined to send home as bearers of the despatches (containing the intelligence of this event) two of his lordship's aide-de-camps, one to proceed by the usual sea-voyage, round the Cape, and the other overland with the duplicate, to ensure the early arrival of the news to the government in England. The senior aide-de-camp of the governor-general was appointed to the first of these duties, and his lordship fixed upon me for the latter. I could not but be well pleased with the prospect of proceeding by a route which was out of the ordinary track; and the service met my wish and intention, which had ever been to return to Europe overland. The idea also of crossing India and so many countries which lay in my route, was highly gratifying to that earnest love of research which I had long indulged. The dependent situation in which Scindiah had placed himself by entering into our views, rendered it unlikely that the division of the army under the command of the governor-general in person would meet an enemy in the field; I should therefore by crossing India be employed, while all would be in a state of inactivity in our camp.

The greatest difficulty, however, which presented itself, was that of travelling over the Peninsula while in so perturbed a state, and to select the most practicable of several routes which were suggested: one through the Rajahpoot provinces, bordering upon the desert, into Guzaraut; another by Scindiah's camp, with escorts of his cavalry, by Oojein to Surat through Khandeish; and a third by being passed from one division of the British army to the next; but all these were so extremely uncertain and dangerous, that they were given up in succession. The only remaining way, which it was at last determined I should take, was by Nagpoor, crossing the Nizam's dominions; from thence through those of the Peishwah, by Poonah to Bombay, where orders had been sent to prepare one of the Company's cruisers to take me up the Red Sea to Suez. We learnt by the late communications from our consul-general at Cairo, that no difficulty would present itself in the desert, nor was there any danger of being plundered by the Bedouin Arabs, since, to use Mr. Salt the consul's own words, "The road from Suez to Cairo was as open and frequented as the road from Calcutta to Moorshedabad." This happy change was stated to have been brought about by the present Pacha of Egypt, a man of very superior abilities, under whose government that country enjoys a tranquillity previously unknown to it for a long period of years.

In the journey before me I expect to meet with every civility from his highness, as mutual tokens of good will had passed between him and our governor-general; and last year the latter sent two young elephants as a present to the Pacha.

On my arrival at Alexandria, if the plague should not be in the country, and I should be able to procure clean bills of health, I intend to hire a vessel for the nearest port in Europe; but if this scourge, fully as bad as the Pindarries, should be at that time ravaging Egypt, I should then on the spot act according to circumstances, and perhaps go to Constantinople, and through Hungary and Germany to England. It had been my wish to have taken another route by the Persian Gulf, by Bassorah, Bagdad, and through Asia Minor, to Constantinople; but that by Egypt was fixed upon, for, when practicable, and at the proper time of the year, it is the most expeditious.

I had flattered myself with not being more than three months on my journey, allowing three weeks to reach Bombay; but I was speedily led to despair of accomplishing it in so short a period. After my arrangements were made, intelligence was received of the treachery and hostility of the Peishwah having burst into a flame; his army, amounting to nearly 40,000 men, having attacked our small force, consisting of but three battalions, posted at his capital, on the 5th November. After a sharp action on the evening of that day, the enemy was repulsed, and had retired much disheartened. This rendered my passing through his territory impossible. I was in consequence directed to proceed from Nagpoor to Hyderabad, and from thence to Goa, where the Portuguese viceroy would forward me to Bombay; but I was to act according to events as they arose. It was settled that Captain M'Ra, the senior aide-de-camp, should proceed this morning, as the same d'ak bearers carry us both in our palanquins the first fifty miles. He then passes into our territory, and I strike to the southward, through the independent states of Bundelcund, in the direction of the river Nerbuddah.

The most serious cause of alarm in crossing India is that of falling in with some of the disorganized savage hordes of horse, ever on the move in this country, on plundering expeditions, or seeking service. Amongst these are of course included the Pindarries, who have announced their intention to murder or maim all the British, or those employed by them, who may fall into their hands; in the latter case by cutting off noses, upper lips, &c. In the present state of the country I lay my account with encountering many difficulties before I reach Bombay; but the route by Hyderabad and Goa is so far out of my way, that I will, if possible, make the attempt to pass through the Peishwah's dominions, where I hope, by the time I arrive, tranquillity will be re-established. I have, however, but little better treatment to expect from the sirdars or chiefs of this sovereign, should I become their prisoner, than from the Pindarries; for during the late disturbances at Poonah they made prisoners two officers, brothers, and report says, with a brutal ferocity of the deepest and unfeeling barbarism, executed them in the most ignominious manner.

We have heard of the Peishwah's army having been put to flight on the 17th ultimo by the division under General Smith, which had moved from its position in advance on the Godavery to the assistance of our small force in the vicinity of Poonah. We have also intelligence of Holkar, or rather Holkar's mother, the regent, having taken the field against us, and moved down her army from the north-west upon Indoor, her capital, assigning as a reason, that as the head of the Mharatta empire has gone to war with us, she feels it her duty to follow his example. But if she continues this threatening attitude, it is to be hoped that a good account of her will be given, either by Colonel Adams, Sir John Malcolm, or the Bombay army.

However, the worst intelligence received within the last week (which, if true, will add to my difficulties), is that of the Nagpoor post having been stopped, and no letters received for several days from that quarter. In India this is looked upon as a convincing proof that all is not right in the direction where the interruption takes place; but even before this suspicious circumstance very serious doubts were entertained as to the fidelity of the Rajah. Indeed it was certain that he intended to oppose us; but the severe chastisement the Peishwah has received will, it is conjectured, prove a lesson of prudence and caution to his highness, if he has not already gone too far. As my route, for about 300 miles, lies through the very heart of this sovereign's territory, all my embarrassments will be doubled should he be engaged in hostility against us, adding to my risk both of danger and delay; but as I agree with Pappenheim, who "thought many things were done by the mere resolution to do them," I shall quit the camp to-morrow morning.

Brigadier-general Hardyman, in consequence of the indications in that quarter, has been ordered from his covering position at Rewah to move down into the Rajah's dominions, and to march on to Nagpoor should he be informed of any act of hostility having taken place at that capital.

It had been not only my wish but my intention to have remained a few days longer at head-quarters, in hopes of hearing of some signal blow being struck against the Pindarries; but I hasten my departure, considering the state of the country, and intending to join General Hardyman on the frontier of the Nagpoor dominions, as I could not allow the opportunity of so good an escort to escape me.

I have heard this morning that Major Richards, who is with

seven companies stationed at Jubbulpoor, near the river Nerbuddah, about a hundred miles within the Nagpoor dominions, has reported that a large force is collecting in that town, and he expects he shall be obliged to retire upon Colonel M'Morrin at Gurrawarrah, to the south of the river: if this be so, and they continue to assemble troops at Jubbulpoor, which is directly in our road to Nagpoor, we may have to fight our way to the capital. General Hardyman has a force sufficient for the undertaking, consisting of a very fine regiment of native cavalry (the 8th Bengal, which I saw reviewed two years ago at Sultanpoor, on the Ganges, and it equalled in its movements many of the finest regiments I have seen on Hounslow Heath,)—his majesty's 17th regiment of foot, a battalion of the 8th Bengal native infantry, and four guns.

Lohargong, 11th December, 1817.

On the morning of the 8th, before the break of day, I quitted the camp, and left the army advancing to the banks of the river Scind, for the frontier of Scindiah's territory, in consequence of two of the Pindarry durrahs, or tribes, having moved in the direction of his camp, as before mentioned, and its being impossible to say what effect 20,000 horse might have on the feelings of his durbar.

I had sent my palanquin forward to Emrokee, where we had been encamped the day before, and my elephant carried me from the camp to the spot where I was to take my final departure. I must confess that though even with the prospect of returning to my native country, which repays an Englishman for many years' toil and absence, I turned my back on my fellow soldiers with a very heavy heart, regretting the loss of so many friends and companions, never perhaps to meet them again. Whilst at Emrokee, during the time my servants were preparing my palanquin, I could not help taking a rapid view of my situation, and the obstacles and dangers of the undertaking presented themselves most forcibly to me. I was in the centre of Bundelcund, one of the most inland provinces of India, setting out to cross the whole of that continent, the greatest part of which belonged to princes at war with us, or at best but jealous, envious, cold-hearted friends. I reflected on the extreme difficulty I should have to combat in judging of the degree of risk to be avoided or encountered in certain situations, to escape the imputations either of rashness or want of enterprise. I certainly felt myself absolutely forlorn, and the busy scene I had been so long accustomed to was strongly contrasted with the stillness around.

But three days before I had been with some of my companions on a neighbouring hill, viewing the busy camp of 80,000 souls at the foot of it, spreading over the wide extended plain, with the buzz of voices, lowing of cattle, roaring of camels, and the smoke of innumerable fires ascending on all sides, when the whole country around was covered by a moving host.

Under the walls of a small fort, with none but my palanquin bearers and servants around me, I now stood almost alone in the centre of a plain, too extensive for the eye to reach its limits, and the only vestiges of the crowd which had trod down the growing wheat in the adjoining field three days before were the marks of thousands of feet, uniformly in one direction, and the carcase of a buffalo, a sacrifice to the last day's march, covered with voracious vultures. I took leave at this place of every thing that belonged to me, excepting my palanquin, four baskets containing my clothes, which were slung from the ends of two poles, resting on the shoulders of the same number of bearers, a bag of biscuit, my telescope, sword, and pistols, and I proceeded to the town of Erij through the melancholy vestiges of the pestilence which had carried off thousands. The remains of the poor wretches, who had fallen victims to its rage, lay on the road-side, torn from their graves by the hungry wolves; and the horrid state in which they were, half devoured, half decomposed, exhibited affecting proofs of our mortality in its worst shape, and did not by any means tend to dispel my gloomy thoughts.

This destructive complaint, the cholera morbus, called by the French mal de chien, and trousse gallant, had shewn itself early in the autumn in Calcutta, but by the activity of the magistrates and medical gentlemen, after the public notice of a remedy, consisting of the liberal use of laudanum and calomel, its ravages had in a great measure been arrested. This was in a city; how dreadful and destructive must it have been in a moving camp remote from assistance, and where, as in all Indian armies, eight or ten followers on an average accompany every fighting man! It certainly surpassed the most afflicting conception I could have formed of such a visitation; and had the wives and children of those in the camp been equally exposed to the contagion, it would have become still more terrific. It began to shew itself in the centre division about the 10th of November, and by the 16th was at its height. The progress of the disease was so rapid (a locked-jaw coming on in the course of a very short time), that many servants or followers, seized on the line of march, died in a few minutes; and those who were obliged to go some distance from the camp in their several occupations, such as the grass-cutters to procure forage for the animals, and the camel-drivers accompanying their cattle to graze, suffered dreadfully. The ravages among the troops were at one time very alarming, and the number of our servants affected brought it home to the officers.

The sun was braved by every one, and on all our tables stood always ready small bottles of laudanum and other remedies. The mode in which the medicine was administered was so simple, that all the officers became expert and successful practitioners, the professional men being much too few to meet the exigencies of the duty.

Our tents were crowded with the sick, dying, and dead; and in addition to the horrors of the scene, it was most distressing to see the almost universal apathy with which the natives conducted themselves towards each other, and the general want of sympathy so common amongst them. I had under my hands, during the course of the malady, twenty-nine patients, of whom twenty-three recovered; and I never quitted them till compelled by its attacking myself. It was in one or two instances, where considerable anxiety and feeling had been shewn between relatives and when success had crowned our exertions, very delightful to receive the burst of gratitude from them; and their natural untutored manner of shewing it, by throwing themselves at our feet, and embracing our knees, had an unaffected and primitive appearance that carried my mind back to the earliest ages.

Excepting in two instances which came to my knowledge, every idea of cast, prejudice of religion and impurity, yielded to its violence, and not one of those under my charge refused to take medicine out of a wine glass from my hand. The instances I allude to were of two Bramins, I believe writers or clerks in the offices of the adjutant-general and judge-advocate. These men, from a dread of being defiled, refused to take any thing but from the hands of each other, both stating that there were none in the camp of so high and pure a cast. Being seized at the same time in different and distant parts, this refusal of all remedies offered them proved fatal, and they equally fell victims to what they fancied a religious and commendable principle, and were doubtless looked upon as martyrs. It was observed that those who lived on grain and simple diet were the first to fall a sacrifice. The Mahometans, who have no scruples about the use of animal food, suffered less; and the Europeans, who lived still more generously, suffered least of all.

It is worthy of remark how careless we all became on many points, which, under different circumstances, would have annoyed or shocked us. I recollect having left the dinner-table to visit my patients; I found that one, a woman, who had been brought to me in the worst stage of the disease, had breathed her last, and as the native servants shewed some dislike to carrying the body a few yards from the tent, to give them an example, I carried the head myself,—so used were we to such scenes. To prove the extent of the alarm throughout the camp, it may be repeated that the followers who fled from the army, added to those who died, in ten days reduced it in number from twenty to twenty-five thousand souls.

On the 19th November we crossed the river Betwah, and as if an iron curtain had dropt between us and the avenging angel, the deaths diminished. Those attacked were in trifling numbers, confidence and security again appeared in the countenances of all, and in a few days the number of graves on the outside of the camp reminded us alone of what had passed.

Erij has been a place of considerable importance. Its numerous mausoleums with domes bespeak it a Mahometan city. One of these was of very peculiar construction, being a dome raised on four half arches, or rather a dome acting as a keystone to four unfinished arches. It appears that the Mahometans are most anxious to lay their bones and those of their friends in good substantial buildings, while during their lives they inhabit very huts. This I conceive originates in a fear of shewing their wealth, which under despotic governments always creates jealousy and suspicion; and a traveller of the seventeenth century in this country accounts for the splendid tombs of the Mahometans by their king being heir to all their wealth, and these erections the only property they could call their own.

The palanquin bearers were laid in relays, sixteen in a set, from Erij to Lohargong, 150 miles to the southward, on the frontier of the Nagpoor dominions. The distance of these relays in India is from twelve to sixteen miles, but I have known bearers on an emergency go on to twenty-four miles. I trusted, should every thing remain quiet, to have found others continued on to Bellary, sixty miles farther to the south, and from thence to the capital. The bearers were better than I expected, the Bundelahs, or inhabitants of Bundelcund, being far from celebrated for this kind of service. Their dress is usually a green quilted cotton coat, and a turban of the same, in which they differ from all the Hindoos, whose dress is white. After changing bearers at Erij, I proceeded to Bamoory, and thence to Kyrooker, having passed through the finest country I ever saw. The eye could not reach the extent of the wheat just above the ground, this being the rubbee, or spring harvest. The insulated piles of enormous stones so general throughout Bundelcund, and sometimes placed in regular ranges, increased in number, and were a relief to the eye after the dreary plains of Bengal, Behar, and the Doab. I passed a very handsome stone fort in the course of this stage, but the name has since escaped me. Every village yet seen out of our territory has a small fort of greater or less respectability, and the houses of the inhabitants are built around within matchlock shot. What a miserable state of society does this defensive precaution bespeak! I suppose our barons' castles in England in feudal times were surrounded in a similar manner by the huts of their vassals. These forts are in general of mud, but from six to twelve feet at the bottom of the wall are often of masonry. They are surrounded with a deep ditch, and the defences consist of small round towers connected by curtains. Some of them have two or three lines of these walls and towers within each other. On the glacis are generally large excavations for grain; but this of course is only in dry situations. It is before such forts that we have lost more officers and men than in any other situation, and for the same reason that we have so often failed before fortresses in Europe,—treating them too lightly. The mud walls receive the shot without being shattered, and they are in consequence very difficult to breach. It was very late when I reached my next stage, Koochaicher, having been obliged to walk the greatest part of the way, on account of the weakness of the bearers. I thought we should have remained all night in the ravines on the banks of the river Desaun, which I crossed near this last place, which is a camel dauk station, and the surwars or riders told me that letters had passed from the southward; but I could not learn from what distance. I was most anxious, and should have been most happy, to have heard of letters from Nagpoor having been forwarded to head-quarters, as this would have shewn that the road was open, and all quiet at that Mharatta capital.

It was midnight when I reached Keitah, one of our most advanced cantonments. I continued travelling all night, and at daylight on the morning of the 9th found my bearers much tired. About nine o'clock the vicinity of Mahobah was discovered to me by the number of temples, tombs, and ruins, some of them beautifully picturesque, scattered on all sides.

This country is undoubtedly one of the finest for a draftsman I ever saw: every tree, hut, and native, is of a peculiar character, and the drapery in the dress of the people renders them always good objects for a foreground.

While admiring the splendid remains around me, my eyes were most pleasantly refreshed by the sight of the top of a white tent, on approaching which I observed several of our Sepoys bivouacked under some small trees in a little bottom, and about 100 horses picquetted near them. I went up to the tent with the confidence which an Englishman feels in meeting unexpectedly with a countryman in a far distant land, particularly in India, which I have ever found to be the true country of hospitality.

On inquiry I learnt that the tent and detachment belonged to Cornet Smallpage of the 8th native cavalry, proceeding in charge of remount horses for the regiments of cavalry to the southward. I was not disappointed, nor was my confidence ill placed. This officer on his return from riding received me with the utmost urbanity and kindness. By some mistake, no bearers had been laid at this stage, and I was obliged to remain till two o'clock to refresh the others, and procure some assistance from the town, which promised but little from its depopulated and ruinous appearance. Of all helpless situations in the world that of being left by the side of your palanquin without bearers, many miles from assistance, is the most deplorable, but in this instance it had occurred under more fortunate circumstances. Having at length obtained sufficient bearers to carry my palanquin, and a horse from my hospitable new acquaintance, I continued my journey.

Near Mahobah is a most splendid tank, formed by raising a vast dam of large granite stones across a valley from hill to hill, and the country inclining towards it accumulates during the rains a body of water nearly two miles in circumference.

The ruins of Mahobah are very extensive; and there was once a stone castle or fort of considerable strength on a rocky height above the town: it doubtless was at some former period a very large and opulent place. The heat was excessive as we proceeded, and I absolutely despaired of my palanquin reaching the next stage. The country gradually altered as we advanced to the southward; the insulated hills became ranges, and reminded me much of some of the mountains in Spain. The inhabitants have availed themselves of the declivities of the country to form several tanks on the same principle as that at Mahobah; and I conceive it was from the advantage of irrigation from these that the country was a perfect garden. At six I arrived at a very large town on a high hill, belonging to the nana of Jaloan. His officers informed me that Ghoorah, where my bearers were stationed, was two coss * further; I however persevered, and about ten arrived at that town. From hence I proceeded with fresh spirit to the village of Purswah, where I was detained several hours, the men who carried my baskets having probably lain down to sleep during the night. It was near eight in the morning of the 10th of December when they joined. The country from this place becomes hilly; the whole face of it is

* A lineal measure which differs in length from one mile and a half to three in various parts of India, but upon an average may be taken at two miles.

covered with dwarf trees, and is of a steril and uncultivated appearance. I crossed the river Kane, about fourteen miles from Adji Ghur, which is at this time of the year not above ancle deep, though in the rains it must be a very respectable stream. There is a distinct view of Adji Ghur from its banks. As I approached this celebrated fortress, which is, most unaccountably, omitted to be mentioned in the Ayen Akbaree, my bearers became fatigued, and I was obliged to walk: the road was most execrable, and the ghaut, which passes close under the hill on which the fort is built, hardly fit for led horses or mules. I was too late to see the interior of the fort, as the table land is 800 feet above the level of the country. Very fortunately I found at the foot of the hill the tent of an officer, who was dining in the fort, but came down about an hour after my arrival, and was, as is customary in this country, most liberal in the assistance he gave me. He had arrived from Lohargong for treasure, and informed me that no letters had been received from Nagpoor, with which state it was the general opinion we should have war. After taking some refreshment, I started from this place, having refused his kind offer of reposing in the tent for the night, although warned that I had a very bad ghaut to pass before I arrived at Punnah. Adji Ghur is one of the most celebrated hill forts in India, not only on account of its strength, but of its former sanctity. It owes but little to art, and is, I am told, about three miles in circumference. The wall is built on the edge of the table land, and, when manfully defended (if I may judge from what I saw of it), must be almost impregnable, as the garrison would only require to roll stones over the ramparts to crush the assailants. When we attacked it some years ago, the governor, a rebellious Zemeendar, though he repulsed us in an attempt to storm, thought it prudent to evacuate it. This desertion of his fort having left his family at our mercy, occasioned one of those extraordinary instances of fortitude and contempt of death which sometimes occur amongst the Hindoos. The females of the Zemeendar's family were to be removed on our taking possession of the fort, and a venerable relation was sent to prepare them. His stay was long; but the sacredness of the Zunnana* debarred all entrance, till the length of time became totally unaccountable, and the door was at last burst open. The horrid scene which presented itself was hardly to be borne; the women, eight in number, and the person who had gone into their apartment, were found dead, and weltering in their blood; and this sanguinary act must have been consented to by one and all, as had any resistance or violence been used by any of the party, it would have been heard by those on the outside.

The only cause which could be assigned for this sacrifice was their having existed in the fort at the same time that our troops were in it, and some idea of pollution conceived by the women from our proximity.

This is the most unaccountable instance of which I have ever read in Indian history of that horrific immolation called the Joar, which originates in a high-spirited though perverted feeling, and is understood never to be practised but when death alone can save the high-minded Hindoos, their wives and daughters, from the brutal treatment of an inhuman enemy†. The last instance I am aware of, except during the late incursions of the Pindarries into Guntoor, occurred in the reduction of a Polygar's fort, by an ally of M. Bussy in 1757. The most celebrated siege in Indian history, by Akbar, which ended in the fall of Chitoor, in A. D. 1567, was marked by this sacrifice. The garrison, seeing no hopes of a successful defence, performed this horrid rite, and put all their wives

* Women's apartment.

† The antiquity of this custom may be learned from Arrian. This historian, in speaking of a certain Brachman city, to which Alexander laid siege, and where a party of the Malli had fled, states, that some of the Indians, seeing the place ready to be taken, set fire to their houses. Quintus Curtius, on the same occasion, relates, that when the townsmen saw that he obstinately resolved to continue the siege, despairing of safety, they set fire to their houses, and burnt themselves, their wives, and children.

and children to the sword, and burned their bodies, with that of their chief, whom Akbar had killed by a musket shot from his own hand. The fathers, husbands, and brothers, having sprinkled their clothes with yellow dust (the colour of despair), felt themselves bound by honour not to be long separated from their families, and perished to a man.

The remains of some splendid Hindoo temples are still left in the interior of the fort. Adji Ghur is, however, in every point of view, inferior in strength and Hindoo remains to Callinger, a fort at some distance from it. The tanks for water, cut out of the live rock, are very fine in both.

From the fatigue I had experienced since I quitted head-quarters, I passed the ghaut asleep in my palanquin without being aware of it, and reached Punnah in the middle of the night. Here the usual accident of having lost my baskets detained me above an hour.

The rajah of this place is a man of the most horrid character, though he boasts of being the head of the oldest family in the province of Bundelcund. He is a most shameful drunkard, and it is said murdered his wife with his own hand. His territory, owing to his bad government, was overrun with robbers and murderers: fortunately I saw neither one nor other. I reached Kukkerittee, two coss short of this place, a few hours after daylight; and, travelling across a dreary plain, arrived here about the middle of the day. The want of personal security evinced by the peasantry out of the British territory is very striking. The moment you cross the frontier, all the ryots are invariably armed; and even the men who drive away the birds from the fields, or attend the plough, are seen with a shield hanging on their backs, a spear or matchlock against a neighbouring tree, and a sword in their sash, though perhaps in every other respect almost naked. All the villages I have passed through in Bundelcund are very neat; and in the more inaccessible parts, in front of each house, is a small raised terrace, plastered over with cow-dung, where the inhabitant was seen sitting, the very picture of content and peace. I found Major Aldin, who commands at this post, at the door of his bungalow. He received me with the greatest kindness; and I am his guest during my residence here. I was naturally anxious in my inquiries, made almost the first moment of my arrival, for news from the southward, and was very much chagrined to learn that there could not be any doubt of a rupture with the state of Nagpoor; Major Richards's letters stating as a reason for his retiring from Jubbulpoor to Garrawarrah, the increasing force of armed men in that town and neighbourhood. Indeed no doubt could be entertained of the hostile intentions of the Soubah of Jubbulpoor, as previous to Major Richards's movement he had desired that our various safeguards might be removed from the town. This unpleasant news was confirmed by Cornet Kennedy, of the 6th Bengal cavalry, who had advanced about seventy miles in the direction of my route, on his way to join his regiment at Nagpoor, but having failed in his attempt to join Major Richards, had been obliged to return from decided signs of approaching hostilities. I was thus placed in rather an awkward predicament, and had it not been for General Hardyman's advance I could not have proceeded any farther to the southward.

I found here Captain Hicks of the Bombay army under singular circumstances. He had been sent into Hindoostan to raise a battalion for the Peishwah's auxiliary force, but as we are now at war with his highness it may appear curious that this reinforcement, consisting of about 700 recruits, should be permitted to proceed. But the disciplined troops, with European officers, in the service of the native princes, are nearly the same in every point of view as our own Sepoy battalions, with this difference, that they are paid by the native prince, and carry his standard. Yet if we break with him, they, in common with our regular Sepoys, act on our side. This was the case on the late affair at Poonah. Major Ford's battalions in the Peishwah's service (to which the battalion raised by Captain Hicks is a reinforcement) co-operated with our force, and behaved well. Their uniform (as I perceived by a small detachment of disciplined Sepoys which Captain Hicks has for his guard) is red and blue, very similar to the English foot-guards. Every thing intimated the hostility of the Nagpoor government. As one proof of this, it may be stated that the first division of these recruits, consisting of 400 men, under the command of a soubidar, which had advanced to a place called Cheparrah, half way on the road to Nagpoor, was there stopped, plundered, and ill treated. The soubidar, of whom Captain Hicks speaks very highly, was made prisoner and put into irons, and 3000 rupees of the public money for the subsistence of the division seized upon. The recruits had fallen back on this place by twos and threes, but a considerable number of them were missing, and had probably deserted.

Captain Hicks has since joined with 300 more fine young men, re-organized the whole, and intends to move on the first opportunity. There is an officer of the Madras European regiment, Captain Williams, at this place, who has been resident in the island of Amboyna. He is attempting to join his regiment, which is at present with Sir Thomas Hislop. It was evident from all these tokens of threatening rupture that the mouldering embers were on the point of blazing out. In our situation we could not but be anxious about the results, as our progress was of course retarded, and the question how we could proceed with safety to the southward left undecided.

We were not long in suspense. Major Aldin received a communication from Major O'Brien, who commanded the 8th Bengal cavalry belonging to General Hardyman's force, that his regiment would be at Bellary on the 14th instant, and that his majesty's 17th regiment of foot would arrive the day following. The 8th native infantry cannot join the remainder of this corps till the 27th instant, but I trust we shall not wait for it. I in consequence determined to push on to Bellary by the 15th instant, and an arrangement was made for the officers, recruits, &c. waiting here, to join the troops at that place. It was settled that they should march the next day, but as I had relays of bearers it was not necessary that I should set out till the 13th, so as to arrive with them on the 14th at Sirnuggur, which is, I find, on the frontier. Small escorts of cavalry are laid on with my bearers.

I have written to Major O'Brien to request an escort of his regiment from Bellary on the morning of the 15th to protect us.

This place (Lohargong) has been a military station about six or seven years, and is the post of communication between Bundelcund and our troops in the Nagpoor dominions, and at Hosseinabad. It flanks the Pindarry country. It was from this post last year that Captain Ridge, with one squadron of the 5th native Bengal cavalry, cut down or put to flight near 4000 Pindarries. In addition to five companies of Major Aldin's regiment, a russollah, or troop of 120 men and horses of the second Rohilla irregular horse, and two six-pounders, are stationed here, and in peace a squadron of regular cavalry. Accounts have just been received that my bearers at the last stage to Bellary, with my escort of thirty horsemen belonging to the rajah of Punnah, have been driven in.

Lohargong, December 13, 1817.

By letters yesterday from Hosseinabad our doubts as to the intentions of the court of Nagpoor were resolved, for accounts have been received of a severe action having been fought at that city on the 26th and 27th of last month. The contest is stated to have lasted for eighteen hours, and to have terminated in the enemy's being totally repulsed. Our loss is supposed to be very heavy,—three officers killed, seven wounded, and three hundred men *hors de combât*. Mr. Sotheby, an assistant to the resident, who was at Khanpoor in October last, being the bearer of some communication, and in charge of presents from the rajah to the governor-general, is mentioned as being amongst the wounded*. We had at Nagpoor only two weak battalions of the Madras army, and three troops of the 6th Bengal cavalry. Colonel Gahan, with the remaining three troops of the 6th cavalry, and nine companies of the 22d Bengal infantry, had arrived as a seasonable reinforcement two days after the action, from the 5th division of the army of the Dekhun.

It was further reported that the rajah had asked for a suspension of hostilities after his repulse, which was granted him, as we were too weak to hope for any thing from another battle; but as orders had been sent to other disposable divisions to move towards Nagpoor before I quitted head-quarters, I trust these will be sufficient to settle matters in that quarter.

This evening I walked round the cantonments, and I think their situation has been ill chosen: about 1400 yards to the east of their present site a gentle hill rises, forming a glacis around it capable in a few hours of being made very defensible, which would have been a preferable situation. Government has been at the expense of deepening a tank, and digging two fine wells of forty feet deep, the last twenty through a bed of rock.

I saw the russollah of horse on parade this evening; they are not good, but make a showy appearance at a distance, being uniformly clothed in red, with high blue caps ornamented with brass. Their horses, being their own, are hardly capable of service. They are armed with a regulation pistol, spear, and sword, and about half the number with matchlocks. A very smart standard, with the arms of the company embroidered in gold, was carried by one of their officers, and the russollah was headed by a fierce looking kettle-drummer, whose whole execution consisted in thumping the parchment with the utmost violence. The officers had splendid horse furniture, and small silver peacocks on their horses' heads.

* This gentleman was killed.

We made them sling their matchlocks, draw their swords, and charge at speed, which they accompanied with loud yells. Some of the men had at least twenty yards of match about their persons, similar in appearance to a large ball of packthread. The receptacles which contained their powder and ball are unwieldy, and as they never make use of cartridges for their pieces, they are a long time in loading. They have a sort of foppery with respect to their sword-belts, which are in general very broad, and handsomely embroidered; and, though on horseback, they wear them over the shoulder.

To my great surprise, on entering the breakfast room this morning I found Lieutenant Smallpage, whom I little expected to have seen again. On considering the cause of my pushing forward, he had, with a proper zeal and discretion, determined to do the same, and by well-judged forced marches, his detachment of remounted horses will arrive to-day. It is his intention to join us at Sirnuggur on the morning of the 15th, and move on to Bellary with us. By letters received from head-quarters this day we learn the Baie, Holkar's mother, has so committed herself that she will be most severely dealt with. The vicinity of this place and the country between it and Bellary to the Pindarry country would always have rendered it necessary to have had escorts, and thirty horsemen were placed at every stage on my route from hence to Bellary. I leave this to-night at nine.

CHAPTER V.

Quit Lohargong—Escort—Disadvantage of the matchlock—Monkeys—Sirnuggur—Reports from Bellary—Patrole—Quit Sirnuggur—Irregular horse—Unsettled state of Indian society—Pindarries—Colonel Skinner—His Corps—Pay—Bad discipline—Independent states of Bundelcund—Bellary—Arrival of the 17th Regiment—Soubah of Jubbulpoor collecting troops to oppose us—General Hardyman's force—Major O'Brien—Intelligence department—Hircarrahs—Their fidelity—Fort at Bellary—Singular situation of affairs at Bellary—Tacit agreement—Troops in the fort offer to surrender if their arrears are paid up—Declined—Mharatta colour—European furniture—Bellary—Hindoo temples—Gondwannah—Ragojie Bhoonslah—Pindarries—Reflections—Happiness arising from the strength of the British government—Khelaut received by the Rajah of Nagpoor—Khelauts, or dresses of honour—Arabs—Intercepted letter from the Soubah of Jubbulpoor—Orders sent from Nagpoor to oppose us—Miserable policy of the native powers—Accounts from Jubbulpoor—Major Richards—Bramin saves his life on account of his sanctity—Intercepted letters of importance—All on the alert—Sehora—Strong country—Bownies—Superstition of the natives—Tanks—Intelligence of the enemy—River Herne—Letter from the soubah—Absurd and faithless communication—Vaqueel's answer—Enemy's position and force.

Bellary, 16th December, 1817.

ON the evening of the 13th I quitted Lohargong with an escort of thirty of the Rhohilla horse. The route, as far as Pipparah, was over an extensive plain, but at the last place I began to ascend the hills, and crossed a very abrupt range on a road in many places little better than a pathway. They were covered with trees of a very stunted growth, and thick underwood. The next escort I had of the Rajah of Punnah's horse were the best irregulars I had seen. They relieved the Rhohilla horse at Pipparah, and appeared very independent fellows; and where the country permitted, kept crossing the front of my palanquin at a gallop, tilting with their long spears. They had their matches lighted during the night, and I conceived for some time they were fire-flies. This circumstance must have made all night enterprises and attempts at surprise before the introduction of the flint lock most precarious. This disadvantage is noticed in the Memoirs of James II. lately published by Dr. Clarke.

While walking, I came unexpectedly on seven or eight large monkeys, about the size of a child four years old: they were very wild, and would not allow me to approach them.

I reached Sirnuggur about five o'clock on the evening of the 14th, and found the officers, recruits, &c. encamped on the banks of a stream to the south of the village. The people of the country informed us that our troops had entered the town of Bellary, and that the head man had fallen into our hands. The cavalry they had in that place was stated to have fallen back on Jubbulpoor.

In the dusk of the evening, as we were walking out, we observed a small detachment of cavalry moving towards us, which proved to be a patrole of Major O'Brien's regiment, consisting of a havildar, or serjeant, and twelve men. They brought a letter from Major O'Brien to inform me of his having arrived at Bellary, and that the 17th regiment would move in the next morning. Cornet Skepton also forwarded a letter to me, stating that he had moved twelve miles to the north of Bellary, and that he should be ready to proceed with me at an early hour the next morning. A led horse for me accompanied the patrole. These few men had a most soldier-like appearance, and the havildar particularly struck me. They had all buff belts and gloves, which, added to their undress dark blue jackets, reminded me of a regiment of French hussars.

The fort of Sirnuggur, as they are pleased to dignify it with the title, consists of four stone houses connected by a wall very capable of defence, if not attacked by artillery. I did not quit Sirnuggur on the morning of the 15th, as I waited for Lieutenant Smallpage and his detachment. We, however, started about ten, under a most motley escort, consisting of the party of the 8th cavalry, sixty of the Rajah of Punnah's horse, and about thirty of the Rhohillas. These irregulars are very bad, and appear much like the class of Indian soldiers whom Lord Cornwallis said he would rather fight than pay. This has however been proved to be a very erroneous opinion by the rapid increase of the Pindarries, and it has been found necessary, in a political point of view, to have some thousands of them in our service. Indeed it is possible more than we have at present will be called for by the sudden change we are endeavouring to make throughout India this year, in putting down the predatory bands. The state of internal commotion we have seen in this country for the last hundred years has formed a class of society whose manners we cannot hope at once to alter, and these mercenaries, at least for the present generation, must not if possible be left without employment. It will take time to alter the feeling of these persons, but at present it would be hopeless to expect them on a sudden to convert their swords into ploughshares.

However, by the great work now going on, the destruction of the nest of plunderers to the north of the Nerbuddah, and the occupation of their territory, a blow will be given to the roaming dispositions of thousands. Till time, that grand reformer, aided by the strong arm of British influence, shall work a great and decided change throughout India, the majority of these freebooters must find bread, and by equally dividing this restless class among the native powers according to their means, we must, *malgré* Lord Cornwallis's maxim, thus support them for some years. We have at present in our service, under the Bengal establishment, 7000 of them. One of these corps, under the command of Colonel Skinner, a half-cast gentleman in our service, consists of 3000 horsemen.

It is a circumstance worthy of remark, and which at the same time shews how strongly tradition has handed down accounts of the Macedonian conqueror, that Colonel Skinner has, for his conduct and gallantry, gained from the military population of Hin-

G. Fitz-Clarence del.   RHOHILLA HORSE.   SKINNERS' HORSE.   Engraved by R. Havell & Son.

IRREGULAR CAVALRY.

Bengal Army, 1817.

London, Published April 1819, by John Murray, Albemarle Street.

doostan the name of Alexander, or Secunder, as it is here pronounced.

The irregular cavalry throughout this country being mounted on their own horses is one of the principal causes which militates so much against them; as should they in action or otherwise lose their horses, they lose their bread; the dread of which must be a great drawback on a man's exertions under fire. Our regular native cavalry having no feeling of this description towards their horses, are by no means sparing of their own persons. Colonel Skinner has to a certain degree obviated this feeling in his corps, by establishing a fund for saving a small monthly sum from the pay of each soldier, who comes on this for a part (I believe only a part) of the value of his horse, should he be lost. These Hindoostanee horsemen receive twenty-two rupees a month, and for this sum mount themselves, provide their own food, and find provender for their charger, and ammunition. This would appear a very small sum in Europe, taking the rupee at 2*s.* 6*d.* The expense of a horseman complete per annum would be under thirty-six pounds. The generality of them however are little better than Pindarries, but they are of service as escorts, and when in our own provinces assist the police. Those I saw appear to be under no sort of discipline, and are by all accounts unprincipled barbarians. I was informed of a circumstance which will place them in a proper light. Near Punnah one of these unconscionable ruffians having a dispute with a man and his wife about the payment for some trifle, seized their daughter, a girl of thirteen years old, threw her across his horse, and fairly carried her off. On complaint being made to the officer commanding at Lohargong, he sent after the detachment of horse to which the offender belonged, who receiving information of the pursuit left the poor girl in the plain, and was never discovered. In our own provinces they cannot commit these excesses, our police being too active, and punishment too certain. I have frequently mentioned the difference between our provinces and those not under our government: this requires some explanation. Sajapoor, where I left head-quarters, was in the territory of the Rajah of Simpter, Erij in that of the Nana of Jaloan. Adji Ghur pertained to us, but the territories of the independent chiefs of Bundelcund are so intermixed, it is impossible to know one from another. The part of Bundelcund not under our immediate government is ruled by near forty petty chiefs, and extends from the river Chumbul north, to Bogulcund on the south, forming a chain of small states, not unlike those of Germany, between us and the territories of Scindiah. Our possessions are so indented with theirs, that it is never known when on the verge of the frontier, to whom the country belongs, which is only ascertained by the villagers paying their rents to their respective sovereigns.

These states are all Hindoo, having formed part of the Mharatta empire, and paid tribute to the Peishwah till the treaty of June last, but since that period they look up to us as their head. This difficulty of marking the boundaries between these jarring chieftains often led to serious quarrels, until they bound themselves to look upon us as arbiters in all cases of dispute. Whenever our influence is strong enough, it is a standing rule in our Indian policy to insist on this agreement, on the principle that even a neutral power must in some measure feel the effects of war carried on in its vicinity, and on the ground of our anxiety to keep the continent of India in tranquillity.

To return from this digression: about ten miles from Bellary I found Mr. Skipton with the remainder of the troop, and proceeded through a woody country over several small ranges of hills, till we came directly above Bellary, which is situated in the plain. The view was very extensive, and the white tents dotted over the country improved the landscape. We were at first under some apprehensions that the 17th regiment had not arrived, as there were but a small number of tents, but were soon satisfied on this point. On entering the camp we found they had just marched in, after a journey of seventeen miles, and were only beginning to pitch their tents. On my arrival I waited on General Hardyman, who received me with the utmost attention. He did not intend to stay for the other battalion of his force, but the animals belonging to the 17th regiment being fatigued with their long march, he meant to halt on the 16th (to-day) but to march on the following day.

A blow in this quarter would at this moment be very opportune, and it is hoped we shall reach Jubbulpoor, the capital of the provinces of the Rajah of Nagpoor, north of the Nerbuddah, in three days from this place. The courage and determination of the soubah and his troops will, I have no doubt, like that of Acres in the Rivals, "ooze out of the palms of their hands," if we do not move down quick upon them; and delay may make them think better of it and disperse. By reports from the southward they are stated to have collected 5000 men and 5 guns at Jubbulpoor. The force under General Hardyman is not in all 1100 men, but being nearly half Europeans, and the rest so fine a regiment of cavalry, it is competent to beat five times its number.

Major O'Brien of the 8th cavalry gives me a place in his tent during the time I remain with this force. This officer has charge of what they call in this country the intelligence department, and is convinced the enemy will not fight us, unless he receives considerable reinforcements which he expects from the southward. The intelligence department and the peculiar manner in which information is obtained in this country in the presence of an enemy, and the slender support upon which it rests, surprised me.

Major O'Brien has sixty pairs of hircarrahs, who are men of very low station, but enterprising; they receive only five rupees a month each, but rewards are held out to them for successful exertion. It is from them and them only he obtains information of the situation, strength, and movements of the enemy, and after digesting their various accounts he moves the corps according to the judgment he forms on the result.

These poor fellows run dreadful risks, but are well remunerated if they succeed in carrying letters to any post difficult of access, or are found to bring in good information. On my expressing my fears as to the possibility of their being bought over and betraying us when their small stipend was considered, I was assured that they are to be trusted with the most unlimited confidence; so entirely indeed, that the general has not placed any picquets at night distant from the camp, being contented with a chain of sentries a few hundred paces around, as the first we should hear of the enemy must be from these hard working fellows, who lie in the jungles and on the roads, and never fail to discover any hostile movement.

They always travel in pairs, and are put to most extraordinary shifts to secure themselves and the despatches. It is much apprehended that several from this force have been seized and put to death by the enemy. The fort in the centre of this town still remains in the hands of the enemy, but no act of hostility has taken place; on the contrary, we have been up to the gate, talked with their sentries, and have a guard of sepoys within 100 yards of it. They appear to me to carry on war in a very singular way in this country, and the situation of affairs here is singular. We are at war with the Rajah of Nagpoor, and are aware of an action having taken place between his troops and a detachment of our army, yet a column moving down towards his capital enters a town belonging to him, where a garrison of 200 men are posted in a fort; by a sort of tacit agreement no act of hostility takes place, and they do not fire upon us, though they will not permit us to enter. The rajah's flag flies on its walls, and yet we have a guard of thirty armed men, in no manner annoyed, close to their gate. This seems to be rather inconsistent on both sides, but our orders are to proceed to the capital; and if the intermediate troops belonging to his highness are as civil as these, and do not oppose our advance, I do not see why we should quarrel with them. The troops in the fort offered in the course of last night by an emissary, sent to Major O'Brien, to evacuate it if we would pay them their arrears. The 8th infantry not being up, the general intending to move on, the fort itself being of no importance and not in our power to garrison, and the 17th regiment being weak, as its flank companies are detached with the centre division of the army, their offer was disregarded.

We have as prisoners three of the principal men of the town, one of whom we intend to leave here, taking on with us part of his family as hostages. Major O'Brien and myself went in the evening of yesterday through the town and vicinity. In the principal bazar stands a most immense brickdust-coloured flag, the Mharatta colour; and, as I am told, used throughout the empire. Confidence has been restored; the inhabitants of the town are returning from the jungles, and we have been enabled to procure some flour and grain. We must take with us all we can get in case of being obliged to proceed the whole way to Nagpoor, for the country to the south of the river is nearly a desert. We inspected the gate of the old Gond fort, which is little better than a strong house; two of its sides indeed are covered by a large tank, but one of its angles is a heap of ruins, and forms at this moment a practicable breach. Close to the gate, and to all appearance neglected, stands a bullock cart loaded with European furniture, I suppose for some house at Nagpoor. It was probably seized on its way down, and those in charge of it driven away. Some of the smart cane-backed chairs are damaged, but eventually the rest of the articles may reach their destination. The ruins of what was once the principal part of Bellary extend on all sides, and there are some fine Hindoo temples in its neighbourhood. This is the first town of the ancient Hindoo province of Gondwannah, or the country of the Gonds, which constitutes the greatest part of the present dominions of the Rajah of Nagpoor.

Ragojee Bhoonslah, the Mharatta general, and relation to the Rajah of Satarah, conquered this province about the middle of the last century, imprisoned the Gond rajah, founded Nagpoor, and established the present dynasty on the throne. Bellary, in common with the other towns in its vicinity, has suffered so much from the Pindarries, that I am surprised it has not been totally deserted. I have often reflected how it was possible for a state of society to continue in so wretched a situation as it has struggled with in these countries for the last fourteen years. The industrious ryot, or husbandman, had always before his eyes the possibility, and far from improbability, of being tortured to point out his little saving, of having his hut burnt, and the females of his family abused or carried off.

I am only astonished at the perseverance of these industrious cultivators, who, when sowing the land, must be aware that it is at least problematical who shall enjoy the profit after the crop is reaped.

How fortunate it has been for this country that circumstances have brought a foreign and generous nation from another quarter of the globe, and raised it to so high a station and such political strength, that it should be able to destroy this host of banditti, when the native courts might have looked in vain amongst themselves for the power or combination to accomplish this most desirable object.

During the whole of yesterday and to-day pairs of hircarrahs have arrived from Jubbulpoor and its vicinity with various intelligence. There is a corroboration of what had been reported at head-quarters previous to my departure, that the Rajah of Nagpoor before the late action had received a khelaut, or dress of honour, from the Rajah of Satarah, the puppet of the Peishwah but in whose name every thing is ordered, and directions to assume the functions of general-in-chief of his armies.

Investing a person with a dress of honour is the mode the sovereigns of India take to shew their approbation, and on receiving any new title or post a khelaut always accompanies it. When I was presented to the King of Delhi in 1815, his majesty gave me one of these dresses, but of most miserable materials. The ceremony is to put it on over the European dress, with a turban tied round the cocked hat, which has a most extraordinary effect. The whole dress is made of muslin worked in gold or silver. The king, with his own hands, tied on the false jewels to ornament my turban.

But when the house of Timour was at its height of power these khelauts were often of great value. It is a very particular honour throughout the East to receive a dress from the king's wardrobe, or one he has worn himself. We see the same custom in use at Constantinople; the grand seignior sending dresses of sable as marks of his favour. There appears to have been no decided rule for such gifts; and we find that Shah Jehan on the completion of his new palace at Delhi, and on taking possession of it, presented all his court with khelauts. They are even sent on the death of a relation as a testimony of condolence. In this case they are always dyed black or green; but there are other tokens of mourning in Hindoostan besides a change of colour in the dress, such as dirty clothes, disordered turbans, and neglected beards. Our government, I have been told, present on certain festivals green khelauts to the mollahs, or priests in the Mahometan cities. We also find that it was sometimes customary to present the rannies, or Hindoo female sovereigns, with dresses of honour, and that they preferred those of men to such as were proper for their sex.

The accounts inform us that the Arabs in the service of the rajah behaved at Nagpoor with the utmost gallantry, and the hircarrahs state that troops are moving from Jubbulpoor to this place; and if we required any confirmation of the rajah's hostility, a letter we have intercepted from the Soubah of Jubbulpoor, Rainjee Thatia, to the chief here, who is in our hands, would put at rest every doubt upon the subject. It commands him in general terms to oppose the Inglaiz behauders *, and mentions that orders have arrived from Nagpoor to that effect; he is also required to entertain all the Pindarries he finds fit for the service, and acknowledges the arrival of fifty. What a pernicious example does this afford of the conduct of the native courts; not looking beyond the present moment, they thus take into their pay these lawless wretches, who on being again discharged will plunder their whole country! A letter was received late last night from a reporter belonging to our government at Jubbulpoor, who has in consequence of his connexion with us been confined and ill treated, but by some means succeeded in writing to us. He states that the force collected there does not exceed 4000 men, horse and foot, and eight guns; and that the soubah being a man of no great spirit we should meet with but little resistance if we pushed on. When the troops at that place heard of our arrival they assembled in great confusion round the Thatia.

Three hundred horse left Jubbulpoor yesterday for this place, and they continue to take into their pay all the matchlock men who offer. We have been very anxious to receive some intelligence of Major Richards; and in the course of to-day an hircarrah has arrived, who left Colonel M'Morrin on the 10th instant. He is one of four who had two letters between them for General Hardyman, but they had been seized by the enemy. This hircarrah had, however, escaped; and in failure of the letter was desired to say that Major Richards had joined Colonel M'Morrin, and that in consequence of hordes of horse surrounding them they were marching for Hosseinabad. They have a large convoy of

* Behauder, a title used in India, meaning gallant, brave, noble,—generally applied, like our word esquire, to the name of a person of respectability.

clothing and stores of all kinds with them for Colonel Adams's division. Within a few hours after the arrival of this hircarrah, another of the three who started with him got to our camp; he also had been taken, and only saved his life in consequence of being a Bramin.

While we halted this day (the 16th), Major O'Brien and myself rode out to the front, and by accident fell in with two natives, who he thought looked suspicious. On searching them, we detected a letter rolled up in the corner of one of their sashes. We returned to camp with our prize, but found some difficulty in translating its contents, as it was in the Mharatta language It has, however, proved to be of some consequence:—the Thatia has promised to assist the garrison of this place with two pieces of cannon, 500 horse, and 1000 matchlock men. They are to arrive to-night, and the chief here is desired not to be afraid. This intelligence of course has had due attention paid to it. Some patroles have been ordered out, and the 17th regiment directed to sleep with their accoutrements on; the quarter-guard and inlying picquet to be doubled; though it is not thought likely that the enemy will approach in the night.. Orders have been delivered out for marching at daybreak, and the hircarrahs affirm that we are to be annoyed on the road.

Camp near Pannuggur, 18th December, 1817.

The night of the 16th passed without alarm, and we reached the vicinity of Sehonra yesterday in very good time, though the distance was twenty-two miles, the enemy not having shewn himself upon the road. We heard indeed of 50 horsemen and 200 matchlock men to the left in the jungle, but no one saw them. All the towns and villages were deserted, but we made prisoner the chief man of one of them. He had barricaded his house, but we entered by escalade off the back of a camel. There was much jungle on both sides of the road, and we passed through some places where 100 light infantry might have stopped us for hours. We observed some very splendid bownies, or wells, with flights of steps down to the water, and generally ornamented on the level of the ground with temples. It is a maxim with the superstitious Hindoos, that he whom heaven blesses with a son, who digs a tank or bownie, and plants a grove of fruit trees, has done his duty in this world, and has an indisputable right to eternal happiness hereafter. This is all in favour of the rich, and particularly hard upon the poor, as their want of means diminishes the chance of their salvation.

Our camp yesterday was by the side of a very splendid tank, and we passed several others of considerable circumference. We hear the enemy is drawn out in front of the town of Jubbulpoor with the determination of fighting us. The general marched this morning (the 18th) at daylight, and passed near the fort at Sehonra, but out of reach of fire. Our road crossed the river Herne in this day's route over a bridge made for our battering guns, which accompanied Colonel Adams's force. An active enemy would have destroyed it. On the march two hircarrahs met us from the soubah with a letter, of which the following is almost the literal translation.

"To my friends the English gentlemen," after expressing a desire for an interview, &c. "Be it known to you that some difference having existed between my master and the English resident, Mr. Jenkins, which is now, by the blessing of God, settled, and the original friendship restored; and orders having been received by me notifying the same, I have therefore desired the agents of your government to go and procure whatever they require. On your arrival at Bellary you acted harshly. You have nothing to fear from me. I have sent a vaqueel (or agent) to you to explain every thing, and always write your answer in the way of friendship. Your approach I have notified to my master. A letter will arrive in a few days from the burra sahib* (Mr. Jenkins), which I will forward

* Literally "great gentleman," a term made use of by the natives to those of superior rank, or holding high official situations.

to you: till then commit not any act of hostility. The people you have seized at Bellary are of no consequence, but simply servants earning their bread, placed there for form's sake."

The vaqueel, however, who was to explain every thing, took fright some distance off, and it was at first settled that no answer should be returned, as it was impossible we could refrain from hostilities if the force collected at Jubbulpoor did not disperse, our orders being positive to march to Nagpoor, and our route lying through that town. The intercepted letters would alone have been sufficient for us to have acted upon, but as we knew of actual hostilities having taken place, there was no question about believing our enemy with respect to "friendship being restored." It was ultimately determined that a letter should be sent without compliments, stating that we should arrive at Jubbulpoor the next morning, and if the soubah was as amicably inclined as he wished us to believe, he would come out in person to meet the general.

The road was extremely bad to-day, and the guns and rear-guard joined us very late. The hircarrahs, who left Jubbulpoor at twelve o'clock, state that the force there consists of 500 horse, 1000 matchlock men, and 4 guns; and that they are drawn up across the road in front of the town, being fully bent on disputing our passage. This place is only sixteen miles from Jubbulpoor.

Eleven o'clock at night.

More hircarrahs have arrived, and all are in the same story, that the enemy intend to fight; but unless they are more numerous than we are led to suppose by the last accounts, it is thought they will not oppose us.

CHAPTER VI.

March from Pannuggur—Sculptured bull—Fine country—Hindoo temples—Account of the enemy—Communication of an absurd nature from them—Answer only verbal—Enemy's position beautiful—Gasconade—Our force halt opposite the enemy's centre—Disposition—Attack the enemy—Cannonade—Charge of cavalry—Lieutenant Pope's gallantry—Enemy's artillerymen behave well—Their guns taken—Rockets—Seventeenth regiment storm the height—Defeat the enemy's infantry—No operations against the town—Message to the enemy—Threats—Submission—Enemy's guns—Careless with powder—Enemy's loss—Enemy evacuate Jubbulpoor—Prizes—Standards captured—Wrought iron balls—Jubbulpoor—Fort—Cantonments belonging to Major Richards—March from Jubbulpoor—Pass of Gurrah—Inhabitants—History of this district—Conquered by the Mahometans—Joar—Distress of the natives—Reflections—Enemy's defeated cavalry—River Nerbuddah a sacred stream—Geographical division of India—Hindoostan and the Dekhun—Accident which occurs to the author—March from Tulwarrah—Arrive at Pipparee—Brinjarries—Manners and customs—Dhoriah—Enemy at Sirnuggur—Dhoomah—Bad ghaut—Accounts received of a second action at Nagpoor—Rajah our prisoner—Arabs and Phitans still in arms against us—Lucknadown—Letter from the resident at Nagpoor—Orders to halt till further orders—Two squadrons given as an escort for the author to Nagpoor—Move to Chipparah—Inquiries for the soubidar belonging to Captain Hicks—Retaliation of the recruits—Mode of concealing grain by the natives—Means of discovery—Halt—Nurella—The long-lost soubidar—Account of his escape—Doolies—Mohargong—Despatch from Mr. Jenkins—Puzdar—Forest and jungle—Tigers—The hircarrah's dread of these animals—Dungertaul—Forest—Tigers in great numbers—Tank—Ramteek—Sacred spot—Jungle—Party of the enemy's cavalry cut to pieces—Accounts from Nagpoor—Arabs come to an agreement—Accounts of the defeat of Holkar—The Mharatta confederacy—Proclamation—Arrival of a troop of cavalry from Nagpoor—Accounts state the Peishwah is still in the field—Ramteek—Seclusion of Women—Prejudices giving way—March to the banks of the Kunnain river—Difficulties of passing through the country—Change of climate—Hawks—Grand falconer.

Camp, Tulwarrah Ghaut, on the banks of the Nerbuddah,
20th December, 1817.

YESTERDAY the fatigue of all was so great that I, among the rest, was too tired to write a line. At daylight we began to move, skirting the town of Pannuggur on our right, and one of the magnificent tanks, so common in this part of the country, on our left. Pannuggur appears to be a town of considerable antiquity, and we passed a very curious sculptured bull placed on a very high stone altar. The huts of the inhabitants are of a particular construction, the side walls consisting only of mats plastered with mud. The whole country, for the last three days' marches, was a perfect garden richly cultivated. A great number of spires of Hindoo temples raised their pinnacles in the centre of the town, but we had no time to visit them, as every report confirmed the intelligence of the determined face the soubah and his troops were about to show. Six miles short of Jubbulpoor we met a single horseman, a very fine looking old man with a long white beard, bearing a letter for the English general, which stated that the soubah did not wish any act of hostility to ensue between us, and informed us that his troops were on the road, and that he was fearful if we approached any nearer some quarrel might take place among the soldiers.

This silly communication only deserved the answer given, which was verbal to this effect, " remove the troops, and let the soubah meet the general." I thought the old messenger looked very uneasy at this laconic reply.

We continued to move on, and crossed a stream with very bad banks, which obliged us to halt to allow the guns to join us.

I rode forward to reconnoitre, and the country being flat, I was with difficulty able to get a good view of the enemy, but on turning the corner of a wood they at once broke upon me in their position.

With my telescope I counted every man who showed himself over the strong rocky hill on which their right rested. This was covered with the most picturesque groups of armed men; some with matchlocks, others with spears, some resting on their shields: many standards were waving in the wind, and the pleasing variety of the colours of their turbans, coats, sashes, &c. made their position, with the strong marked rocky back ground, a perfect picture.

With a design I suppose of frightening us and by way of a foolish gasconade, they continually fired their matchlocks in defiance. On the left of this theatrical group, in the open ground, were posted four pieces of brass cannon glistening in the sun, strongly supported with masses of infantry; and upon the left of these appeared from 800 to 1000 horse drawn up in the front of their tents with their kettledrums beating. At times a single horseman dashed out, and, advancing towards us at speed, turned his horse short round within a few hundred yards, and retired tilting at the tufts of grass, and brandishing his long spear apparently to dare us to the fight. Their whole force must have exceeded 3000 men. The bugle from the rear sounded the advance, the guns having passed the difficulty, and the column, marching between two small villages, halted opposite the enemy to make our disposition for attack.

Two squadrons of cavalry under Major O'Brien were sent round their left to cut off their retreat to the Nerbuddah; our four guns were placed in the centre, masked by the cavalry of the advance under Cornet Kennedy of the 6th native cavalry, who had handsomely expressed his wish to do duty, during the service, with Major O'Brien's regiment. These afterwards became a reserve which covered the right flank of the infantry. Three companies of the 17th regiment were posted on each side of the guns, two companies in reserve in rear of them, and a squadron of cavalry, under Lieutenant Pope, was placed as a reserve in rear of the left. The baggage was concentrated in charge of the rear-guard, a mile in the rear, near a tank.

As soon as all was arranged, the whole advanced slowly towards the enemy, as the bullocks which draw the cannon in India are very miserable substitutes for horses, and the guns are generally left behind after the first fire. About eleven o'clock, having arrived opposite the enemy's centre, our cavalry was withdrawn from before the artillery, and the answer to the general question if

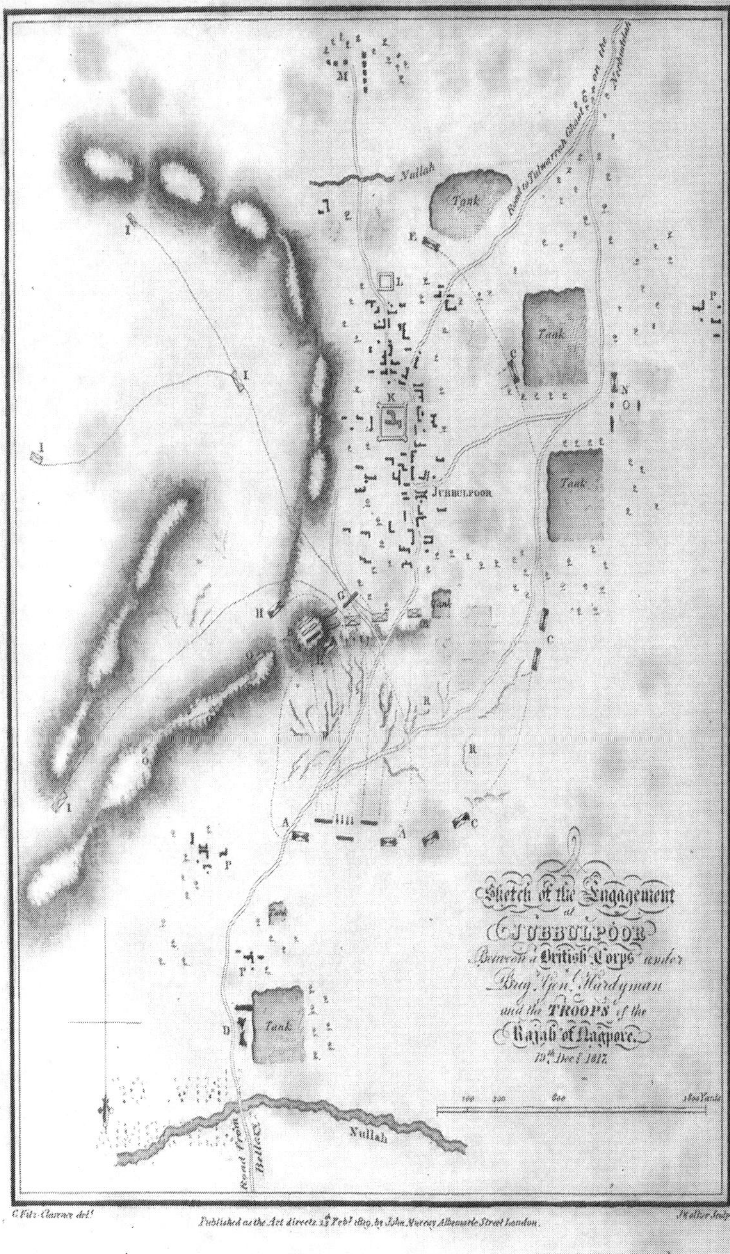

G. Fitz-Clarence delt. Published as the Act directs 23d. Feby. 1819, by John Murray Albemarle Street London. J. Walker Sculpt.

REFERENCES TO THE ENGAGEMENT OF JUBBULPOOR.

The British troops are coloured red—the enemy's yellow.

A. Brigadier-General Hardyman's disposition; four guns in the centre, three corps of the 17th on each flank, with two corps and 200 of the 8th cavalry in reserve.

B. The position of the enemy; their right on a strong stony knoll; their cavalry with the left on a tank, and their centre garnished with four guns.

C. Two squadrons under Major O'Brian moving on the flank and rear of the enemy.

D. The baggage and rear guard assembled at a tank.

E. Lieutenant Pope's squadron charging the guns in flank, exposed to the fire from the infantry on the hill.

F. Left wing of the 17th, storming the hill.

G. Right wing of the 17th, covering the captured guns.

H. Cornet Kennedy, 6th Native cavalry, after supporting Lieutenant Pope, threatens the rear of the enemy's infantry.

I. The enemy's broken cavalry.

K. The Fort.

L. The Tope Konnah, where considerable progress had been made for the increase of their park.

M. The cantonments lately occupied by Major Richards.

N. Our camp after the action.

O. The retreat of the enemy's defeated infantry.

P. Villages, the names not known.

R. Broken ground and small ravines.

all was ready, being answered in the affirmative by Lieutenant D'Oyley, our right gun opened at eight hundred yards with Shrapnell shells. Had the enemy reserved their fire for our word of command we could hardly have fired more together; both shots must have been in the air at the same moment; and for about ten minutes the fire was pretty sharp on both sides, but as we were moving up towards them their shot flew over our heads. I offered my services, which the general was so kind as to accept. In a few minutes the enemy began to waver on their left, and the general ordered Lieutenant Pope's squadron to advance towards their right and centre. This officer at a hand-gallop passed under the fire of the enemy's infantry on the hill, and with a most brilliant charge took their guns.

The sirdar of artillery and his men behaved nobly; the former wounded Lieutenant Pope in the body with a spear, but was shot dead by the havildar whom I formerly mentioned as commanding the patrole the day before I joined the camp. Till he fell they fought bravely, and were pistolled at their guns; but their cavalry fled. Cornet Kennedy was now ordered to charge their infantry, which had come down into the plain; but they regained the height, and fired heavily upon him, and threw many rockets amongst us: I had never seen them before, and even asked what they were. The general then brought up the left wing of the 17th to the foot of the hill, which, with all their hearts and every possible exertion, they ascended under a heavy but ill-directed fire, and gained the summit; shot, bayoneted, or put to flight the defenders, and seized their standards. Cornet Kennedy, who had passed round to the other side of the hill, cut down all who attempted to retire in his direction; many, however, escaped along the ridge. At the foot of the hill near the town it was with the greatest difficulty I could save our reporter who had written to us when at Bellary. He had escaped from his confinement, and rather rashly entered into the *demêlé;* I could hardly persuade the troopers to believe him a friend, and indeed if he had not mentioned to me the name of our political agent in Bundelcund, he would have been killed in an instant, as the sabres were lifted to destroy him. The regiment formed near the captured guns, and the general being desirous to act up to his orders in moving on to Nagpoor as soon as possible, would not lose time or men in attacking the town. We proceeded, therefore, to the right of the road, and encamped about a mile from it, as soon as all opposition outside was ascertained to be over. All who approached were fired upon from the houses, but the general sent in to say he would open his guns upon the town if all the armed men were not out of it by ten o'clock at night. This threat brought out many of the town's people and bankers, the latter of whom are usually in India looked upon as neutral, from the use they are to both partics. They entreated the general not to carry his threat into execution, and promised not only the evacuation of the place by the troops, but a surrender of seven more guns in the fort, and the general gave his word they should be well treated on these conditions. The guns we took in the field are cast brass with iron cylinders, two of them three, and two six pounders, but they are so thick that, till I looked at the bore, I thought they were six and nine. Six tumbrils with their bullocks fell into our hands, with much ammunition, and great store of balls, grape, and chain shot. They appear to be very careless with their powder, as large quantities of it lay loose near the guns. The enemy's loss in men must have been considerable, as in so limited a space, excepting at Talavera, I never saw so many dead bodies; and in a small Hindoo temple on the summit of the hill, not thirty feet square, lay forty-two of the dead, heaped on each other. The cotton clothing of many was set on fire by our wadding, and smothering in their quilted jackets, burnt till it reached their powder flasks, and these exploding, disfigured the bodies horribly. Two of their wounded sirdars remained in the town, but the *Bapo*, the military man who commanded in the action (the soubah being a civilian), fled from it, though wounded in the arm, by what they called a grape shot, but doubtless a ball from one of the Shrapnell shells. Our threat had so good an effect that our hircarrahs reported in the evening it was not only possible but safe to go into the town, and Major O'Brien, accompanied by Lieutenant Smallpage, went through it on an elephant at ten at night, though I thought it rather a rash undertaking. We have heard that the soubah was anxious to meet the general, but the sirdars dissuaded him. The soldiers of the two regiments took many prizes of arms, money, horses, cattle, &c. and have had regular auctions in their lines, which have occasioned much amusement. Some of the arms taken were very handsome, and two English blunderbusses were found upon the field. Seven standards in all, of green and red, and white and orange silk, have fallen into our possession; several of which have hands embroidered on their centre, and in one of them a dagger with seven balls; they are ornamented with silver tassels, but are far from being superb. I have asked the officers of the 17th to give me three, which I intend to take on with me as far as I can, and if possible, to England, though they will be very cumbersome. The carriages of the guns and tumbrils have hands painted on them in red, and the only explanation I could get of this emblem, used here as well as on the colours, is that it is meant for poujah (worship). Several of our wounded are hit by lead slugs, others by wrought iron balls; two officers of the 17th regiment, and a native officer of the 8th cavalry, are among the number, besides Lieutenant Pope, whose wound is feared to be dangerous, and causes great regret, as all in the field witnessed his gallantry. The general's syce, or groom, was killed by his side, but our loss otherwise has been trifling.

This morning (the 20th) before we marched I went through the town, and think it one of the best I have seen. I am not surprised at this, as its wealth ought to be great, from the richness of the country from Bellary to Jubbulpoor. I trust the forfeiture of so fine a province will be part of the punishment of this faithless rajah. The fort, surrounded by houses, is miserable, but might hold out for some time against an enemy without artillery. We found some swivels and a horse load of rockets, which we brought out with us. In the *tope khonnah*, or artillery ground, was an iron four-pounder mounted and loaded. Very considerable progress had been made in forming new wheels, gun-carriages, &c. We then proceeded to the cantonments lately occupied by Major Richards, if they deserved that name, for I never before witnessed such miserable habitations for Europeans; they were very slight, consisting of the frame of a house covered with mats and whitewashed: some parts had been burnt. The general before we left Jubbulpoor ordered all the enemy's guns to be burst except those taken in action, which we carried with us. I was employed all this morning by his order taking the ground in the neighbourhood, as he wished to send a sketch of the action to head-quarters. Before we quitted the ground, we passed the two hircarrahs of the enemy we had taken at Bellary guarded, and the general with much kindness liberated them. I was much amused by the mode in which they expressed their thanks, pulling up the grass which grew by our feet, and filling their mouths with it. We marched at twelve o'clock, and about two miles southwest of Jubbulpoor traversed the strongest and most difficult country I ever saw. The town of Gurrah, once the capital of this province, is built in a most singular pass, and extends through and along the face of a mountainous ridge about two miles. Had they opposed us here, and not in the plain, it is possible our further operations to the southward might have been suspended. The rocky heights to the back of the town were covered with the inhabitants, the town itself being nearly deserted. The fine country from Bellary, we learn from Dow, once formed a little independent Hindoo principality;

of which this town was the capital. It fell under the power of the Mahometans, in the reign of Akbar, not without a severe contest, the troops of the emperor being opposed by the reigning queen Durgetti, at the head of her army. The war was concluded by the fall of the strongest fort, and the annihilation of the whole of the garrison, after they had performed the horrid and despairing rites of the joar by the destruction of their wives and children. The plunder was immense, and 1000 elephants are stated to have been taken. As we passed through the town it was painful to see many women and girls by the side of the road, as if too unhappy to exert themselves, or dreading the worst that might happen to them, bewailing their fathers, brothers, and sons killed the day before; wretched victims taken from their homes to support a cause in which none of them were interested. Patriotism does not exist among the natives of India, and they could not be bound by feelings of gratitude to their prince, who has allowed them, without any exertion on his part, to be plundered by the Pindarries for fourteen years past. The people throughout India, being brought up under a despotism, are as confined in all their sentiments of liberty as in their other ideas, and consider themselves as belonging to the sovereign whose officers are placed over them. Thus having no incitement of a virtuous or generous nature to take up arms, their only motive is that which predominates in all despotisms, fear; and through dread of punishment when called upon, they blindly range themselves under the standard of the sovereign, though without any motive in the quarrel. In the present instance, indeed, it is impossible they could feel anxious to support a government which has not acted as the guardian of their peace and homes; and in all probability they would be thankful to come under our rule and protection. But though fear is the predominant feeling, we have both witnessed and felt that they are occasionally actuated by principles of fidelity and military valour.

I rode forward to this place, and found that forty of the enemy's cavalry had left the other side of the river this morning. With a childish feeling of ambition, I made every exertion to cross the river Nerbuddah, which runs between steep banks close to the town, in order to be the first to enter the Dekhun, in which I succeeded. This river is now about three feet deep, and the stream one hundred yards across, with a fine pebbly bottom; but in the rains it must be as large as the Thames at Richmond. It is one of the first order of rivers and a sacred stream, all rivers not being equally so esteemed throughout India, in which there are I believe only twenty-eight thus venerated. On crossing, it used to be customary in the Mahometan armies to give a largess to the troops and followers. The geographical division of India is not generally known in England. Hindoostan does not properly include Bengal nor the country south of the Nerbuddah, the latter of which is called the Dekhun as far as the river Krishna, and was a much later conquest of the Mahometans than their more northern possessions. The troops cross the river to-morrow, and we continue our march towards Nagpoor.

Cheeparah, 26th December, 1817.

I have been prevented writing regularly by a severe accident which befel me on the evening of the 20th, and it is now with difficulty I can hold my pen. It was determined to destroy the guns taken from the enemy, as carrying them on increased our difficulties, and at the hour appointed I went to see the order executed, when an unlucky spark set fire to a considerable quantity of powder near the spot where I was standing, which, exploding, burnt me severely in the legs, hands, and face. The whole of my clothes were either burnt, or torn off me by the artillerymen, and my hair and feather were much singed. On the 21st we marched to Pipparee, having passed the river without difficulty. I have been obliged ever since the accident to be carried in my palanquin, not being able to ride. We had an alarm this day (the 21st) that the enemy had attacked our rear, but it proved to be nothing but a few horsemen who had talked to our brinjarries. These are a class of itinerant merchants who travel over India with many thousand oxen laden with grain. It is by these people that the Indian armies in the field are fed, and they are never injured by either army. The grain is taken from them, but invariably paid for. The head of the brinjarries has peculiar privileges at the courts of the native princes. They encamp for safety every evening in a regular square formed of the bags of grain, of which they construct a breast-work. They and their families are in the centre, and the oxen are made fast outside. Guards with matchlocks and spears are placed at the corners, and their dogs do duty as advanced posts. I have seen them with droves of 50,000 bullocks. They do not move above two miles an hour, as the cattle are allowed to graze as they proceed on the march. On the 22d, by the mistake of our guides, our advanced guard went one way, and the column another; and it was very late in the evening before the error could be rectified. The next day we marched to Dhooriah, and heard of a force of the enemy about twelve miles to our right at Sirnuggur, but being out of our way, our orders would not admit of our approaching them. The country was extremely steril, and covered with dwarf trees and small bushes, and the road lay over several ridges of small abrupt hills with some bad passes for the guns. On the 24th we marched to Dhoomah by a very long and bad road. About three miles before we arrived at our ground, we ascended the worst ghaut we had seen, and the artillery were only got over it by manual labour. When we reached the village it rained, and we had hardly got under cover in a house before one of our videttes reported the advance of a body of infantry, which on nearer approach proved to be a party of thirty men. On inquiring who they were, and whence they came, we learned that they were fugitives from an action which had been fought at Nagpoor on the 16th, between General Doveton and the rajah's troops, and that our forces had captured all their guns and elephants, and made the rajah himself prisoner. The Arabs and Pithans were stated to have taken post in the palace, where they continued to defend themselves. We, of course, continued to advance, until stopped by a letter from the resident, which we received on the morning of the 25th, on arriving at our ground at Lucknadown. It was brought by two hircarrahs, and was from Mr. Jenkins himself, announcing that the rajah had come into our terms, and directing the general to halt until further orders. As it was my duty to proceed on as fast as possible, and I had in my possession a written authority to demand escorts, General Hardyman ordered two squadrons under Major O'Brien to move on towards Nagpoor till we should fall in with another escort from thence, or, if not, to continue with me to that capital. I have written to Mr. Jenkins to send an escort to meet me, with bearers for my palanquins, and to lay others on the road to Bombay or Hyderabad, as he may think fit. According to these orders and arrangements the general's force halted this day (the 26th), and Major O'Brien with the two squadrons, Captain Hicks with his recruits, and the officers whose regiments are to the southward, and myself, moved hither this morning, to the south of the river Payen Gunga. This is the place where the first detachment of Captain Hicks's recruits were dispersed and ill treated. We have made inquiries about the soubidar who was taken prisoner, but have gained little information respecting him. He was last heard of at a fort off the road called Soune. Some of the recruits, acting from a very natural spirit of retaliation, went sauntering through the town, where they had been previously abused; and the features of some of their former persecutors having left a strong impression on their memory, they first seized and secured them, and then set to all together with bamboos and thrashed them to their hearts' contents.

We were not aware of their thus taking the law into their own hands until after the affair was over. I am happy to say that the surgeon has this day pronounced Lieutenant Pope to be out of danger.

We have procured some grain from this village. It is customary for the natives to bury their grain in magazines formed beneath the surface of the ground, which have earth strewed over them, and are thus concealed from a hostile army. In order to detect them, persons with long sticks, with iron ferules and rings, thrust them deep into the ground in the neighbourhood of the villages, and from the noise of the rings judge if they have hit on one of these magazines.

On the banks of the Kunnain, January 2d, 1818.

Having marched ten days without a halt, we gave the horses a day's rest on the 27th, and resumed our route on the following day to Nurella, through a better and more open country than we had seen since we crossed the Nerbuddah. On the march a most miserable object presented himself to us from the jungle, so emaciated and weak, that it was with difficulty we could learn from him that he was the long lost soubidar, whom Captain Hicks could hardly recognise; so altered and reduced was he by cruel treatment. Our inquiries concerning him during our advance had undeceived his captors, to whom he had always affirmed that he belonged to the Peishwah; but from the time they heard that we interested ourselves about him, he was treated with the utmost barbarity, and almost starved. The preceding night, finding us in their vicinity, they carried him out into a wood, with the intention, as they told him, of hanging him. The poor wretch, seeing the necessity of exertion, asked leave to drink from a neighbouring stream, and collecting his little remaining strength, ran into the jungle and escaped. He was put into a dooly and brought on. A dooly is a sort of palanquin for transporting the sick or wounded; they are made very light and carried by four men, and so contrived as to serve for a bed whether in motion or at rest.

On the 29th we marched to Mohargong, and received a despatch from Mr. Jenkins for General Hardyman, counter-ordering his former directions, and desiring him to move on to Nagpoor, as General Doveton's force would probably be required to act to the westward. On the 30th we marched to Puzdar, through an amazingly thick forest, and had we been opposed by an active enemy, an hundred light infantry must have destroyed us all. Till we descended a ghaut about nine miles from our ground, we had been moving on a table land which we ascended near Dhoomah. The view from the top of the ghaut was most dreary and discouraging. The eye could not reach a patch of cultivation, and nothing but the tops of trees were visible. It was land unprofitable for man or beast, and it was with difficulty we found ground to encamp on. The jungle and trees were absolutely intermixed with our tents and horses. One of our brinjarries was sprung upon by a tiger from the jungle on this day's march, and was severely wounded, though he escaped with life. In this village we also found a servant belonging to an officer of the 6th Bengal cavalry, who, on his road returning from Nagpoor, had half his face carried off by one of these animals. I laughed at the fears of the hircarrahs when they stated that they did not like to pass through the jungle on account of the tigers, but it appears they were well founded. The following day we marched to Dungertaul. The wilderness that surrounded us could not be surpassed by the wildest parts of America: our flankers encountered the greatest difficulty in passing at any distance from the road. In the jungle we found no less than three bodies half devoured by the tigers, and saw a very large mark of a tiger's foot where it must have crossed the road. From all these circumstances I am convinced that these animals must be in vast numbers in these unfrequented wilds. The ground on which we encamped was good, about one hundred acres having been cleared for cultivation. I was much pleased with the situation of a tank of above fifty acres of water near this village. It is surrounded by hills or rather rocks of granite, with the luxuriant foliage of the tropics every where overhanging the water, and producing a reflection nearly as vivid as the original. Hundreds of monkeys were amusing themselves on the branches; and the dam which confined the water was a fine piece of masonry. On the 1st of January, 1818, we marched to the neighbourhood of Ramteek. On our approach our hircarrahs reported that 500 matchlock men had taken post on a height above the town with some pieces of cannon, in a pagoda celebrated for its sanctity, as the name implies, being called the Hill of God; but as 200 cavalry were never intended to escalade pagodas, we moved to the right of the town, and encamped very quietly in the neighbourhood. We did not clear the jungle till within three miles of Ramteek. The light manner in which we treated our enemy in moving through the jungle made me, used as I had been to European warfare, often very nervous; but those about me seemed perfectly convinced that there was no enterprise in the enemy. Still when in the forest with a thick underwood up to our very tents, I frequently shuddered to think of the consequences if they should unexpectedly attack us. In the course of the morning some of the natives came in from the town, and informed us that parties of the enemy's cavalry were still in the neighbourhood, and that a body of them had been surprised and cut to pieces half-way between Ramteek and Nagpoor a few days since.

In the course of the day we received advice from Mr. Jenkins that he had granted the Arabs their own terms, and that our flag had been hoisted on the palace the day before under a royal salute. These accounts also informed us that Sir Thomas Hislop had on the 21st ultimo, near Oojein, attacked and totally defeated Holkar's army, with the loss of all his guns, and 2,500 men left dead upon the field. Our loss was estimated at 30 officers and 700 men killed and wounded. So much for the Mharatta confederacy! Their head defeated in two actions and a fugitive; the Rajah of Nagpoor our prisoner, after having been unsuccessful in a similar number of engagements; Holkar totally defeated, and Scindiah under the supervision of 12,000 British bayonets! The people of the town also brought us a proclamation signed by Mr. Jenkins, and published the preceding day at Nagpoor. It stated in general terms that our relations of amity with the rajah had been re-established; but it was observed that it had not the rajah's seal. The inhabitants of Ramteek nevertheless promised to furnish us with supplies.

A troop of the 6th Bengal cavalry arrived in our camp about three o'clock in the afternoon, having left Nagpoor the same morning. General Doveton had sent them to act as my escort, but as no bearers accompanied them, I could not move faster than by the regular stages. The officer who commanded gave us many particulars of the late actions, and mentioned that the Peishwah was still in the field with a large body of troops. In the evening I went into the town, and found it very rich and populous; its situation is uncommonly strong, being covered on two sides with defensible hills, and on the others by large and deep tanks. The receipt of the proclamation seemed to have set the inhabitants quite at their ease; and the number of women in the bazars selling vegetables, grain, &c. denoted our having quitted the provinces, which, from a long continuance under the Mahometans, had fallen into the selfish and jealous system of hiding their females from the eyes of the world. The following anecdote will shew how much the prejudices of the people are giving way to more liberal ideas. It is customary in the autumn at a Hindoo festival, called the Doorga Poujah, for the natives of wealth in Calcutta of that persuasion to give great assemblies, which are frequented by the Europeans of both sexes. The Hindoo women, far from partaking of the festivities, are only allowed to sit with screens before them so as not to be seen. The difference being pointed out to one of these entertainers, he remarked that it was an absurd custom, and that he trusted to see it done away, as it had only been introduced by the Mahometans; and that now we were their rulers it would be better to assimilate on this point with us, as it was originally their own custom.

This morning, January the 2d, we marched to this place through a fine champaign country, forming a most delightful contrast with the dreary forest to which we had been so long accustomed. We are near the scene where the party of the enemy were surprised the other night by Major Munt of the Madras cavalry. I have heard from Mr. Jenkins this morning, who, I am sorry to find, says that it will be with the greatest difficulty I shall be able to cross the country to Bombay, as the whole, particularly the Peishwah's dominions, is in a very turbulent and unsettled state, and in all directions overrun by detachments of the enemy's horse. I regret this much, as I fear I shall be longer going to England this way than the despatches by sea. The heat is considerably more oppressive within the last few days in consequence of our having moved so far to the southward, and we have been obliged to put on our summer clothing. The difference of latitude between the spot where I left the governor-general's head-quarters and Nagpoor is about four degrees and a half, Erij being about 25° 47″ N. L. and Nagpoor 21° 14″ N. L. Near this situation the former resident to the court of Nagpoor built a house on the banks of the river, and being fond of hawking, called it Falconer's Hall. It has been burnt down by the rajah's troops. Hawking is a very favourite amusement throughout the East, and hawks are looked upon as part of the state of the Indian sovereigns. The Arabs are particularly attached to the pastime. In the Ayen Akberree no fewer than ten kinds of hawks are mentioned; and the grand falconer at the court of Delhi was a man of high rank, as was anciently the case at the courts of England and Scotland. We have seen great numbers of antelopes in the ravines near the camp.

CHAPTER VII.

Arrive at Nagpoor—Contrast of civilized life with what we had lately seen—Ladies—Visit General Doveton—Camp—Troops at Nagpoor—Difficulty of the author in continuing his route—Hospitality of the resident at this court—The Seta Buldy hills—Strong position—Accounts of the action of the 26th and 27th November—Bravery of Arabs in the rajah's army—Mode of fighting—War cry—Intoxicating drugs—History of the Arabs in the service of the sovereigns of India—Abyssinians—Abyssinian Omrahs—Arab village—Situation of the followers of our troops—Panoramic view from the summit of the Seta Buldy hills—City—Camp—Field of battle—Foragers—Christian Sepoys—Reflections on the Christian religion with reference to the conversion of the natives—Difficulties—Castes—Hopelessness of conversion—Excommunication, or loss of caste—Ram Mohun Roy—His great learning—A reformer—His eloquence—General knowledge—Liberal feelings—Bramins interested in keeping the lower classes in darkness—Lost caste—His person and manners—Anxious to visit England—Tolerant sentiments of the Hindoos—Captured guns—Large guns—Dutch guns—Venetian sequins—Coins—India always draws the valuable metals to itself—Twelfth light infantry—Madras Sepoys—Madras Sepoys small men—Bengal troops formed of full-sized men—Field of battle of the 16th—Gog and Magog—The city of Nagpoor—Jumma Talao—Batteries against the city—Tanks—Suburb burnt—New wall not finished—Gateway—Main street—Mhuts—Old palace—Women's apartments or zunnana—Small horse—Elephants—Many captured—The city—The rajah—Mhun Bhut his adviser—The author's intended route—Dowlutabad and the caves of Ellora—The author's escort—Nizam's cavalry.

Nagpoor, January 5th, 1818.

AS we approached Nagpoor on the morning of the 3d, we saw the white tents upon the Seta Buldy hills, and the whole country became enlivened by the various strings of returning foragers crossing the plain from every direction, and all verging to one point. I am the guest of Mr. Jenkins for the time I remain here, and the kindness with which he received me has been very gratifying. Several ladies appeared at the breakfast table, who have no other homes than the residency, as the cantonments, with all their property, have been lately burnt by the mischievous and savage enemy. It will be readily conceived how pleasing was the contrast of this display of civilized life after what I have been describing. These ladies had, it seems, experienced many inconveniences, hardships, and even dangers during the late disturbances, having been at the foot of the hill in the house during the time of the action, when several cannon shot struck the roof.

After breakfast, having expressed my wish to take the earliest opportunity of paying my respects to General Doveton, an elephant was ordered for me, and Major O'Brien and myself proceeded to the camp. It covered so extensive a piece of ground that I am persuaded the Madras army must in the number of followers exceed our Bengal armies. Their wives and children, I have understood, always accompany the Madras Sepoys in the field, which they never do with the Bengal troops. Part of the camp was on the plain, and its two flanks on ranges of hills made a most magnificent appearance. Near the hill was the Bengal force, and over the residency the white tents of the two gallant battalions, who had defended the hills, rose one above another on the very site of their victory. The whole country was brightened by these temporary habitations. There were collected in the vicinity of Nagpoor three regiments of cavalry, 1000 of the Nizam's regular horse, a troop of horse artillery, foot artillery, and ten battalions of infantry. I learnt from General Doveton that I could only proceed with escorts by daily stages, and that he had one ready for me whenever I required it. I consequently stated that I should set out on the 6th at daylight, as I hoped before that time to have all the papers and information I might require. Before I took leave of the general I expressed a wish to see a regiment of the Madras native army, and he was so kind as to direct the 12th light infantry to be paraded the next morning at break of day, and arranged that his aid-de-camp and myself should afterwards proceed over the field of battle of the 16th December, and return to his tent to breakfast. We then visited Captain Fitzgerald, whose conduct had been so conspicuous in the first action. The residency appeared a perfect hotel, as in reality it has been since the breaking out of the disturbances, for all who present themselves are welcome. Such hospitality must have been not a little expensive, for at such a distance from the coast every thing is excessively dear, and wine and beer, and all European articles, perform a journey of five hundred miles before they reach this capital. Nothing but a government can afford to give breakfasts, dinners, &c. for thirty or forty persons daily for six weeks or two months. In the evening I accompanied Captain Lloyd, the commander of the residency escort, who was wounded with four balls in the late action, over the Seta Buldy hills, the position occupied by our troops on the 26th and 27th November. It is extremely strong, and it was truly fortunate so good a post offered itself in the vicinity of the residency. The summit of the largest of the two hills was at the time of the action a Mahometan burial ground, but many of the tombs have been destroyed to face the works we are forming. As they were all of masonry, I conceive the fragments from them must have been most destructive during the cannonade. There are many trees amongst the tombs, and all are marked by the shot; some, indeed, look to be dying from the wounds they received. Several of the enemy's captured guns are now posted on the hill, which has in appearance become a little fortress. The smaller hill, which is joined to the larger by a broad saddle, was at the time of the action almost a cone, but has since been flattened at the top, and a small redoubt formed on it. This hill was at a very critical moment carried by the enemy's Arabs, who seem to have behaved extremely well, but were unsupported by the remainder of the rajah's army. Their manner of advancing was exceedingly imposing. Being perfectly undisciplined, they advanced in a crowd; the bravest being in advance, and taking high bounds, and turning two or three times round in the air, they rushed forward to the sound of small drums, accompanied by the perpetual vociferation of their war cry, *deen deen Mahomet* (the faith of Mahomet). This sounds at a distance like ding, ding, which is often used instead of the correct expression. The war cry of the Hindoos is *hurry hur*. The Arabs are represented as having fired very fast, which is hard to be accounted for, when it is considered they do not use cartridges. In approaching to close quarters, having no bayonets, they fight with shields, swords, and daggers, and sometimes take *bang* or opium to inspire them with courage, though it is as strictly prohibited by the Koran as the drinking of wine.

The Arabs in the service of the native princes have at all times been celebrated in the armies of India for their courage and other military requisites. They were undoubtedly introduced into the country during the remote ages, and from the effeminacy of the inhabitants of the Malabar coast, the crews of the vessels carrying on the trade between Arabia and India must, at an early period, have found it worth their while to become mercenaries. They are taken notice of as being settled below the mountains in Tabrobana (Ceylon) by Pliny. Marco Polo speaks of large numbers of them on the Malabar coast; and Barthema mentions that 15,000 settled at Calicut, and that they had the character of being good soldiers. We hear of them in the armies of the princes of the Dekhun, where they were more respected than in Hindoostan, though they were sometimes employed by the kings of Delhi. Till of late years there was a colony of them at Lucknow, called Shahzadas, and in 1759 M. Bussy had 500 Arabs and Abyssinians in his service. Of the latter, also, many have been enrolled in the armies of India, and we find a large body of them in the service of the King of Bejapoor in 1657. Guzeraut was entirely in the hands of an Arab aristocracy till 1802, and we still see them in the service of the Peishwah and the Rajah of Nagpoor.

The Abyssinians however appear to have risen to higher official situations than the Arabs, for we read of Abyssinian omrahs in the courts of the Dekhun, and in the year 901 of the hegira we observe one of this nation, of the name of Dustoor Dunar, holding the government of Culberga; and in the instance of Malik Amber, an adventurer, whom I shall presently have occasion to mention, we find him approaching to almost regal power.

But to return to the situation of Nagpoor—The Arab village, their former cantonment to the eastward of the bottom of the hill, had been burned. The situation of the followers of the army, including the wives and children of the Madras Sepoys, must have been most distressing during the action, as they were crowded on the reverse of the hill, and many were killed by the shot that flew over it. From the top of this eminence the view was most extensive and almost panoramic. A magnificent tank, called the Jumma Talao, about three quarters of a mile long, extends from the suburb of the city, which is nearly due east of the residency, to the Arab village at the foot of the Seta Buldy hills, and the palace, city, and our batteries raised against the latter, were clearly discernible. To the south-east, and round to the south of the residency, is the field of battle of the 16th December, and the plains on which the columns of attack were formed. To the west the whole of the country was whitened with tents, with the residency bungalows, and huts of the bazar at the foot of the hill directly beneath: and to the north a plain extended, bounded by the hills near Ramteek, covered with elephants, camels, and foragers coming in from a great distance; our army, and still more that of the enemy with their numerous cavalry, having devoured every herb within some miles. In walking down the hill I passed over several graves ornamented with a cross; and I found, on inquiry, that within reposed the remains of some Madras Sepoys, who had been converted to our faith, and had fallen in the late action.

I cannot but express here, though with sorrow, that I am not surprised our religion is held in disrepute by the natives of India.

Being from its very essence anxious to receive into its bosom any proselyte who offers, the missionary, too ready to go through the forms, dubs christians the vilest wretches of the lowest class, or of no caste, whose ideas can hardly reach any persuasion except that which is imposed by early education or fear. Their desertion from their former faith can be founded only on self-interest, and the gratification of eating what they choose, of swallowing arack, and calling themselves of "*master's caste,*" and fancying themselves of master's religion. What has made the Hindoos, I conceive, think ill of us, and look upon our religion as degrading, is this reception into its communion of the lowest castes, and outcasts, whom they hold in the utmost horror, and whose very touch they avoid with as much circumspection as we should the contact of a leper. The natives consequently deem all Europeans, from their indiscriminate "good-will to all men," to be of the lowest and vilest caste; because, according to their ideas, outcasts only would admit outcasts. But nevertheless the superiority of our genius and intelligence makes its due impression in maintaining our estimation amongst them. M. Sonnerat tells us that some christian missionaries, aware of the detestation in which the lowest castes are held by the higher, and desirous of appearing like the Bramins, refused to associate with the despised race, or to admit them into the pale of the church, but were very properly reprehended by the apostolic legate for the distinction they had made, as being inconsistent with the first precepts of the christian religion. The truth is, that a Hindoo of rank or family would, in changing his religion, have to contend not only with those bigoted principles indelibly ingrained in his nature, but with the dreadful consequences of excommunication, by which he would forfeit every object of enjoyment, as well as respect and birthright. Is it not quite hopeless therefore to expect a genuine and sincere conversion of these people to the christian tenets? and would it not be doubly impracticable, should the missionaries attempt to extend their labours beyond the meanest classes above-mentioned, whose abjuration adds still another difficulty with regard to the higher orders, who could never endure to be classed with outcasts?

There has never been, to my knowledge, an instance of any Hindoo of condition or caste being converted to our faith. The only conversion of any kind, if it can be called so, that has come within my observation, was that of a high-caste Bramin of one of the first families in the country, who is not only perfectly master of the Sanskrit, but has gained a thorough acquaintance with the English language and literature, and has openly declared that the Braminical religion is in its purity a pure deism, and not the gross polytheism into which it has degenerated. I became well acquainted with him, and admire his talents and acquirements. His eloquence in our language is very great, and I am told that he is still more admirable in Arabic and Persian. It is remarkable that he has studied and thoroughly understands the politics of Europe, but more particularly those of England; and the last time I was in his company, he argued forcibly against a standing army in a free country, and quoted all the arguments brought forward by the members of the opposition. I think he is, in many respects, a most extraordinary person. In the first place he is a religious reformer, who has, amongst a people more bigoted than those of Europe in the middle ages, dared to think for himself. His learning is most extensive, as he is not only generally conversant with the best books in English, Arabic, Persian, Sanskrit, Bengallee, and Hindoostanee, but has even studied rhetoric in Arabic and in English, and quotes Locke and Bacon on all occasions. From the view he has thus necessarily taken of the religions, manners, and customs of so many nations, and from his having observed the number of different modes of addressing and worshipping the Supreme Being, he naturally turned to his own faith with an unprejudiced mind, found it perverted from the religion of the Vedes to a gross idolatry, and was not afraid, though aware of the consequences, to publish to the world, in Bengallee and English, his feelings and opinions on the subject. Of course he was fully prepared to meet the host of interested enemies, who, from sordid motives, wished to keep the lower classes in the state of the darkest ignorance. I have understood that his family have quitted him; that he has been declared to have lost caste, and is for the present, as all religious reformers must be for a time, a mark to be scoffed at. To a man of his sentiments and rank, this loss of caste must be peculiarly painful; but at Calcutta he associates with the English. He is, however, cut off from all familiar and domestic intercourse; indeed from all communication of any kind with his relations and former friends. His name is Ram Mohun Roy. He is particularly handsome, not of a very dark complexion, of a fine person, and most courtly manners. He professes to have no objection to eat and live as we do, but refrains from it in order not to expose himself to the imputation of having changed his religion for the good things of this world. He will sit at table with us while the meat is on it, which no other Bramin will do. He continues his native dress, but keeps a carriage, being a man of some property. He is very desirous to visit England and enter one of our universities, where I shall be most anxious to see him; and to learn his ideas of our country, its manners, customs, &c. I have heard of another Bramin in Bengal, who, within the last three years, has written a book to prove that Christ and Mahomet are incarnations of Vishnu; and this belief is perfectly consistent with their religious opinions, as Sir William Jones informs us the Hindoos believe that the Deity has appeared innumerable times in many parts of the world for the salvation of his creatures, and though we adore him in one appearance, and they in others, yet we adore, they say, the same God, to whom our several worships, though different in form, are equally acceptable, if they be sincere in substance. Nay, one of their authors asserts, that Almighty God delighted in the various forms of religion, just as he delights in the various face of nature which he has created.

On our return from the hills, we went to the spot where the guns, to the number of sixty-five, taken from the enemy on the 16th, were stationed, and where they made a very splendid show. They are of all sizes and shapes, and the carriages from a wooden platform on wheels to our most finished conveyance. Two large guns, about twenty-five feet long, which were great favourites of the rajah, had not been brought in, their weight being immense. These have been christened by our officers Gog and Magog. I was surprised to find many Dutch guns among the rest, though their having found their way here is not more singular than the following circumstance.

When the Rajah of Rewah was to pay us, about five or six years ago, a sum of money, to the astonishment of the collector he offered in part several thousand Venetian sequins in gold. I am well aware of the prevailing trade running through the hands of this republic before the discovery of the Cape of Good Hope; yet that these coins should have made their way into a country certainly seven hundred miles from the sea, is a circumstance worthy of remark. The sequin is still well known in India by name, though it is corrupted into the word *chikeen:* its value is four rupees. The Spanish dollar is current in China; and, from the vast quantities drawn to that country annually in exchange for its tea, has become almost a drug. Roman coins have at different times been found in various parts of India. This is easily accounted for, from the ancient complaint; that India has at all times attracted the gold and silver of Europe to itself. It remained for an European power, by establishing a pre-eminent government on the spot, to return to Europe in private fortunes, and by other means, a portion of this wealth.

On the 4th, at daylight, I proceeded to General Doveton's

tent, and, accompanied by his aide-de-camp, saw the 12th light infantry put through five or six movements. They appeared to be stouter men than the generality of the Madras sepoys, these being smaller than the Hindoostanee natives who form the Bengal troops: the latter would not yield the palm to the finest picked regiments of the European princes, and in all probability would surpass them. Their individual and collective courage is proverbial. In 1815 eight grenadier battalions were formed in Hindoostan from the grenadier companies of the regiments of infantry of the Bengal presidency, and they were certainly the finest troops I have ever seen on any service. This battalion of light infantry is one of the battalions of the 12th regiment of the Madras native infantry. They moved in the most perfect manner, and their equipment is well calculated for the peculiar service for which they are designed, though the sword fixing on the musquet may be found fault with. They are armed with a light firelock, something heavier than one of the old cavalry carbines, and considerably shorter than the musquet generally used by the regiments of infantry. The uniform of the officers, covered with gold, is too conspicuous, and totally inconsistent with their description of duty. This regiment was not inferior to the finest British light infantry regiments we had in the peninsula, and recalled to my memory the light infantry companies of the German legion.

We then proceeded, with a strong escort of cavalry, to the ground of the battle of the 16th, which lies to the south and south-east of the town, and met, drawn by many yoke of oxen, the two large guns before mentioned. Several other guns, with broken carriages, lay strewed on the plain, and are to be brought into the residency as soon as convenient. In the evening of this day I went to the city to see the gate and wall, where an attack had failed on the 24th ultimo, after the rajah's army had been dispersed, and the Arabs defended the city. The Jumma Talao, a fine tank, extends nearly the whole way from the residency to the city, and is about three quarters of a mile long, and four hundred yards broad. I was told that nearly 40,000*l.* was expended on its construction. The batteries raised against the gate and wall were formed on the dam of earth round this tank, which had been thrown up from it. This, though a noble tank, is inferior to many others I have seen. In the ruins of the ancient city of Gour, to the east of the Ganges, opposite Rajmahl, there is one of a most extraordinary length and breadth, being part of the ancient Hindoo remains when it was the capital of Bengal. After viewing the defences from the spot on which our batteries were erected, we examined the wall, which is miserable; and the suburb on this side has been burnt to the ground, or destroyed by our fire. In the front, and to cover the bottom of the wall, which we had battered, runs a fine piece of masonry which I suppose to be what in this country is called a rainnee, similar to a fausse-braye. I was informed that the late rajah had begun it after the war of 1803, intending to wall in the whole city; but about five years after its commencemnet it was given over. The foundation is laid all round the town, and in some places is ten feet above the ground, and I think about fifteen feet thick, with round towers at short distances, considerable segments of which protrude from the wall, and flank the curtain between them. The gate on which our principal fire was directed was totally blocked up with fragments of the wall; so much so that we could not enter it, but went round by a breach to the right, which, when the city was occupied by the Arabs, had been defended by an entrenchment, and barricaded with carts. In the main street leading from the gate of the palace are several Braminical mhuts, or, as we improperly call them, pagodas, from forty to fifty feet high. They are of white stone, beautifully carved, but the sides they present to the gate have been much damaged by the shot which flew over it. The old palace stands about three hundred yards within this gate on the right-hand side of the street, and the new palace immediately opposite. The stone for building the walls of the city and the palace came from the Seta Buldy hills, and the quarries from which it was taken tended much to the strength of our position during the late action. The old palace was commenced by the Rajah Moodajee, and was finished before 1790. In 1754 the army of Salabut Jung, accompanied by the French troops under M. Bussy, penetrated as far as this capital, and signed a peace under its walls. The old palace has been shattered by the shot, but it is not materially injured. We entered a court-yard in front of it, through a very handsome grey-stone archway, and found it full of Sepoys, as a garrison of two battalions in the city were parading for the evening roll-call. The front of the palace can boast of nothing very particular, but on entering it, the first quadrangle surrounded with a colonnade of superbly sculptured black wooden columns about thirty feet high, with a very handsome entablature and cornice of the same materials, is very striking. The whole is paved with stone, and in the centre is a basin and fountain. This court is about seventy yards square, and has an appearance of barbaric magnificence and unstudied architecture which is far from unpleasing. To reach the upper apartments we passed between two walls up a miserably dark flight of steps, and found the rooms mean and gloomy. I was very glad to reach the top of the building, which has a flat stuccoed roof with battlements, much shattered by our fire. We had here a very good view of the different courts of the palace, all small excepting the one I have described, though a similar colonnade on a reduced scale runs round them all. Two of these, with apartments between and about them, and a colonnade two stories high, were for the zunnana or women's quarters. They had all been removed to the southward at the beginning of the disturbances. Every court has a bath and fountain in the centre, and curtains to raise or let down at pleasure, to shelter those in the colonnade from bad weather or cold. I made my way with much difficulty into these apartments, but did not observe in them any thing remarkable. On each side was a kitchen, fitted up with stoves and lighted by windows forty or fifty feet from the ground (the ceiling being at the height of the house), and the smoke must have found its way through them or the roof, as there were no chimneys. In short, from what the zunnana presented, the description of the ladies' apartments in the Arabian Nights' Entertainments was far from realized in his highness's palace. At one of the corners on the terraced roof was a small octagonal wooden pavilion, fitted up with some paltry mirrors. This building had suffered severely from the cannon-shot. Having descended from this, we inspected the stables, where we saw an elephant which had been hit by a spent cannon-ball, and had a very deep dent on its side from the blow, but the skin was not broken. Our principal inducement however for visiting the stable was the fame of a little horse four years old, and only thirty-three inches high. This diminutive creature was, I think, the most beautiful model of a horse in miniature I ever saw. It was very playful, perhaps vicious, and when I stood across it on tiptoe it attacked my knees on its sides, striving to bite them. There were but five or six other elephants in the stables, though the rajah has many more. Our cavalry in the action of the 16th took forty-five, for which it was understood his highness had offered, and we had accepted, a lac of rupees. We next proceeded through the city, which is in a most miserable state, with only one or two of the streets paved. The suburbs on all sides have suffered more or less from fire, and as our elephants squeezed themselves through the narrow streets we saw some poor creatures just returned from the jungles, to which they had fled for protection, bewailing with their families the loss of their all, and lighting fires from the fragments of the roof of their huts and furniture to defend them against the cold of the approaching night. These conflagrations and demolitions were the work of the Arabs, who, before they marched out, plundered even their master's palaces.

On the day of my arrival I made inquiries as to the situation of the rajah, who I found was a prisoner in a tent in the residency grounds. Thus true Mharatta treachery had met its reward. Four mounted troopers and eight sentries formed a chain round his tent, and secured him from escape. He asked as a favour that the sentries over him should be Bramins from Hindoostan, that no Mharatta might see him in his present humiliated situation. His guard was accordingly furnished by the Bengal troops. Two tents off, equally well watched, was his principal adviser, Mhun Bhut. He gave himself up on the morning of the 1st instant. This wretch, a Bramin, long before we imagined that the discontent of the court of Nagpoor would have grown into open hostility, had boasted in the city that he had recommended the rajah to attack the residency, in violation of all the laws of nations. He practised but too successfully on the youth and inexperience of his sovereign.

Captain Hicks with his recruits intends to come on with my escort, and I have found here a friend of mine, Mr. Elliott, an aide-de-camp of Sir John Malcolm's, son to the governor of Madras, who being in bad health wishes to accompany me for change of air, and to prosecute his route to Bombay, if he shall be able to continue moving with celerity. Our route from hence to Arungabad, the principal city of the Nizam in Berar, and seat of the viceroy, is seventeen days' march through Ellichpoor and Jaffierabad, though the daily stages are very long. An idea of travelling to the southward was early given up on account of the great distance of the rajah's frontier in that quarter, and the equal necessity of my moving with escorts. The river Wurdah is no farther than three days' march in the direction in which I am to move, and we then enter the Nizam's country. Mr. Jenkins, with the greatest kindness, as I cannot yet ride from my accident, has lent me an elephant as far as Arungabad. As I am very desirous to see the fort of Dowlutabad, as well as the celebrated caves of Ellora near that city, I have written to our resident at the court of the Nizam, at Hyderabad, to procure permission from his highness to see the interior of the fortress. My escort is to consist of one jemidar, or native subaltern, and 35 men of the regular Bengal cavalry, 200 of the Nizam's reformed horse, and a company of his regular infantry. These last are nearly as good as our own Sepoys, being under European officers; and the horse, having a British officer at the head of each thousand, are the best of the irregular cavalry in the Nizam's pay. There are four thousand of them divided into as many corps, which are reckoned very good and trust-worthy, as they have at times behaved themselves so as to merit that character. If it is true, as reported, that the country from hence to the river Wurdah is overrun with the enemy's cavalry, this escort might make a very tolerable defence. The road I have to travel from hence to Poonah, the capital of the Peishwah, is near 490 miles through Arungabad and Ahmednuggur, which is 60 miles from that capital. The distance from Nagpoor to Bombay is under 600 miles. A led horse is to accompany my escort, should it be necessary, and in the event of my being able, to ride him.

I shall now, as far as I may feel myself permitted, relate what I have learned of the late events at this capital.

CHAPTER VIII.

LATE EVENTS AT NAGPOOR.

Accumulation of troops at Nagpoor—Hostile reports in the city—Coincidence of the arrival of news—Duplicity of the rajah—Reinforcements—The rajah receives a khelaut or dress of honour from the Peishwah—The resident's remonstrance—The rajah quits the city and enters his camp—Hostile accounts—Preparation to repel threatened hostility—Critical arrival of the troops from the cantonments—Friendly assurance of the resident—Remonstrance of the rajah—Hostile preparation of the enemy—Effrontery of the Mharattas—Position of the Seta Buldy hills—Neighbourhood—Strength of the brigade—Military precautions bring on hostilities—Cantonments burnt—Resident sends for reinforcements—Dangerous situation of the followers—Morning of the 27th November—Attack of the Arabs—their success—Captain Fitzgerald turns the tide of victory in our favour—Arabs repulsed—Our loss severe—Cessation of the action—The rajah sends in to the resident—On a tacit suspension of hostilities the enemy's army fall back from their advanced position—Colonel Gahan arrives with a reinforcement—Major Pittman arrives with a reinforcement—General Doveton arrives with his division—Terms offered to the rajah—Preparation for the attack of his army—Rajah's attempts at evasion—Columns formed for attack—The rajah surrenders himself—The enemy's artillery promised to be given up—Detail of the troops for attack—The treachery of the enemy's sirdars—Their total defeat, and capture of their guns—Arabs throw themselves into the city—Negotiation with them—It fails—Account of the city of Nagpoor—Batteries open on the Jumma Derwaseh—Assault—Repulse—Severe loss—Detachment of the enemy surprised in the neighbourhood—Arabs capitulate—British take possession of the city—Detachment moves against Ghun Put Rao.

AT this Mharatta court, up to the middle of November, all appeared tranquil; the usual amicable communications passed between the resident and the durbar, and it was fully expected that the contingent of 3000 cavalry and 2000 infantry was preparing, and in a state of forwardness to act with us against the predatory hordes, or to cover the country from inroads, according to the terms of our treaty. However favourable were outward appearances, a correspondence was reported to be carried on between the rajah, the Peishwah, and the Pindarries; and rumours from Poonah stated that it was the intention of the Peishwah to break with us, and that he expected the rajah would join him, as bound by his duty to the Mharatta confederacy. What gave plausibility to these accounts was the great accumulation of force at Poonah, and the raising of troops through the rajah's territories, for he called upon all his feudatories, and had even recruited his army in districts out of his own provinces.

By the 14th of November the rajah had collected round him about 8000 cavalry and the same number of infantry, of which 3000 were Arabs, with a large train of artillery. Various hostile reports were at this time circulated in the city, and it was even stated that some of the Mharatta sirdars had been recommended to send away their families. This assemblage of troops had a most serious and suspicious appearance, as it was simultaneous with the augmentation of the Peishwah's army at Poonah, and perfectly inconsistent with the language of the rajah, who had always, when pressed on the subject of his contingent, excused himself by alleging his want of means. All these reasons, in addition to many others, created a very considerable uncertainty as to the intentions of this court, and it was impossible to divine what the cold weather might produce. The news of the treaty with Scindiah, and of the Peishwah having gone to war with us and of his failure on the 5th November, arrived at Nagpoor on the same day, and appeared to make no alteration in his highness's durbar. His language was particularly friendly, but the same evening he gave dresses to several of his sirdars, ordering them to raise more troops at a higher rate of pay. In the course of the next three days it became evident from various circumstances that nothing but a commanding force at his capital could keep him from becoming our open enemy, and it was deemed requisite to send for the detachment which had been held in readiness from the fifth division of the army of the Dekhun. Colonel Gahan, who commanded this detachment, consequently marched from Sindkairah on the 20th November, being at that time 170 miles from Nagpoor. As a further indication of the hostile mind and duplicity of this prince, he accepted at this time a khelaut of honour from the Peishwah, the assuming of which was to be attended with great pomp, and our resident was invited to be present. This of course was declined, and a remonstrance was made, though the rajah endeavoured to excuse the act by stating that the khelaut had been despatched from Poonah before a rupture had taken place. The ceremony was given out to be on occasion of his taking the command of the Mharatta armies, being the sena putty, or hereditary general-in-chief, which is in the family of the Bhoonslahs of Nagpoor. The latter part of this farce consisted in his going into his camp, and remaining there for three days, his troops welcoming him with uncommon magnificence and parade. The whole was evidently an excuse to get among the soldiery; and from this moment the natives looked upon war as certain, and our resident was convinced that it was a decided proof of his union with the Peishwah. Every report from the city announced the intention of attacking us, and on the 25th all communication between the residency and city was at once put an end to. Information was received that the contingent had been ordered into the city, and the accounts from the different camps stated that the troops of the rajah were getting under arms.

Up to this period the resident had hoped by a semblance of confidence not to precipitate matters, but it was now a useless risk to keep it up any longer; and for the general safety of the mission, as well as of the lives of the troops and their families, it became absolutely necessary to concentrate. The troops from the cantonment two miles distant were ordered in, and on their arrival they were moved to the hills above the residency. As they reached the summit to take up their ground, some of the Arabs in the service of the rajah were observed ascending the other side from their village at the bottom where they were cantoned. They, however, fell back on the critical arrival of our troops. At the time of this disposal of our force, the resident, Mr. Jenkins, sent to the rajah to assure him he was not acting from any hostile feeling, but adopting a precautionary measure to which he was compelled by the appearance of all around. On the evening of this day, the resident sent his moonshee* into the rajah's camp, with a statement of his doubts relative to the late events; and it was upon this occasion that the first remonstrance was mentioned on their part. This reasoning, with the sword in his hand, was a decided proof of the rajah's war-like intentions, though in answer to Mr. Jenkins, the minister said his highness had no inimical views, and they all offered to bring about a reconciliation, and even talked of an exchange of visits the next morning. On the 26th in the morning, the rajah's troops were seen busily employed in bringing out guns, and pointing them at the Seta Buldy hills, and from their movements it appeared as if they only waited to be fully prepared in order to attack us. They nevertheless, with the effrontery and treachery so usual among the native powers (as we have so recently seen exemplified at Jubbulpoor), in the face of their dispositions, and when by every rule of war we should have been fully justified in firing on them, again sent for the resident's moonshee, but Mr. Jenkins desired him to intimate to the durbar, that all negotiation was a farce under such manifestations of hostility. About sunset they again sent in, but it was impossible to comprehend their object, as the interview was abruptly broken off by the commencement of the firing.

The Seta Buldy hills, which had been fixed upon for our defensive position, consist of two eminences of nearly equal height to the east of the residency, and presented a very strong post. The separate knolls, about three hundred yards from each other, were joined by a broad saddle. The most southward of these hills was flat on the summit, having been used as a Mahometan burying-

* Native interpreter and secretary.

ground, and capable of holding from one to two battalions in column; but the hill to the north was almost a cone, and could only cover a few men, and allow place for two guns. The whole range was from three hundred and fifty to four hundred yards long, and from two hundred and fifty to three hundred broad, in general steep, and in some places rendered inaccessible by stone quarries. Immediately to the west of the hills are the grounds of the residency, containing six or eight houses, and the huts of the bazar. The Jumma Talao, a large tank, about three quarters of a mile long, is situated due east, about five hundred yards from them, and extends to the suburbs of the city. At the foot of the Seta Buldy hills on the east, north-east, and south-east sides, are the cantonments of the Arab troops in the rajah's pay, within two hundred yards of their summit. On every side a vast undulating plain of several miles extends, being excellent ground for cavalry. The families of the officers, soldiers, and followers, accompanied the troops to the residency, and took shelter in the houses, grounds, and west face of the hill, while Mr. Jenkins's residence was given up to the ladies and their children. The whole of our force was under 1200 men. The 24th Madras native infantry was posted on the smaller hill; the 20th regiment and the resident's escort on the larger; and three troops of the 6th Bengal cavalry, with 100 infantry, in the residency and its grounds. Two pieces of cannon were posted on each hill.

At sunset on the 26th, Colonel Scott, who commanded, thought it necessary, from the number of men in the Arab village, to place sentries close up to it, which produced at first a remonstrance from the Arabs, and on our refusal to withdraw (at the same time stating, it was only a military precaution), a fire of musketry from them, and a severe desultory action commenced, accompanied by a very heavy cannonade and flights of rockets. All the gentlemen of the residency immediately repaired to the scene of action, and, as is always the case in India, the civilians emulated the military. As soon as the sword was thus fairly drawn, and the scabbard thrown away, the flames and smoke which ascended in the direction of the cantonments, declared the fate of the houses and property of those engaged in the defence of the hills, and the inveterate spirit of the enemy. His fire was particularly destructive on the smaller hill, and in the course of the night it was found necessary to form a breastwork of bags of grain to shelter the men from the musketry of the Arabs posted in the village below. At midnight Mr. Jenkins thought it expedient to write to Major Pittman, who was in Berar with 1000 reformed horse, and two of the Nizam's regular battalions, to join him, though it was quite uncertain whether the hircarrah could escape the numerous troops and emissaries of the enemy. The messenger, however, a voltinteer, succeeded in delivering his note. The Sepoys during the whole night endured the painful reflection that many of the shot which passed over them fell amongst the defenceless multitude of their wives and children assembled on the reverse of the hill towards the residency.

At daylight of the 27th, the whole force of the enemy was seen from the hills. Thirty-five guns were firing from the rajah's army, and the village below was crowded with infantry, and the plain around covered with immense masses of cavalry. At eight o'clock the Arabs made a most desperate charge, sword in hand, from the village, on the small hill, and succeeded in gaining possession of it and the guns, and the flight of our defeated troops spread an alarm among the defenders of the larger hill, which was much increased by the guns we had lost being turned upon them, and the action was looked upon as more than doubtful.

The cavalry under the command of Captain Fitzgerald, consisting of 250 men, had been exposed all night to a battery of guns pointed against them, and the cannon-shot which came over the hill. Their commanding officer had been unsuccessful in his repeated applications since daylight to quit the residency grounds,

REFERENCES TO THE BATTLE AND CITY OF NAGPOOR.

The British troops are coloured red; the enemy's yellow; the dots are skirmishers.

a Position of the battalion 24th Madras native infantry, and afterwards of the Nagpoor escort, and 50 men of the 20th native infantry, and two guns.

b Position of the battalion 20th Madras native infantry, Major Jenkins's recruits, and two guns; and also 1st position of the Nagpoor escort.

c The hill that was taken by the Arabs from a party of the Nagpoor escort and 50 men of the 20th native infantry, but regained by them with the assistance of a portion of the 20th and 24th native infantry, led by various officers.

d A deep quarry, under cover of which the Arabs approached to within thirty yards of our men on the hill, and surprised them.

e An empty rocket and powder magazine belonging to the Bhoonsla.

f First position of the troops of the 6th Bengal native cavalry, with skirmishers thrown out, occupied by them from sunset till ten o'clock.

g Second position of three troops of the 6th native cavalry, occupied by them from 10 o'clock at night till 10 o'clock on the morning of the 27th. At eight o'clock the two parties posted to the north, joined the party to the west, which was drawn up at the residency gate, where a company of the 20th native infantry was also posted.

h Third position of three troops of the 6th Bengal native cavalry, after having repulsed the enemy's charge, routed a portion of his infantry, and taken two of his twelve pounders.

i Fourth position, or one troop 6th native cavalry, which charged a body of Arabs, destroyed about 40 men, and checked their last meditated attack on the northern hill, and secured the possession of the two six pounders taken by the infantry from the enemy.

j The guns spiked by the infantry after having driven the Arabs from them, who opposed them with showers of grape.

k The two six pounders taken by the infantry; they had been drawn upon the northern hill by the Arabs, who kept up a severe fire from them, and one of our six pounders which they had captured; all three were left on the hill when they were driven from it.

l The large camp, called Súke Durah, in which the Bhoonsla pitched his tent; it consisted of about 15,000 men.

m The camp of Gunput Rao Soubahdar, consisting of 5000 horse and 2000 matchlock men.

y The enemy's cavalry, collected after their discomfiture.

BATTLE OF THE 16th DECEMBER, 1817.

n General Doveton's disposition.

o Colonel Scott taking possession of the first battery without opposition.

p Enemy's troops.

q General Doveton forms line about 1000 yards from the enemy's position.

r Enemy's position.

s Horse artillery and cavalry.

t Enemy's defeated troops.

DIFFERENT QUARTERS OF THE CITY, &c.

1 Resident's compound.
2 Village or bazar of Setabuldee.
3 The Sepoy's lines of the Nagpoor escort.
4 Myna Baeeka bazar.
5 The Jumma Talao.
6 The dam of the Jumma Talao.
7 The park or shed for cannon.
8 Garee Khanus.
9 Suneecheeree market or Pate.
10 Hindoo pagodas.
11 Gunees Pate or market.
12 Chimna Bapoo's garden.
13 A pucka enclosure called the Imambara.
14 A small nullah, its source at the Ambajeree tank, four miles distant.
15 A small nullah, its source at the Telinkoree tank cantonments.
16 A small nullah, its source in the Huzaree Pahars, or hills to the north-west.
17 Soubadar Gunput Rao's cantonment.
18 Major Jenkins's cantonment.
19 The made road to Colonel Scott's cantonment.
20 The road through the rajah's garden to ditto.
22 The old road to cantonments.
23 The arsenal.
24 Narrain Rao Vakeel Ka Pate or market.
25 A shed for cannon.
26 Seerus Pate or market.
27 The Toolsee Bagh.
28 The Bhootea Durwazee.
29 The Toolsee Bagh Ka Durwazee.
30 A gate.
31 A small gate.
32 The Oomrer Durwazee.
35 The Boodwar ditto.
36 The Jumma ditto.
37 The Ambaree Kham.
38 The cannon foundery.
39 The residence of Sawat Khan.
40 The palace of the Bhoonsla, or Rajah of Nagpoor.
41 The stables of the Bhoonsla.
42 The Old Killa, and residence of Rajah Boorunshah.
43 The residence of Bowanny Kalao.
44 ———— Gunput Rao Soubahdar.
45 ———— Mahajee Naick.
46 ———— Surdur Bapoo, the prime minister.
47 ———— Jeswunt Rao.
48 Mungutwarre Baka Baee Ka Pate.
49 Etwaree bazar.
50 Lindu Palao's.
51 Longunge.
52 The residence of Piderce Nana, Sahib's banker.
53 The residence of Himmut Buhadour.
54 The Boodhwaree Bazar.
55 The Hunsapooree.
56 The residency of Davy Sing.
57 Goolgunge.
58 Rooce Gunge.
59 Lukker Gunge.
60 Buger, ditto.
61 Lall ditto.
62 Mussan ditto.
63 Mangulwaree-appa Sahib ka Pate.
64 Kalua Talao.
65 A good Pucka well.
66 Mr. Forster's tomb.

G. Fitz Clarence delt.

Published as the Act directs 1st Feby 1819 by John Murray, Albemarle Street London.

J. Walker Sculpt.

and charge the host of enemy's cavalry on the plain, as a desperate alternative to being destroyed in a state of inactivity. At this critical juncture, when the enemy's hopes were at their highest, and our infantry most disheartened, Captain Fitzgerald dashed out of the ground of the residency at the head of his small band, charged the enemy's cavalry, broke them, put them to flight, seized and turned their guns upon them, and by this unexampled exertion gave confidence to our infantry, who, taking advantage of some confusion amongst the enemy occasioned by the explosion of a tumbril, rushed on them and regained the hill and guns, our cavalry cutting up some fugitives in the plain below.

This was the only serious attack; and by twelve o'clock the firing, which lasted eighteen hours, had ceased. Our loss was heavy, consisting of four European officers and 100 men killed, and 11 officers and 203 men wounded. Six pieces of cannon were taken by the cavalry. The loss of the enemy must have been above 400 Arabs, and perhaps 200 Mharattas. Mr. Sotheby, assistant to the resident, was killed during the time the Arabs held the small hill. The situation of the ladies of the officers was very distressing; they were exposed to a certain share of danger, and had the additional misery of knowing that their husbands were in still greater peril.

The rajah, as soon as the action was over and his repulse complete, sent to the resident, representing that all that had passed was not only contrary to his wishes, but even to his orders, and that he was most anxious to put an end to hostilities. After much negotiation, the resident stated, that unless the troops were withdrawn, this could not be assented to; and, in consequence, during the evening and night of the 27th, the enemy's army fell back to the south side of the town and encamped. A tacit cessation of hostilities was thus agreed to. It was evident that this was greatly advantageous to the British, as the overture originated with the superior, though defeated, enemy; and our force was on the point of being augmented by Colonel Gahan's detachment, which was expected in a few hours. The rajah was completely disheartened, while on the contrary Mr. Jenkins only waited for reinforcements to act offensively. The troops were employed all the 28th in putting the hills in a state of defence, and on the morning of the 29th Colonel Gahan arrived, making the situation of all at Nagpoor comparatively secure, though not strong enough for the measures contemplated. The rajah had his ministers continually with the resident, assuring him of his desire for a reconciliation, though intelligence from the city stated that warlike preparations continued, and that fresh infantry daily arrived. After what had occurred, it was impossible to look to his professions, but only to his actions; and these, as the labours in his arsenals continued, argued strongly against such assurances.

On the 5th of December Major Pitman arrived with two battalions belonging to the Nizam, and 700 reformed horse. He had received the letter from our resident, written on the night of the 26th ultimo, on the following day at Mortagapoor, in Berar, and had made every exertion in his power to join. After the arrival of this corps, the resident found himself strong enough to repel any attack the enemy could then have made upon him.

Affairs continued in this situation until the 12th, when General Doveton came up with a regiment of cavalry and the light infantry of his division, and the remainder of his troops joined him on the 13th. The rajah having up to this date continued his hostile preparations, no time was now to be lost in bringing matters to a settlement; and one day being allowed to refresh the troops after their fatiguing march, terms were proposed to him on the evening of the 15th. They were framed upon the basis of placing us in the condition in which we should stand after a successful general action. These were the surrender of the rajah's person, occupation of the city by the British troops, the delivering up of all his artillery, and the removal of his army from the position they then held. The alternative was, his highness's camp being attacked on the 16th at daylight. This brought on a negotiation, which terminated in the rajah's promising to surrender at seven the next morning; and the attack was not to take place until after that hour, should he not be as good as his word.

The baggage, camp equipage, and followers, were on the evening of the 15th collected under the Seta Buldy hills, where they would be covered by the 20th and 24th Madras infantry, and one battalion of the Nizam's. The remainder of the army slept upon their arms, to be ready, should their assistance be required on the following day.

On the morning of the 16th December, at six o'clock, the rajah again sent in, stating that the Arabs would not allow him to surrender himself, and proposed to postpone the execution of the terms for two or three days. This preposterous attempt at evasion was treated with the most unexampled forbearance; the emissary being desired to return to his master, and inform him, that the resident would grant until nine o'clock to give himself up, and if he did so, some longer time would be given for carrying the other terms into execution; but should there be any delay, the British troops would instantly advance to the attack of his army. In the mean time General Doveton moved down to the plain to the south of the residency, directly opposite the enemy's camp, and formed the troops for the attack. Before nine o'clock, when the expectations of all were raised to the highest pitch, and all those not employed with the division intended to attack were assembled on the Seta Buldy hills, four horsemen plainly dressed were seen urging their horses at speed towards the residency, and forcing them up the steep face of the hill. The foremost threw himself off his horse, and, with an hysteric laugh, advanced to Mr. Jenkins, and proved to be the rajah himself; and they proceeded together down the hill to one of the houses. Our resident did every thing to persuade him that this was the only step he could have taken to save himself.

On the request of the resident to receive the artillery, and that the rajah's army should be withdrawn, his highness craved more time, and expressed his apprehension that the troops would not be induced at once to submit. But the resident, determined to take advantage of the impression made on them by their prince having given himself up, and of the effects of General Doveton's threatening disposition, only gave till twelve o'clock for the surrender of the artillery; and Ram Chundur Woug, who had accompanied the rajah, was sent to cause it to be carried into execution, by his highness's army falling back, and leaving the guns for us to take possession of them. He returned before twelve o'clock, and stated that this had been done.

General Doveton, at the hour appointed, had formed the troops under his command, in order to be fully prepared, as the general expressed himself in the private account of the action of this day, to frustrate all Mharatta artifices, and only waited with anxiety to put a finishing stroke to the war. The disposition was as follows:

The cavalry, under Lieutenant Colonel Gahan, consisted of the
Horse artillery,
Bengal gallopers,
Madras gallopers,
6th Regiment Bengal cavalry,
6th Regiment Madras cavalry.

Under the command of Lieutenant Colonel M'Leod were
6 Companies His Majesty's Royal Scots,
1st Battalion 12th light infantry,
2d Battalion 13th regiment native infantry,

1st Battalion 22d regiment Bengal native infantry,
Flank company 1st battalion 2d regiment native infantry.

Under the command of Lieutenant Colonel M'Kellar were
One Company of His Majesty's Royal Scots,
2d Battalion 24th regiment native infantry,
Brigade horse artillery.

Under the command of Lieutenant Colonel Scott were
One Company of His Majesty's Royal Scots,
1st Battalion 4th native infantry,
Detachment artillery,
Sappers and miners,
One company 2d battalion 14th regiment native infantry.

The reserve battery was commanded by Lieutenant Colonel Crasdell, and the farther reserve, it is believed, consisted of the reformed horse, and one battalion of the Nizam's.

A few minutes before noon the two hircarrahs, who were to direct the general to the spot where they stated the guns had been assembled by the rajah's order, having arrived requesting a detachment to take possession of them, the general, on questioning them, was impressed with the conviction that all would not be as we might wish, and that it was more than probable several of the chiefs would not consent to give them up as was supposed. He therefore instantly determined to move on with his whole force in open columns of companies, with the several reserves in line, the horse artillery and cavalry keeping in the plain to the right. Orders were given that no act of hostility should take place on our part. On the approach of the troops to the first battery, which was drawn out to oppose the left, the enemy quitting their guns, left them in our hands, and Colonel Scott's division was left in charge of them. The several divisions continued to advance, and on approaching the Mharatta camp, in a few minutes a very heavy fire of grape was opened along the whole of the enemy's line, beginning first on the cavalry from the gardens of Suka Durrah. The whole army advanced with the greatest steadiness, and, on the heads of the columns clearing some enclosures, line was formed in a soldier-like manner, and the whole then advanced intrepidly upon the guns, when a volley and a charge of bayonets carried them, and the enemy fled, leaving their camp standing. The cavalry charged a large mass of the enemy's horse, who dispersed, and forty-five elephants fell into our hands. This gallant affair, which only cost us 120 men killed and wounded, placed in our possession seventy-five pieces of cannon. Three thousand Arab infantry threw themselves into the city, which was very strong, from a number of stone palaces, &c.

The 16th and 17th were employed by the rajah to induce them to leave it. His highness paid them their arrears, and they were offered from us every security for their march out of the rajah's territories, but without effect, and General Doveton was in consequence obliged to commence hostilities against them, and that part of the city which they occupied. Lest we should not succeed with the means we had on the spot, the general ordered up his battering train, which he had left at Akolah.

Nagpoor is surrounded by an imperfect wall with round towers, in circumference about three miles. About three hundred yards from the west gate, or Jumma Derwaseh, within the walls, stands the palace, a very strong stone building, to reduce which a battering train was required, together with experienced sappers and miners, (of whom the Indian army is much in want). The neighbouring houses also being of great strength, could not be carried by assault without a great loss of men, and risk of failure.

The suburb is very large, containing many stone houses, and, including the city, is seven miles round. The Arabs, who had taken post within, were particularly effective behind walls.

A commanding situation on the banks of the Jumma Talao was fixed upon for the erection of our batteries, within two hundred and eighty yards of the Jumma Derwaseh, and by the exertions of Captain Davis of the engineers, and the selection of such of the captured guns as were of sufficient calibre to be useful, they were opened on the morning of the 21st December, with a view if possible to effect a breach in the old palace wall. The experiment of that day, however, having convinced General Doveton that this object was not attainable with such ordnance, the firing was directed on the gateway, with the intention of laying it open, so as to enable the troops to establish themselves in that advanced position. On the evening of the 23d December the commandant of artillery and chief engineer reported that the battering had produced such an effect as to render a lodgment practicable with little loss, and this was confirmed by every information the general could obtain. A combined attack on the gate as well as on the Toolse Baug, and another advanced position (with a view of closing on the enemy) was directed to be carried into execution on the 24th in the morning, when the additional corps had moved down for the relief of the several posts. The attack on the Jumma Derwaseh was made under the general's own eye, that of the Toolse Baug by Lieutenant Colonel Scott, and the other under the command of Major Pittman.

The troops rushed from the battery about half-past eight o'clock, on a signal preconcerted with the leaders of the other two attacks. But those who advanced to the gateway found it was not sufficiently wide to admit of a section entering at once, and the enemy having taken the precaution of lining, with bodies of Arabs, several stone houses on both sides of it, as well as of the street leading to it, which could not be perceived from the battery; the attacking body, after having been exposed to a heavy fire for some time, was obliged to take shelter in the adjoining huts and behind the mud walls, from whence the attempt was kept up. Finding however little or no probability of their being likely to obtain possession of the gateway, the general recalled them from the assault. The columns under Colonel Scott and Major Pittman were more successful; but from the failure of the principal attack, they were ordered to take up their former ground. Our loss, including these attacks, was very heavy from the 19th to the 24th December, consisting of one European officer, 19 men killed, and three field-officers, one captain, three lieutenants, two ensigns, and 71 Europeans wounded; and one native officer and 34 Sepoys killed, and five native officers and 145 men wounded. The evening of our failure in the attempt upon the city, Major Munt of the Madras cavalry surprised and cut to pieces a body of the enemy, amounting to 400 men, on the banks of the Kunnain, about ten miles from Nagpoor.

On the morning of the 25th December the Arab chiefs in the place made a communication of their willingness to evacuate it, on certain conditions being granted to them; and having the next day sent out their principal chiefs, or peer zadahs, to conduct the negotiation, the several points were satisfactorily settled by the resident and the general, with the Arab and other forces, who evacuated the city at noon on the 30th, when the troops took possession, and the British standard was hoisted on the palace, under a royal salute.

The Arabs were allowed free and safe conduct through the rajah's territory, with their families and property; and after an exchange of hostages, for which service Lieutenant Sheriff was selected on our side, they marched for the frontier. Previous to their quitting Nagpoor, they plundered the palaces, and committed many excesses. Colonel Scott was appointed to command the city with two battalions. This convention with the Arabs left General Doveton's division disposable, as soon as General Hardyman's corps should arrive, which was again directed by our resident to advance to Nagpoor, that General Doveton might be at liberty to return to Berar, and subsequently into Khan'deish to undertake the siege of Asseer Ghur, as he had been originally ordered by Sir Thomas Hislop. The battering train belonging to General Doveton, which had reached the banks of the Wurdah river on its way from Akolah, was remanded to Ellichpoor. On the morning of the 6th of January a detachment of four squadrons of cavalry and two battalions of infantry, under the command of Colonel M'Leod, was ordered to disperse a force of 4000 horse assembled about forty miles to the south of Nagpoor, under the command of a chief named Ghun Put Rao, who having received information of the movement, retreated out of the rajah's country into Berar, with the intention of crossing the Nizam's territory to join the Peishwah.

CHAPTER IX.

The author leaves Nagpoor—Delays and mistakes—Length of the column—Arrangements for the march—Rencontre with some British officers—Mad elephant—Indian ruse de guerre—Villagers present nuzzurs—Anecdote—Arrive at Gorar—Arrangements in camp—Jemidar of the Nizam's escort—His field equipment—Want of discipline in the native armies—State of the country—Tigers—Arrive at Kotal—Hostility of the inhabitants done away—Elephants—Anecdote of one—Their Docility—Use made of them in India—Used as executioners—Cruelly treated—Females preferred for riding—Equipments of these animals—Employed in war—Cased in iron—Burst open gates—Swivels used on their backs in the time of Akbar—Used at the siege of Chitoor—In war in Africa and Asia—By Europeans only for baggage, &c.—Ceylon elephants the best—Reservoir of water—Carry the standard—Singular honours—Ensigns of royalty in India—Umbrellas—Arrive at Pettah—Arrive at Aumnair—Wurdah river—Flag—Opium—Chinese consume large quantities—Much taken by the natives of India—Fatal effects—Monument to commemorate the burning of a woman—That sacrifice continues—Mahometans tried to put a stop to it—Leave necessary—Antiquity of the custom—Supposed origin—Anecdote—Mahometan tomb—Arrive at Singure—Religious feelings of the jemidar—Some account of his Russollah Barghirs—Sillidars—Proportional expense between Hindoostan and the Dekhun—Dress of the irregular horse—Quilted jackets—Trade between Persia and Arabia in horses to India—Mounting the British cavalry—The northern traffic in horses lately terminated—Mharattas value their mares—Cutch horses—Anecdote—Charms tied on the horses—Jemidar most scrupulous respecting his religion—Arrive at Ambarrah—Newab Salabat Khan—His jaghires—His troops—His son Namdar Khan—The hilly country around Gywul Ghur—Gonds—Conversation with the jemidar—Prejudices—Religious discussion—Apt remark of the jemidar—Arrive at Dewulwarrah—Message from Namdar Khan—Vaqueel—Arrangements for meeting Namdar Khan—Dreadful occurrence—Tigers—Apathy of the natives.

Gorar, 6th January, 1818.

AFTER the usual inconveniencies and delay at starting on a first day's march, we quitted the residency at an early hour, and on our arrival at General Doveton's camp, to our astonishment, neither the baggage nor Captain Hicks's recruits made their appearance, though positively directed, and after an hour passed in inquiries, we put ourselves *en route*, leaving fifty of the Nizam's horse to bring them up, should they, on discovering their mistake, come to the place of rendezvous. We were under some apprehension that they might have accompanied the column of baggage belonging to a detachment which had marched the same morning to act against a force already mentioned, about forty miles to the southward, but the nature of my duty did not admit of my being detained. After we had proceeded about four miles, our guide, whether from ignorance or perverseness it is difficult to decide, declared that he had no knowledge whatever of the place we were going to, and we were consequently obliged to halt to procure another. A trooper who had gone to the left, though unsuccessful in finding a villager, brought us information of all the baggage and recruits being about a mile in that direction on a parallel road. We then halted, and sent back to the camp to beg a fresh guide, but before he reached us we found a man who stated that he had been several years an hircarrah to Mr. Elphinstone when resident at Nagpoor, and that he knew the whole road to Ellichpoor. We were soon overtaken by two of General Doveton's hircarrahs, whom we dismissed after they had ascertained that the volunteer guide was well acquainted with the road. It was necessary to halt every two or three miles, as our baggage, which was found to be very considerable, extended far to the rear, and the whole column consisted, with the recruits and followers, of about 1500 souls.

Some slight disposition was made on the march, and all were informed that it was never to be deviated from. An advance of twenty of the irregular cavalry preceded my elephant and Mr. Elliott's palanquin. The jemidar, with the detachment of regular cavalry, immediately followed the elephant; 150 of the irregular horse (which had all joined) marched in their rear; the company of infantry behind them, then the baggage and recruits, and thirty of the irregular horse; and twenty of Captain Hicks's old disciplined Sepoys armed, formed the rear guard. The flank patroles were furnished by the Nizam's horse, and we tried to be as compact as we could, though from the heterogeneous character of our column, we did not succeed so well as we wished. Our road lay across an extended and somewhat barren plain.

About twelve miles from Nagpoor, we met three officers of the Madras army coming from Ellichpoor with a strong escort. They informed us that the road was open and free from the enemy, but they cautioned us to avoid a mad elephant at Kotal, where we are to halt to-morrow. He is stated to have belonged to the rajah, and to have broke away from the engagement of the 16th, his mehout or driver having been killed. The country and crops have sustained much damage from him, and he has even killed several people. Our cavalry in the action at Nagpoor shot many of the mehouts, to prevent the escape of the men of rank, as it is an Indian *ruse de guerre* for the master, when closely pressed, to take the place of the driver, and thus save themselves by assuming a more humble character.

The people from the villages came out to meet us with presents of fowls, eggs, and milk. They were in a dreadful state of alarm, which we attempted by every means in our power to allay. The chief man of each village offered his nuzzur or present of a rupee or two in a white handkerchief with trembling hands, and I was obliged to receive them, as the refusal would cause apprehension, the acceptance of them being an assurance of good will and approbation. The first time I refused the money, but the jemidar of the Nizam's horse rode up to the side of my elephant, and in the most respectful manner represented to me the necessity of acting otherwise. I cannot account for the origin of this eastern custom, of an inferior never approaching a superior without a gift, unless it is with the idea, in this quarter of the world of universal despotism, that all is at the mercy of the strongest. Thevenot tells us that two envoys of the French East India Company, owing to a want of knowledge of this custom, quarrelled with the Banians, to whom they were recommended at Bourhampoor in Khandeish. On their arrival at that city the Banians approached them with basons full of sweetmeats and rupees in their hands, as a token of esteeming themselves their inferiors, and to compliment them; but the Frenchmen, imagining the twenty-five or thirty rupees offered them were a sign they were thought to be poor, and given from a charitable motive, flew into a violent passion.

The only person to whom British officers offer nuzzurs is to the King of Delhi, as we hold Bengal under his firmaun. The officers who have commands in the service of the native princes, on their appointment and introduction to the durbar, present them as being viewed in the light of servants.

We have made a march of sixteen miles, and are encamped on the banks of a small stream. The different descriptions of troops have had their places for encampment pointed out to them, and this is to be continued for the future. The regular cavalry on the right, the infantry in the centre, and the Nizam's horse on the left. Our tents in the rear, with the baggage and recruits. The twenty old Sepoys belonging to Captain Hicks take the rear guard. The jemidar of the Nizam's horse has been directed to send small detachments, consisting of five men mounted, about a gunshot to the front, rear and flanks, and to keep four men in the village at night. All have been ordered to sleep in their clothes, and on their arms, and the drummer is stationed at the door of my tent to beat the assembly at any hour. The recruits belonging to Captain Hicks take the out-sentry duty at night, and being all double have received orders to make no disturbance should they have reason to be made uneasy by any movement in their front, but quietly to report it. The jemidar of the Nizam is directed to keep his men, who are all Mahometans, on their ground, should any alarm take place, as they have no particular uniform, and are dressed like the enemy; and he has been informed that we are determined to fire on any horseman in our front, or out of their known position, as the enemy might otherwise ride up as friends, and when near or on our flanks assume their real character. He is also to keep them collected till one of us join him. Two very handsome horses with superb caparisons belong to this jemidar, who is himself dressed in a vest of green English broad-cloth, laced with gold, and very rich embroidered belts. A shield of buffalo's hide with gilt bosses is hung over his back. His arms are two swords and a dagger, a brace of English pistols, and he has his matchlock carried before him by a servant. His name is Salee Mehumed Khan, and he appears to like conversing with us, though in a very diffident manner. He has a very good field equipment, consisting of a capacious tent and six camels, and at our halts has a large horsecloth of green, red, and yellow, spread on the ground for him to sit upon. The russollah or troop has a most splendid pair of kettle-drums, and two gaudy embroidered standards. The first drum is to beat at half-past three tomorrow morning, and the second for moving off our ground at four. The jemidar has been desired to procure guides from the village for the march, and to continue the practice daily.

Kotal, January 7th, 1818.

We left our camp this morning long before daylight, and the Nizam's horse did not, I suppose, calculate on my stirring so early, as they did not overtake us for many miles. To give an idea of the want of discipline and disregard of orders in the native armies it will be sufficient to state that the Kings of Delhi were often obliged, when moving from one ground or encampment to another, to threaten to burn the tents of those who were tardy in striking them, and sometimes even to carry the threat into execution. The country was in great part covered with jungle, but well cultivated around the villages. These are all built at the foot of small mud forts, a too certain sign of suffering from the inroads of Pindarries. On the march I saw a small seat in a tree, which the jemidar informed me is used as an ambuscade for a tiger, the country being overrun with them; and when the vicinity of a road is rendered particularly unsafe by being haunted by one of them, the best shot in the village takes his post in the seat in the tree, with a sheep or goat as a bait under it, which in the night by its cries allures the tiger, and he becomes an easy mark to a rested matchlock.

On our approach to this place I despatched some horsemen to find out the situation of the mad elephant, which gave us much cause for uneasiness, as mine has shewn some symptoms of not being on his best behaviour, and if they had met they would doubtless have fought; but happily the mad one is on the other side of the town, and we hope to pass him before daylight to-morrow morning. The people of the village threatened to fire on the horsemen sent forward if they attempted to enter it; but on our arrival, and sending a corporal of the regular cavalry to the huckeem* to state that I would feel obliged by their seizing any one of my camp followers who might be found plundering, they argued, as I expected, that no harm would be done them, and established a little bazar in our camp. They also promised to drive the mad elephant off the road, but the poor creature is so thin and reduced that he can hardly walk; about twenty men having lately surrounded him with long spears, with which they have continually tortured and wounded him, and he is nearly dead with irritation and misery. At certain times of the year elephants go mad in quest of the females, and become totally ungovernable. During the time our camp was at Erij on the banks of the Betwar, in Bundelcund, one of our largest elephants fell into this state, and although he had the mehout's son on his neck, broke away, and rushed close to the head-quarter tents. The mehout with a long spear attempted to bring him to order, thrusting it deep into the root of his trunk, and while giving directions to his son how to treat him, the animal watched his moment and rushed at him. The poor wretch saw his danger, and in attempting to fly fell over

* Chief of the village.

some tent ropes, and was pulled back by the trunk of the elephant and kicked to death. The animal then rushed to the river with the son of the deceased on his back, and what is remarkable, in passing some clothes spread out on the ground to dry, stopped short, and gave them up by his trunk to the boy, who to humour him pretended to put them on. A stronger elephant was at last brought to charge him, and his gallant mehout managed him so well that the mad monster was obliged to give way, and being quite fatigued, in passing through some deep ground allowed himself to be chained and secured. Accidents frequently occur when they are in this infuriated state. When we were encamped at Puzdar one of Major O'Brien's elephants got loose and killed a man, who had opposed his going across the camp at night.

The astonishing docility and gentleness of these animals always made me delight in viewing them, and the variety of tricks that they are continually playing is very entertaining. They will frequently on being teased by the flies walk up to a tree, break off a branch with their trunk, and rid themselves of their minute enemies. This prospective advantage in their judging of a future effect from a natural cause perhaps exceeds instinct. Elephants have been, according to the earliest accounts, used for pleasure, war, and burthen; and the first person who succeeded in reducing them to slavery must have been of a very determined character. Diodorus Siculus and Arrian speak of these animals being trained for war in the Indian armies which opposed Alexander. They were so disposed in the army of Porus, being placed at equal distances from each other with lines of soldiers connecting them, as to resemble the walls of a city, the former appearing like towers, and the latter like the walls. Indeed it was natural they should have been applied to military purposes soon after they were first tamed, from their enormous power, and imposing appearance; and though when not enraged they have, in common with other animals, a dread of man, yet the mehout can always make them attack one, and they have been commonly used as executioners. The command the mehout has over them is surprising, and the brutality with which they are sometimes treated makes it astonishing that they do not crush with their enormous force the wretch who lords it over them, and who, as a wanton exercise of his insolence, with one foot upon the trunk, and holding by his tusks or ears, often obliges the animal to lift him on his head. When he does become violent, as I have mentioned, he is, as may be well supposed from his vast bulk and strength, a most formidable object, and for this reason the females are preferred for the howdah, or to ride on. Their number is what the native princes most pique themselves upon, and, from their superiority over the rest of the brute creation, they must have been very early used by the sovereigns and great men of the country. They are extremely lavish of expense in their equipments; and it is a very common thing to see silver gilt howdahs: the Peishwah had one richly ornamented with glass. In war the sovereign or commander-in-chief of the native armies always rode upon an elephant; and in Indian history it will be seen that a number of battles have been lost from the chiefs quitting their elephants, and being supposed by their troops to be slain, as they no longer appeared in their former elevated situation. These animals were cased in iron, and the war howdahs secured by plates of brass. They were sometimes employed in storming or assisting the soldiers to ascend the walls of fortresses without a ditch, and putting their heads against the gates to burst them open; for this reason the gates have in many instances large iron nails, a foot long and an inch square at the base, to prevent their pressure. To counteract this, the elephants had iron plates on the front of their foreheads. In the time of Akbar they were used in war with swivels on their backs; and at the siege of Chitoor they were introduced into the fort to destroy the garrison, who refused to receive quarter, having given themselves up to despair. Dow tells us that the scene was most shocking. The brave Rajahpoots, rendered more valiant by desperation, crowded around the elephants, seized them even by their tusks, and inflicted upon them unavailing wounds. The terrible animals trod down the Indians under their feet "like grasshoppers," or, winding them in their powerful trunks, tossed them aloft in the air, or dashed them against the walls and pavement. They have indeed been used in war in all countries. The Ptolemies and Hannibal trained the African elephant for their armies, and Marco Polo speaks of them in the army of the grand khan of Tartary, carrying from twelve to sixteen men on their backs*. This I conceive to be impossible, unless they were upon two stages. In the European armies they have been wholly given up for war, excepting to carry baggage, and sometimes to assist the artillery. The only notices we have of them in the history of wars in Europe are that of those brought into Italy by Pyrrhus, and by Hannibal into France and Italy: the former are said to be the individual animals brought by Alexander from India—a proof of their longevity. Those of Ceylon are preferred to all others; and the natives pretend that all other elephants, being aware of their superiority, *salam*, or pay obeisance to them. We find elephants have been at times broke in to ride with the bridle, and that Assud Khan, one of the kings of the Dekhun, was the first to attempt this novel system. The elephant has a peculiarity which I do not think has been taken notice of by any naturalist. It has a reservoir to hold water, which it draws at pleasure, by introducing its trunk into its mouth, and uses it principally in cooling itself, by blowing the water under its stomach. This reservoir must contain several pints. In the native armies the standard and kettledrums are carried on an elephant at the head of the army; and Marco Polo tells us that the grand khan, in one

* Elephants are known in a domestic state in Timbuctoo, as I was informed by Hadjee Talub Ben Jelow, the governor of the princes of Morocco, who had lived in that city long, and used the Arabic word *feel* for this animal, and described it perfectly.

of his expeditions, and in action, was stationed in a large wooden castle borne on the back of four elephants, whose bodies were protected with a covering of thick leather, hardened by fire. This castle contained many cross-bow men, and on it was hoisted the imperial standard. The zerrie puttah, or standard of the Mharatta empire, was also carried on an elephant. It was a particular honour to hold the fan or umbrella over the head of the sovereign when on his elephant, the latter being a particular mark of distinction, included among the ensigns of royalty, which, with others, are to a certain degree peculiar to India. Ferdozi, in speaking of the ensigns of royalty which were sent by Mahmood, nephew of Mehumed Ghori, to Koutoub, mentions a throne, umbrella, standard, and drums. At the court of Delhi no one is permitted to use an umbrella in the king's presence; and Arrian takes notice of the umbrella being carried over the heads of the people of rank in India. Before the time of Feroz the Second the imperial umbrella was red, but he changed it in 688 to white. We also learn that the kings of the Dekhun used different coloured umbrellas*.

We are strongly encamped to-day with one flank on a wood and the other upon a stream, which turns and covers our rear. To-morrow we cross the Wurdah, quit the country of the Rajah of Nagpoor, and enter that of the Nizam.

Aumnair, January 8, 1818.

We passed the dreaded elephant before daylight with safety. The country belonging to the Rajah of Nagpoor, which we have crossed, is in part beautifully cultivated, though not by any means equal to the provinces north of the Nerbuddah. We observed on the march a large town, which is only divided from this place by the river Wurdah, and is not mentioned in our route. It is a very considerable place, with the remains of a strong fort, and appeared

* Since I have returned to England, I find the people of rank in the Loo-choo Islands use the umbrella in a like manner.

opulent. They even called it Pettah, the town being doubtless at one time dependent on the fort, which now appears dismantled. This town, outside of which we are encamped, is large and populous. No villagers came out to meet us, and they are far from being so civil since we crossed the river; but the reason is obvious, we are in a friendly country, the Nizam being our ally. They do not therefore feel that great eastern motive, *fear*. The Wurdah is a very miserable stream at this time of the year, and we passed it with the greatest facility. It runs over a rocky bed, and below our camp forms a number of small cascades. We found the flag in the town changed, the moment we crossed, from the brick-dust colour of the Mharattas to the sacred green of Mahomet; and the number of poppy fields showed that we had again approximated the dissipated followers of that prophet. The production and sale of opium is one of the monopolies by which the Company make such large sums annually. The quantity imported into China is inconceivable; and the Chinese would feel as miserable without this horrid drug as we should be if deprived of their tea. Though the use of it is prohibited under the heaviest penalties, they risk every thing to procure it. The natives of India chew it, or rather swallow it in pills, which throws them into a state of intoxication, more pleasant they say than that produced by drinking fermented liquors; but it leaves them, on recovering, in the most dreadful lassitude; and after having given way freely to its use, and becoming fond of it, the period between the restoration from its effects and a fresh dose is so extremely painful, that few have firmness enough to bear up against it: thus, by habitual repetition, they render themselves more and more incapable of being weaned from it, and in a few years destroy themselves. The eyes of those who are addicted to it have a shocking inflamed appearance; and the most intelligent servant, after taking it, becomes more or less like an idiot. They also smoke it, and gradually use it in such large quantities as would totally overpower the senses of a person unaccustomed to it. The ministers of the Rajah of Nagpoor, during the late disturbances, when their miserable prince became half paralysed with his fears, gave him quantities of this intoxicating and exhilarating drug.

The river Wurdah is now the boundary of the Rajah of Nagpoor's country, who, at the peace of 1803, ceded all west of it, that is Berar, except five districts.

We saw, in the course of this day, a small brick building, which is always erected on the spot where a woman has burnt herself with her husband. This horrid ceremony is not decreasing; and so careful are we of not interfering with the religious opinions of the natives, that it is permitted throughout our provinces, though not within the Mharatta Ditch at Calcutta, which bounds the jurisdiction where the English law is in force. We learn from both Tavernier and Bernier that the Mahometans were as anxious for doing it away as we are, and that it was under their government necessary to ask leave, as it is at present under ours; so that our magistrates and police officers invariably see that force is not used. Thevenot also tells us, that the Great Mogul and other Mahometan princes had ordered their governors to employ all their diligence in suppressing it, and that it required great solicitations and considerable presents to obtain permission. The antiquity of this custom is very great; for Diodorus Siculus, when he mentions Alexander's entering the country of the Catheri, relates that by the law the living wives were burnt with their dead husbands. The same author affirms it to have had its origin from a woman having poisoned her husband. Within the last two years, circumstances caused inquiry to be made with respect to the burning of women in the neighbourhood of Calcutta, which excited much notice with many comments, and had become known to the natives. A widow who was about to burn herself, after having walked three times round the pile, which is part of the ceremony, seeing a number of

English gentlemen spectators, walked up and addressed them. She said she was anxious to do away the impression which the English entertained, that the women who thus sacrificed themselves were previously stupified with various drugs. She denied this, offering herself as a proof to the contrary, and of their motives being good, arising from a religious feeling of its being acceptable to the Supreme Being, and that attempting to dissuade them from it was not only cruel, but impious. She then placed herself by the side of her deceased husband, and went through the remainder of the ceremony with equal heroism.

On the outside of this village is a very handsome tomb of stone to the memory of a Pithan Sirdar, who died here. It is a square building, rising into a fine dome about sixty feet high, with a stone tank in front of it.

Singuré, 9th January, 1818.

We have made a march of 20 miles to-day, moving parallel to the range of mountains which skirt the north of Berar: on the other side of them a plain extends to the river Nerbuddah. We passed close to a mosque, and the moment the minarets appeared above the trees, the scrupulous jemidar of the Nizam's horse asked permission to quit the line of march, with a few of his men as devout as himself, to offer up prayers. As it is not only liberal, but good policy to show a respect for all religious opinions, since they tend more or less to the good government of society, it was granted him.

The jemidar, with much sociality, comes into our tent, sits down on a chair, enters into conversation with us, and seems tolerably well informed. He says his native home is in the neighbourhood of Jeypoor. The men under his orders are almost all mounted on his own horses, and he receives 40 rupees per month for each complete horseman; and after the first expense of the horses, saves considerably out of his allowance. These are called barghirs, in contradistinction to those mounted on their own horses, who are called sillidars, and of whom he has not above 20 with him. The difference in the expense of provisions and equipments between Hindoostan and the Dekhun may thus be estimated. Here the horseman complete receives 40 rupees per month; in Hindoostan only 22, and this is of course the standard for calculating every thing. The irregular cavalry throughout India are mostly dressed in quilted cotton jackets; though the best of their habiliments are not, as I supposed, stuffed with cotton, but a number of cotton clothes quilted together. This serves as defensive armour, and when their heads are swathed round, and under the chin, with linen to the thickness of several folds, it is almost hopeless with the sword to make an impression upon them. They also at times stuff their jackets with the refuse silk of the cocoons, which, they say, will even turn a ball. There is, in England, a similar idea respecting a silk handkerchief. They are in common but badly mounted; and it is a mistaken idea that the generality of Indian horses are of a valuable breed, for the Dekhun has always been supplied from the Persian Gulf, and Hindoostan with horses from the north-west. It is curious, that Cosmas reports from the testimony of Sopatrus, as mentioned in the Periplus of Dr. Vincent, that horses were brought from Persia, and that they paid no duty on entering India; and Cæsar Frederick mentions the same thing on the coast of Canara. Marco Polo, in speaking of Mahaba on the western coast of India, states that horses were brought from Ormus, from Diufur, and Arden, and that 5000 were supposed to be annually imported. The cavalry of Madras and Bombay will always obtain plenty of horses from this ancient branch of commerce, which still exists in full activity; but under the Bengal presidency, were it not for the Company's stud, which is a very fine establishment, I do not think they would be able to procure enow, as the dealers who used 12 or 14 years ago to bring strings of fine Tourkee horses from beyond Kabul, have of late relinquished that traffic, either on account of the heavy duties they are obliged to pay on passing through the various states, or perhaps of being intercepted by the Seiks. There was once, however, a particularly fine breed of horses in Hindoostan called the jungle tarzé, but it is now almost extinct. The Mharattas, like the Arabs, are extremely careful of their mares; the former have been known to give 5000 rupees for one. The breed of horses in Kutch is very fine; they have a peculiar dip in the back, and their superiority over the other horses of India is accounted for in the Ayen Akbaree, by the following anecdote. A long time ago an Arab merchant ship was wrecked on the coast of Kutch, and seven chosen Arab horses were saved from the wreck, which are reported to have been the progenitors of the present race. From a like incident, the breed of horses called galloways derive their origin: some Spanish horses having been on board of some of the ships of the Armada, stranded on the shore of that county in Scotland. The jemidar has one of the Kutch horses, and as he is very superstitious, all his stud have tuzveez or charms, consisting of small scraps of parchment, with sentences from the Koran written on them, wrapt up in little bags an inch square, tied round their legs and necks. He affirms that he does not smoke, because his prophet disapproves of it in the Koran, and when I have sent for him, I have found his five periods of prayer in the course of the day interfere very much with his duty. We are encamped on the Wurdah, which here runs between steep banks.

Ambarrah, January 10, 1818.

Our route to-day has been through a very rich country, and we are at present encamped in the jaghire of the Newab Salabat Khan, of Ellichpoor.

He is a very respectable man, and a very fine old soldier, much attached to the British government. He holds a considerable jaghire under the Nizam, on military tenure, furnishing a brigade of two battalions of infantry, 2000 horse, and four guns. The infantry have some European officers, though the newab commands. He is just now absent from Ellichpoor with Colonel Deacon in the neighbourhood of Arungabad, and I fear I have no chance of meeting him. His son, Namdar Khan, is however at Ellichpoor, and General Doveton having written to him to inform him of my passing through his estate; he has ordered provisions of every kind to be brought us from the villages, and it is with difficulty I can make the villagers accept of any remuneration. The hills to the north of this belong at present to the Rajah of Nagpoor, being part of some mehals which were left to him to the west of the river Wurdah, after the treaty of 1803. In these hills is situated Gywul Ghur, a fort taken by the Duke of Wellington in the same year. Some Gonds, the original inhabitants of Gondwana, before the conquest of the Mharattas, are in arms in these regions, but it would be only waste of time to reduce them.

We had a very long conversation this morning with the jemidar, Sallee Mahomet Khan. He came into our tent whilst we were at breakfast, and we invited him to partake of our fare, which he declined, saying he had previously taken some refreshment. As he had on some former occasions evinced great liberality of feeling, I asked him if he refused from a belief in any impurity arising from eating with us, which is so common among the Mahometans in India, as they have imbibed many of the prejudices of the Hindoos. He stated that his refusal of our offer did not spring from that motive. This circumstance introduced a long discussion on the subject of our religions, and produced some controversy. However, on taking leave, he remarked with great aptness and good humour, "there is but one God and one Ellichpoor. Two roads lead to that city, one by the village we are now in, and the other by Omroutee;" and suffered us to draw our conclusion. The illustration was very happy, and we were much pleased with his remark, as he has, during the time he has accompanied us, shown that he respects the ordinances, and firmly believes the religion in which he was brought up, but does not despise or condemn the tenets of others.

Dewulwarrah, January 11th, 1818.

Our route this day has continued parallel to the range of mountains to the north, and the face of the country is well cultivated. About six miles from this place we met a jemidar, with a very civil message from Namdar Khan, that understanding I was to arrive at Ellichpoor on the morrow, he had ordered a gentleman to receive me on the ground I should encamp on to arrange our meeting, as he intended to come out himself and accompany me into the city. Soon after our breakfast, the approach of this vaqueel was announced: he appeared to be a coarse vulgar man, dressed in a red silk suit, with many hircarrahs and attendants. He informed me his name was Muste Khan, and that it was his intention to return in the evening to Ellichpoor, with the information at what hour I might be expected, as the general,—so I found Namdar Khan desired to be called,—would come out of the city three or four miles to receive me. He brought me a present of baskets of fruit, and two goats, for which, particularly the latter, I was most grateful. The young newab is said to be rather of a dissipated character, and to give much trouble to his father.

A very curious circumstance occurred almost under our view this morning on the march. About half an hour before daylight, as we were passing through a village, we were arrested by most dreadful cries, so heart-rending, that Captain Hicks and myself stopped the elephant to inquire into their cause. It appeared that two brothers, one 10 years of age, the other younger, having heard our advanced guard pass, came out, through curiosity, from a cottage about 20 yards from the road. The former was immediately sprung upon by a tiger in the middle of the village, and carried off; the youngest ran in and informed the mother, who uttered the exclamations of distress we had heard. The tiger must have been within 20 yards of our elephant, and I am surprised he did not show symptoms of alarm, as they are generally very susceptible of fear in the vicinity of these animals.

There is some consolation, but of a painful kind, in knowing that the tiger, in springing on a living animal, generally fractures the skull of its victim with a violent blow of its paw, thereby rendering it insensible in a moment. There was no chance of recovering the poor boy, as the tiger went off into the jungle immediately, doubtless to his most secret haunt to enjoy his horrid repast.

I have often been surprised at the apathy of the natives of India, but in nothing more than the carelessness with which they permit the high grass which communicates with the thickest jungle to grow up to the very doors of their houses, serving as a cover to the tigers.

CHAPTER X.

Meet Namdar Khan—His sewarry—Our reception—The newab's dress—His mania for English manners and customs—His cousin—Proceed to the city—Conversation—Ignorance—Gate and wall of Ellichpoor—The newab's palace—Garden—Pavilion—Breakfast—Indian etiquette—The various apartments of the family—Youngest son of Salabat Khan—Return to our tents—Information of an action near Poonah—Vaqueel of the Soubah—Interview with the Soubah—Hindoos always employed as ministers of finance—Dinner—Nautch women—Wine—Toasts—Take leave—Arrive at Omery Comery—Arrive at Coleplaiser—Mode of supplying the troops in India—Bazars—All trades to be found in them—Immense numbers of followers attached to the Indian armies—Quantity of baggage—Flag to each bazar—Fikirs—Multitudes in the time of Tavernier—Their penances—Measuring their length, &c.—Superstition—Other penances—Braminical religion—Horrid rites—Ghauts—Sierra.

Omery Comery, January 10th, 1818.

YESTERDAY I was so fatigued with the officious attention of the newab, that I could not put pen to paper, but I was nevertheless amused at times with the singular scenes we witnessed. We started very early from Durwulwarrah, in hopes of encountering the general as near the city as possible, in order to shorten the time we should be in his society. About four miles from it, however, we descried his sewarry*, as it approached ours, which was better looking, though not so numerous. His suite went off to the side of the road, and he got out of his palanquin and came forward to receive us. Captain Hicks and myself dismounted from our elephant, and walked forward to meet him. It required all the good breeding I was master of to refrain from laughing. A modern equipped Othello stood before us. He had on an immense cocked hat, with a long queue doubled up to his head, hanging in an enormous loop. He was dressed in a red coat laced with silver, very large epaulettes, a silver star embroidered on his right breast, and a French grey pair of loose trowsers, not long enough to hide another pair of

* The retinue of a great man.

red silk under them, the latter dangling over his shoes upon the ground, for he had no boots; and to complete his toilet, he had a grenadier officer's regulation sword. He shook hands with both of us, as it appears to be his anxious wish to copy all our manners and customs, and then introduced us to his cousin Golaim Hossein Khan, the son of his uncle Futteh Jung. His was a grotesque imitation of European dress, entirely in compliment to us; but the cousin was in the Mahometan costume, and embraced us in the native manner. The general came up on my elephant, and Captain Hicks and the cousin mounted one belonging to the newab, and we proceeded to the city in the most imposing attitude. I conceive he must have been accompanied by 800 men of different descriptions, horse and foot, and my 300 soldiers, joined to these, made a very respectable appearance. He continued chewing pawn and cardamoms, and lolled his tongue out of his mouth, covered with these nasty ingredients; yet he did all in his power to be polite, and that he failed was not his fault, but his misfortune. The only blame that could be laid to his charge was his ever having attempted so hopeless an undertaking: but we must not criticise him too severely, as he meant well. After I had overcome the difficulty of sitting by his side, the next was to find conversation. I judged correctly in supposing that he would be pleased with remarks upon his person, and stating how very much flattered we were by our manners and dress being so correctly followed by a person of his rank. He said he was anxious to go to England, but disapproved of the sea voyage. I recommended to him the travels of Aboul Talub Khan, in the Persian language, as giving a very correct account of our country. He answered he had heard of it, and had requested Mr. Jenkins, at Nagpoor, to procure it for him from Calcutta. As a specimen of his ignorance of geography, he asked me if I was going to that city, though it was east of us, and I was travelling west; and pointed out to me his howdahs, which had been made there by Mr. Jenkins's order. He inquired my rank, and I thought seemed disappointed when I told him I was so low in the army. Thus, for once, captain was not a good travelling name.

I had not been ten minutes with him on the elephant before he pointed out to me Gywul Ghur rising among the hills on our right, and apparently about twenty miles distant. I fully anticipated what was to follow this introduction, and heard with the utmost patience an account of the great and strenuous exertions the newab Salabat Khan had constantly made to prove his fidelity and affection for the Company; and, the Rajah of Nagpoor having now forfeited all by his late conduct, how very desirable and how very acceptable the mehals west of the Wurdah, with Gywul Ghur, would be to the newab. I made answer that I thought he deserved this reward, hoped he might receive it, and then stated that I knew nothing at all about it, and hope I left him in a very happy state of uncertainty as to the meaning of my answer. We entered the city through a gate of beautiful architecture, built, as well as the wall, of sand-coloured stone. I believe the gates of the Prince's stables at Brighton must have been taken from this, as they are much alike, but what I now speak of is much higher, and more splendidly carved. The wall appeared to be about sixty feet in height, with very handsome battlements, but is not above four feet thick. It is only carried in part round the town, the present newab's father not living to finish it, and it being reckoned ominous for a person to continue any building, when the projector has died before it is completed. In consequence of this preposterous idea, many imperfect works are left throughout the country to fall to ruin; and a son feels no pleasure, but on the contrary dread, in pursuing perhaps a favourite design of his father. This city is the capital of Berar, and was plundered in 1583 by Koka, Akbar's general. Near it is Argaum, where the Duke of Wellington, in 1803, defeated the Rajah of Berar, with great loss. The city has been very much benefited by the old newab, and all the bazars and houses near his palace are of brick, though his own residence does not make a very showy appearance. It has an open space before it, where two six-pounders were posted, with small union flags placed on their carriages. We entered it through a high gate, and advanced between two lines of Rhohilla infantry, armed with matchlocks, spears, and bows and arrows, who *una voce* set up a tremendous shout, calling on God to bless the newab. We alighted at the gate of his apartments, and passing a curtain entered a small garden, with fountains and cypress trees, surrounded with high walls. In the middle stood a covered pavilion, open on all sides, with several verandas furnished with sofas and glass shades for lights, and in the centre a breakfast-table, spread with every thing requisite after our manner. Soon after our arrival the table was covered with pilaws, curries of fowls and vegetables, plates of hard boiled eggs, and in the centre, by way of ornament, in a salad-bowl, a large white unboiled cabbage, which the general believed to be an article of English fare. Our entertainer helped himself without ceremony, after seating us and placing his cousin at the bottom of the table. The former used a knife and fork in his mania for our customs, but the latter eat in his native manner, with his right hand, having servants ready with a bason and towels to wash occasionally. As to their visitors, we sat much in the same situation as the guests at the dinner of the ancients in Peregrine Pickle; and though all very hungry, none appeared to volunteer for the forlorn hope of tasting the dishes before them. I, however, at last mustered courage to help myself to the mess nearest me, but was immediately satisfied as to its ingredients being a villanous compound, as far as I could guess, of gooseberry tart, garlick, and chillies. The evident repulse I had met with, which it was impossible to disguise, warned my two friends from falling into the same mishap, and we sat in mute despair, wishing in vain for the end of the detestable meal. The hard-boiled eggs would have been most palatable, but there was no other bread than the common India cakes, baked on an iron plate, of a consistency not unlike leather. There was a brown-coloured water served up as coffee, but this was wholly inadmissible. I had not a hookah, and etiquette would not allow our host to smoke if I did not, it being in India considered the height of ill-breeding to smoke before an equal if he has not his hookah. After some little time two were brought in; he was quite satisfied, and I was not sorry, as I wanted something to refresh me, and tobacco is an excellent stimulant. I was very desirous of returning to my tent, which had been pitched outside of the city by my escort, as I had excused myself from taking up my quarters in the house offered me, which I had not seen; and hoping it would produce an opportunity for our taking leave, I proposed to the general to visit it as well as the old newab's house, and those of his brother and nephew.

We first proceeded to the house of the brother, which consisted of a large court-yard with a fountain, some plantations of shrubs along the walls, and a large elevated veranda at each end with small rooms off them. In one of these verandas is a sort of throne, resembling a box at a theatre, not above eight feet from the ground, with a ladder to afford access to it. The inside is lined with small mirrors, like those in the back part of a tradesman's shop in England, one over the other, without either taste or judgment, and of no particular pattern, the intention appearing to be to cover the wall at all events. It required I think about three tiers of these mirrors, including the frames, to reach the top. The residence belonging to the newab Salabat Khan is similar, but somewhat larger. The women's apartments of course we did not see. A son of the newab's, two years old, passed through whilst we were here, accompanied by a number of boys, five or six years old, as his attendants. Namdar Khan brought him to us, but he began to yell violently, I suppose from the same cause an English child cries the first time it sees a black footman. We were then taken to our "house," as he was pleased to call it, which consisted of a yard, a fountain, and veranda, not unlike a second-rate dog-kennel. After promising to dine with him at six o'clock, we were relieved by his quitting us, and made the best of our way to our camp outside the city, passing through a similar gate to that by which we had entered, and with some cold meat made up for the loss of our breakfast.

When we had been some time in our tent, two officers of the royals passed. From the uniform of one of them I knew him to be a surgeon, and invited him in, not only to see our sick companion, but to obtain some news. They stated that a very severe action had taken place between Poonah and General Smith's camp, which had originated in one of our battalions having been ordered back to the city, and on its way having fallen in with a large body of Arabs, who were, though greatly superior, totally defeated, with the loss of 500 men. Our loss was reported to be very heavy, including two officers killed.

This was a very unpleasant piece of intelligence, and I am quite at a loss to conceive how I shall ever reach Poonah; for if a battalion cannot move without being attacked, I can hardly expect to be able to have an escort sufficiently strong. I had sanguinely hoped that by this time the Peishwah's dominions would have become perfectly tranquil, and that I should have been enabled to travel dauk, from Arungabad to Poonah; but it seems the Peishwah is still in the field with a large army.

About two o'clock a vaqueel from the soubah arrived to learn at what hour he might pay his respects to me: this was arranged to take place at four o'clock in the afternoon. At that hour he came with a numerous suite, sat half an hour, talked incessantly, used immense quantities of snuff, and at last departed, leaving three sheep, as many fowls as would furnish a poulterer's shop, and vegetables, sugar, and spices for a year's consumption. This gentleman is an Hindoo, and is the government collector of the Nizam. It has almost invariably been the custom in the Mahometan states to have Hindoos for their ministers of finance.

At six an elephant arrived to carry us to dinner into the city, where we found six or seven officers of the 2d and 13th Madras native infantry. We dined in the apartment of Golaim Hossein. Until dinner was ready, a company of Nautch women were introduced to sing and dance. Our repast appeared to be of the same kind as that in the morning, with the addition of some excellent little patties. I was much surprised at finding Madeira and Claret on the table, and fancied the general was in jest when he asked me to take some with him; indeed, I could not believe I saw correctly, when, doubtless scandalizing the many rigid of the faithful who stood around, he, with the greatest *sang froid*, hob-nobbed with me, and tossed off a bumper of Chateau Margeaux. From this time till after dinner he never ceased drinking to every one, qualifying the wine with glasses of cherry brandy; and the moment the table was cleared he stood up, and gave first "the Company," with three times three; then "the King;" and, last of all, a safe journey to me. If he was aware that the latter meant the sovereign, I conceive he must have concluded "the Company," by giving it the precedence, to have been, like Stefano in the Tempest, viceroy over him. I was of course obliged to propose his health, the health of his father, uncle, and cousin; and, seeing my friend any thing but a sober follower of the Koraun, I broke up the party from table. We then adjourned to the singing and dancing of the Nautch women, and the newab again called for wine, and toasted them all by name till the libations had evidently considerable effect on his senses; and as I found, though mine was a Christian head, that I could not hold out much longer, I wished him good night, and was truly rejoiced to find myself once more in my tent, being to march this morning at three.

We set out about that hour, and for some time lost our way in the dark, but reached this earlier than might have been expected, being twenty-four miles from Ellichpoor. The range of hills to the north has been visible all this day, but we have increased the distance from them very perceptibly.

Coleplaiser, January 14th, 1818.

After a march of eighteen miles we reached this place, which is totally deserted, and falling into ruins; I have consequently been obliged to send back three miles to procure provisions for the troops. It may appear extraordinary that I had not taken the necessary precautions for furnishing my little detachment with necessaries; but in India the mode of supplying troops in the field with provisions is totally different from that of every other country in the world.

When a force takes the field, government arranges so as to have sufficient stores of grain carried by the brinjarries: a bazar, or travelling market, with every thing that can be required, accompanies the army at the private risk of these individuals; and an Indian soldier on service, or in cantonments, is bound to subsist himself from his monthly stipend. Government sells to these private venders in the bazar the provisions it has brought into the field, and they again retail them to the troops at a moderate profit. My detachment was not numerous enough to make it worth the while of any person to form a bazar; and it was to be supposed that I could always find provisions in the towns near which I encamped for so small a body of men, nor should I have been deceived, except in an instance like the present, when a town named in my route as a halting-place proved to be abandoned. In these bazars every trade or calling exercised in a city is to be met with; and it is the various tradesmen and their families belonging to them who so much impede the movements of the Indian armies, and create so great a difficulty for defending and covering such a multitude on the march, that a force so circumstanced has not inaptly been called a large baggage guard. Every person quits the cantonments with an intention of being equally as comfortable in the field; each subaltern has his chairs, table, and bed, besides his tent; and some regiments take their messes into camp with them. I was informed that a regiment of dragoons, under the Bengal presidency, took the field with fifty fat oxen, and 120 dozen of claret, besides other wines and requisites. In addition to the general, or, as it is called, the Sudder bazar, every regiment has its own; and the facility with which they find their places in camp is extraordinary. Each bazar has a high flag in its centre; and on this being raised, when arriving on a new ground, the different strings of people are seen dividing off to their several distinct and well-known standards.

In the numerous accounts of Indian armies published in England, notice has not, I believe, been taken of the fikirs, who attach themselves to regiments while in the field, and who live by begging. When troops are coming off the march, and approaching their new ground, these vagabonds, who live on the superstition of the natives, seat themselves about a mile from the camp, and spread a coloured carpet before them to receive the offerings of the Sepoys. They have a small flag near them, and beat a tom-tom, or drum, accompanying it with a begging whining song, and their carpet is very soon covered with pice (a small copper coin) and cowries. The fikir who had attached himself to the cavalry brigade, with the centre division of the Bengal army, displayed a very gay standard, consisting of a black horse on a white ground; and I was often tempted, by my gratitude to him for the information he gave us that we were approaching our destination, after a long march, to throw him a rupee. Tavernier tells us, that in his time it was calculated there were no fewer than 800,000 Mahometan fikirs, and 1,200,000 Hindoo fikirs; but they must have been much reduced in number since that period. Many of this class of holy mendicants make vows of painful penances. I have seen some who have allowed their hands to remain so long clenched, that the nails have grown out through the back of the hand. I have also seen others, whose arms held upright over the head had become stiff in every joint. They occasionally undertake to measure their length from their homes to some sacred temple or ghaut; and I had an opportunity of witnessing one in the neighbourhood of Calcutta who was performing this penance. He laid himself upon the ground on his face, and then getting up, advanced two long steps about equal to his height, then again lay down, and continued this absurd pilgrimage as long as I observed him, and doubtless to his destined spot. But the most singular penance I ever heard of was in Bengal. At a certain feast in the autumn, a number of Hindoo devotees erect a large mast in an open place in the neighbourhood of the village, with a moveable yard across the top of it. From this yard a rope with an iron hook is suspended, the end of the yard being brought down near the ground; a Bramin passes the hook through the muscles of the back of one of the devotees, between the shoulders, and, the lever being depressed at the other end, the miserable fanatic is drawn up in the air, and the yard being moved round upon a pivot with great rapidity, he, swinging out in almost a horizontal position, amidst the screams and shouts of the crowd, throws flowers to them. There is a precautionary large loose loop put round him, in case the muscles of the back should give way. They have also a superstition that a man about to be executed imparts a sanctity to all he touches; and, in a manner similar to this, he always throws flowers amongst the crowd, who eagerly scramble for them. At the same time of the year other devotees, accompanied by tom-toms and conchs, march in procession about the villages, five or six men being fastened upon a bamboo; that is to say, a long thin slice of bamboo is passed through their sides, about an inch under the skin, and continually kept soft by applications of grease. I saw another wretch who had passed an iron bar, larger than a common sized pencil, and four feet long, through his tongue. The Braminical religion appears to me to have become of a more sanguinary cast in Bengal than in the upper provinces.

But the most inhuman of all their barbarous customs is the following. When a sick person is given over, by way of ensuring him eternal salvation they carry the helpless creature to the banks of the river, and stuff his eyes, mouth, and nose with clay: should he recover after this extreme unction, he loses caste, and becomes an outcast from his friends and relations, and virtually dead to the whole world. Some anxious expecting heirs, it is supposed, take their fathers down to the water side at a very early stage of illness; and I have no doubt numbers would recover if they did not undergo this horrid rite.

I find I have several times mentioned the word ghaut for mountains, which requires some explanation. Custom has brought this word into use in a similar manner as the Spaniards apply the word sierra, or saw, to a range of mountains: originally only those with irregular tops, like the teeth of a saw, were so called, but in time they have given the name to the whole ridge. A ghaut means a pass, and is even used for a ford across a river. The whole range of hills now takes the appellation, from the natives being accustomed to employ the expression of passing the ghaut for passing the mountains; and thus they have by degrees become synonymous.

CHAPTER XI.

Arrive at Culmeshur—Akolah—The Aumildar's son—Accounts from Arungabad—Unsatisfactory intelligence respecting the road through the Peishwah's dominions—Arrangements for seeing the caves of Ellora, and Dowlutabad—Action at Corry Gaum—Defeat of the enemy at Sirnuggur—Reflections on India—Zemeendary system—Refractory landholders—Change which the British have made—Instance—Arrive at Bottalo—Arrangements for the camp—Tumblers—Liberality of the Newab Namdar Khan—Cheapness of the necessaries of life in India—Cowries—Bearers—Prejudice—Loss of caste—Customs in a great degree immutable—Example—Hereditary trades—Arrive at Omerapoor—Lucknawarra ghaut—Hindoo temple—Mhut—The bull Nundee—Fanaticism of the Mahometans and Portuguese—Arrive at Chandee—Deserted—Reflections—Names common to the Mahometans and Christians—Account of the tribute called choute—Arrive at Jaffierabad—The Aumildar—Altar—Pindarries—Generally destroy life—Mahometans respect the ashes of the dead—Similarity of customs in different nations—Casuistry of the natives—Sago—Determined to set out from Jaffierabad—My escort to follow—Arrangements.

Culmeshur, 15th January, 1818.

WE have this day almost lost sight of the ghauts to the northward, and the country through which we have marched has been rich and well cultivated. We passed under the high and handsome walls of Akolah, a considerable city, which, inferring from the numerous ruins in its neighbourhood, must at one time have been much larger. Indeed I am of opinion, from the remains of an old wall, extending to a great distance, that it must have been removed from its original site, as is not uncommon in this country. The Aumildar, or chief man, sent his son out with an imposing suite to meet me, and present his nuzzur. He informed me that he had, according to my request, sent all kinds of provisions to our ground at this place, which is four miles to the west of Akolah. Soon after we had advanced beyond the town we met a shuter surwar, or man mounted on a camel, from Captain Sydenham, the political agent in Berar, stationed at Arungabad, to whom I had written from Nagpoor, requesting him to provide every thing to accelerate my movements. This letter was any thing but satisfactory, for he stated that no one could pass from Toka, or the river Godavery, the frontier of the Nizam's and Peishwah's dominions, to Poonah, without a strong escort, as the emissaries of the latter were on the road, with orders to murder all persons who had any correspondence with the English. He has, however, promised to lay dauk bearers some distance from the other side of Jaffierabad on to Arungabad; and I have written to him to have the goodness to arrange that I shall be able to see the greatest curiosity of manual labour in the world, excepting the pyramids of Egypt—I mean the caves of Ellora, and also the fort of Dowlutabad. After marching from the 16th to the 22d, the day on which my escort will arrive at Arungabad, it will be absolutely necessary to give the men and our camels a day's halt at that city, and I hope, by pushing on before them, and by overtaking them after they have passed through it, to be able to see these remarkable places, without impeding my progress an hour. The Peishwah's army is stated to be in very considerable force, so that there will be great difficulty and risk in attempting to proceed from the other side of the Godavery, as we shall then find ourselves in an enemy's country, but I must attempt it at a happy moment when his troops are off the vicinity of the road.

The action of the single battalion, of which we heard when at Ellichpoor, appears to have been as severe as possible, and fought under the most distressing circumstances. It took place at a village named Corry Gaum, and strongly proves how inferior are undisciplined courageous thousands to disciplined courageous hundreds. Our battalion consisted of 500 men, who for a whole day successfully opposed ten times their number. Colonel M'Morrin has also returned upon Gurra Warrah, and defeated the troops at Sirnuggur, which we left to our right, when moving down to Nagpoor, taking all their guns, and putting them to flight.

I should think the number of defeats in all quarters, and in every way, must convince these unruly and unprincipled people how unavailing it is to strive against our power. I do not see any cause which at present exists in India, from the Mahometans or Hindoos, or any native power, to shake our government over this part of the world, that is to say, if we respect the prejudices of the natives, do not attempt to subvert their religion by the introduction of our own, and if our military force is kept up in the highest and most efficient manner, both in quality and numbers, and is not permitted to dwindle into police officers and their assistants. Above all, by being exactly strict and honourable in all our intercourses with them, most scrupulous in the distribution of justice in our civil courts, and rendering them, by our commanding military force, secure in their homes, (to which they have been long unaccustomed) they must, and undoubtedly will become excellent subjects, and attached to our rule. But the first and leading maxim, never to be deviated from, should be constant and most serious notice of the slightest insult, or even neglect from any native power; and a few rigorous examples will prevent the chance of their future recurrence. They must already have seen the steady settled system upon which we act, and be fully aware that they cannot expect or hope for half measures from us. To exemplify this, though on an inferior scale, the alteration which has taken taken place in the zemeendary system under our government may be adduced. It was the custom throughout India, and still continues so in the countries under the native rule, that should a landholder fancy his mud fort strong, and the power of the government from which he held his estate not equal to its reduction, he would refuse to pay his rent, defend his fort for a few days, sometimes beat off, or more frequently make terms with his master, who was generally satisfied with two-thirds of, or less than his due. From an act of this description being viewed by our government in the light of decided rebellion, and no compromise being admitted, nothing of the kind ever occurs now in our territory; whereas, in consequence of the remissness of the government of the Newab Vizier, battering trains, and our best battalions of Sepoys, are once or twice a year sent into Oude to enforce payment of arrears from these refractory subjects. The like happens under every native government. When I was, in November last, at Jalaoun, in Bundelcund, a fort belonging to the nana of that place, I went to see the guns in his tope khonnah or artillery ground. One of the gun-carriages was much shattered, and bore the marks of shot. On inquiring when it had been exposed to fire, I found it had been employed against one of these lawless zemeendars about four months before, and one of the golundauze then present had been shot through the body*.

When I thus point out the probable safety of our dominion in this country, I cannot but remark, that the dangers arising from colonization are great and imminent, and all hope of suppressing it is fast giving way to an increasing population of the offspring of European fathers and native mothers.

Bottalo, 16th January, 1818.

We have performed a march of about twenty miles this morning, and the road for the first part was extremely bad. I have made some small alteration in the position of the troops in camp, having removed forty of the Nizam's horse from the front line, and posted them so as to form a rear guard, and placed the twenty armed old Sepoys, belonging to Captain Hicks, as a disposable

* It has often been remarked by our medical men, how much stronger the probability is of the recovery of the natives than of Europeans from similar severe and dangerous wounds of this description; the former being accustomed to plainer food, and consequently being in a better habit of body.

force, to move to the rear or flanks as may be deemed necessary, since we are too weak to afford flank picquets. I shall attempt to procure another company of infantry from Arungabad or Tòka, and then we shall be strong enough to bid defiance to all roving parties.

We had not been long on our ground when a noisy and tumultuous set of nautch women and tumblers took the camp by storm with their tom-toms beating, insisting on exhibiting before us, and, when ordered away, becoming extremely obstinate, and apparently determined to make good a lodgment in the very heart of our position. But we at last got quit of them.

As we still continue in the newab Salabat Khan's jaghire, the villagers are ordered to furnish us with fowls, eggs, fruit, &c. and the kuckeems or chief men think they have a right to hold conversations with us at their leisure, and squatting down at the entrance of the tent to ask all sorts of absurd questions. If this is to be the price of their civilities, I would gladly dispense with all the advantages. The extreme cheapness of every thing in India renders the offering of the products of the village of no importance, and a rupee or two thrown in return generally covers the expense. In Bengal the necessaries of life are so cheap, from their abundance, that their value in small quantities cannot be estimated in metallic coin, and they make use of small white shells, brought from the Laccadive Islands, as the medium of exchange. In Calcutta, as I have been told, 5200 of them equal a rupee, and Marco Polo takes notice of their being used in the dominion of the grand khan of Tartary. I have, from curiosity, sent this moment into the bazar to inquire the number of cowries (the name of these shells) in a rupee, in the country where we now are, and find that, being at a considerable distance from the sea, 3520 are the full change for that coin. In England it will hardly be conceived that any article of food can be so low priced as I have stated, but from this source originates the small wages of the servants. The bearers at Calcutta receive five rupees a month, equal to 12*s.* 6*d.*, out of which they clothe and feed themselves, and yet save money. The class of servants who generally come from the province on the coast, between the presidencies of Bengal and Madras, called Orrissa, return it is said an annual sum to their friends and relations of three lacs of rupees, or 36,000*l.*, though I think this exaggerated. Their number is very great, as almost every European has his palanquin, which is carried by them. It is usual to have a set, consisting of a head bearer, a mate, and eight or ten others. They are all Hindoos, and very scrupulous as to the rules and customs of their caste. They will bring a glass of water to an European, but will not take it from him, as the touch of his lips has defiled it. However, in cases of illness I have seen them behave better, wave these foolish ideas, and act with less prejudice. They are bound among themselves not to perform any duties but what are assigned to them, and should any one of them transgress, the rest inflict upon him loss of caste, and refuse to eat, smoke, or associate with him. But the penalty of a large dinner to some Bramins and many of their caste, at their expense, places them again within the pale of communion.

It is inconceivable to what extent the natives carry these ideas of caste and custom. Because it is the usual duty of the lowest caste to grind corn by a handmill, the Bramins and Rajahpoots will eat the grain parched on the fire, or starve, rather than make it into flour with their own hands. On our advance from Jubbulpoor we had no fewer than 9000 Brinjarry bullocks laden with grain with our corps, but still we ran a risk of a number of the natives starving, as we had not persons enow to grind it; and though the troops were idle after they had cleaned their horses, and had sufficient handmills, yet no flour being in the bazar for them to purchase, the Hindoos declared they would not perform that office;

and, though greatly in want, sat down and refused to make any exertion whatever, so that numbers went without food, except parched grain, for many days. It is the same with their trades; the father delivers his own down to his son, who does the same to his offspring, and thus, through twenty generations they never improve or degenerate, and from the apathy consequent upon this, appear to have lost all inventive ideas. They are nevertheless very dexterous imitators.

Omerapoor, 17th January, 1818.

A long and fatiguing march of twenty miles has brought us to this place; and since we ascended the Lucknawarra pass, we have been almost surrounded by jungle. This ghaut is not of any consequence in a military point of view, as the continuation of the range of hills to the right and left is in every part passable for cavalry. Yet some one has built on the summit of the hill, across the road, a large arched gateway, flanked with towers: it is without a staircase to the top, and now falling to decay. We have passed many large villages, totally deserted, from the continual ruin brought on them by the plundering parties of the Pindarries. These freebooters were too strong for the inhabitants to defend themselves against them, and the poor wretches who escaped from former spoliations have taken refuge in the towns and cities; but in a few years the former of these must have shared the same fate, had not our government taken steps for their protection, and for the punishment of the robbers.

We are well encamped in the angle of two streams; and even the junction of these small rills offers an opportunity for the Hindoos to display their superstition. A very curious black stone temple stands in the angle, the blocks not very large, and presenting no other carving besides being hewn into coarse columns and rafters, with others piled on them to form a sort of roof in a pyramidical shape. It is about eight feet high. Above this small temple is a modern mhut, uniting the Hindoo and Mahometan architecture. Opposite the door is a very curious stone bull, three feet long and two feet high. The head is much disfigured; I suppose by the zealous Mahometans, who, like the Portuguese, attempt to destroy all the vestiges of the religion of Brama.

Chandee, 18th January, 1818.

We arrived here after a long march, and found this village, like the generality of those above the Lucknawarra ghaut, entirely abandoned, the Pindarries having nearly depopulated the country. It is a pleasing reflection that our armies have saved the few remaining towns; and I trust the total extirpation of these robbers will be effected before next year.

We have had no intelligence from Bombay, nor from Mr. Elphinstone, our former resident at the Peishwah's court. He is not at Poonah, being with General Smith's army in pursuit of the Peishwah; but we may indulge a hope of hearing from Captain Sydenham, our political agent in Berar, to-morrow, on our arrival at Jaffierabad. Jaffier is one of the few names common to us and the Mahometans. They have also Moses, Ibrahim (Abraham), and Yusef (Joseph), Daoud (David), Yacob (Jacob), and Daniel. Abad is a city, or any place with a large population; its literal meaning is "populous," and sometimes it is used for "inhabited." Nearly all the cities built by the Mahometans have this addition to the name of the founder; thus Shah-Jehan-Abad, Acbar-Abad. The Hindoo designations of these two cities are Delhi and Agra, and are those generally in use.

By the accounts we received from Arungabad on the 15th it is stated, that the moment the Nizam heard of the defection of the Peishwah he declared war against him, but in all probability as much from a wish to do away the claim for the arrears of choute as a desire to act up to his treaties. The history of this extraordinary tribute, arising out of the Mharatta mode of warfare, is so curious, that I cannot refrain from giving some account of it. As early as the latter end of Aurungzebe's reign a proposal was made to that prince, by the Mharattas, to receive from him the demukki, or tenth handful, that is to say, a tenth part of the revenue of the Dekhun; and upon this condition they engaged to discontinue their practice of plundering the country annually: this met with a decided refusal from so high-spirited a prince. In Behauder Shah's reign, that sovereign having chosen for his residence the city of Lahore, which was at a great distance from the southern provinces of India, the Mharattas took advantage of it, and obliged all the imperial provinces of the Dekhun to pay them a fourth part of the revenue, which is the meaning of the word choute. In the vice-royalty of Hossein Alli Khan, a new arrangement was made with the Mharattas, the tenth part of the revenue being added to the quarter which they had before received. At one time this tribute was as high as one-third of the revenue, and the Mharattas had their own officers for its collection. In 1753 Bengal and Bahar were obliged to pay this impost.

Nothing could be more ruinous or more disgraceful to a government than this shameful compromise; yet from the mode of warfare of the Mharattas, whose example we have since seen followed by the Pindarries, it was difficult if not impossible to meet them on equal terms; and, as we have witnessed in the governments of the Dekhun, it was thought better to yield a portion without the country being ravaged, than to allow them to live at free quarters. This extortion led to consequences still more disastrous to the existence of the government, for the ryots excused themselves from paying the revenue, by pleading the sufferings they had undergone, as was the case in the provinces plundered in 1812 and 1815 by the Pindarries.

Jaffierabad, 19th January, 1818.

On our approach to this place, we were informed by the advanced guard of a body of 200 horse being in our front, and we halted till the escort was assembled. They, however, proved to be the guard of the Aumildar of the city, who had come out to meet us, and presented me his nuzzur. We left the town to the right, which appeared to be of considerable size, and, crossing a large stream, encamped on the opposite side. In the centre of the stream, on a detached rock, appeared a small altar, with the sacred bull, but so near the water that it must be covered in the rains. On dismounting from my elephant, the Aumildar informed me that bearers, or bhoeys, as they are here called, were ready to carry me on to Arungabad; one set of fourteen being ready at this place, and two others of the same number in each being on the road, all belonging to the viceroy, Rajah Govind Buckish. But I have not found, as I hoped, a letter from Captain Sydenham.

We have not been able to gain any political intelligence from the Aumildar, who calls himself a relation of the viceroy, and, I suppose, trusts to this for impunity, as he has not prepared any provisions for us. We can only learn from him that he was dreadfully alarmed last year by the Pindarries. They did not, however, enter the city, but contented themselves with plundering the villages around. He adds, that they did not murder any body. This must have been a very humane troop, not to have marked their route by blood.

We are encamped near the remains of a Mahometan burial-ground, of which, I believe, the Nizam's troops do not approve, as they expressed a wish to move higher up the river. The Mahometans venerate much the spot where a body has been buried; so much indeed, that, as long as one stone remains upon another, they never use the ground, or hazard the disturbing of the ashes. I have often, when walking, been asked in a respectful manner by persons of that persuasion to turn to the right or left, to avoid stepping over a grave. It is usual, when passing the tomb of a saint, to throw a stone on it. I have heard of a similar custom in Scotland, of throwing a stone on a cairne, as a token of respect. So rigid are they with respect to not invading the repose of the dead, that when I was at Delhi, in 1815, it was mentioned as a strong instance to prove the influence our resident at the imperial court had obtained over the natives, that he had persuaded the inhabitants to remove a burial-ground, which was in some inconvenient situation. It is very amusing to remark the ingenious casuistry with which both Mahometans and Hindoos reconcile their consciences to what is contrary to their customs in cases in which they have been brought into difficulties. The clerks in our offices are often Bramins, yet they use the quill, though feathers are looked upon as impure. Some years ago the Hindoos in Calcutta discovered that sago was not a grain, as they had previously supposed, and the alarm amongst them was very great; but the Bramins, who had partaken of this food in common with all the rest, reflected that the condemnation of an individual, when all were equally guilty, would be an incongruity, and ought not to be permitted. The discussions upon so weighty a cause were at last compromised, in full conclave, by declaring it lawful to eat sago, though it was not grain! Potatoes, which have been introduced by us, are now freely used by all, though roots are prohibited by their law; and, if report speaks truth, so are some liquids containing alkohol, also introduced by Europeans.

As the bearers are stationed, and I am anxious to secure time to visit the caves of Ellora and the fort of Dowlutabad, and as there is no intelligence of any of the enemy being on the road, I have determined to push on this evening. I shall take with me twenty-five of the Nizam's horse, having already despatched the same number about twelve miles on the way; and the jemidar, whose family reside at Arungabad, has volunteered to go on with me, though it is about sixty miles from hence, and he has already travelled twenty. I leave Captain Hicks, Mr. Elliot, and the escort, to follow by daily marches; and I shall hope to see them on the morning of the 22d in Arungabad. I was desired by General Doveton to leave the regular cavalry at this place; but, as I have not heard from Captain Sydenham as to the prospect I shall have of a relief at Arungabad, I shall carry them on with my escort at least to that city.

CHAPTER XII.

Leave Jaffierabad—Messenger from Captain Sydenham—Arrive in sight of Arungabad—Fountain—Walls of the city—The city in ruins—Received with great kindness by Captain Sydenham—Most satisfactory news—Treaty with Holkar—Flight of the Pindarries—The Peishwah's army—Enemy's horse on the road between this city and Poonah—Arrangements for escorts—For visiting the caves of Ellora—Captain Sydenham's residence—Cypress trees—The city—Inferior mosque—Vaqueel of the Rajah Govind Buckish—Arrangements—Ghun Put Rao—Visit from the viceroy—Conversation—Tomb—Similar to the Tarje—Inferior in its materials—Minarets—Mosques—Mode of worship among the Mahometans—Marble trellis—Shah Jehan's munificence—Fine view from the top of the minarets—French redoubts—Fiker's tomb—Tame fish—Water-mill—Aurungzebe's palace at Arungabad—History of the city—English sailing boat—Magazine—Assier Ghur—Arrival of Captain Hicks and Mr. Elliott.

Arungabad, 20th January, 1818.

I LEFT the camp at Jaffierabad at four yesterday evening, and found the rajah's bearers very good. The jemidar continued the whole way by the side of my palanquin, and we had the advantage of a fine moon, during the early part of the night. About twelve o'clock I met a messenger from Captain Sydenham, who stated that he had not written to me, supposing I could not have advanced so fast, but that he had sent an express to Colonel Deacon, who was posted at Jaulna, to order 200 cavalry and a guard of infantry on each stage of the road between Jaffierabad and Arungabad. His letter also contained a very kind invitation to make his house my home, during my stay at Arungabad, and extended this polite offer to my two companions.

After travelling all night, I came in sight of this city about seven o'clock, and was exceedingly pleased with the view it presented. The trees interspersed among the houses, and the dome and minarets of a large tomb, which at a distance appeared like the tarje at Agra, diversified the scene, and I congratulated myself on the good accommodation which awaited me within the walls. I observed a large fountain or spring issuing from a tablet of stone, similar to those by the road-side in Spain. The walls are of the kind common to cities in India, but low, with round towers; and there was a heavy gun on one of them near the gate. On entering it, the city presented the usual scene of ruin and desolation; as is almost universally the case in this country, where one sovereign builds and inhabits a city to give him the credit of having founded it, and which is deserted by his successor for a similar reason;—hence the numerous cities half peopled throughout India. I passed through several inhabited parts of the town, which were separated from each other by large intervals covered with ruins. I arrived at Captain Sydenham's some time before breakfast, who received me with the greatest cordiality. Several ladies, who had moved from their houses in the neighbourhood to that of Captain Sydenham, on approach of a body of the enemy's cavalry, met me at breakfast: I was very anxious to learn what intelligence had been received from all quarters, and found it most important, and tending greatly to show the consolidation of our Indian empire. It appeared that, after the action of Sir Thomas Hislop with the force of Holkar, negotiations were opened for the conclusion of a treaty between us and the defeated enemy; and within a few days a subsidiary treaty was signed on the 6th instant, on terms highly gratifying. The several divisions were in pursuit of the Pindarries, who had, with the loss of their families, baggage, property, &c. fled to the north-west, but not without great reduction of their numbers.

But I was more interested individually with respect to the state of affairs in the province which bears the name of this city, as I was to pass through the largest part of it, which is under the dominion of the Peishwah.

It appears that the flight of the Peishwah's army has been unceasing, and that our pursuing army has continued to follow its steps, but without any action of consequence having taken place.

It is reported that the Peishwah has fled into Rye Ghur, a strong fort, where his wives and treasure have been placed. Although his main army is for the present removed from the road between this city and Poonah, yet large bodies of horse are hovering around. My escort will however be strong and efficient, and I have also written to Colonel Deacon, who is near Jaulna, to request him to send me thirty regular cavalry, and 100 light infantry, to meet me at Toka, on the frontier of the Peishwah's country, which will give me, with my Bengal cavalry, sixty regular troopers, 200 reformed horse, and 200 infantry, so that I need fear nothing but encountering the Peishwah's army.

Captain Sydenham has been so kind as to arrange every thing for my visiting the caves at Ellora, which village belonged till lately to Holkar.

The garrison of Aurungabad consists of only one battalion, not sufficient by any means to defend its extensive walls.

Captain Sydenham's house was given him by the Nizam. It was formerly the residence of the soubah of the city, and with some little additions, is now a very comfortable habitation, consisting of several small yards paved with stone, with fountains and large pieces of water in the middle of each, and closed verandas at the ends. I am in a tent pitched upon the top of a high terrace, surrounded by balustrades, in the midst of a garden, with fountains and cypress trees; the latter are common in the Dekhun, though none exist in Bengal or Hindoostan. This evening Captain Sydenham, and myself, in his curricle, went through the city, which is mean, but some of the streets are good. The mosque, having no minarets to it, though ornamented with a fine tank of masonry in front, cannot be called handsome. Almost every house has a fountain in its court-yard.

A vaqueel from the Rajah Govind Buckish waited upon me this morning, to know when he should call upon me; which ceremony is fixed for to-morrow, and I am to return the visit on the 22d instant. My present intention is to give our camels one day's halt on the 23d, and order them on to Toka, where I shall join them on their second day's march.

Arungabad, January 21, 1818.

Intelligence has been received this morning that Gun Put Rao, the sirdar of the Rajah of Nagpoor, who had collected troops to the southward of that town, and against whom the detachment was sent on the morning I quitted Nagpoor, arrived at Sirpoor on the 13th instant, about 100 miles south-west of Jaulna, in the centre of Berar: he has consequently been moving nearly parallel with us all our route. He is reported to have 4000 cavalry with him. This has interfered with our arrangements for viewing Ellora and Dowlutabad, the precautions taken for intercepting this chief being such, that an escort cannot be spared for us. Captain Davies's force, which was to furnish our escort, has been ordered to the north-west, to prevent his passing into Khandeish, and Colonel Deacon to the southward, to intercept his junction with the Peishwah. It has also made a very considerable alteration in other respects, but our escort is to be furnished from this garrison.

According to our arrangement, about three o'clock the viceroy arrived, and we had a conversation of above half an hour. He is a quiet looking man, but I am told able, and well informed, particularly in the history of this country, and of Persia. I was anxious to learn from him if any reliance could be placed on the stories respecting the date of the formation of the Ellora Caves, as mentioned in the Asiatic Researches. He answered that they had no correct accounts whatever of their date or founder. He asked me concerning my route to Ferungistan, the land of the Franks or Europeans, and inquired if I passed through Arabistan (Arabia),

Misr (Egypt), or Romé;—this last is the utmost extent of their ideas in geography, and is far from meaning any part of Italy, but the provinces of the eastern Roman empire. The rajah was also curious to know the age of the governor-general, the number of his children, and if he understood Persian; with regard to all which I satisfied him. Before he took his leave, I presented him with a necklace, armlets, and a sprig of jewels for his turban, to the amount of 3000 rupees, and poured some attar of roses in his handkerchief, and gave him two pawns*. He was accompanied by an immense suite, I suppose 500 persons, and offered me 100 horse for my escort from Dowlutabad to Toka.

After dinner I proceeded with Captain Sydenham to see the tomb I had observed at a distance on entering the city. Tavernier states that it is sacred to a wife of Aurungzebe, but I was informed it had been raised to the memory of a daughter of that monarch, the founder, or perhaps improver of this city, which bears his name. The inclosure around the tomb is very considerable, and must, I am persuaded, consist of 30 acres laid out in gardens. The gateway is something like, though inferior to, the tarje at Agra: indeed the whole building is copied from that beautiful structure, but has all its defects, with but few of its beauties; and the materials are much coarser and inferior. It is, like the tarje, octagonal, raised on a high terrace, with a dome, but unlike it in the four clumsy minarets at the corners of the terrace. These steeples have generally an unpleasant appearance, and it is only at the tarje where the lightness, beauty, and costliness of the materials make them admissible. This tomb has the same number of mosques as that at Agra, one to the east, the other to the west, but that facing Mecca is the only one complete, having a wall on the west side, while the other is open like a pavilion; consequently the former

* A pawn is a small packet consisting of spices, chunam, and the betel nut, wrapped up in the pawn leaf, and presented on taking leave.

only can be used for prayer, it being the Mahometan custom during devotion to face towards the holy city. The tombstone in the inside of the building at the tarje is on a level with the top of the terrace, and the body is placed below; but here you descend by many steps as if going into a bath, the whole being lined with marble. The tomb is surrounded by a very handsome eight-sided screen of white marble trellis of so fine a quality, that the least slip of the chisel would ruin a whole slab of great value and minute carving. At the tarje, they tell you, each time the workman succeeded in perforating the marble without endangering the whole, he received a rupee as a reward. In this respect the tomb here is equally rich, but it wants the beautiful mosaic work of flowers in different coloured stones round the top and on the pilasters. The windows are also fitted with the same beautiful trellis-work; and on the outside of the building, the first slab about three feet high, and the dome, are of marble, but the rest is patchwork, being of stone, from the neighbourhood, stuccoed. The materials of the tarje consist of white marble alone, ornamented with black, and the mosaic is formed with coral, cornelians, bloodstones, and other coloured stones. Altogether it is so superior in every way to this tomb, that it forms as strong a contrast as the abbey church of Westminster and St. Margaret's. This, however, is stated to have had large sums expended on it by a relation of the emperor during his absence, which his majesty, from his penurious spirit, and I think not without reason in this instance, refused to reimburse him from the imperial treasury. The tarje was built by Shah Jehan, the father of Aurungzebe, to the memory of his favourite wife, and he expended 700,000*l*. upon it, exclusive of the marble, which was a present from one of the Rajahpoot sovereigns.

I went to the top of one of the minarets, whence the view was fine and extensive. Captain Sydenham pointed out the circuit of the city walls, Aurungzebe's palace, and two small redoubts, probably raised by the troops under M. Bussy, during the short time the French were predominant in the Dekhun, before the recall of that officer by M. Lally.

We then proceeded to the fiker's tomb, which is nothing more than a Mahometan monastery built over the grave of a saint. The only difference is, that the inmates of the above are Peer Zadahs, or descendants of the saint. The building consists of some light arched pavilions and mosques, intermixed with trees, vines, fountains, and large pieces of water, which contain immense quantities of tame fish. These have so far overcome the dread of the human figure, as almost to eat out of the hand. There is a water-mill on the ground, looked upon by the natives as one of the wonders of the world. This is, I believe, almost the only one in the whole country, and probably erected by some Europeans. The arts of life are still in so rude a state in India, that there are neither wind nor water-mills, and grinding is performed by a hand-mill.

Colonel Deacon having declined to assist me with any part of his force, I shall be obliged to take on all the cavalry I brought from Nagpoor; but Captain Sydenham will give me 100 fresh infantry from the Nizam's battalion in garrison here.

Arungabad, January 22, 1818.

At daylight this morning I accompanied Captain Sydenham on his elephant to see the ruins of the palace erected by Aurungzebe, and was much disappointed in them. Even when newly built, the royal abode must have betrayed his majesty's parsimonious spirit, and have been greatly inferior to those of Agra or Delhi. The remains are fast mouldering to decay. They are even unsafe to pass through, and are only fit haunts for jackalls, owls, and bats. Arungabad was originally only a village called Gurkah, but accounts differ as to the person who first raised it to the rank of a city. Malik Amber, an Abyssinian, who held a small independent sovereignty in the beginning of the 17th century, of which Dowlutabad was the capital, is supposed to be its founder. But in all probability it bears the name of him to whom it owes the greatest part of its grandeur, if not its foundation. After we had viewed every thing worthy of attention, we proceeded to a large tank, on which Captain Sydenham had an English sailing boat built at Bombay, and brought thence on men's shoulders. This piece of water is supposed to have been the inducement for Aurungzebe's removing hither from Dowlutabad. We next visited the magazine in the centre of the town to see an 18 pounder, intended to form part of the battering train to reduce Assier Ghur, should it not be delivered into our hands. I procured 100 muskets with bayonets for Captain Hicks's recruits, and the 100 infantry are to have their ammunition increased to 100 rounds a man, as it is apprehended our difficulties will increase after passing the Godavery.

It appears that the hope of the surrender of Assier Ghur is but very faint, as the killidar, it is believed, has received a lac of rupees from the Peishwah to defend it to the last. This fortress is one of the strongest in India, and deemed nearly impregnable, if properly defended. It is stated to have been built by Assa Ahir, who gave it his own name, but the word has been by time changed into Assier Ghur. Assa was a zemindar of an illustrious family of Khandeish, which had dwelt on this mountain, as well as ruled the district, for 700 years. In 801 of the hegira, it was seized by stratagem by Nuzzur Khan Feroki, who set up a new monarchy in the province of Khandeish, where he had previously commanded as governor. The fort remained in the hands of the descendants of Nuzzur Khan till the reign of Akbar, when it was taken by one of his generals. It afterwards fell into the hands of the Mharattas, and Scindiah took possession of it when he was supreme at Poonah. In 1803 it yielded to the Duke of Wellington; but was delivered up on the treaty of peace.

Captain Hicks, Mr. Elliott, and the escort, have arrived, and I have arranged with them that they are to give rest to the animals to-morrow, to march half-way to Toka on the 24th, and reach that place, which is on the Godavery, on the 25th, being the Peishwah's frontier, where I shall join them the same day. Captain Sydenham and myself, after the rajah's fête to-night, quit this city for the Caves of Ellora, and I shall not return here, but take leave of Captain Sydenham at Dowlutabad on the night of the 24th.

CHAPTER XIII.

NARRATIVE OF THE OPERATIONS OF THE ARMY OF THE DEKHUN.

Sir Thomas Hislop marches from Charwah—His route—Arrives at Oojein—Negotiations—Hostility of Holkar—Pacific feeling of the British—Holkar's minister quits the camp—His army in position on the Sepra river—Preparing for battle—Revolution in his camp—Dubious conduct of the Sirdars—Unjustifiable and open hostility on the part of the enemy—Sir Thomas Hislop determines to attack them—The British still anxious for a pacific arrangement—Fruitless communication—Hostile language of the enemy—Reflections on the moderation and forbearance of Sir Thomas Hislop—Army moves on that of Holkar—Their position—Action commences—Arrangements—Storm of the enemy's line—Severe loss by their destructive fire—Gallantry of the enemy's artillerymen—Total rout of the enemy—Pursuit—Sixty-three pieces of cannon taken—Our loss—Sir Thomas Hislop halts at Meinpoor—Bombay force—Sir William Keir's route—Arrival at Rutlam—Sir Thomas Hislop moves from Meinpoor—Junction of the Bombay force near Taul—Advance reaches Mundissor—Arrival of Holkar's vaqueel—His head-quarters at Purtaub Ghur—Ordered to move next day to Rampora—Suspension of hostilities—Pindarries much reduced—Treaty signed with Holkar.

THIS city (Arungabad) being the point of communication between the army of Sir Thomas Hislop, Bombay, and Hydrabad, I have been informed of the particulars which brought on the action at Meinpoor, and terminated in the treaty with Holkar, and shall here state in a general manner what came to my knowledge.

His excellency Sir Thomas Hislop, when at Charwah on the 26th November, determined to move north across the Nerbuddah, from which he was not far distant, and commenced his march on the 27th. On the 2nd December he was to the north of the river; on the 6th his head-quarters were at Bhyawul; and on the 12th he joined the force under Sir John Malcolm, who had been waiting for him from the time Holkar evinced a hostile disposition. On the 13th Sir Thomas Hislop's head-quarters were near Oojein, Scindiah's capital, and on the 18th at Paun Behar.

Negotiations had for some time been carried on between Sir John Malcolm and Holkar, and subsequently under the direction of Sir Thomas Hislop, in hopes of persuading the young prince, or the Baie, to see their own interests. But we could only get the customary professions of amity, which are usually in Mharatta politics a mere cloak for deceit; and on several occasions our unfortunate followers were killed or wounded, and our cattle carried off by the cavalry of this prince. On the 19th, the vaqueel of Holkar, who had been some days in the camp, negotiating with Sir John Malcolm for the conclusion of an amicable arrangement, quitted it, and did not return as was expected. From this circumstance, and from the doubtful appearance of affairs, the commander of the forces judged it advisable to advance with his army on the 20th towards the position which it was known the army of Holkar had taken up on the left bank of the river Sepra, near Meinpoor. At that date the head-quarters were established within eight miles of the enemy, (for no doubt could be entertained how they stood affected towards us) at Arnea; and it is particularly worthy of remark, that on that day no friendly communication of any kind was received from the army of Holkar, so that, all dissimulation being laid aside, we had reason to look for instant acts of hostility; and every information brought in by the hircarrahs confirmed the opinion that the troops were preparing for battle. By the ukbars, or written reports from the enemy's camp, as well as from the intelligence of all the hircarrahs, it appeared that a sudden revolution had taken place in the durbar of the young prince. On the 19th instant the Regent Baie, and her minister Gunput Rao and his adherents, had been seized and put into prison by the chiefs of battalions Roshun Beg, Roshen Khan, Ram Dun, and Guffoor Khan, who had got possession of the sovereign, and mounted over him a guard of Sepoys with guns. Great rejoicings were stated to have ensued in camp on this change of councils, and the battalions were said to be ready to sign an acquittance for the whole of the arrears of their pay. Although the chiefs, into whose hands the young prince had fallen, pretended great friendship to the British, and even advised one of our news-writers in camp to tell Sir John Malcolm that those who were the enemies of our government, and wished to march to the Dekhun, had been seized, yet they neither sent back Meer Zuffir Ally, the vaqueel, nor made any other direct communication whatever. On the contrary, on the evening of the 20th, a large body of horse advanced within three miles of the British camp, and a party of about 200 attacked a small number of Mysore horse, within sight of the picquets, killed one man, and wounded several others. This attack differed from the former outrages committed by Holkar's troops, inasmuch as it was obviously not made for plunder, but on a principle of premeditated hostility.

Under all these circumstances, Sir Thomas Hislop determined to attack the army of Holkar, having previously, out of regard for the youth of that ruler, and the inefficiency of his authority over his troops, manifested a forbearance which must mark to all the world the moderation of the British government. The hostile and aggressive spirit of the faction which controlled the counsels and durbar of Holkar being placed beyond the reach of doubt, he determined neither to permit his army to maintain an attitude of defiance, nor to continue a negotiation which had evidently become insincere on their part. Thus situated, the British force had no alternative for self-defence and the vindication of the national character, so that the immediate attack of the enemy was arranged. Sir John Malcolm, however, to give the friends of peace (if any such had influence) still another opportunity of saving the young prince, and preserving his dominions, prepared, by desire of Sir Thomas Hislop, a friendly letter, to be conveyed to him, if opportunity occurred, previous to the battle. On the morning of the 21st of December, the army was put in motion, and advanced towards the adverse camp; and on the march a pair of camel hircarrahs met it, with a letter from the maha rajah. It was of the same unsatisfactory nature as all the preceding communications, and Sir John Malcolm gave in reply the letter he had in readiness, which was intrusted to the hircarrahs, with directions to use the utmost expedition for its delivery.

As the army approached still nearer the enemy's position, a pair of Sir John Malcolm's hircarrahs presented themselves, with an answer to a letter they had received from his moonshee to Meer Zuffir Ally. The purport of it was absolutely hostile, as might be inferred from the following passage: "The sirdars have resolved on war, but they may be conciliated by proper means; yet they are the troops of Holkar." The letter concluded by referring for the rest to the hircarrahs, which was decisive, as they had nothing to say, but that Holkar's army was prepared for battle.

Thus the conduct of those who exercised the functions of government for Holkar ever since the design of the Peishwah was known; the negotiations carried on with that chief while he was at war with the British government; the assembly of the whole of the army at Meinpoor with the avowed intention of proceeding to the Dekhun, to support the Peishwah; the delays and evasions practised in the negotiations with us; the non-compliance with the just and moderate propositions made for an amicable arrangement; and, above all, the acts of unprovoked hostility committed by their troops, fully justified Sir Thomas Hislop in attacking them from the day he had arrived at Oojein. Indeed, had it not been for the nonage of the prince, and the disorganized state of the government, nothing could have warranted the forbearance which had been exercised towards them.

When our army arrived within four miles of their position,

the khass* paiega, or household cavalry, of 4000 horse, was pushed across the river to harass its advance. On our arriving near their army, they were found strongly posted, with the river Sepra between the armies, their left protected by the bed of the river, and their right by a very difficult ravine; while their line, which could only be approached by one ford practicable for guns, was covered by several ruined villages. After reconnoitring, Sir Thomas Hislop, finding that to turn their flank would require a long detour, and perceiving at the same time that the bed of the river offered considerable shelter for the troops during their formation, determined to attack them in front, and ordered the advance of the columns to the ford.

Some light troops were immediately crossed, followed by the horse artillery; and four guns were posted on the right bank, so as to enfilade some of the enemy's guns, which were directing their fire on the passage of the stream. The troops as they crossed were formed, under cover of the bank, in the bed of the river, and took up the position assigned to them; the cavalry and Mysore horse on the left, where the enemy's principal body of horse were stationed; and the 2d brigade of infantry, and the light brigade, in front of the ford. The first brigade of infantry, after forming, ascended the bank, and, in co-operation with the light troops, moved rapidly to the storm of the enemy's batteries. The advance of this corps was the signal preconcerted for the general attack of the whole line. The troops no sooner shewed themselves above the bank than the men began to fall very fast; but the whole moved on with rapidity, and the charge was performed with

* The body guard of the Grand Khan of Tartary, consisting of 12,000 horse, Marco Polo tells us, was called khasitan:—may not this be derived from the same word khass-paiega, or household troops, خاص with the Persian plural an? the literal meaning of khass being favourites of a king, those armed by their employer, belonging to a king, excellent, superior, royal.

REFERENCES TO THE BATTLE OF MEINPOOR.

The British troops are coloured red—the enemy's yellow.

¶ Position of the Commander-in Chief at the commencement of the action.

a. The British cavalry, under Brigadier-General Sir J. Malcolm, K.C.B. K.L.S. dispersing large bodies of horse.

b. The British troops, advancing in column.

c. The rockets and horse artillery, under Major Noble, C.B. covering the advance of the troops.

d. Position of Holkar's army. ’ His cavalry.

e. Foot artillery in Battery.

f. Foot Comps. H.M. R S.
4th ditto. M. E. R.
2d. batt. 14th. N. I. } Colonel Scot.
Light brigade, ... Major Bowen.
} The grand attack led by Brigadier-General Sir J. Malcolm, K.C.B. K.L.S. &c. &c.

g. The charge and retreat of the enemy.

h. The 2nd position of the enemy.

K. The enemy's camp left standing.

y. A bank (to cross the ravine) cut through.

··· The only fords for infantry.

|| Not fordable.

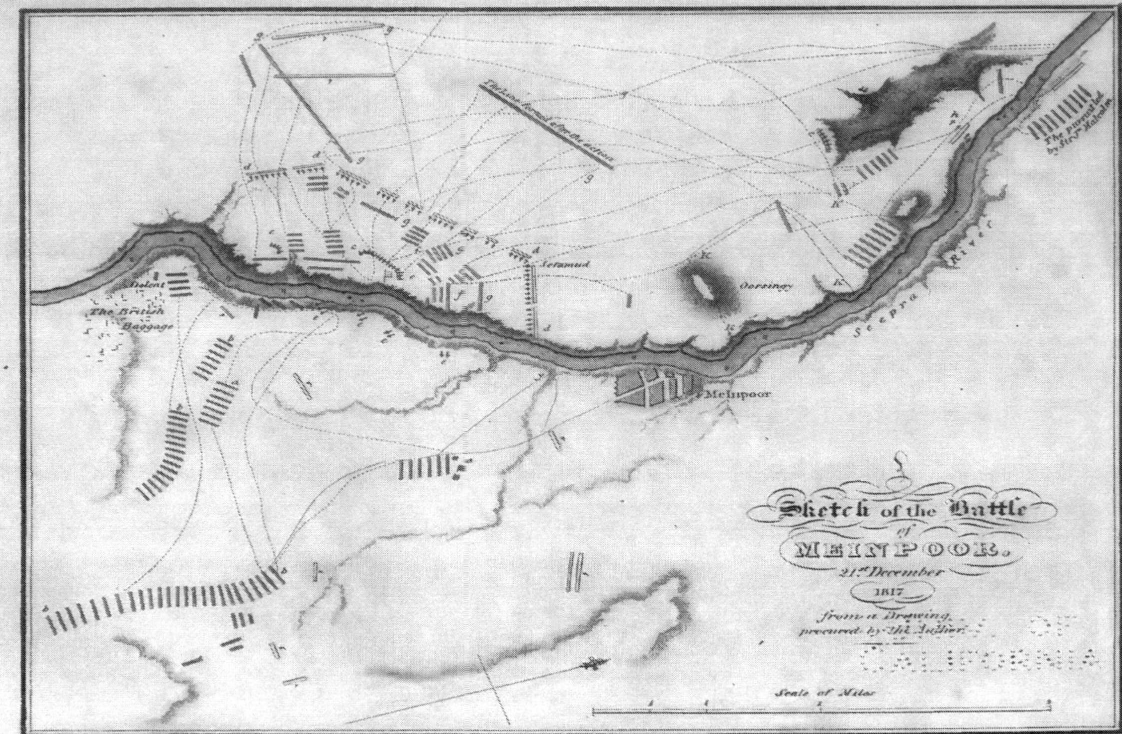

G. Fitz Clarence del.t

Published as the Act directs 24th Feby 1829 by John Murray Albemarle Street London.

J. Walker Sculpt

an ardour and gallantry that could not be surpassed; the European regiment being led by Sir John Malcolm. The enemy's fire was destructive, but the troops pushed forward in the most undaunted manner. Ill supported by their infantry, the artillery was yet pointed with dreadful precision; and its discharge continued till the brave men who served the guns were bayoneted in the act of depressing them. The enemy's cavalry fled from the field, and escaped almost entire. Their infantry did not behave well, and were nearly all destroyed, for hardly four battalions out of fourteen escaped from the sanguinary rout. Our cavalry, supported by two corps of light infantry, were ordered in pursuit on the right bank of the river, and the Mysore horse on the left. The result of this action, which lasted from noon till almost three o'clock, was the capture of the whole of the enemy's artillery, amounting to 63 pieces of ordnance, and the complete defeat and dispersion of their army, with a loss of 5000 men. The general direction of the pursuit and flight was towards Rampora. The conduct of the officers and troops was most commendable, and the names of those who particularly distinguished themselves are mentioned in Sir Thomas Hislop's despatch, containing an account of the battle.

Our force in the field was about 5500 regular troops, fourteen light guns, and 3000 Mysore horse; that of the enemy consisted of fourteen regular battalions about 500 each, sixty-three guns, and about 20,000 cavalry. The loss we sustained was very severe, as it amounted to three European officers and 171 men killed, natives included, and thirty-eight European officers and 569 men wounded. Sir John Malcolm joined in the pursuit with the light corps, and a few days after beat up their quarters, took their camp, and all their baggage, 8000 bullocks, and 100 camels; while Sir Thomas Hislop found it necessary to halt in the vicinity of Meinpoor for several days, to establish the hospital, and to concert other ultimate measures.

Having now brought the operations of the army of the Dekhun down to the defeat of Holkar on the 21st December, it will be necessary to trace the march of the Bombay force, which was ordered to advance into Malwa, to act in conjunction with that under Sir Thomas Hislop. The contingent of this presidency, consisting of 5800 men, and a body of the Gwykwar's horse, under the command of Major-general Sir William Keir, marched from Baroda, the capital of Guzeraut, on the 4th December. On the 7th he moved from Jerode, in the vicinity of Baroda, and arrived on the 8th at Wuzulpoor, and the following day at Godra; where ascertaining that considerable credit had been attached to a premature report of his arrival at Dhawud, which might have induced Sir John Malcolm to hasten his arrangements, he came to the determination of divesting himself of every incumbrance, by leaving his heavy guns, baggage, and stores at Godra, and pushing on to Dhawud, through a strong and jungly country, inhabited by a tribe of professed plunderers. At this place he arrived on the 13th or 14th (accounts differ), and there is reason to believe continued his route towards Malwa, farther than Jerré. The disaffection of the native powers towards us appearing to spread, the Bombay government became desirous of having an overpowering force near the capital of the Gwykwar, and on this account resolved to recall the division moving into Malwa.

Sir William Keir obeyed this command, which he received on the 16th, and was on his march back to Jerré on the 17th. This movement was countermanded by Sir Thomas Hislop; and the general returned again to Dhawud on the 19th. He had met with much annoyance from the barbarous excesses and rapacity of the bheels on his line of baggage, by which he lost upwards of thirty followers, and several Sepoys, while the banditti were hid by the thickness of the jungle. He continued his route, and on the 20th was on the Annass, at Lewghur on the 21st, at Pellowud on the 22d, on the left bank of the Myhee on the 23d, and on the 24th at Rutlam, where, in consequence of the events which had taken place in Malwa, he was ordered by Sir Thomas Hislop to halt till further orders.

On the 25th December, Sir Thomas Hislop, who still remained at Meinpoor, received authentic intelligence that Holkar and his court, with a considerable number of horse, who had fled to the northward after their defeat on the 21st, had halted and assembled at Seta Mhaw. He thereupon directed Sir William Keir to detach two squadrons of His Majesty's 17th dragoons and a native flank battalion to form a junction with the advanced guard of his excellency's army under Sir John Malcolm at Koondlahon on the 27th; and, in co-operation with this last force, consisting of four horse artillery guns, four squadrons of regular cavalry, two light battalions, and 2000 Mysore horse, proceed against the power of Holkar, to strike a decisive blow at the only remains of his army.

Sir Thomas Hislop having succeeded in obtaining excellent accommodation in Meinpoor for the reception of his numerous wounded, garrisoned the town with a battalion of native infantry, four guns, and 200 Mysore horse, under the command of Major Moodie, and sent orders to Sir William Keir to advance with his division on the banks of the Chumbul, intending to form a junction with it on the 29th or 30th.

His excellency marched from Meinpoor, it is believed, on the 28th December, and formed a junction with the Bombay force on the 30th near Taul, this last having moved by Phinka. The advanced guards of both armies, under Sir John Malcolm, reached Mundissor on the 31st December, and the main bodies advanced in two columns towards that place, and again joined at Mundissor on the 1st January, 1818. It was the intention of the commander of the forces to move with the whole upon the Pindarries, and, if possible, to annihilate them at one blow, having directed Sir John Malcolm to halt until the arrival of the main bodies. But the appearance of the vaqueel, Meer Zuffir Khan, from the Maha Rajah, in camp on the 31st December, bearing a preliminary agreement, signed by Mulhar Rao Holkar, differing somewhat in form, but not in substance, from what Sir

John had transmitted, and which had been approved by Sir Thomas Hislop, altered the plan of operations. The vaqueel stated that this pacific measure had been produced by the advance of the corps under Sir John, and by their knowledge that he had separated from his heavy baggage, and intended to pursue them with increased rapidity. The head-quarters of Holkar had halted at Purtaub Ghur, within eighteen miles of Mundissor. In consequence of this pacific offer, Sir John Malcolm desired that Tantiah Jog, the person who had the principal management of affairs belonging to Holkar, should come into the camp that evening, and the army of that prince was directed to move to Rampora the following day. It was also most positively promised that the camp of the Pindarry Kureem Khan, who, having fled from General Marshall and Colonel Adams, had joined the army on its retreat, should march to a distance from it immediately.

The submission of Holkar, which obtained for him a suspension of hostilities, had the necessary effect of destroying any hope which might have been formed, either by his own confederates or the Pindarry chiefs. At this period the Pindarries were much broken and reduced, having been severely handled by the pursuing columns. The durrahs of Kureem and Wussul Mehumed had particularly suffered, and that of Chetoo had also lost several guns and much baggage; and subsequent to this they were all much dispersed by pursuing detachments from the Bombay army.

During the negotiation of the treaty with Holkar, Sir John Malcolm displayed the greatest promptitude and ability, and it will ever stand as one of the most advantageous for our interest in India. It was one of those few desirable steps required to consolidate and strengthen our empire, and to place the states dependant on us on the surest foundation; affording the happiest prospect of a long series of peaceful years, and promising permanent tranquillity to a most disturbed part of India.

CHAPTER XIV.

PERSONAL NARRATIVE RESUMED.

The Rajah Govind Buckish's reception and house—Illuminations—Strange difference in customs—Mode of eating—Persian dinner—Bread with poppy seeds—Wine—Return to the rajah—Fireworks—Singers and nautch women—Salaries—The Catalani of the east—Mimics—Anecdote—English song—Rajah's anecdote of a singer in Mehumed Shah's reign—Take leave—Presents—Travel all night—Ghaut above Dowlutabad—Road—Extensive table land—Karguswarrah—Paper manufactory—Mahometan tombs—Rowsah—Tombs of the saints—Importunity of the Peer-Zadahs—Aurungzebe's tomb—Wooden screen—Tombs—Their decorations—Drums—Nobut—Tents and escort—Proceed to the caves of Ellora—Reflections—Hill of red granite—Keylas—At first disappointed—The area—The temple in the centre—The sensation when viewing it—Entrance—Statues of elephants—Much mutilated—Description of the stupendous work—Seen to great disadvantage—Steps—Sculptured records—Entrance to the great temple—Gigantic porters—Interior—Lowness of the roof—Pillars—Medallion in the centre—Aurungzebe's intolerant spirit—Sanctum sanctorum—Porticos—Caryatides—Bridge—Five smaller temples—Coating of sand—Halls in the cliff—Decorations—Comparison of the Indian and Grecian pillars—Classical ornaments—Cistern of water—Ideas of the Sepoys—Measurements—Proceed to the other caves—Dūs Avatara—Teen Taul—Do Tual—Bhud cave—Bramin and Bhud religion—Return to Keylas—Tiffin—Beef—Extraordinary changes—Anecdote—Caves to the north—Cascade—Dooma Leyma—Indra Sabha—Other excavations throughout India—At Mavelipuram—Miserable communication at Ellora along the face of the hill—Cave at Elephanta, at Carli, at Salsette, at Guyah—In Gondwannah—Arrangements for proceeding across the country—Salee Mehomet Khan—Escort from the Rajah Govind Buckish.

Rowsah, 23 January, 1818.

LAST night about seven o'clock we proceeded to the residence of the rajah, which is nearly opposite the great mosque. We were received by him at the door, and conducted into a very handsome veranda, well lighted with chandeliers; in front of it a large piece of water, and fountains, on the other side of which, reflected in the water, was a very splendid illumination, with many globes and differently shaped figures formed of lamps, continually revolving, which had a very beautiful effect. The floor of the veranda was covered with white cloth, and Captain Sydenham took off his shoes before he went upon it; but I declined following his example, being in boots, and having appeared in them at the court of Delhi before the king. This point was settled by Lord Lake' stating, after the battle of Delhi, when he was to appear before Shah Allum, that boots were a part of his dress as a soldier, and that he could not appear without them. It is curious how directly opposite our ideas on this subject are to those of the natives in India. A Mahometan servant will hide himself, should he be without his turban when you come upon him unprepared, and he dare not enter your room without leaving his shoes at the door. What a revolution must take place in England before a footman may with propriety come into a room with his hat on, and without his shoes! The rajah brought his son, a fine boy, to see the show, telling us that his other child was ill with the small pox. After seeing some very bad mimics, we were informed that our dinner was ready, and proceeded to another court, where in a veranda, very elegantly lighted, we found a table furnished with Captain Sydenham's plates, knives, forks, spoons, glasses, &c. these not being known in the east, where they always eat, and even help you, with the right hand. An excellent Persian dinner was served up, consisting of some very good dishes; and the bread, with poppy seeds in the crust, was very delightful. Our repast had, however, one advantage over those of Persia; our beverage being madeira, hermitage, and claret; at which, after sitting an hour, we sent to inform the rajah we were about to return to the veranda. Some bad fire-works were exhibited, being inferior to the generality, as the natives are very successful in these matters, but the short notice I had given did not permit the powder to dry. After we had seen these, a celebrated singer was introduced, who sung tolerably well, not only Persian, but Hindoo songs, accompanied by tom-toms, and two instruments not unlike guitars. This man, with the set of mimics, and two sets of nautch women, are always in the rajah's pay, and are part of his household and state. He receives 300 rupees a month, equal to 37*l*., and the mimics and nautch women from 300 to 400 a set. I am told that a singer, a woman at Hyderabad, is in such repute, that she will not sing under 500 rupees a night. She must be the Catalani of the east. These mimics are the worst kind of buffoons, and accompany their acting by silly remarks, and execrable attempts at wit. I recollect seeing a set when I was in Hindoostan in 1815, who, in ridicule of our cutchery or court of justice, went through a trial, in which the judges were supposed to be Europeans. The offender, when about to enter on his defence, is interrupted by a servant who announces that dinner is ready, and the judges start up, pronounce the prisoner guilty, condemn him to be hanged, and run off to table. It is almost needless to remark how little this buffoonery is justified by the actual practice of our courts in India, and the classical English reader will at once apply to this specimen a line of one of our great poets. Yet the performance, however it may be regarded as a piece of impertinence, is a proof among many others of the mildness and toleration of the British government; since even the public actors feel that they can take such liberties with impunity. After several songs, our singer stated that he had been in Calcutta, and knew an English song; and to my surprise, began to the same tune as that in which he had been chanting his Persian,

> I care for nobody,
> Nobody cares for me.

This was all he knew, and was well enough; but in repeating it several times it became

> I care for no-
> -body no ca-
> -re for me, I
> -care for nobo-
> -dy no ca

to my infinite amusement. The rajah, I thought, fancied I was treating his singer with great disrespect on my laughing at him, and, to raise him and his *meticr* in my opinion, began a long story about a singer who was performing before Nadir Shah after his capture of Delhi. At a nautch given to the conqueror by his prisoner Mahumed Shah, the former was so pleased with him, that he promised to give him any thing he asked. The patriotic and disinterested singer immediately answered, "the occupation of the city by your army has raised the price of flour to an exorbitant height; make it cheaper*."

After we had seen both sets of nautch women and more fireworks, we took leave, and the rajah presented me with presents similar to those I had given him the day before, with the exception of two small bottles of attar of roses, and immense wreaths of roses thrown round our necks. We reached home by eleven, slept in our palanquins, were taken up at three by our bearers, attended by 50 infantry, and I awoke this morning at the foot of the ghaut, near Dowlutabad. Having slept in our dressing-gowns, after changing we proceeded to walk up the ghaut, paved by some devout person, who, to transmit his renown to his successors, has placed two small pillars, with his name and date, about half-way up the hill, which is very steep. The stones used in making the road have evidently been taken from some building of great beauty, which had probably fallen to ruin in the neighbourhood, as some of them are very elaborately carved. As we ascended, we had an excellent view of Dowlutabad, which, from this spot, appears impregnable. After passing the small pillars, the road winds round, and the hill intercepts the prospect of that wonderful fortress. On reaching the summit, at the close of a very fatiguing walk, we found an extensive table land to our right. The steep face

* This anecdote is, I find, somewhat differently related by Dow.

of this elevated ground is similar to that which overlooks Ellora, to which it is continued by the same range, but turning to the north at right angles with that which we ascended, having therefore a western aspect, and runs nearly north and south. We mounted Captain Sydenham's horses, though I was still suffering from my accident, and went on about a mile and a half to the village of Karguswarrah, or Paper Town, so called from a large manufactory of that article being established in it, in consequence of the advantageous vicinity of some large tanks of spring water. Paper is made in India, though leaves are still used for writing upon. The houses are of hewn stone, badly joined, and not half inhabited. The number of Mahometan tombs on this table land, some of them large and of superior workmanship, extends all the way from the road over Dowlutabad, to the town of Rowsah, about eight miles. This name implies a burial-ground, and the place became thus celebrated from several Mahometan saints being interred here; and therefore all the devout followers of the prophet, who lived and died at Arungabad, wished their bones to repose in their vicinity. Here Aurungzebe is buried. We entered the town, which is surrounded by a stone wall, through a handsome gate of the same materials. The houses are more connected than those of Indian towns in general, and reminded me of a Portuguese town of the second class. We then proceeded to the tombs of two saints, where a similar body of Peer-Zadahs, as at the fikir's tomb, pestered me in the most importunate manner for alms; and after threatening to horsewhip them all round, at the risk of being maltreated, I was obliged to give them ten rupees, to save myself from being torn to pieces. This forced charity went very much against my will, as of all the useless and abominable institutions which have arisen from superstition, none is worse than a monastic life, as it implies a renunciation of all the respectable duties and social ties of life. The first establishment was mean, but contained the bones of the emperor Aurungzebe within its walls. This tomb is characteristic of the failing of that monarch, and by its meanness exemplifies the ruling passion strong in death. It is a plain Mahometan tomb, covered with a green cloth, in a wooden screen of trellised laths, not even painted. His majesty's executors have acted up to his wishes. He was removed from Ahmednuggur, where he died, and was afterwards buried here. We next proceeded to the tomb of the saint, and were not, as I expected, asked to take off our shoes. The doors of the outer wall are plated with silver, but of no great value. The body is interred in a small house about the shape of a common dog-kennel, though much larger; and through the doorway I saw the floor was covered with a brocade cloth of gold, with flowers strewed around, and a few lamps lighted hanging from the roof, intermixed (from the gloom of the interior I could not ascertain) with what I supposed to be a number of glass balls, full of, or lined with quicksilver, also pendant from above. Some tombs of members of the same family are near this, inclosed in a very handsome trellis of red stone. As we returned, I saw an immense pair of drums, used at the religious feasts held here once or twice a year. They were in the shape of kettle-drums, and at least five feet high, and six in diameter. The continual beating of the nobut, or great drum, is one of the highest signs of rank and power, and over the gate of every palace is a gallery or balcony, where this noisy instrument is beat at certain hours in the day and night. One of them is always carried on an elephant before the commander of a native army. At Morshedabad, when I was there, the newab had them continually beat. Four gates to his palace had each a nobut, and each of these sounded a quarter of each hour, and made the most horrid din imaginable. It is very lucky for his newabship that he cannot be prosecuted for a nuisance. After seeing other tombs of no interest, we proceeded to this ground, where we found tents, and a very strong escort.

I now find myself within a mile of the wonderful Caves of Ellora, and am only waiting till after breakfast to visit them: I cannot help congratulating myself on the enviable situation in which I am placed, as all antiquarians, and indeed all who have any laudable curiosity, would delight to be by my side. As but few, however, can partake of this pleasure, I shall attempt, and hope to give, a satisfactory description of them *.

After breakfast, taking 50 Sepoys for our escort, we proceeded in our palanquins towards the caves, distant about a mile; and I do not recollect that I ever felt more anxiety and impatience, or expected more delight, than on this occasion; and I have by no means been disappointed.——Having returned, though dreadfully fatigued, I will not permit my feelings to pass away, without recording them on a more secure tablet than that of my memory. My eyes and mind are absolutely satiated with the wonders I have seen: the first are weary with objects so gigantic and extraordinary, to which they were totally unaccustomed; and the latter has been so much on the stretch, being crowded and overwhelmed with ideas so overpowering and various, that I despair of ever forming any calm judgment upon them. The gross superstition, the cause of their formation, becomes even respectable and venerable, from the admiration which I experienced of these early and stupendous works of human genius, of unremitting toil and perseverance. I felt a sensation of gratitude, and almost of esteem, towards the religion which had effected a labour so immense and remarkable. Every thing around me spoke of other times,—of individuals, nations, and arts, long since passed away; and I took a hurried view of the present state of India, looking in vain for any power or class of men, great,

* Since I have arrived in England, I have seen views of these excavations, published by Mr. Daniell, and should be doing him an injustice, did I permit the opportunity to pass, without remarking that they are (like the rest of this gentleman's works throughout India, of which I have seen great part) inimitable.

or I may almost say omnipotent enough to venture on so prodigious an undertaking—a work which has successfully withstood the barbarous attempts of the Mahometans, and outlived the name or era of its founder, which is hidden in the most remote antiquity. The Bramins, and the Hindoo nations, in their original purity, long before our era, who had here concentrated their religious institutions and power, and made the very mountains subservient to their superstition, and the various changes which had taken place throughout India within the last 2000 years, all passed with the velocity of a vision; and as I stood in Keylas, casting a rapid glance from those ages concealed in impenetrable darkness, in which the stupendous monuments of art before me had arisen, down to the present moment, I sought in vain for any incident in the lapse of time, which could convey an equal conception of the power of man over matter. And here that national and personal vanity which I have already confessed prompted me to ask myself whether the object of amazement, next to this in the history of India, was not that of the inhabitants of an island in the outskirts of Europe, unknown even by name in these regions, till they were seen first as merchants, and then as conquerors; and who, during little more than half a century, had by a gradual extension of military operations, terminating in those which formed the subject of the despatches with which I was charged, established over the country an influence or dominion, which may now be said to be universal. These ideas, with the magnitude of the works around me, all tended to set cool reflection at defiance; yet the multitude of fast-forming and overwhelming thoughts have left an indelible though indistinct impression, and now only present the difficulty, in putting them on paper, of repressing their rapid rise, and allowing the tumult of my mind to subside.

A period of time has elapsed, since the first excavation of the Caves of Ellora, so immense, that even their sanctity has been effaced;

for though containing in a perfect state the deities at this moment worshipped in the Hindoo mythology, yet no pilgrim now visits them, nor are they in any manner, or to any one, (except a cursory traveller) an object of veneration. Whatever may have been the cause of the erection of the stupendous buildings in Egypt, or the religious feeling which prompted their construction, I am not surprised that a satisfactory account of their founder and era has been lost in ages so remote, as to leave in existence no remains of that worship, except themselves and tradition. But *here*, where the very same religion still maintains its ground, that these surprising monuments should be held in such a degree of disrespect cannot well be explained, unless upon the supposition that the excesses of the Mahometans, who entered the most sacred places, may have rendered them impure, and thus have deprived them of their former holiness.

We descended the face of the hill, which is of red granite and very steep, and enjoyed a fine view of the extensive plain beneath us, with the village of Ellora about a mile from the foot, embosomed in trees. The rest of the plain had however rather an arid appearance. About two-thirds down the hill, which, Captain Sydenham informed me, was hollowed for near two miles into vast halls and chambers, we came in front of the great excavation, called in Sanskrit, Keylas, or Paradise. From having had my expectation raised to the highest pitch, I was in the beginning greatly disappointed. The first object which strikes the traveller is a gateway, having apartments over it, connected with the sides of the hill by two walls with coarse battlements, and apparently built across an old stone quarry; and above, and on each hand within the gateway, are seen a confused crowd of pagodas and obelisks, so that should a stranger view it from the outside, not being aware of the peculiarity of the work, he would wonder at the taste of thus burying so many buildings in so obscure a situation. But on approaching the wall and gate, you search in vain for the usual separation of stones in building, and the whole is found to be one mass of rock. This is however capable of being accomplished by manual labour, without any great exertion; and it is only on entering the gateway, and passing into the immense area, two hundred and forty-seven feet long, one hundred and fifty broad, and one hundred feet high, and viewing the principal temple supported by stone elephants, and bearing in mind that this stupendous, yet elaborately worked mass, is formed of kindred material with the coarse perpendicular wall of stone which shuts you in on three sides, that the astonishment and admiration is felt, which, far from wearing off, I think increases on reflection. On entering the gate (1), which has several rooms over it, the first object which presents itself, immediately opposite, is a colossal figure about ten feet high, surrounded with sculpture, and two small elephants joining their trunks above his head. This important personage is in a sitting posture, and, by being daubed with red paint, is rendered, if possible, more hideous than when he started from his mother rock. The openings into the area are to the right and left, (2) (2). Facing these openings, in the bottom of the area, stand two stone elephants, (3) (3), of the size of life, both more or less mutilated, and with no other decoration than two coarse ropes carved round their bodies. It is from the vicinity of these elephants that the eye and mind first explore and comprehend the whole of the exterior of the great pyramidical temple, 90 feet high, in the centre of the excavation. The minute and beautiful carving on the outside is very happily contrasted with the cliff around. From the elephants, about 30 feet further, are two beautiful obelisks, (4) (4), stated to be 38 feet high, covered with carving, and not only light in appearance, but much relieved by each compartment or story being variously and beautifully sculptured. These are very perfect. The main temple, (5), stands rather towards the further end, than in the middle, of the area, and is connected with the apartment over the gate, (6), by a small temple, (7), in which stands the bull Nundee, and beyond it, by a sort of bridge, (8), directly over the figure seen on entering, and over the openings (2) (2), into the area opposite to the elephants, all similarly cut out of the solid rock. The bull is not large, and rather disfigured. The centre temple has several smaller, and not so high, beyond it, (9) (9) (9) (9) (9), which, from the neighbourhood of the elephants, appear attached to it, but are not so in reality, except by the floor of rock, which leaves the whole, as if supported by the statues of animals, projecting more or less from the solid mass; some with half their bodies protruded from it, others with only the heads and fore-quarters. The principal of these are elephants of the size of life, and lions larger than life, and some imaginary animals. For the sake of diversity, these statues are all in different attitudes; several in fierce conflict with their neighbours, and all looking as if executed at the whim of the workmen. The feet, talons, ears, trunks, tusks, &c. have suffered much; it is supposed from the intemperate zeal of the Mahometans.

The distance from the sides of the temple to the face of the scarped rock is not more than forty feet on each side, and it is painful to look up for any length of time. The flights of steps, of which there are two, (10) (10), ascending to the floor, supported by the animals on which the temple is formed, are on each side, and rather beyond the smaller temple which contains the bull Nundee. Between the principal temple and the gateway, on the outside walls, there is much sculpture in nine rows of figures, about a foot long, of men fighting: some armed with bows, others with clubs and long straight swords. On the right side, among others, are some figures in cars, with two and four wheels, drawn by horses, and monkeys seem in every part to be very active, and by no means second-rate performers. This is supposed to allude to the conquest of Ceylon by Rama; but as I do not understand the Hindoo mythology, I shall not attempt to unravel the meaning of these carved records, as doubtless they are, but leave it to others who are versed in "mystic lore." It may just be mentioned that the image of Hunomaun is represented in heaving rocks to form the bridge between the continent and Ceylon. The steps turn inwards about half their rise, and meet on an uncovered landing place, (11), between the small temple containing the bull, and the great temple, about three or four feet below the level of the latter. The door, facing the west, (12), twelve feet high by six broad, ornamented with colossal statues on each side, is now before you; and on ascending, I believe, four steps, and passing between the gigantic porters, you arrive at the great chamber of the principal temple: though, for the first few minutes after you enter, the gloomy light does not permit you to see distinctly, which, added perhaps to the dead silence, the massy pillars, and the Goliah-like figures at the other end, but partially discerned, together with the feeling inspired in the area, tends to absorb the faculties; yet I gazed in mute admiration. The interior, from the door to the recess at the other end, is one hundred and three feet long, sixty-five wide, and the height but seventeen; and I think the lowness of the roof adds materially to its effect. The size of the pillars, being in thickness out of proportion with their height, bespeak the weight above, and excite the peculiar sensation of a desire to crouch when inside. It was then I felt the real circumstances of the mighty work around me. Here had the perseverance of man ornamented a mass coeval with the world; and which, differing from all other temples on the face of the earth, had grown like a statue from an uncouth block, under the hands of an artist: and my feelings did justice to the designer and workmen. It is sustained by four rows of pillars, not above four being of the same workmanship, the shafts minutely carved, but the capitals quite plain; and the roof, between these supports, appears resting on an imitation of great beams, crossing and fastened on the capitals of the columns. The roof is plain, excepting the centre, which has a round medallion in basso relievo, representing a man between two female figures; though that on the left is almost destroyed, and appears, by accident or design, to have been detached from the roof and to have fallen, leaving a mark of what is the original colour of the stone, nearly the whole of the interior having been blackened by Aurungzebe, who, to show his contempt for the opinions of the Hindoos, filled it with fuel which he caused to be set on fire. It would, however, almost have bid defiance to his cannon; and, with the other caves in its vicinity, exists to this day, a wonder of the world, only equalled by the pyramids, and likely to stand to the end of time, as firmly as the neighbouring hills. Opposite the entrance is a recess, (13), the sanctum sanctorum, with a group of colossal figures on each side, whose heads touch the roof. This recess runs back about forty feet on the outside, beyond the back wall of the temple, and contains the lingam. On each side of the centre of the great chamber, protruding into the area, are open porticos, (14) (14), and their roofs supported by pillars resting, like the other parts, on elephants. The four centre pillars of the interior of the temple are wanting, thus leaving an open passage from the door of one portico to the other. These are rather below the level of the floor of the temple, and are richly sculptured throughout, and instead of pilasters to uphold the roof, on each side of the doors from the main temple are two female figures, twelve feet high, whose heads, touching the cornice, appear to bend, yet in a graceful attitude, under the weight they sustain. It will be recollected and observed how strong a similarity these figures have to the Caryatides of the Greeks, and I believe it would be a difficult question to solve, whether the Indians borrowed them from that people, or *vice versa*. The porticos have seats, on one of which I attempted to cut my name at the expense of my knife. From that which is to the south of the temple, there is supposed to have been, and appearances countenance the idea, a bridge, (18), thrown across the area to the excavated halls of the cliff, with which there is now no communication from below, as there is with those on the northern side. Behind the recess, or sanctum sanctorum, (opposite the principal entrance), which runs backwards outside the temple near forty feet, (13), is a balcony or open gallery, (15) (15) (15) (15) (15), which passes from two doors, (16) (16), one on each side of the colossal groups, out of the great chamber, round its side, and the end of it, and has five smaller temples, (9) (9) (9) (9) (9), of a similar shape to the principal one, two on the sides and three at the eastern termination, which complete the whole structure. They are all sculptured in the same manner, and supported by the animals beneath, of which I fancy there must be in all from eighty to one hundred. The roofs of the great and smaller temples gradually rise to points, and the outside walls of all are carved in pannels of grotesque and obscene figures. The whole has at some late period received a coating of sand-coloured plaster, which has been painted over in different colours, and even now, though more than half destroyed, takes much from the sculpture. The architect was not content with performing this gigantic work in the centre, but has excavated the face of the cliff on each side three or four stories, (17) (17) (17), each twenty feet in height, and of considerable depth; these last I had not time to enter, as the other caves I had to visit extended to the north and south, about three-quarters of a mile each way. When one considers the immense labour expended on Keylas, where nothing but the chisel and hammer could be used, which differs from nearly all other temples, in not being built, but formed by the superfluous rock being torn from it, and the construction of which is so contrary to the usual principles, (as blocks of stone were carried from, not to it, for its completion), one hardly knows which to admire most, the projector, or the person who carried the design into execution. Yet I feel almost a partiality for the former; for in what an original and expanded mind must the

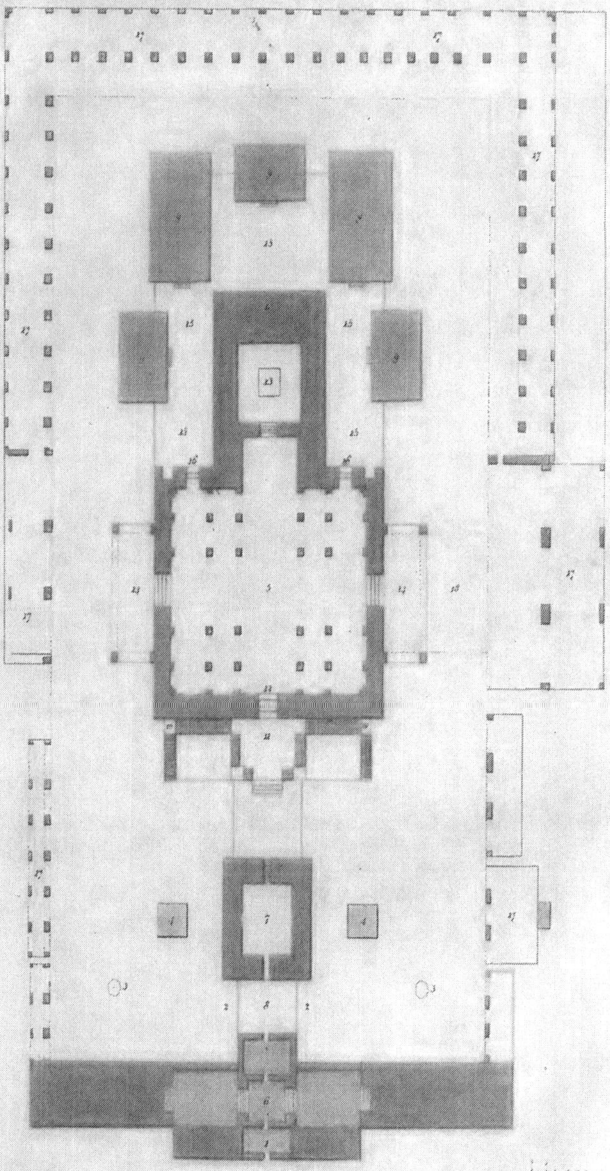

PLAN OF THE GRAND TEMPLE, KEYLAS.

J. Walker sculp.

idea first have been conceived of hollowing out and decorating, by the hand of man, a very "rib of the world," spurning the detail of piecemeal building, and thus taking advantage of the primeval materials placed by nature on the spot, and wresting from her very bowels a place of worship. Some of the sculptured decorations, and the taste in the ornaments, would do credit to the best period of the Grecian school, though in general an evidently uncultivated style of architecture predominates; and the irregular shapes and devices on the shafts of the pillars, with their plain capitals, in the principal temple, are, in my opinion, more rich than the plain Grecian pillar with its ornamented capital, though not so chaste. The fluting of the Corinthian order is but a poor attempt of this description. Some of the minute ornaments are even classical. I observed, in several instances, the bust of a man from the head to the middle, ending in a scroll or flourish, &c., and the wings of birds having similar terminations. The lions' heads, with flourished ornaments from their mouths, I have often seen used in modern furniture in Europe. Nearly the entire bodies of the largest figures project from the wall, and there is not, throughout the whole, a single arch. Immediately on the outside the gateway is a cistern of very fine water, which being also cut out of the granite rock, would in any other spot be a curiosity in itself, but here, for an extent of nearly two miles, man has gone beyond himself; and Captain Sydenham heard one of the Sepoys lecturing another before the rest, for expressing doubts of its being the work of the gods. The plan and some of the most important measurements of this extraordinary place, which Captain Sydenham assured me were perfectly correct, I have taken from the Asiatic Researches.

DIMENSIONS OF KEYLAS.

	Feet.
Gateway, height	14
Passage of the gateway, having on each side rooms fifteen feet by nine .	42

	Feet.
Inner area or court, length from the gateway to the opposite scarp . . .	247
Ditto breadth	150
Greatest height of the rock, out of which the court is excavated	100

CENTRE.

Balcony over the gateway, fourteen feet by eight, and eight high. A room within it nine feet square, and about nine high. Another within it, same dimensions. One on each side from the centre, twenty-two by fifteen each. Bridge, twenty feet by eighteen, with a parapet three feet six inches high. Ascent by nine steps from the bridge into a distinct room, in which is the bull Nundee, sixteen feet three inches square. Another bridge, twenty-one feet by twenty-three feet broad, leading to the upper portico of the temple. This portico, with the parapet wall, is eighteen feet by fifteen feet two inches, and seventeen high; within, a bench that is rounded off four feet high by three feet seven inches broad. You can enter this portico from the gateway by a passage, that the filling up of the rubbish has afforded, but the proper passage is by flights of steps, of thirty-six steps each, leading up on each side the body of the temple.

GRAND TEMPLE.

	Feet.	Inches.
Door of the portico, twelve feet high by six feet broad; length from the door of the portico entering the temple to the back wall of the temple	103	6
Length from the same place to the end of the raised platform behind the temple	142	6
Greatest breadth of the inner part of the temple	61	0
Height of the ceiling	17	10

Two porches on each side measured, without, thirty-four feet ten inches by fifteen feet four inches. The particulars of the intricate measurement of this fine temple will be best understood from the plan formed on the spot.

Height of the grand steeple or pyramid computed about ninety feet from the floor of the court, and of the smaller ones about fifty. Height of the obelisks about thirty-eight feet. Base eleven feet square, being eleven feet distant from each side of the room in which is the bull Nundee. The shaft above the pedestal is seven feet square. The two elephants on each side of the court or entry are larger than life*.

Having gratified our curiosity in this part, we then proceeded to the southward, along a bad and dangerous path, to visit the other caves, of which the first was 103 feet wide and fourteen feet high, but I saw none at all like Keylas. This was called the Dus Avatara, or the ten incarnations of Visnu: it is supported by several rows of pillars, and penetrates into the mountain forty-six feet, terminating in a recess. On the sides, in compartments, are groups of figures, as high as the roof. The supporting columns in the cave are not ornamented, being plain and massy. We last of all passed into the Do Taul and Teen Taul, two very fine caves, similar to that I have just mentioned, except that one consisted of two stories, and the other of three. They contained groups of gigantic figures, from five to six or more in a compartment.

I was much amused by a Bramin who accompanied us, and, as we passed each, named the principal deity represented, with as much *sang froid* as the exhibitor of a collection of pictures. To attempt to remember all is impossible, as I have, in six hours, gone over what would take the same number of days. In one of the three caves I have mentioned, I entered a small room, out of which three doors led into dark apartments; but it would be a fatal step to any one who attempted to advance, as they are large caverns full of water. The most southern cave I visited is, for several reasons, the most remarkable after Keylas, though not so

* They did not appear to me to be beyond the natural size.

large or curiously wrought. It is similar to the interior of a chapel, having an arched roof, and the only one so formed amongst so many. It has a line of columns passing down each side, of quite plain shafts, little or no capitals, and, without any real use, a representation of arched rafters, as if supporting the rock above. At the farther end is a figure in a sitting posture, with a tree spreading over him. This cave is in length seventy-nine feet, forty-three in breadth, and thirty-eight high from the centre of the arch to the floor. In short, this is, whether antecedent to, or of later date than the rest, of a totally different style, and even apparently belonging to a different religion; and I find I am borne out in this idea, as all the other caves are supposed, by persons who have studied the subject, to be of the present Braminical religion, but this to be of the religion of Bhud. Out of this arises a very interesting question. All accounts of the Hindoos speak of a most dreadful persecution carried on by the Bramins against the sect of Bhud many years ago, and the subsequent expulsion of the latter, whose doctrine at this day extends over Ceylon, Thibet, Tonquin, Cochin China, throughout China; exists largely in Japan; and is, without doubt, the religion which has the most numerous followers in the world. Next to this, I suppose, the Christian can boast the greatest number of believers; then the Mahometan; and lastly, the Braminical; being the four principal religions which divide the habitable world.

It is well known that the Bramins were successful in driving out their opponents, and establishing their own faith, which has never since been shaken. Which then of these caves is the oldest? It is not likely the Bramins would make excavations of such magnitude near a place of worship formed by the adherents of the detested religion, nor is it possible that the Bhudists could have excavated their temple after the Bramins had completed Keylas, as they have never since been powerful enough, and but very thinly scattered throughout India. The Bramins, although they admit that Bhud is the ninth Avatar, or incarnation of Vishnu, and the last that has appeared on the earth, always speak of the sect which takes its name from Bhud with the utmost hatred, and distinctly assert that the religion which goes under that denomination is false, and fabricated by some impostor. Sir William Jones supposes that Bhud was a reformer of the doctrines contained in the Vedes, as he disapproved of sacrificing animals; and thinks there may have been two of this name, the latter a disciple assuming the same character, and who, attempting to overthrow the whole system of the Bramins, drew down the persecution from which the Bhudists fled. It is not likely, when we consider the very tolerant principles of the religion of the Bramins, that the persecution could have originated with them; but very probable that it was produced in their self-defence, against some reformer, such as Sir William Jones speaks of. But though we now see the Bramins, from their success, completely masters of all Hindoostan and the Dekhun, still the question remains unanswered as to the greatest antiquity of the two religions.

The name of the river which divides Hindoostan from the Dekhun being the Nerbuddah, or river of Bhud, and a sacred stream; the great extent of the relics of this religion, not only at Ellora, but I am told in the caves at Carli, and those in the island of Salsette, near Bombay; the excavation at Navilipuram; the vast prevalence of this religion at the present day; and the ninth avatar of the Braminical religion bearing its name, would induce a belief that it was antecedent to that of the Bramins. The Bramins themselves, which strengthens this opinion, told Captain Wilford * that

* I find, since my return, that Mr. Dubois agrees with me, that the Bramins came from the north, or north-west, and that we must seek for their origin amongst the northern mountains; their books make frequent mention of two celebrated mountains remotely situated beyond the most northern boundaries of India; one of these mountains is named Maha Mena, the other Mandura.

they came originally from the north into the plains of Hindoostan, and were not aborigines of India; and though it is probable that in the time of Alexander the Braminical religion was established in Hindoostan, and probably in the valley or plain of the Prasi and Gangarides, and may even have extended to a Hindoo principality south of the Nerbuddah in this vicinity, still from all accounts it was not till a much later period that it extended itself further to the southward. There is, therefore, the strongest reason to believe that the Bramins have spread themselves from the northward, gradually to the most southern parts of India; and Mr. Chambers thinks the religion of Bhud was known and prevailed on the coast of Malabar, so late as the ninth century of our era, (as an idol named Bhud is mentioned by two Mahometan travellers in that century), and in Guzaraut in the 12th century, as D'Anville quotes an Arabian geographer, who states that the sovereign of Guzaraut, at that period, professed the religion of Bhud. Still we find that the Mahometan conquerors at a very early period destroyed some highly celebrated Hindoo temples in this province; but as they did not study the history of the natives until the time of Akbar, and in all probability did not discriminate between one religion and another, it is possible they may have been Bhud temples. And yet no account exists of any violent persecution by the Bramins since the establishment of the Mahometans: it must therefore have taken place before the year 1000 of our era. Mr. Gentil also adduces a strong corroboration of the late introduction of the Bramin tenets into the southern parts of India, and proves that a recollection still existed of the more ancient religion. He mentions having seen a statue in the plains of Virapatnam, which the natives told him was the god Baouth, who was now no longer respected, for that his worship and festivals had been abolished ever since the Bramins had made themselves masters of the people's faith. From the Braminical religion having extended itself from the northward, it is natural to expect that the remembrance of what preceded it should be strongest in those countries which continued the longest attached to their ancient faith; and the failure of its introduction into Ceylon is accounted for, not only from its insular position, but from its being the point to which the persecuted must have fled. Indeed, it is not improbable that the fabulous story of the expedition against the island by Rama, may have been an incursion for the prosecution of this inveterate hostility.

From these various authorities, from which and the want of authentic records it is very difficult to form a judgment, we can only collect that the Bramins have expelled the Bhudists, and established their own faith in place of the faith of Bhud; and it is not impossible, from the caves of both religions being upon one spot, that they may have been but schisms from each other, and that the two sects, out of respect to their common origin, may have continued together in a peaceful, though different course of life and opinions, for perhaps one or more centuries; and have refrained from violent measures, until ambition, or some worse passion of the human mind, fanned the flame which led from dissensions to open war, and ended in the expulsion of the Bhudists. We find from the history of Cashmir, that these two religions have in that country existed together at the same time; and the most powerful sovereign, who reigned as Dr. Buchanan supposes in the third century of our era, tolerated the doctrines of Bhud, after his predecessor had established those of Bramah; and it was not until the year 342 A. D. that the Bramins got the better of the Bhudists, and burnt their temples. As to the antiquity of the two religions, if we allow the figure of Bhud to be the personification of fire, as some of the statues representing this deity have a small flame on the tops of their heads, and that one of the earliest religions among mankind sprung from a natural respect towards the sun, and also grant that the Bramins come according to their own admissions from the northward, the preference seems due to that of Bhud.

After viewing this cave, I became excessively fatigued from the heat of the weather, and we returned to Keylas. I gave up, with great regret, the attempt to sketch the great temple and area, being well aware that the pencil must at all times be superior to the pen in describing buildings or scenery; but I found it would require more hours to draw the complicated mass before me than I should be enabled to afford, having still to examine the caves to the northward. I was well pleased to find a table spread in the centre of the principal chamber of the temple, and most happy to eat some slices of a round of beef, to invigorate us for our further progress. The beef relished uncommonly well, and suffered nothing from the idea of feasting on the flesh of the most sacred and venerated animal of the Hindoos, in their most singular temple, where 100 feet distant was a statue of a bull, once in this very place an object of adoration. What revolutions must have taken place, and what number of ages elapsed, to have brought about these changes!

After tiffin, the name given in this country to the meal we call lunch, we amused ourselves with shooting at the paroquets and other birds, which seek refuge in the holes in the rock on the cliff around. This pastime gave rise to an instance, common amongst the Sepoys, of the effects of the introduction of our discipline, and the regard paid to it. I shot a paroquet, and ordered a Sepoy, amongst others attending, to bring it me from the area into which it had fallen. We had been, previously to this, in conversation with the havildar, a Bramin, being curious to know his opinion of the caves, and of their origin and founders, and the subject had led us to religious points. The Sepoy who had gone to pick up the bird being a Bramin, Captain Sydenham remarked that he ought not strictly to touch a feathered animal, more particularly when dead; but the havildar made answer that he was fully aware he ought not to do so, but that he knew our discipline, and of course he could not but obey. About the time we were leaving Keylas, the chief man of

Ellora came up to pay his respects to us. We informed him, that his whole village and district had been ceded to us by the late treaty with Holkar, and he replied that he was most ready and willing to become our subject.

We then proceeded to the principal caves to the northward, by a worse and more dangerous path than that to the south, and saw many small excavations, not longer or deeper than fire-places, and like them in form, the sides being coarse pillars supporting a cross carved stone. There were even several ranges of these. At the distance of about half a mile, we passed near a high cliff, from which in the rains a large water-fall projects itself. At this time the body of water was diminutive. The height of the fall must be 80 feet, and we went under it, after scrambling along the cliff at the imminent risk of our lives, (for what reason I never yet have ascertained), while every one else passed round the cascade by a tolerable path. We reached the entrance of a cave, and ascended it by a steep flight of steps, at the top of which were two lions very well carved, in a crouching position. This cave is unlike the flat-roofed caves to the southward, being higher than any of them, with but few pillars, and none in the centre; and the statues, of which there are a great number, being of equal height with the roof. The sanctum sanctorum is here in the centre, in a small room about twelve feet square, with four doors, and the intermediate wall covered with colossal figures. On the opposite side to the steps by which we entered, the architect, I suppose not secure of the continuation, or consistency of the mass of stone from the vicinity of the stream, has cut deep into the mountain the whole length and height of it parallel to the cave, which is about 100 feet, to satisfy himself of its being fit to work upon. This probationary excavation is about twelve feet wide, and my companion having fired off his fowling-piece, the birds issuing from the holes, occasioned such a noise, as made me draw back, fancying the whole mountain was coming down. I am convinced that fear arises, next to what precautionary nature has given us for self-preservation, from entering into scenes to which we are not accustomed; and that the most admirable sort of courage, called self-possession, is only to be acquired by being used to trying situations of all kinds, or the determination of a mind made up to meet certain crises, however novel, with fortitude. In this instance, my mind, being overcharged with wonders and thoughts on the novelty of all around me, gave way to this sudden, turbulent, and distracting noise, which I confess dismayed me, and nearly put me to the rout.

We now continued along the face of the mountain about half a mile further, and came to an excavation of a different kind, of most beautiful workmanship. This is called Indra Sabha. The rock has been cut out so as to produce an area of about 60 feet square, the western face being open, but the other three supported by pillars of very minute workmanship. It forms three distinct caves, each at right angles from that nearest to it, full of compartments of figures not above eight feet high, which is about the height of the roof. The floor here is also carved with much beauty, and the whole is fully as well executed, if not better finished than Keylas; though as to size they bear no comparison whatever. A figure in one of the groups is pointed out as a miser, and the statue is like a skeleton with a skin on. The bones, &c. are admirably done, though there are not enow of ribs. All the statues in all the caves are quite naked. In front of the recess at the end are two small pillars not eight inches in diameter, which emit a hollow, not unmusical sound, when struck repeatedly with the heel of the hand. In the area of this cave, formed by the three sides of sculptured rock, stands a small temple 18 feet square, and 27 high, something like the smaller ones at Keylas, though more elaborately wrought; and on the right side of it, there is a single pillar 24½ feet high, surmounted by a lion. Among the bushes, totally out of sight, are the remains of an elephant as large as life. There were other caves in the neighbourhood, but it was impossible for me to visit them, being pressed for time; indeed I regret that Keylas was the only excavation I had time to view with the attention it deserved.

These are not by any means the only excavations of the kind in India. The sculptured ruins in the neighbourhood of Satras, on the coast of Coromandel, about 40 miles to the southward of Madras, called Mavilipuram, are something similar in general character and design, though on a much inferior scale,* the two largest temples being 30 feet high and 20 broad. These solid stone pagodas, which are stated to appear as if cut out of detached rocks upon the spot, resemble in design the great pyramidical temple of Keylas, and the smaller one of Indra Sabha, at Ellora. There are also striking resemblances of the elephant as large as life, and of the lion much larger and well executed, nearest to the two principal of these pagodas. In the area of Indra Sabha, and that of Keylas, are elephants, and in front of the former cave in the jungle near the entrance, I discovered another figure of an elephant much mutilated. The proportions of the elephant and lion are like those supporting the temple in Keylas; but here the want of natural proportion between the two animals is accounted for, by the necessity of their being of equal height, to receive the floor of the great temple, which they bear on their backs. But the size of the lion at Mavilipuram must have originated in the exaggerated idea of that animal, unknown as it is on the coast of Coromandel, or within 500 miles of it. The caves in the east side of the rock at Mavilipuram also resemble the minor caves at Ellora, being hollowed out to the size of a spacious room, with two or three rows of pillars left, as a seeming support to the mountainous mass of stone which forms the roof. The workmen have,

* Vide Asiatic Researches.

however, been more attentive in the communication from one piece of sculpture to another at Mavilipuram than at Ellora. Here nothing but a miserable path, in some places very dangerous, runs along the face of the hill. Conceiving that the work would be incomplete without communication, I looked for a road, but did not see any, even at the base of the hills. On the contrary, the country is furrowed out far into the plain in small ravines, and water-courses formed during the rains, by torrents rushing from the table land above. At Mavilipuram there is stated to be an inscription; and Thevenot says there is another on one of the obelisks, which I had not time to examine minutely, at Keylas*. The marks of the mason's tools are described to be evident on the rocks at Mavilipuram; they are equally so at Ellora, and the instrument does not appear to me to have been larger than a common sized pointed chisel. In addition to these caves, there are others at Elephanta, an island in the harbour of Bombay, and in the island of Salsette, and at Carli, all of which it is my intention, if I have time, to visit in the course of my route. There are others scattered over India. Mr. Harrington mentions some in the neighbourhood of Guyah, near Patna, and that the entrance to one of them is very curiously wrought with elephants and other ornaments. It is, however, extremely possible that still more may exist, of which we have not yet any information or accounts, as Captain Blunt, who traversed through the interior and wildest parts of Gondwanah, in the vicinity of a village called Mera, discovered a Hindoo excavated temple, formed in the side of the rock, the base of which was 50 feet by 45, and the height, supported by pillars, 15½. The shafts of the pillars are stated to be very much diminished, and appearing as

* In the fifth volume of the Asiatic Researches are some ancient inscriptions taken from Ellora, and translated by Lieutenant Wilford, but throw no light whatever upon the age or founder of these vast remains. Two short sentences (where they are taken from is not said) speak of the Bhud religion.

if attempts had been made to destroy them. This cave contained some images, and a cell for the lingam, which had been removed. At some distance to the north-west is another cave of smaller dimensions; and to the northward is another of two stories, which I conceive to be similar to the Do Taul at Ellora. Anquetil du Perron and Thevenot have visited these caves, and of late years a great number of Europeans have seen them. Thevenot notices the multitude of tombs spread over the table land above, and mentions the mosques over the town of Rosah. His account of the caves, however, is confused, and extremely imperfect: he particularly notices Keylas, the Teen Taul, and the arched Bhud cavern, and says, in passing under the masses of rock, when he considered the weight above him, he could not help trembling. I am not surprised, however, that he does not give a better description; for he states, that he was only two hours in viewing what it took me a whole day, and that very superficially, to visit. The tradition at that time amongst the Hindoos of Arungabad was, that all these pagodas, great and small, were made by the giants, but at what period it was not known. He calls Rosah, Rougaique *.

* Since my return to England, I have read Mr. Legh's travels, in which he speaks of the excavated temple at Guerfeh Hassan, which this traveller calls a stupendous monument of the labour bestowed by the ancients on their places of devotion. Although this appears to me to be of a similar character to the caves I have seen in India, I do not think it goes any further to prove an affinity between the two nations or religions than a similarity of design in the construction of caves. By the measurement given, 140 feet, it is only inferior in size to Keylas at Ellora; but from being covered, and of a lower style of workmanship, it by no means equals the latter, and may be ranked with Elephanta. In the excavation of which Mr. Legh speaks, the columns are ornamented by colossal statues of priests, but none of those at Keylas appear to be of this description, though the Braminical string is seen on some of the figures; but this I believe is worn by some of the incarnations of Vishnu. These figures are analogous to the Persians of the Greeks, and corroborate the assertion of, I believe, Denon, that they probably have had their origin in Egypt. The female figures, representing the Caryatides of the Greeks, we have seen at Ellora. The four niches, containing each of them three figures, in the first chamber of the temple at Guerfeh Hassan, are thus far as to position similar to those in the *Das Avatara* at Ellora; but it

I have written to Colonel Burr at Poonah, to request escorts to meet me half-way from that city to Seroor, and to Captain Gibbon at Ahmednugger, who is now acting as government collector for the districts lately forfeited by the Peishwah, on the same subject, and I hope to hear from them on my route. Salee Mehumud Khan has come out here to receive my orders, being 16 miles from Arungabad; and he and his men ought to accompany Captain Hicks and Mr. Elliott, as their escort to-morrow at three o'clock half-way to Toka. This is a very unpardonable piece of conduct, and I think he wished to get my permission to remain. The hundred horse from Rajah Gôvind Buckish have come into camp, to act as my escort from Dowlutabad to-morrow evening.

would have been extremely curious if in the *Sekos*, or shrine, the altar, which is stated to be about three feet three inches high and three feet broad, had any appearance of ever having the *Lingam* on it; as in all the caves containing the *Lingam* on an altar of these dimensions but one at Ellora, there is a small chamber similar to this, though I do not recollect any figures being in them, as in this in Nubia.

CHAPTER XV.

Dowlutabad—Pettah—Enter the second wall—Irregular Sepoys—Minaret—Son of the governor—The native princes jealous of their officers—Miserable state of the artillery in the native fortresses—The citadel—Height of the scarped cliff—Causeway—Entrance—Enter the subterraneous passage—Communication with the ditch for water—Singular mode of defence—Deemed impregnable by the natives—Road to the summit very steep—Doasdo durwaseh—The summit of the rock—Anecdote from Tavernier—Extensive view—Works of the Pettah—Cistern—In all probability the ancient Tagara—Hindoo name Deoghur—Fell early to the Mahometans—Malik Caffoor—Name changed to Dowlutabad—Absurd scheme of one of the emperors of Delhi—History of the fort—Malik Amber—Dowlutabad taken from his son—Mahometan princes distrustful of their officers—The city moved to Arungabad—Falls into the hands of the French—Delivered up by them—Abyssinians—Adventurers—No hereditary nobility—Foreign influence—Reflections.

Dowlutabad, January 24, 1818.

AT daylight we were taken up by our palanquin bhoeys, and as I had not shaken off the fatigues of the day before, I did not awake until I found myself within the pettah, or outer wall of this stupendous fortress, which contains the town. The hill which forms the citadel, and the main strength of the place, was towering above us. The scarped rock, appearing to cut off all communication from those below, and the towers, buildings, and trees, impressed me most forcibly with the idea of the flying island of Laputa in Gulliver's Travels, and I felt most anxious to reach the very apex of the hill. I proceeded through the gate of the second wall or fortified place, where about 100 irregular Sepoys were posted as its guard, and these were all the troops I saw. After leaving another barrier of stone behind me, I passed near the foot of a minaret, apparently 120 feet high, and erected, as I was told, in commemoration of the first capture of the place by the Mahometans. The son of the governor, who was acting as his deputy, met me at the last gate outside the ditch, and presented me his nuzzur. So jealous are the native princes of their officers, that I was informed the family of this young man are kept at Hydrabad as hostages. I accompanied him to the narrow causeway which crosses the ditch, but went first to the right, to a sort of tower or cavilier, on which is planted a very heavy brass gun, but as I did not measure its calibre, I only supposed it equal to throwing a ball of sixty pounds: like the generality of the artillery in the forts belonging to the natives, the first discharge would dismount it. Already, from the age of the carriage on which it rests, and the weight they have to support, the trunnions have sunk several inches into the wood, and even bent the iron work. Hence, not being above 100 yards from the ditch, I had a very good view of the fortress, which has a most imposing appearance. It is formed of an insulated hill of granite, about 3000 yards from the range of hills to the northward and westward, and presents to the view a shape not unlike a compressed beehive, except that the lower part, for one-third of the way up, or perhaps less, is scarped like a wall, and presents all around a perpendicular bluff cliff. I should think it must be about 500 feet to the summit, which is almost a point. The scarp of the rock, down to the edge of the counter-scarp, may be 150 feet, though the governor stated it to be eighty yards; the breadth of the ditch seventeen, and that of the water eighteen. Suppose the scarp below the glacis be from thirty to forty feet, this, added to 150, will make nearly the whole height of the scarped cliff. Up to the ditch, including the outside walls of the pettah, I had passed four lines of walls and gates, and it was very easy to account for this lavish number of defences, for had they not "worked up" the quantity of stone taken from the rock, it would have formed a small hill. The causeway across the ditch will not admit more than two persons at one time, and a building, with battlements, defends it on the other side. This causeway, the killidar assured me, could be destroyed in a few minutes, which, from its being of stone, I did not readily believe.

Had I not been informed how I was to ascend the summit of the perpendicular cliff, I should have despaired of ever reaching it, as no visible means presents itself, and all is alike steep and forbidding; though one may, with an attentive eye, discover a small window, about half-way up, in the face of the rock. I was anxious to proceed, being determined to mount to the top; and the governor led the way through an excavation, into the heart of the rock, so low that I was obliged to stoop nearly double; but after a few paces, a number of torches shewed me I was in a high vault, and we began to ascend on a winding passage, cut through the interior of the body of the hill. This is described by Dow as a staircase, instead of which it is only a gradual slope. This passage was about twelve feet high and the same broad, and the rise regular; and at certain distances from this dismal gallery were trap-doors, with flights of small steep steps, leading to the ditch below, only wide enough to admit a man to pass, also cut through the solid rock, to the water's edge, and unexposed to the fire of the assailants, unless they were on the very crest of the glacis. I suppose we were four or five minutes in reaching the window I had seen from below, and, after resting, we continued to climb. As I observed a passage leading off from the one in which we were, I followed it, and to my surprise found it led back, forming a retrogressive semicircle, to our road; and on the sides of it were many recesses, with shelves for depositing stores. We might have been, in all, ten minutes mounting by torch-light, and came out in a sort of hollow in the rock, about twenty feet square. On one side, leaning against the cliff, was a large iron plate, nearly of the same size as the bottom of the hollow, with an immense iron poker. On the besiegers having gained the subterraneous passage, this iron is intended to be laid down over the outlet, and a fire placed upon it. I observed a hole perforating the rock about three feet in diameter, which is meant to act as a bellows to the fire, and the current of air which came through it was so strong that I could hardly stand against it. From its strength, and these various precautions, this fortress is deemed impregnable. There are some small houses, towers, and gates on the road to the summit, which is very steep, and in some places covered with brush-wood. But the house of the governor is a most excellent habitation, surrounded by a large veranda, with twelve arches, hence called the doasdo durwaseh, or twelve doors. The road, and the only one to the top, passes through this house. Above this, the ridge is very narrow, and on the peak, on which flies his highness the Nizam's flag, on a stone bed, not many feet broad, stands a large brass twenty-four pounder.

This is the gun Tavernier mentions in the following anecdote. It being the custom to have many European artillerymen in the service of the Mogul, one who had been unsuccessful in his repeated applications for leave to return to his native land was informed, upon some occasion when the sovereign passed by the neighbourhood of this fortress, that if he succeeded in placing a gun of this size in the most commanding site in the fortress, he should have leave granted him. Being stimulated to exertion by the promise, he succeeded in the attempt; and the gun will probably remain to the latest period as a proof of his enterprise. This cannon, and two three-pounders lower down the hill, are, I believe, nearly all the artillery on the rock itself.

From the flag-staff the view is most extensive and beautiful: I plainly distinguished Karguswarrah and Rosah, over the range of hills. The works of the pettah are not continued round the base of the hill, but only on the eastern side, and though numerous, are miserable and contemptible. The outward wall is, it is said, 5000 yards in circumference.

After resting from the fatigue of ascending, which was very great, we returned down the hill, and saw a tank or cistern, about 100 yards from the summit, cut out of the rock, and containing, I should think, forty hogsheads of water.

It seems evident that this place is the ancient Tagara; and its present diminution in size may be accounted for from the seat of government having been removed to Arungabad. It is likely, from the vast labour and time employed upon the face of the scarped rock, that it must have been the citadel of a place of great importance; and the vicinity of the caves of Ellora induces a belief that they were probably hollowed out near the population of some great city. The Hindoo name for this fortress is Deoghur, a name by no means applied by way of excellence, as it is common to forts throughout India. There is one in Guzeratte, and another in Bundelcund. It remained in the hands of the Hindoos till the year 695 of the hegira; and it is remarkable, that, though supposed to be the strongest place in the Dekhun, it was the first which fell to the Mahometans, on their earliest invasion south of the Nerbuddah. It was at that time in the possession of a Hindoo prince named Ram Deo, and surrendered to Sultan Alla, who was then general of the imperial forces, and commanded an expedition, which deserves no other appellation than that of a predatory incursion. In 707 of the hegira Ram Deo was again vanquished by Malik Caffoor, an Abyssinian, whom the conqueror had left as his deputy. But a pacific agreement was at last entered into, and he was no longer troublesome to the Mahometans. His son, however, from some cause which is not known, was closely pressed by Malik Caffoor, who, through his interest at Delhi, received orders to strip him of his dominions; and in 711 of the hegira, he seized the young rajah, and put him to death. In the early part of the fourteenth century of our era, the emperor Mahomed the third, son of Tonglick Shah, having conquered great part of the Dekhun, and being much pleased with its situation and strength, attempted to make Deoghur his capital, the name of which he changed to Dowlutabad, or the fortunate city. To people his new metropolis, he depopulated his ancient capital Delhi, by driving, with the utmost cruelty and tyranny, the inhabitants from their homes, 800 miles to the southward. But this violent and wild scheme naturally failed, though not before he had ruined or rendered miserable many thousands of his subjects. Mahomed Shah dug the reservoir of water near the summit of the rock, and added a ditch. I conceive that this does not mean the ditch at the base of the cliff, although one of my accounts states that it was not there when in the hands of the Hindoos: but, as it would have been incomplete without, the probability is that the first founder must have formed it. Subsequent to this, in 744 of the hegira, when the Mahometans were driven out of the Dekhun by the sovereigns of Arinkil and the Carnatic, it still remained in their possession. About the year 1595 we find this fortress in the hands of Ahmed Nizam Shah, of Ahmednuggur; and on the fall of this dynasty it was taken by Malik Amber, an Abyssinian slave, who, by his vast talents both in the field and cabinet, almost acquired sovereign power. In A.D. 1634, Mahabat Khan, a general of Shah Jehan, captured it from Sidi Amber, a son of Malik Amber, but I do not know by what means. Ever after, the governor of this fortress was independent of the viceroy of the province, to prevent the latter, in case of revolt, from having so strong a place to depend upon. The frequent instances of treachery and rebellion, from the want of moral principle, were so common among the Mahometan governors, that, as a precautionary measure, Akbar and Jehan Guir made a practice of changing their governors every three years; and we find from Marco Polo, that the Grand Khan of Tartary pursued the same course. Thevenot, at the time he visited it, states that it was a place of great trade. He did not enter the fortress, but describes it as a hill of an oval form; and Tavernier says it is one of the best fortresses in the Mogul's country, and that the gunners in it were generally Englishmen or Dutchmen. He had evidently not seen the inside, as he would naturally have mentioned the subterraneous passage. But in speaking of the difficulty of access to it, he says the road will not admit of above one horse or camel at a time. The seat of government having been removed from its vicinity to the present site of Arungabad, has of course ruined the city dependent upon the fortress.

In 1758 this place fell into the hands of M. Bussy. On the recall of this officer by M. Lally, it returned to its old master, the Nizam; and the French lost, by this inconsiderate step, their footing in the Dekhun, which they have never since regained. The fortress is certainly very strong, and I do not think it would submit but from famine. Shells with short fusees might be effective, but in this case the besiegers would avail themselves of the subterraneous passage, as a bomb-proof. However, though it would have been a good *point d'appui* for the French, still to others it can under no circumstances be of the least importance, as it does not command any road, pass, or country.

It may appear extraordinary that an Abyssinian, as we have seen in the instance of Malik Amber, should have become so great and powerful; but it proves how fated the inhabitants of India have ever been to be ruled by foreigners. Indeed this region has been, from the earliest ages, the sport of revolution; nor is there, in the history of any other, so many instances of sudden vicissitudes of fortune, nor of the rapid rise of so many daring and able adventurers. Among the natives, this was the result of there being no hereditary nobility, the great pillar of political stability and cohesion, as is exemplified in Europe. The field was open to all who could boast more talents, and often more vices, than their fellows. Foreigners have at all times had the greatest influence throughout the country. The feeling of the Mahometan conquerors naturally respected those, who from the north-west brought to their recollection the country from which their forefathers originally came; and we find the Arabs and Abyssinians, from the remotest period, playing a great part in the Dekhun. The extraordinary rise of Malik Amber and of George Thomas* are examples; and any one who has viewed the state of society in India under the native princes will probably agree with me, that should our Indian empire ever fall to pieces, or by the pursuit of a tame or weak system be reduced to debility, an individual of talent, backed by a sum of money, would acquire prodigious control, and even territorial possessions. I am convinced that an European with abilities might, as long as his funds lasted, (and in India, where possession of a country gives right to the collection of the revenue, he would never probably be in want of them) not only gain a footing by well arranged plans, but could not fail of making himself an independent chief, and perhaps establish a dynasty.

* This adventurer, an Irishman, came to India in a British ship of war, in 1781 or 2, having served as quarter-master. He quitted this ship at Madras, and joined the Polygars, but in 1787 he arrived at Delhi, and entered into the service of the Begum Sumroo. On a dispute with this sovereign, he entered the service of the Mharattas; he continued increasing in power and character, till he formed a small independent territory in the Hurrianah, and at one time commanded a little army with a well-organised train of artillery. In 1801, he however fell under the increasing French army of M. Perron, in Scindiah's pay, and died near Berhampoor in 1802, in comparative poverty.—*Vide Franklin's Life of George Thomas.*

CHAPTER XVI.

Intelligence of a corps of the enemy—Arrive at Toka—Officer commanding the post—River Godavery—Village inhabited by Bramins—Sungum—Human Sacrifice—Bheels—Savage tribes throughout India—Introduction of the Bramin religion—Instalment of the prince of Biccaneer and Jeypoor—Camp—Ghun Put Rao—Salee Mehumed Khan—Bombay troops—Improper conduct of the irregular cavalry—Picquets—Approach of a body of cavalry—Mode of raising troops in India—Bad system—Quit Toka—Leave the cavalry of the Nizam on our ground—The author at once becomes captain of a caravan—Alarm—Confusion—False report—Discipline unknown to the irregular horse—Arrive at Sooné—Unpleasant reports—Sooné belonging to Scindiah—Agriculture—Population of our provinces—Advantages of our rule to the natives—Mr. Burke's invectives—Reflections on our government—Canal of Ali Murdhan Khan—History of this nobleman.

Toka, 25th January, 1818.

I QUITTED my kind friend Captain Sydenham at nine o'clock last night, and arrived this morning at three in a village where my thirty regular Bengal cavalry and a fresh set of bearers were posted. I did not intend to proceed from this place to Toka until the arrival of Captain Hicks and the escort of infantry, as we had received intelligence in the course of the day before of a Zemeindar, about five miles from that place, having assembled 200 Arabs and 300 horse in the Peishwah's interest. But as there remained several hours of darkness, I hoped under cover of it to push on to this place, in which I succeeded, having arrived within sight of it at seven o'clock in the morning. The town made a very good appearance, the houses being all of stone, and several stories high. I sent a serjeant to inform Mr. Arden, the officer who commanded this small post, of my approach, begging him to inform me where I could find ground to encamp on, and he sent an orderly as a guide for my escort, and one to conduct me to himself.

Having crossed the Godavery, I found him on the bank ready to receive me, and accompanied him to his house in the town. The part of the river I forded is not above knee-deep, but immediately opposite and above the town it is impassable. The village appears to be situated on a sungum, or angle formed by two rivers, of which the Godavery is much the largest, and Mr. Arden informed me it was a present from the Peishwah to its sole inhabitants the Bramins, the spot being a sacred one. Nearly all the angles formed by the junction of two rivers are sacred, and the most celebrated throughout India is that at Allahabad, at the conflux of the Ganges and Jumna. Here many sacrifice themselves annually by drowning, or waiting in the water till the alligators carry them off. The Godavery is one of the sacred rivers, and is called the Gunga of the Dekhun. My two fellow-travellers had not arrived, and, by answers to my anxious inquiries if the road on to Ahmednuggur was open and safe, I learnt that large bodies of the enemy's horse were moving in all directions, and the Bheels on the alert to act against any thing to which they felt themselves equal. These are a savage race of men, who have neither partaken of the civilization nor prejudices of castes of the Hindoos, and are in a most barbarous state of society. The Bheels extend throughout the province of Arungabad, Khandeish, the Concan, to the north of the Nerbuddah, and throughout Guzeratte; and under the name of Koolies, form one of the savage tribes spread through the Rajahpoot provinces. They are supposed to be the Aborigines of the country, and strongly corroborate the idea, that the Bramins and their religion have been introductions of a later era. Similar tribes extend over nearly the whole of India, in the same manner as the Bheels. I have remarked that a great part of the Rajah of Nagpoor's dominions is inhabited by Gonds, who are stated to have been the original possessors of that district, and though they now belong to the Hindoo religion, they have much fewer prejudices than others of the same faith, and have no idea of impurity from poultry and fowls. In Bengal, the Ram Ghur Hills, almost within the last 30 years, were inhabited by a race of savages, till civilized by Mr. Cleveland. And in the other wild parts of India they exist under the name of *Getes, Bhattees*, &c.: Abul Fazel mentions them under the name of Bunmanies.

From what I have before argued on the subject of the northern origin of the Bramins, added to the consideration of the military character, and the profession of arms standing so high as only to be inferior to priesthood, it may be thought not impossible that the Hindoo religion was introduced by conquerors at a very ancient period, like that of the Mahometans, from the north: for Indian annals prove that the natives of this country have always been liable to conquest; and it is curious to remark, that the general course of history from the earliest ages strengthens the supposition, as the northern nations have at all times conquered the less hardy kingdoms of the south. The Goths overrun Europe; the Pithans and Moguls the country of Hindoostan; the Tartars China and Thibet; and we have only one exception to the contrary, in the conquest of the Arabs and Saracens, which was guided by a religious fanaticism. A confirmation of this theory is, that in the Rajahpoot states in Biccaneer and Jeypoor the sovereigns are still installed or enthroned by the class of persons, whom tradition alleges to be the original inhabitants of the country. In the first of these states they are called the Jets or Getes, and in the latter Meenkas; and the reason assigned for this custom is, that they were in possession of the country before the arrival of the Rajahpoots. I cannot pass over the very remarkable custom or ceremony which takes place on installing the Rajah of Jeypoor. The chief of the Meenkas cuts the rajah's great toe, and marks his forehead with the blood.

After my two companions had joined me, having promised to

dine at four with Mr. Arden, we proceeded to the camp, which I found very well posted, about half a mile from the river.

In the course of the morning we received an account of Gunput Rao having moved towards the Godavery, and of its being supposed he would cross it at a large town about 30 miles down the river, called Monghy Puttun, this day, on his way to join the Peishwah. About two o'clock I received a note from Mr. Arden, intimating the arrival at Sooné of Lieutenant Hamilton with 200 infantry, who are to act as my escort. I think I shall now be strong enough to cope with any adversary I may meet, and trust to reach Ahmednuggur on the 27th.

The conduct of Sallee Mehumet Khan, and the irregular horse, has been represented to me as being excessively remiss. Captain Hicks reports that he has not seen him since he quitted Arungabad, and not above half his men have come on. He has, however, since arrived in camp, and his men have dropped in by twos and threes; but as this piece of neglect had so soon followed his absurd excursion to Rosah, I showed that I was much displeased with him. He seemed to feel that I was annoyed, but though he said he had come 30 miles that morning, I would not allow of his excuses for not being ready with 24 mounted men at six o'clock; as I determined to post some light cavalry picquets round us at night, so that it should not be from want of precaution if we got into any scrape. The jemidar has informed me, that he left at Arungabad 20 sick and lame horses tired out by my rapid march.

The rajah, Govind Buckish, having at my request furnished me with several pairs of hircarrahs, I have sent some to Sooné, and others to villages upon my flanks, and I trust I shall be aware of the vicinity of any of the enemy's troops. I have also given directions for the horses to remain saddled all night.

I have been very much pleased with the appearance of the

detachment of the 4th regiment posted at this place, being the first of the Bombay native army I have seen. They are stouter than the Sepoys of the Madras army, and appear in very fine order, though disfigured by a very ugly cap, to describe which would be totally impossible.

Sooné, January 26, 1818.

After dining yesterday with Mr. Arden, I returned at six to the camp to place the cavalry picquets, while Captain Hicks posted the infantry sentries as usual. But to my astonishment, none of the Nizam's horse were ready, and the difficulty I had to turn them out cannot be conceived. The jemidar alleged as an apology that the horses were being cleaned, and the men cooking their dinners; and did not appear to be aware of this incorrectness in point of military duty, after I had warned him in the morning. About eight I succeeded in procuring the number of men I required, and taking a serjeant and two of the regular cavalry with me, I galloped round, though quite dark, and posted six small picquets of four mounted men each, causing one man to continue mounted, and allowing the other three to sleep, being well aware that I was now on hostile ground. These were about gun-shot in front of the infantry sentries. I proposed that the serjeant, and two regular cavalry who accompanied me, knowing the road round the picquets, should act every two hours as patroles, taking a fresh man with them, so that three times in the night a double patrole would go round the cavalry picquets. After I had posted them, I returned to see if they were all upon the alert, and had I been an enemy, could have passed between them, as their burning matches showed exactly where they were stationed. This I obviated, by placing the mounted men who had their matches lighted about 200 yards to the flank of the other three, and it was past nine before I returned to my tent.

About 11 I received a note from Mr. Arden, with the information that what we had heard in the morning concerning Gunput Rao was correct, being corroborated by an express to me from Captain Sydenham. This was fated to be a night of uneasiness. About 12, a body of horse appeared in front of the camp, and were stopped by the picquets. Their sirdar, after stating they were friends, presented a note directed to a British officer at Poonah, being a recommendation for their reception into the auxiliary horse at that place, and they desired to be admitted into the camp. This was of course refused, and they were ordered to take post in front of the picquets.

This mode of recruiting throughout India is the usual manner of assembling the armies of the native princes. Upon a larger scale, an officer of character receives an order to raise so many men, infantry or cavalry, getting a certain sum for each man and horse per month. These in general are like Falstaff's ragged crew; and as they do not receive above half what is given to their chief, they are of a most miserable description, and few of the sovereigns, or their lieutenants, ever inspect their armies.

This morning before three we quitted our camp, and I suppose the jemidar and his men had not recovered the fatigues of their march the preceding day from Arungabad, as they all remained on the ground, not one of them being ready to accompany me. To my astonishment, though the regular cavalry had been saddled all night, and the order was general and positive, when I rode up to awake the irregular cavalry, I found they had not a single horse ready, and we proceeded without them, having the advantage of a fine moon, and our road lying across an extensive plain. I was this day for the first time, except on the excursion to the caves, able to ride, having only completely recovered from my accident at Jubbulpoor, the effects of which incommoded me most seriously during the whole of my march. After proceeding about eight miles, the irregular cavalry overtook us, and the jemidar of the small corps of about 40 men, who had presented themselves to the picquets last night, offered me his nuzzur; and I told him that if he conducted himself to my satisfaction, I would add my voice to his recommendation. But while I was arranging this, and posting him to the rear guard, thus increasing it to above 60 men to cover the baggage, I was astonished to see the crowds of people and baggage animals I had with me. I must have had from Arungabad from three to four thousand souls, and as many camels, horses, and bullocks; and I found myself at once chief of a caravan of the most motley description. Several merchants at Arungabad had asked leave to accompany my escort, the road to the westward having been so long closed owing to the disturbances in the Peishwah's country, and I granted it to them. But if the few who asked my permission availed themselves of it, immense numbers besides paid me the compliment of trusting to British power and generosity, and accompanied the escort without leave being asked or obtained. They covered the whole line of march; and in this dilemma the patrole upon the right galloped in, informing me that 4000 cavalry were moving upon us. Cornet Elliott immediately mounted his horse, and I sent him to the head of the troops to direct them to move very slowly, while I tried to keep the irregular horse in order. Some of these were loading their matchlocks, others flashing them off, some drawing their swords, and all talking and crowding round me in the utmost confusion. My horse, which I had never mounted before, proved a most vicious animal, and kicked and flew at all the other horses near him.

The news spread to the moving mass of baggage which began to extend all over the country to the left of the road, and I gave up all hope of doing any thing with them. I rode however at a gallop to bring my regular cavalry to cover them, when Captain Hicks met me and quieted the alarm, which had originated in an immense herd of Brinjarry bullocks; and very well satisfied we all were to find it was a false one.

This absurd elucidation of our bustle enlivened us much, and had, at the same time, the effect of bringing along with it the pleasing dramatic associations of old England, by reminding us of Major Sturgeon's adventure, when attacking the gibbet at Hounslow. I speak the Hindoostanee very imperfectly, and though the irregulars seem to be ready enough, yet in the din they all made, being under no sort of discipline and all talking as loud as they could, I think, had the alarm proved well founded, we should have been in a very unpleasant situation.

I found the greatest part of the cavalry belonging to the Rajah Govind Buckish had come on with us, their sirdar not being able to make known to them my orders to return from Toka to Arungabad, as they did not encamp in any regular form; and when the rest moved off this morning, they also accompanied them. Sallee Mahomed Khan was very desirous after this alarm to know if the Bengal regular cavalry were to return with him;—a proof how highly the irregular horse in India respect and look up to our regulars.

On my arrival at this place, I found Mr. Hamilton with 200 infantry, who was on the point of marching to meet me, as a large body of the enemy's horse were moving on to this place. He presented me with a letter from Captain Gibbon, containing the information that 1500 horse, under a zemeendar of the Peishwah named Dhumajee, had set out from the neighbourhood of Ahmednuggur on the 24th (the day before yesterday), announcing their intention to attack this place and Toka. Captain Gibbon also stated that a body of 5000 Pindarries was on the banks of the Godavery four days ago, at a place called Pattery.

It requires some explanation to account for the intention of

Dhumajee to plunder Sooné, as it may naturally be supposed that a town in the centre of the Peishwah's dominions would belong to his highness. But it is a village of Scindiah's. This is very common throughout the Mharatta states, and in Malwa there is more than one instance of a town being divided between Holkar and Scindiah. From the vicinity of these bodies of the enemy's horse, I desired all to be upon the alert, and ordered some of the reformed horse out to patrole around. But they have become extremely sullen, and have as good as refused; and I cannot get them even to move into their place in camp from under the shade of some trees. I think, however, with the 550 men I now have in camp, we ought not to be uneasy about any thing but the long line of encroachers on my protection, who, though I should be fully justified in abandoning them, as they incommode us extremely, still, having thrown themselves upon my generosity, I should be sorry, if I could prevent it, that any harm should befal them. I find this place is about 26 miles from Ahmednuggur, and 14 miles from hence is a very bad ghaut called Wamporah, but on this side and beyond it the road is good.

I have observed that the soil is much more clayey than in Hindoostan, and that the natives turn up very deep furrows with their ploughs, while in the latter country they hardly do more than cover the seed. The astonishing extent of uncultivated though valuable ground, in all parts of India, is hardly conceivable; and though the population at present must consist of from one hundred and eighty to two hundred millions, I am convinced it could subsist three times that number. The number of natives in our provinces, which has been stated at sixty millions, is very much under-rated; and the last returns given in to the governor-general of the population of Bengal, Behar, and Orissa, is thirty-seven millions. This is certainly the most thickly inhabited part of our dominions, but I have no doubt, including the upper provinces and our other possessions, the whole must be double; and should we take the Peishwah's country, in addition to our other late acquisitions, the amount of the population under our rule will be above one hundred and twenty millions. I conceive that this result is likely, as the Peishwah having forfeited the whole by his treachery, great part of his fine country must be ceded to us.

From a feeling of humanity and good-will towards human kind in general, it always affords one pleasure to hear of an extension of British territorial possessions; for even should local motives forbid the introduction of our constitution and laws, still from the benignity of our character, which pervades all our institutions, and which from our mode of education becomes, to a certain degree, engrafted in almost every individual, an improvement of the legislature, and of the general welfare of the inhabitants, are the invariable consequences. And I should be guilty of a gross injustice to my country, if I did not here avail myself of the opportunity, as far as depends on my humble testimony, to do away what has been alleged against our national reputation with respect to our conduct in India. The eloquent virulence of a great departed statesman, when aimed at Mr. Hastings, unhappily recoiled on the British character collectively. At the present day it will not be difficult to exculpate Great Britain from the more serious charges, for, long before the persecuted Hastings had breathed his last, an applauding country had placed him above such imputations; but at the time Mr. Burke made his celebrated remark no one was equal to its refutation, nor will I attempt to excuse the early agents of the Company from blame. But Mr. Burke might have been told, with respect to the minor points of our total disregard of the arts or comforts of the people, that Bengal (we did not then hold Hindoostan) was a different country from Europe, as much in customs as in climate, and that the magnificent monuments he wished us to leave would not only have been superfluous but absurd. Caravanseraies or seraies, as they are called in India, are not required in a country where all travel by water in boats capable of comfort and shelter. Bridges, if erected, would have been carried away by the torrents in the rains. He could not have meant that we should build mosques or Hindoo temples, which, from being raised by the hands of infidels, would not have been accepted or occupied. Canals would have been supererogatory, where Rennell tells us there is no town farther than 25 miles from a navigable stream. Roads, excepting one, and that which follows the course of the river Ganges, thrown up by the Mahometans, would have been equally as useless as the canals, where the travelling by water suits the inactivity of the people, and agrees with the climate and prejudices of the inhabitants. The formation of the great road through Bengal and Behar was effected in 1781 for the purposes of general military communication with the frontier, and for transporting the various implements of European warfare during the time the Ganges was not navigable. We had built a fortress to secure our capital, and unless he would have wished us to have raised triumphal arches or columns to the memory of our many victories, which so zealous an economist never could have approved, I cannot conceive what he would have had us to do. He might have been told we were new settlers in the country, and that we had hardly begun to feel our situation; that the Company held Bengal and their other possessions on an insecure tenure, as their right of territorial possession was much questioned.

But to eradicate any impressions which may remain from his assertion, I must state, that from all I have seen since I have been in this country, the most searching inquiry into its government would only tend to raise the British character higher than ever. Should we lose this empire, it is a happiness to say our name will be revered to the end of time; and though we may not have left piles of buildings as monuments of our dominion, or use-

H H

less masses of frivolous conceited expense, or gigantic altars to impose upon after ages, our government will be ever remembered as having overthrown a barbarous and overpowering tyranny, by the introduction of a mild, equitable, and paternal legislature; for an upright and impartial administration of justice, a security to personal property previously unknown, a vigour unexampled, an extirpation of robbery, and a general diffusion of happiness hitherto untasted. It may be proper here to remark, that certain districts in the southwest of Bengal, in consequence of their vicinity to the uncivilized country of the Gonds, had long been infested by barbarous hordes of robbers called *Decöits*, whose cruelties exceed all description, but that within the last two years these freebooters have been repressed, and the country placed in a state of tranquillity and protection. The exertions of Mr. Charles Oakley, sent expressly for this purpose, were highly eminent, commendable, and successful in effecting this most desirable object.

I wish I could recollect the exact words which the governor-general used in one of his addresses to the students of the college of Fort William: but the sense is strongly engraven on my memory, being consonant with my feelings towards every thing that emanates from Great Britain. His lordship strongly recommended the young men, who were quitting the presidency to hold situations as magistrates and collectors in the distant provinces, to cherish and confine their attention to their duties, and, by their upright conduct towards the natives, to establish a confidence in our justice, impartiality, probity, virtue, and good faith, and make them revere the English name, and hand down to their children's children a remembrance of our mild rule,—which would be more honourable and lasting than inscriptions on tablets of brass, or the erection of marble monuments.

Let us hope that our good sense will ever lead us thus to pay attention to things of real value, and of importance to the whole community, rather than to dazzling with vain show the eyes of a few.

Since the period of Mr. Burke's invective, we have in India, and ought, in the eyes of Europe, to have regained the character which the nation had perhaps lost, in consequence of the actions of a few adventurers; and it is time that the real state of India and of our subjects should be fully known and understood by the whole world. I trust I may assist in removing the veil which has hidden this empire from being seen in its true light, and make all Englishmen feel satisfied of the uprightness of our government and functionaries, and of the advantage those under them receive from British rule.

The present government has also attended to many points of inferior importance, (after that of the happiness of our subjects), which would at any rate save us from so undeserved a rebuke to a great and civilized people. Several of the beautiful remains of the Mahometan sovereigns have been repaired at a considerable expense, and at this moment there is an officer employed to open a canal which has long remained choked up, and which formerly gave fertility to thousands of acres. When India shall again settle into a state of peace and permanent tranquillity from the present active operations, the attention of our government will be turned to a general improvement of the situation of all ranks and classes of the Indian community; and I firmly believe the present extirpation of robbery, and suppression of anarchy, is only the first step to still greater blessings to the numerous population of our far spreading provinces.

The history of this canal which I have mentioned is curious from that of its founder, and being, I believe, unknown in Europe, I will take the liberty of stating the particulars of so noble a work, especially as they may throw light on the policy and character of this interesting portion of the world.

In Shah Jehan's time, the Persian governor of Khandahar, named Ali Murdhan Khan, finding his fidelity was suspected by Shah Abbas, king of Persia, took advantage of his war with the Turks in 1638; and, to save himself from the malice of his enemies, delivered the fortress and province over to the king of Delhi, who received him with every mark of esteem and gratitude, and among other distinctions, conferred on him the government of Cashmir. He was a man of great abilities, and though little can be said in extenuation of his treachery, during the remainder of his life he remained firmly attached to his adopted sovereign, and was by him employed in the highest offices. It may therefore be presumed that nothing but necessity would have driven him to so disgraceful a step. He amassed a fortune so immense, that it was supposed he was possessed of the philosopher's stone; but it is more probable that his wealth was accumulated by the formation of a canal, not for navigation, but for irrigating a sterile tract of ground, between Paniput and Delhi.

This noble canal was about 100 miles from north to south; the water which flowed through it being taken from the Jumna, ninety miles above Delhi, and rejoining that river nine miles below the city. The natives call it Nehur Behisht, or the river of paradise; sometimes the sea of fertility. The revenue of the country through which it flowed was fourteen lacs, but having been neglected and choked up for 100 years, by the political convulsions so prevalent in this region, after the death of Aurungzebe, it does not now amount to more than one lac. Beyond its effects in agriculture, it was of extraordinary consequence to the health of the inhabitants of Delhi. The water of the Jumna, and of the wells, which they are now obliged to drink, is so much impregnated with natron, otherwise called soda, as to prove at times very injurious. The point of the river from which the canal is taken is a great distance from that portion of the country in which the natron is so abundant, and there was a cut made from it to supply the city with wholesome water. There could not therefore be an act of more true beneficence than the restoration of this canal; and so it appeared to the present governor-general, who decided on the undertaking: and the work is now in actual operation, under the superintendence and direction of Lieutenant Rodney Blane, of the Bengal engineers, whom Lord Hastings selected for this duty, on account of the character he had acquired in the scientific pursuits of his profession. There is a fair prospect that the expense of this work will be compensated many fold, not only by the general improvement, but by the tolls taken for water which passes by sluices in the banks of the canal into innumerable channels to water the country on both sides, which will bring back the population, and restore fertility to considerably above a million of acres.

Ali Murdhan Khan was a man of superior talents, and I shall therefore notice a few circumstances of his life, to shew that the court of Delhi could at one time boast of men, who for talents would have been admired at any court. His government of Cashmir was so satisfactory that the superintendance of the Punjab was also presented to him, and he was allowed to hold Cashmir by deputy. He was next appointed governor of Cabul, to regulate that province after the misrule of a former governor. The Usbecks, who invaded his government, were repulsed by him, and he retaliated, by following them into their own country, which he ravaged as far as Balk, and returned with much booty. In 1647, in the war with the Usbecks, he distinguished himself under the command of Prince Aurungzebe, who commanded the army. He afterwards, in 1651, on the nomination of Prince Dara to Cabul, continued in the government of Cashmir, and died in 1656, nominal captain general of the imperial forces. He is stated at the time of his death to have had no less than 16,000 families, who looked up to him as their protector. He died worth 1,895,000*l.*, which devolved to the emperor, according to the eastern custom of the sovereign being heir to all his subjects.

CHAPTER XVII.

Misery of being in camp with undisciplined troops—Advantages of disciplined troops—Prejudices—Singular custom of the Mharattas—Quit Sooné—Wamporah ghaut—Difficult road—Pettah of Ahmednuggur—Captain Gibbon—Escorts—Receipt of letters—Camp—Gate—Monumental tablet—Pettah—Prickly-pear hedge—Fort of Ahmednuggur—Entrance to native forts—Interior of the fort—Vaulted—Once unhealthy—Improvements—History of the fort—Taken by the Duke of Wellington—Guns of large size throughout India—"Great gun of Agra"—Fit object for St. James's Park—Hill forts—Mode of defence—Strength—How provisioned—Rainee—*Fausse braye*—Gateways—Natives defend their forts with great gallantry—Gingalls, or wall-pieces—Bags of powder—Line the ditch with thatches—Success against Hattrass by bombardment—Bheels.

Ahmednuggur, 27th January, 1818.

I ORDERED yesterday a similar arrangement as before, respecting the precautions for our safety; but at the appointed hour neither man nor horse of the Nizam's troops were in readiness, and on my sending for the jemidar, he frankly owned they were so unlike our troops, who had the advantage of discipline, that they were seldom if ever to be depended upon. After waiting above an hour, he furnished me with sixteen dismounted and eight mounted men, and it was near nine before I had posted them round the camp. At twelve I was called and went round the posts, and found two of the picquets absolutely gone away. I immediately rode to the jemidar, whom I awoke, and expostulated with him very warmly on this gross breach of trust, and pointed out to him the unsaddled horses of his troopers, and, to bring it more home to him, his own riding horses not in any way prepared, although ours and those of the regular cavalry had been saddled all night.

The irregulars are, I believe, displeased with being brought beyond Arungabad, as the majority of them have their families in that city; and they appear by no means satisfied with my peninsular ideas of military duty. I look upon discipline in an army to be as great a blessing as organized government, to which it bears an affinity, is to a civilised community; and as no man would, if he could avoid it, live in the latter, without the support and comfort of this great requisite, I hope I shall never again quarter in the same camp with troops thus wholly unbridled and lawless. An officer, with them, is little better than the captain of a band of robbers; and were not my journey nearly at an end, I should feel inclined to dispense with their assistance. They were informed, the day before yesterday, that they would not find corn in Sooné for their horses, nor flour for themselves; and I proposed that they should bring on one day's provision of each with them, and tying my handkerchief, of which they all have several, shewed them how it might be done; but they are so wedded to their own ideas, it had no effect, and I was in hopes they would have gone without, but the civility of the good subjects of Scindiah prevented this, by furnishing them with what they required.

I know of nothing more ridiculous than the childish custom among the Mharattas of adding to a substantive a word of no meaning, which rhymes with it, which they practise particularly when they wish to speak with "a winning fondness." Thus if they want *otthur* (wheat) for themselves, they will inquire if there is not in the bazar *otthur watthur*—*roote* (bread) is *roote poote*—*dana* (grain) is *dana wana*, and thus throughout the language. It is a curious circumstance, which has been remarked to me, that this custom was common in several ancient languages, and is at this day exemplified in our own. For instance, *hurry scurry*, *helter skelter*, and many others.

We quitted our camp near Sooné at an early hour this morning, and about seven arrived at the foot of the ghaut, which presented a very bad road and strong ground. I moved the infantry to the top, while I kept the cavalry below in the plain, and hastened the baggage and merchandize as much as possible; but it required more than two hours before all was over. I do not recollect ever to have seen stronger ground, and had we been opposed, it would have been impossible to have forced it with our small force. In many places it was absolutely necessary for the animals to climb over the rocks. On reaching the top, a fine plain presented itself, and extended the whole way to Ahmednuggur.

The pettah, only lately taken possession of by General Smith, was visible from a considerable distance; but the fort was not in sight till within 1000 yards, the ground gradually sloping towards it. After paying my respects to the officer who commanded the fort, I went into the pettah, where I found Captain Gibbon, who requested me to be his guest for the day. Captain Gibbon informed me that Colonel Fitz Simmons, of his majesty's 65th regiment, had ordered 200 Sepoys and 50 horse from Seroor to meet me half-way at Ragin Gaum; and in the course of the day I received several letters, one of which was from Mr. Elphinstone. But from the number of cavalry and emissaries of the Peishwah surrounding General Smith's camp, the extreme difficulty of sending papers is such, that it only contained the expression of his regret at not being able to give me details of what was passing in this quarter, and mentioned that Mr. Coates, the medical officer attached to the residence, who was left at the city of Poonah, would give me every information I might require.

After breakfast, and promising to dine with Captain Gibbon, I went out to the camp, which I found well posted near a fine stream. The gate through which I passed on my way out of the pettah is close to the site escaladed by the troops under the Duke of Wellington; and on the very spot, in the face of the wall, is introduced a black stone tablet to the memory of an officer of the name of M'Kenzie of the 78th regiment, who was killed there. It is very neat, with his crest above, and some words in the Gaelic language,

—I suppose his motto. This memorial was raised at the expense of Lady Hood, who, while travelling through India, passed this place, and ordered its erection. The names of two other officers of the same regiment, who fell at the attack, are also inscribed on the stone.

About five I got upon my horse, and rode through the pettah to the fort. The latter is about 1000 yards from the former. The pettah means, in India, a town which is dependant on a fort; and there is in general space left between them, so as not to hinder the fire of the fort from having due effect upon besiegers. The pettah is generally surrounded by a wall; in this instance it is not high or thick, but within it is an immense prickly-pear hedge, about 20 feet high, and the first I had seen, though common in native forts. No human being can pass it without cutting it down, and this is a matter of the utmost difficulty, as it presents on every side the strongest and most pointed thorns imaginable. Being full of sap, fire will not act upon it, and the assailants, while employed in clearing it, would be exposed to the enemy's matchlocks from behind, so that it is stronger than any abbatis or other barrier that can be conceived. The pettah was taken by escalade in 1803, by British troops under the Duke of Wellington.

I went on to the fort, and entered it through a small bazar under its walls. The ditch is very deep and broad, and passing over a drawbridge, the road runs nearly round a large *burj* or tower, and is exposed to the flanking fire of the curtain and the other towers. On entering the first gate, I found myself in a small court surrounded with high walls, whence another gate opens into the fort. Thus, should the assailants force the first barrier, they would only gain for themselves a place to be slaughtered in. Nearly all the native forts have similar entrances, though not exactly upon the same system. Almost opposite the gate which opens into the interior of the fort, about 150 yards from it, is a large and high castle or tower, with an arch passing through it, and appearing to me to have been built for the same purpose as the keeps of the old castles in England.

The fort, entirely of stone, is I think nearly an oval, about a mile in circumference, with a vast number of large round towers. During the time it was in the possession of Scindiah, before it fell into our hands, he had added to the walls some useless works of brick and mortar, which have not been removed; and, at the same period, some scaffoldings for musketry were placed over the cannon in the towers, the latter being fired through a sort of port-holes in the wall which continued above them. This fort is, I believe, almost the only one in India of the native construction which has a glacis to cover the foot of the wall, the natives always attaching strength to height, and valuing the imposing appearance rather than the intrinsic strength of a rampart, which consists in being secured from fire. The walls between the towers are not very thick, and the distance from one to the other not above 80 or 90 yards. The whole area within the fort is vaulted beneath for stores, and as usual, when any subterraneous place is formed, the reports of treasure being buried in it are in general circulation. At one time, from the ditch being full of stagnant water, it was the grave of many officers; but of late improvements have been made, and are in progress, an engineer being employed in draining the interior. Barracks are to be constructed, and another gate opened, for at present it has but one.

Ahmednuggur was built in the year 900 of the Hegira, by Ahmed Nizam Shah, king of Bidjapoor, who gave it his own name. Two years subsequent to this, he built the fortress. Ahmednuggur was taken in 1601 A. D., after a long and bloody siege by Prince Daniel, and an unsuccessful attempt to relieve it by the confederate princes of the Dekhun. Prince Murad had been previously beat off in 1595. It was given up by the Peishwah to Scindiah, when the interest of this prince predominated at

THE GREAT GUN AT AGRA.

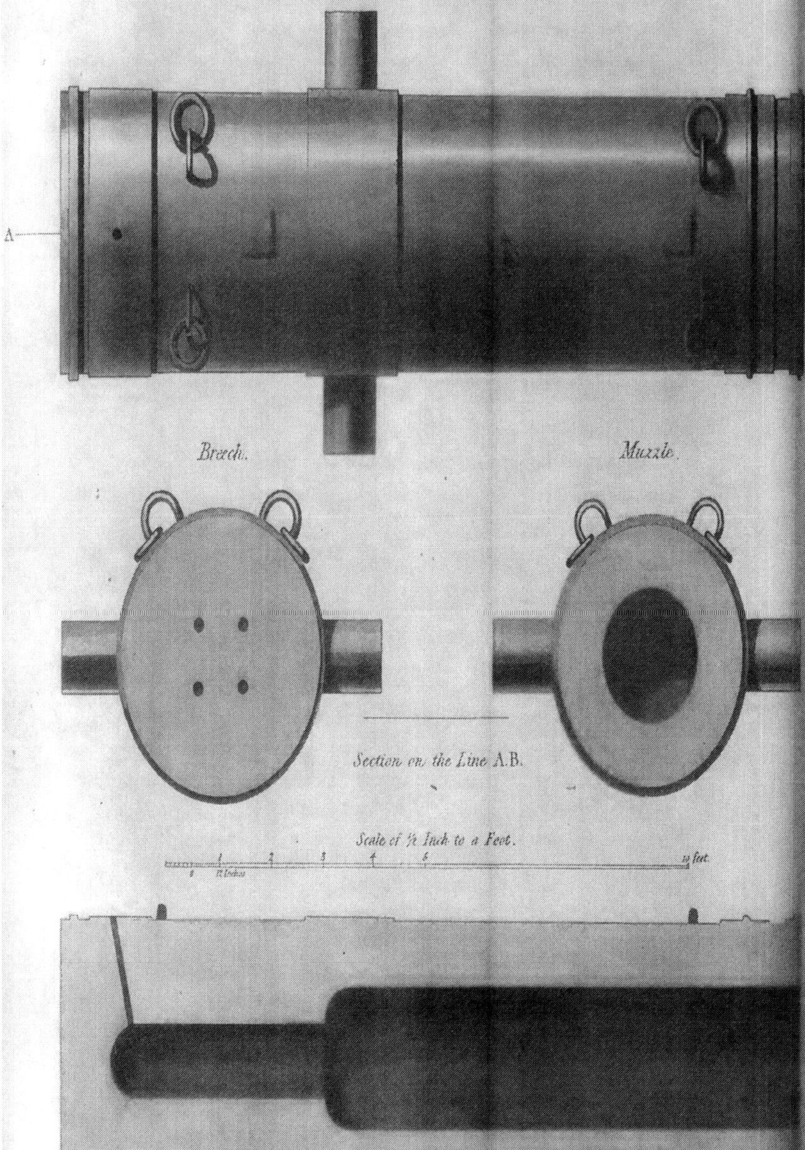

Poonah, as it had previously fallen under the rising power of the Mharattas; and on the 12th of August, 1803, it was taken possession of by the Duke of Wellington, and has ever since remained in our hands, though by all accounts, gold belonging to his highness the Peishwah, then our ally, though now our enemy, was more successful than the steel or lead. There is here a famous gun about 25 feet long, which is stated to have carried shot into the camp of the duke, though out of range of all reasonable weapons.

The natives of India, and indeed of every eastern nation, seem to have been anxious at all periods to render this destructive engine, from its size, more powerful than those of the western world; and I have witnessed some curious instances of what may be called their extravagance in this way. At Agra I have seen a gun more like an immense howitzer, above 14 feet long, 22½ inches in the bore, into which persons can get: the following is a table of its dimensions.

TABLE OF DIMENSIONS.

Nature.	Weight.			Diameter of the					Length of the			Weight of the Shot if Iron.		Weight of the Shot if Marble.	
				Calibre.	Chamber.	Muzzle.	Trunnions.	Base Ring.	Chamber.	Chase, including the Chamber.	Piece.				
	Cwt.	qrs.	lbs.	Inch.	Inch.	Inch.	Inch.	Inch.	Inch.	Inch.	Inches.	lbs.	oz.	lbs.	oz.
1500lbs. brass.	1049	1	4	22 5	10 8	46 5	11 3	48 6	51	159	169 5	1497.39	0	567	0

Weight in maunds 1469.

Value of the gun as old brass, in Sonaut rupees, 53,400; but if serviceable, it may be estimated at one lac and sixty thousand.

This gun was once supposed to contain much gold; and even as old brass, it is valued at 7000*l.*; but if serviceable, it may be estimated at about 18,000*l.* It at present lies near the banks of the Jumna, outside the wall of the fort. An attempt was made to transport it down to Calcutta, but its embarkation failed. I wished exceedingly, when I saw it on my first arrival in India, that it should find its way to England, to be placed in St. James's Park, near the trophies of Africa and Europe represented by the Egyptian gun, and the Spanish mortar from Cadiz, and thus complete the military tribute to the British arms from three quarters of the globe. At Delhi, opposite the Lahor gate, is a gun of a very large bore; and the reader will doubtless recollect the two guns at Nagpoor called Gog and Magog, which were, I think, finer pieces and better proportioned than this at Ahmednuggur, which has drawn from me these observations.

At the siege of Trichinopoly, in the early part of our career, the British used a large cannon, which tradition stated had been sent by Aurungzebe from Delhi, and required a thousand yoke of oxen to transport it. We read that at the siege of Rintinpoor by Akbar, in 1656, the emperor had with him two guns, which threw a ball stated to be more considerable than even that of the gun at Agra. There are also several others scattered over this country, at Dacca, Delhi, &c.

Ahmednuggur appears to me to be very strong, and is one of the few fortresses which the natives have formed, without having some natural recommendation. It is in places almost inaccessible, on the summits of hills, that they usually construct their fortresses, and in the defence of these they use large stones, some round, considerably larger than cannon-balls, and others in the shape of small rollers, which being thrown over the walls, destroy every thing on the face of the hill. From the strength, and almost impracticability of reducing these hill forts by storm or breach, a large quantity of grain, of which the food of the Indian soldier principally consists, is looked upon as the best security, after that of the loyalty of the governor;

and should they also have water, a killidar would be looked upon as very unfortunate or treacherous if he did not hold out till reduced by famine; for the more active parts of a siege are seldom undertaken by the native powers.

The investment of an eastern fortress did not in general consist of any thing beyond a blockade; and it will be seen by a reference to Indian history, that the surrender of these forts has been caused more by treachery and scarcity than by any other means, and that the length of some sieges in this country equal those of Troy, Ostend, and Mantua. The food of the Indians being almost entirely rice, which is perhaps the least perishable of any article of subsistence, the defence of such places may be the longer protracted. Though the natives did not understand the construction or advantages of a glacis, still they saw the necessity of covering the foot of the wall from the enemy's fire when exposed to it, and formed a defence similar to our fausse braye, which they call Rainee. They are very partial to loopholes to fire through, and in the mud forts form them in the walls, of baked earthenware cylinders. The gateways of their fortresses are mostly very difficult of access, the entrance being through several turnings at right angles with each other before you arrive at the body or interior of the place. Each of these narrow and confined lanes is generally enfiladed with guns, and loopholed on every side, so that should the enemy force the outer gate, they find themselves exposed to a continuation of fresh dangers from an invisible garrison at every turn. I am not, however, a good judge of native fortresses, as I have only seen those of Chunar on the Ganges, of Allighur, and of Agra and Delhi. The gates at Agra, Allighur, and Chunar, are examples of this difficulty of entrance.

The Indians, in the defence of their forts, behave with the greatest gallantry and courage, and in this differ from the Europeans, who often fancy that when a practicable breach is made in their walls surrender becomes justifiable. But here all feel desirous of fighting man to man, and look upon the contest in the breach as the fittest occasion for meeting their enemies with their sword and dagger. They use large heavy wall pieces called gingalls, which send a ball of two or more ounces to a very considerable distance. Having no shells or hand grenades, they cast bags of gunpowder into the ditch, which exploding by fire thrown on them, scorch the assailants; and at times they have had recourse to thick earthenware pots with fuses, and full of powder, the pieces of which wounded dreadfully. They have been known to line the sides of the ditch with straw thatches, and by throwing other lighted thatch on their enemies envelope them in flame.

Our success against Hattras has been a wonderful encouragement towards taking all the native forts by similar means, that of bombardment; and from their having no casements, shells are the most effective means for reducing them.

While we were in the fort, we were informed that the Bheels had collected in the Wamporah Ghaut, with the intention of opposing us, having assembled 3000 men, variously armed with matchlocks, bows and arrows. But the appearance of our long line of march, and the numerous followers and baggage, caused them to apprehend they were too weak. I suppose some individuals we had seen on the top of the hill were a party of these ruffians.

I returned to dinner at Captain Gibbon's, and got late to my tent; but previous to dismounting from my horse went 'round the different posts, and to my surprise found all on the alert.

CHAPTER XVIII.

Quit Ahmednuggur—Poonah auxiliary horse—Major Ford's battalion—Road unsafe between Seroor and Poonah—The Peishwah's movements—Strength of the escort—Augmentation of the Bombay army—The Indian army—Extraordinary rise—Fine order—Bengal troops—Warfare in India—Khetri tribe, or Rajahpoots—Bramins bear arms—Alexander—Ancient mode of war—Fire weapons—Chariots—Swords and shields—Ancient armies numerous—Human sacrifices—Cavalry—Little or no discipline in the Hindoo or Mahometan armies—No formations in their battles—Reflections on discipline—Advantage of the flint-lock over the match-lock—Natives have no idea of the value of time in military operations—Steady pace—Armour generally worn—Elephants cased in iron—Chiefs mounted on them—Ancient sieges—Gunpowder—European gunners—Engineers—Cannon like those at Cressy—Light guns in Aurungzebe's army—Bullocks draw the guns—Artillerymen good—Miners—Rockets—Arrows—Regular troops in the service of the native princes use flint-locks—French first aid the native princes—Foreigners common in the Indian armies—Early European garrisons—Portuguese did not drill the natives—The French did so first, but did not succeed so well as we have since done—Retrospective view—Great change—The minimum and maximum of our Indian empire—Dress like the Europeans—European troops, both French and English—Arabs and Abyssinians in M. Bussy's army—Precedence of M. Bussy—Recalled by M. Lally—Native powers attempt to form disciplined Sepoys—French influence destroyed in 1761—Their attempts to re-establish themselves—Vigorous policy of the Marquis Wellesley—Treaty of 1814—First British subsidiary force in 1768—Various subsidiary forces—Inferiority of the undisciplined troops of the natives—Change of dress—Turban—Feathers—Leather—Volunteer battalions—Mahometan and Hindoo prejudices—Siege of Jeypoor—Conduct of Ameer Khan—Retaliation—Anecdote—Mark of caste—Attachment of our Sepoys—Anecdotes—Insurrection at Benares in 1809—Quelled by the Sepoys, although their religious feeling worked upon—Insurrection at Barelly—Anecdote—Conduct of the Sepoys at Poonah—Reflections—M. Lally's conduct towards the Sepoys—His ignorance of the prejudices of the natives—Change of condition among the soldiery of India.

Ragin Gaum, 28th January, 1818.

AT three o'clock we left our ground near Ahmednuggur, leaving the Nizam's infantry, I had brought with me from Arungabad, to return to that city. The country we passed over was in general very barren and somewhat hilly; and when within a few miles of this place, we fell in with several of the Poonah auxiliary horse, who were out patroling. These men had a different character from the other irregular cavalry I had previously seen, were nearly all armed with English cavalry carbines, swords, and pistols, and were dressed in small red vests, with yellow edges, tied on by strings of the same colour. They were generally small men, and not well mounted.

Soon after we had arrived in sight of this village, Captain Wilson, who commanded the escort sent from Seroor to meet me, rode up, and informed me of the strength of his detachment; I found it consisted of some of Major Ford's battalion, formerly in the Peishwah's service, and about half the number of the 2d battalion of the 1st regiment of the Bombay army, which had behaved so gallantly at Corry Gaum, on the river Beemah. Captain Wilson stated that the road between Seroor and Poonah was very unsafe, so much so, that I must take with me a piece of cannon, 100 Europeans, 200 Sepoys, besides all the auxiliary horse that can be collected. But the latter suffered so severely at Corry Gaum, that they are very far from numerous. This officer had been out on convoy duty a few days since, and was surrounded by the enemy's horse, whom he foiled in carrying off any thing, except about twenty bullocks laden with grain.

Captain Wilson brought me a letter from Colonel Burr, who commands at Poonah, and who so highly distinguished himself in the action of the 5th of November at that capital, recommending me not to go on from Seroor if the Peishwah should turn to the northward, and inviting me to be his guest. Captain Wilson however states that the Peishwah has gone to the southward. I have taken up my ground on a very excellent spot, out of gun-shot from the town, which, like Sooné, belongs to Scindiah. I have now near 250 horse in camp, and 400 infantry. I have placed the Poonah auxiliary horse as my rear guard, and all are ordered to remain saddled; and having sufficient force, I shall at night post two flank picquets, of a serjeant and twelve men. These auxiliary horse behaved very well when moving with General Smith, from the Godavery back to Poonah, although he had no regular cavalry in his division.

Captain Wilson has informed me, that in consequence of the late disturbances, the army under the Bombay presidency has been considerably augmented. It had previously consisted of only a troop of horse artillery, a battalion of foot artillery, nine regiments of infantry, of two battalions each, and a marine battalion. The addition consists of two regiments of cavalry, a battalion of infantry added to that of the marine, which has thus been formed into the 10th regiment, and another, the 11th, newly raised, of the usual force.

What an army does the state of this country render necessary! The regular numbered troops alone, exclusive of provincial regiments, invalid battalions, irregulars or auxiliary corps, now under the command of Lord Hastings, as commander-in-chief of India, without reckoning the king's regiments, consist of

6 Troops of European horse artillery,
3 Troops of native horse artillery,
6 Battalions of foot artillery,
18 Regiments of cavalry,
3 European regiments of infantry,
64 regiments, or 128 battalions of native infantry;

and this has grown out of a few petty factories, and the speculations of merchants. The expense of a great part is borne by the native princes.

The immense number and efficiency of our Indian army forms as fair a criterion of our strength and vast possessions as tracing our territory on the map; since, in time of peace, it now nearly equals in numerical force the whole army of the king in the four quarters of the globe, and certainly equals it in discipline and good order. It, however, requires that these corps should be seen to be duly valued; and I will venture to say, that the finest picked corps of the European sovereigns would not, by the side of the Bengal battalions, appear in size, weight of men, or military respectability, superior to them. They are admirable troops, and when it is considered that we have a choice of men from all Hindoostan, and of course prefer the hardy and martial race of Upper India for the materials of our army, where the most powerful and finest men perhaps in the world are nurtured,—men who, by the most violent and athletic exercises, maintain to the last their muscular force and physical energies,—this fact will no longer be looked upon as extraordinary.

War was at a very early period practised as a separate profession throughout India, and was held so high in estimation, that the military, as in ancient Egypt, ranked as a caste only inferior to the Bramins or priesthood, and took the precedence of all others by the institution of their first lawgivers.

In the Rajahpoots of the present day, who have never till lately been completely conquered, we still see the pure Khetri tribe, whose bravery is too well known to require any comment. They are in all probability the Catheri spoken of by Diodorus Siculus; and if a supposition, which has been hazarded, of the introduction of the present Hindoo system and religion, be correct Rajahpootanah was the allotment of the military class. The profession of arms was not, however, confined to these alone; for the Bramins themselves, unlike the Levites of the Hebrews, filled the ranks of the sovereign, and even the sanctity of the priesthood gave way to war.

We find the Indians opposing the army of Alexander with great resolution; and the amazing strength and numbers of the army of the Prassi and Gangarides doubtless tended to make the Grecian army desirous of checking the progress and ambition of its own leader. With respect to their mode of warfare in early times, we have accounts of their using multitudes of elephants, and of their soldiers being armed with bows and arrows, swords, shields, and javelins. Though fire weapons are by name strictly prohibited in battle by the laws of the Hindoos, and guns are mentioned by an historian of good authority to have been used eight hundred years ago, yet it is impossible to say whether by this expression the effects of gunpowder are really meant. There is reason to believe that chariots for war were in use among the ancient Hindoos, in common with all the armies of antiquity, as they are represented with two or more wheels in the sculpture at Ellora, recording (as it is supposed) the expedition of Rama to Ceylon; and are also mentioned by the historian of Alexander. Straight swords and clubs are in the hands of the figures at the same place, though the former at this day are all more or less curved. The shields represented at Ellora are exactly those now used, being circular, and with only one strap for the hand to hold them in the centre of the inside. The ancient Hindoo armies appear to have been very numerous; the slaughter consequently dreadful; and it was sometimes permitted to sacrifice a human being before a battle or expedition of great consequence. The Bramins were ever foremost in the ranks, and when they fell in action in the heat of blood, there was not the same importance attached to it as to their violent death under other circumstances; for by the Hindoo religion, whoever killed a Bramin was doomed in his future state of existence to inhabit the body of an unclean animal for as many years as there were particles of dust absorbed by his victim's blood. It is singular that the early Rajahpoot armies consisted principally of cavalry, though at present they form the best infantry of the British army. But the generality of the ancient armies of India, like those of the middle ages of Europe, were principally composed of large bodies of horse, and the infantry was despised, and considered to be of no value; though our discipline has since proved in India, as it has in all parts of the world, that infantry, when really good, is the strength of the battle. There was little or no discipline in the armies either of the early Hindoos or of their conquerors, the Mahometans of a later period; and, as at the present day, their cavalry appear to have ever moved in goles, or balls, being large congregated masses, and thus made their charge in the shape of a wedge.

The natural bravery of the natives, both Mahometans and Hindoos, was very great till the introduction of an artificial courage by our discipline, which seems to have eclipsed, if not wholly put an end to, the display of individual courage. I never met with any instance of regular formations in the native armies, and I do not believe the practice existed at any period till introduced by the Europeans. The necessity of submitting to discipline, and the confidence inspired by combined and united movements, comes in room of personal prowess, and in aid of that contempt of death and dread of shame in which the spirit of a soldier consists. A disciplined army may, and not without reason, be said to resemble an extensive combination of machinery, the parts of which, inert and inactive in themselves, are by the hand of science and system made to act in unison for the attainment of some object; and by these parts, though they may be damaged in the course of service, still, if repaired by fresh materials, the work is continued.

The Chevalier de Bayard is said to have regretted that the introduction of gunpowder would destroy all true courage: perhaps it may have been remarked on the introduction of discipline, that it might (as it undoubtedly has done) in some degree diminish that generous, warm, enthusiastic valour of old, and the opportunities for its individual display. This has been changed into a passive yet determined obedience, of a quality fully as laudable, grounded on the conviction of its expediency. We have seen in modern armies, that though the individual may not be interested, the very lowest and most debased of human kind may become excellent private soldiers. Bengal, in the time of Lord Clive, furnished good battalions of Sepoys, though the most despised and pusillanimous people: at present they are never received; and among Sepoys the epithet Bengalee is a term of reproach. The great Frederic formed his armies of the lowest and worst class of men, recruited from the various vagrants in the free towns of Germany; and it is well known what noble efforts they made. We all have seen, of late years, a nation which had, for the last few centuries, been far behind the rest of Europe, both in civilization and spirit, by the assistance of British discipline and courage, overthrow the veteran armies of France at the very point of the bayonet, and emulate the heroism of their forefathers in this country and on the coast of Barbary: while an adjoining nation, admitted to be possessed of much higher moral qualities, was most discreditably foiled in the field, in consequence of not submitting to be trained.

When former ages are reviewed with the eye of a soldier, as well as with that of a statesman, it will be seen that the superiority of the Greeks and Romans in the field over the barbarians who opposed them originated in the close form and discipline of the troops. Subsequently their generous and tolerating policy secured what this discipline had conquered. It is a curious circumstance that the state of India under the British should, in both these peculiarities, resemble strongly the state of nations overcome by the Romans. It is discipline, together with a quick firing of the flintlock and field-pieces, which has given us the striking superiority over the natives. It is the steady fire of these that the troops of the native princes cannot face: that regularity of movement, quickness of evolution, and strict and unerring obedience in action, giving union and combination, opposed by confusion, clamour, distraction, and insubordination, must ever secure a commanding ascendancy. The natives have no idea of the value of time in military operations; the most frivolous excuses or causes preventing the movements of their armies, which will always make an active and regular force superior to them. They express their astonishment and the utmost dread at the steady and continued fire of our Sepoys, which they liken to a wall vomiting forth fire and flames.

The firm and regular pace, the first and most necessary part of a soldier's instructions, is quite incomprehensible to them; and in this we again see the almost total change requisite to complete a soldier, as he is not allowed even to use his legs, but in a prescribed manner. Armour was at all times worn on the arms, breast, and head, and sometimes dresses of chain armour were in use, and the war elephants were even cased in iron. The chiefs, from the time of Porus, till of late years, were generally, if not always in action mounted on elephants; and these animals themselves are stated to have taken part in the affray, by wielding immense and heavy chains, and dealing out overwhelming blows. Their sieges were carried on under the first Mahometans in a manner similar to those of Europe before the discovery of gunpowder, not only slowly, but hopelessly; and it was seldom any thing but famine which reduced the garrison. Ferishta mentions, at a very early period, as Dow tells us, that guns were used at the battle between Mahmood of Ghizni and the confederate Hindoo army in 1008, A. D. 399 of the Hegira. But as engines for throwing stones are subsequently spoken of, I am not satisfied that the weapon we now use is meant by that historian.

As early as the reign of Humaioon the Mahometans appear to have understood the use of artillery, and even of shells; but I do not think they had the assistance of European gunners till the latter end of Akbar's, or the beginning of Jehan Guir's reign, when they became extremely common; and artillerymen were the first Europeans to prove the ascendancy in war of the western nations over those of the east. The engines alluded to appear to have been a sort of catapultæ. Any one, ignorant of the English history, might fall into a like mistake, with regard to the use of fire-arms in this country, for cross-bows and archery went by the name of artillery.

The Portuguese found fire-arms in the hands of the natives; and, from several specimens I have seen, (of what date I am uncertain,) the first attempts of the Indians to make cannon were, similar to those mentioned as being used at the battle of Cressy, of bars of iron hooped together. I have, however, in one instance, at Delhi, seen an improvement on this, wedges of iron being placed as radii hooped together, so as to form the gun. Aurungzebe, we learn from Bernier, had light field guns, drawn by horses, which we have only within the last twenty years introduced into our Indian armies, as horse artillery.

For the first time during the present campaign, by way of experiment, in the Bengal army, horses were employed for the foot artillery; bullocks having always been, and still continuing to be, the usual draught animals throughout India; and in the native armies it was not uncommon to see thirty or forty yoke transporting one of their heavy guns. Yet they have been decidedly found most inefficient, from their slowness, being perfectly unable to keep up with the line after the first discharge; and, in case of retreat or defeat, the guns are always left behind.

The artillery at present in use among the natives is generally an iron cylinder, with molten brass cast round it. Their artillerymen are mostly good; but though shells were used by the Mahometans before the reign of Akbar, as stated in Dow's Ferishta, they are at present unknown to the native powers. Mining was common amongst them; and rockets were early brought into use, and are far from being an ineffectual weapon. They have an iron cylinder fastened with untanned leather thongs, and transported on horses or camels, and, on being lighted, an additional impetus is given to them from the foot of the thrower. They will pass through the body of a horse or man. We read of the musketeers in the army of Akbar being armed with very heavy arquebusses, with rests; but the matchlock is to this day the weapon of the country. Arrows were, until very lately, in general use, and are not even now entirely given up; and I have been informed that, during the late war with the Gorkahs, they fired small ones of iron out of their matchlocks. The flintlock, an introduction of the Europeans, is far from being general, and, I may even say, is never employed by the natives: though the Telingas, armed and disciplined after our manner, in the services of Scindiah and Holkar, make use of it. Some good flintlocks are, however, made at Lahore.

No improvement of any kind appears to have taken place in the art of war from the time of Akbar to the middle of the eighteenth century, when the French first, and subsequently the English, when aiding the native princes, changed the whole system, by the introduction of the European warfare, as far as the character and customs of the country would admit.

It was no unusual circumstance for these princes to have foreigners in their service. Arabs and Abyssinians have ever formed part of the armies of the Dekhun; and in Hindoostan the Mahometans have always preferred to those born in the country the Tartars and Moguls who came from the north-west; and Tippoo, at one time, sent to Persia for 1000 horsemen. This feeling had paved the way for the introduction of European mercenaries.

The early garrisons of the forts and factories of the European nations in India did not consist of natives of the country, but of a class, who, in all probability, would not have found employment in any other service, including many Caffres and half-casts, who, from wearing hats, were called by the natives Topasses, from tope, a hat; as the native soldiery of India, whether Mahometans or Hindoos, all wear turbans. There is reason to believe that the Portuguese did not discipline the natives, as we have since done: the French have the credit of preceding us in this system; and here, as in other cases, we have improved on the invention of that nation.

In 1746, at the siege of Madras, we find the French had 400 natives in five companies, whom they had disciplined like Europeans, at Pondicherry. The French, however, never made their Sepoys so good as ours; and it is even supposed that they were not clothed, but only armed like Europeans. This instance in 1746, mentioned by Orme, is the first we have on record; and at this period the English had not adopted the system, as 2000 peons, or irregular infantry, were taken into our pay on the occasion, and 800 or 900 muskets were for the first time distributed amongst them.

It is curious to take a retrospective view of an English factor at his desk in 1746, with a pen behind his ear, trembling at the nod of the meanest of the Mogul's officers, and treated with the greatest insolence and oppression;—with no higher military character under his direction than a peon stationed near a bale of goods; with a jurisdiction not extending beyond a court-yard of a warehouse connected with it; and contrast this picture with the situation of the Company's army in 1817, when 150,000 men, disciplined by British officers, presented the spectacle of as fine an army as any in the world, receiving its impetus of action from a great statesman and general, who held the person of the Mogul a pensioner upon the bounty of his government, wielding the political and military resources of the empire over a theatre of operations in the present campaign, extending from Loudheanah to Guzaraut, in a segment of a circle of nearly 1200 miles. Such are the minimum and the maximum of our Eastern empire!

In 1754, the first king's regiment that ever landed in India, the 49th, with forty artillery-men, under the command of Colonel Adlercron, arrived at Madras; and in the same year the French likewise received 1200 Europeans, including 600 hussars; and, from the draughts which had previously arrived, the two nations could bring into the field 2000 Europeans on each side.

Up to this period, and even later, the progress of the French was very great in the Dekhun; and M. Bussy had, without the appellation, in 1753, a subsidiary force in the service of the Nizam, consisting of a battalion of 600 Europeans and 5000 disciplined Sepoys, posted at Arungabad, besides the 600 Europeans, 400 Topasses, and 4000 Sepoys in the Carnatic. In 1756 he had added four troops of cavalry to his force; and in the early part of the same year had commissioned the French agents at Surat to levy a body either of Abyssinians or Arabs, who, being endued with more courage and hardihood than the natives of the Dekhun, he intended to discipline as the choicest of his Sepoys. Of these 600 had been collected, but were either dispersed, killed, or taken in their attempts to join him at Hyderabad, after his rupture with the ministers of Salabat Jung in that year. The force of the two nations in 1756, on the coast of Coromandel, Orme, from whom the greater part of the historical matter respecting our military career is taken, tells us was 10,000 Sepoys on each side. The pay of the French battalion, in the service of the Nizam, Salabat Jung, was most exorbitant; and M. Bussy took the precedence of all his sirdars. In all probability M. Bussy, from his talents and address, would, after 1758, when he had taken possession of Dowlutabad, have established the French power throughout the Dekhun. He commanded a very fine army, and he had confirmed himself in the strongest influence at the court of the Nizam; but being recalled by M. Lally, the structure which he had commenced, and of which he had firmly laid the foundation, was totally overthrown. In 1757 the regiment of Loraine had been added to the French king's troops on the coast of Coromandel, and the following year the regiment of Lally came out.

It was natural that the native powers, who then possessed military men of genius and talent, should be anxious (seeing the great advantages that troops disciplined after our manner had over their own system) to form in their own services a similarly efficient force. In prosecution of this design, as early as 1752, a Mahometan of the name of Mursapha Khan, who had been previously in command of the Sepoys accompanying M. Bussy from the Carnatic to the Dekhun, and making the most of the knowledge he had acquired in this school, raised and disciplined a corps of 4000 Sepoys, and hired them out to the best paymaster. The King of Travancore, in 1755, by the assistance of a French officer named Launoy, disciplined, in like manner, 10,000 Nairs after the European method.

The French power in India being crushed in 1761, they have since made several endeavours indirectly to re-establish it, at the court of the Nizam, at that of Tippoo, and with Scindiah. At the first of these, subsequent to 1792, the force organised by the officers of this nation consisted of twenty-three battalions, which carried the colours of the French republic, having the cap of liberty on their buttons, and being in a most efficient state. Their attempts to aid Tippoo were of a more open and decided character than those in favour of the Nizam; and the considerable French army which Madajee Scindiah had originally formed, and which under his successor was commanded by General Perron, consisted, previous to 1803, of near 40,000 men. All these various efforts were crushed by the active and vigorous policy of the Marquis Wellesley; and an article has been ever since introduced into all the treaties with the native powers, not permitting them to retain any European in their service for the pursuance of the same object. The treaty of peace of 1814 obliges the French to be content with troops sufficient for police alone, and has rendered it improbable that they will ever gain at any future time, in any part of India, the means or opportunity of annoying us.

The first subsidiary force granted by the British was, I believe, that to the Nizam in 1768, though we had acted previously as auxiliaries to the native princes, not only on the coast of Coromandel, but in Bengal.

The accumulation of the Company's army kept pace with their

accession of territory. The Newab of Oude received, in 1775, a subsidiary force; as did the Rajah of Mysore in 1798. The Peishwah followed their example in 1803. Two years ago the Rajah of Nagpoor was placed in a similar situation, and this year we have seen Holkar obliged to receive the same assistance from us.

Having myself witnessed the inferiority of the irregular infantry and cavalry of the native princes, the astonishing want of discipline, and the difficulty of bringing them into any kind of order, and also their attachment to their ancient habits and prejudices, it seems almost incredible, that in the short period of 60 years, we should have been able to bring about the total alteration that has been made. To point out the difference between the feeling of the natives some years since, the astonishing change they have undergone, and how they give way to a mild, gradual, and well judged encroachment on their prepossessions, when not openly nor rudely assailed, I need only mention, that there is not at this day a man of the highest caste who will not be grateful for European medical assistance, if the medicine be taken from his own vessel, and given him from the hand of one of his own caste; a compliance which would formerly have been considered as the highest pollution. The Sepoys did not for some time give up their native costume, but now the loose Indian dress has given way to the more compact European; and in Bengal the Sepoys, with their faces turned from you, cannot at this day be distinguished from the king's troops.

The gradual change of dress has strongly marked the gradual advance of our conquest over their prejudices. At first they would not wear any thing but the turban; but now the cap of blue cloth used throughout Bengal, and introduced into the armies of the other presidencies, is the French chaco, with only the difference of being lower on one side than the other. In the eighth Bengal cavalry they have absolutely introduced it, so that the European officers and the native men will now wear the same head-dress.

It is contrary to the ideas of the Hindoos, and an act carrying impurity with it, to touch the feathers of our domestic fowl; yet in a battalion under the Bengal presidency, many of the Bramins of the highest caste wear them in common with the rest of the battalion, and would not part with them on any account, as they were given them as a mark of distinction for their conduct, when under the command of Lord Lake.

The Hindoos and Mahometans fasten their vests on different sides, thus marking in a distinct manner the religion to which they belong; and it was for this reason at first difficult to introduce our European jacket without lapels, and single-breasted; but it is now universally in use throughout the whole army. Difficulties were also made, both by the Hindoos and Mahometans, about coming in contact with leather, fearing it might be that of a cow or hog; and in the Madras cavalry to this day, though they use boots and saddlery, they will not wear leather breeches; but in Bengal, all the native cavalry dress like the Europeans. Greater trouble has at all times been experienced in persuading the Madras Sepoys to receive innovations than those of Bengal; and they do not wear pantaloons with buttons, but trowsers fastened with a string round the waist. In Bengal, the Sepoys will even wear cloth pantaloons; and I have seen a regiment of light infantry, a volunteer battalion, returned from Java,* at Barrakpoor, setting all prejudices at defiance, and wearing ammunition shoes and gaiters, and European felt caps and feathers.

The Mahometans, in becoming soldiers, have but few obstacles to overcome; but the Hindoo has a prospect before him of many severe privations in conforming to his duties as a soldier, and to these he submits with the greatest patience. Should he be exhausted with the most parching thirst, I have been informed, he must not drink in the morning unless he has first bathed, which it is often impossible to admit from our strict rules of service, particularly when near an enemy, as all their clothes and appointments must be taken off. They cannot even cook or eat, but almost in a state of nudity; and they have been known to refuse to drink water, though much distressed for the want of it, when it has previously been defiled by other castes.

At the late siege of Jeypoor, by Ameer Khan, the garrison, which consisted principally of Hindoos, suffered much from the want of water; this Mahometan chief having cut the throat of a cow, and thrown her into the tank from which the garrison procured the greatest part of this necessary—thus rendering it in the highest degree impure to the Hindoos. They have occasionally annoyed the Mahometans by slaughtering hogs, and using them in the like manner.

I cannot adduce a stronger instance of the good feeling which has at times been entertained by the European soldiers for the Sepoys than the following anecdote, which speaks highly for both parties, and I heard it from authorities which I have no reason to doubt. The 76th regiment served under Lord Lake for so long a period with the Sepoys, that they had become attached to each other; and the former being aware of the prejudices of the latter, have been known, when they happened to arrive the first in camp, to wait till Jack Sepoy (as they call him) had drawn the water he wanted from the tank or well. Ought not this example, though set by common soldiers, to make those in higher sphere and more civilized countries blush, who have not known how to respect and tolerate the prejudices of their fellow creatures?

The difficulty encountered in ordering or persuading the Sepoys not to wear the mark of caste on their face is unknown in the Bengal presidency, where in all the highly disciplined regiments it is not permitted on parade.

The following anecdote will prove that the Sepoys are heartily and sincerely attached to their officers and our government. During the late events at Poonah, indeed, that attachment was put to a more severe trial than could ever have been expected; and I will venture to say, it is the universal feeling throughout the armies of the three presidencies towards their leaders. The credit of having established this affection is due to the British officers who are immediately placed over them, and who by their justice and mild conduct have so rooted it in those under their command as to extend the principle from personal partiality, to the whole system of our government.

The very touch of a dead body, or any thing deprived of life, would be to a Bramin the greatest stain of impurity which could befall him. But in more than one instance, the native officers and soldiers, many of whom were Bramins, have insisted, from a sense of gratitude, on carrying a European officer to his grave. The lips of a European defile beyond recovery a vessel out of which he may drink; but the Bramins in action have allowed their European officers, and even requested them, to drink in this manner from their vessels. It should therefore be recollected, that all the victories and territories we have gained, and all the discipline which has led to them, are owing alone to our European officers attached to our Sepoy battalions; and that the great machine of our Indian army, which we now see in a most perfect state, should be ever strongly cemented by the attachment of the soldier to his officer. It must on this account be our unalterable policy to prevent the former from thinking, or even suspecting, that he can do without the latter: unhappily a very few officers are posted to each battalion, as all the staff situations throughout India are filled up from the regimental officers, which makes it possible and likely that an evil so much to be dreaded may eventually be felt. I have seen a battalion on parade, after having furnished the necessary officers for camp duty, left with three officers, including the commanding officer and adjutant; and many battalions at this moment have but five officers to do duty. It is evident then that some alteration must and will doubtless be made, by separating such appointments as the commissariat and barrack department from the line, and by the court of Directors sending out cadets, so as always to keep the corps of regimental officers full.

The discipline and fidelity of the Bengal Sepoys have, in several cases, been put to the severest test, even by having their religious prejudices worked upon in points on which they are the most scrupulous.

A strong proof of this occurred in 1809, on the occasion of a dispute between the Mahometans and Hindoos in the city of Benares. Both parties, with the illiberal and intolerant spirit ever attendant on fanaticism and religious persecution, insulted each other's opinion, and defiled each other's places of worship, in the manner most offensive to their respective feelings. The Mahometans cut the throat of a cow, the most sacred animal of the Hindoos, on a stone altar in a sacred tank, within the precincts of the holy city; and the Hindoos, by way of retaliation, killed a hog, the most offensive animal to the Mahometans (who in many points follow the Mosaic law), in one of their mosques. This gave rise to a bloody dispute, and rendered it necessary to call in the military. The Mahometans, being greatly outnumbered by the Hindoos, had been expelled from the city. But the Bramins, finding the Sepoys brought in to quell the tumult, called out to the Hindoos in the ranks, that the origin of the dispute was a religious one, and threatened them with the heaviest imprecations if they acted against them. The Hindoo Sepoys, though in all probability next in the ranks, and touching one of the hated religion, only answered by levelling their muskets, and thus put down the disturbance.

In the late insurrection* at Berelly, when the Pithans rose upon the small force stationed at that place, the Sepoys, though for several days exposed to the utmost danger of being overcome by numbers, and though sorely pressed, fought and quelled the re-

* This insurrection broke out from the Pithans mistaking the intention of introducing a small rate, to pay for a night watch in the city, for some heavy impost; and being worked upon by designing men, attacked our military.

Fitz Clarence fec.t Engraved by R.Havell & Son

SEAPOYS.

of the Bombay, Bengal, and Madras Armies

London. Published April 1819 by John Murray, Albemarle Street

bellion; not a man deserted; and even of the irregular cavalry, though raised in the same city, and acting against their friends and relations, only one man quitted his ranks, and was immediately, for his want of faith, cut to pieces by his comrades. I have understood that the fidelity of the Sepoys, during the late disturbances at Poonah, was exposed to the greatest temptations; and neither bribes, threats, nor cruelty, could induce them to swerve from their duty.

I anticipate no probability of an alteration in their sentiments toward us, as they see the character and success of our government, not depending upon an individual, as among themselves, but supported by the exertions of several hundred functionaries, amongst whom are many military men, superior to their first officers, and who for a period of the last seventy years have almost invariably carried its victorious arms throughout India. In addition to this, the greatest advantages are held out to bind them to us. They have invariably found us just and good masters, paying them their stipends to the hour they were due; and all are deeply interested in the continuance of our rule. The stability of our government is made more secure by the Sepoys being spurred on to general good behaviour, from the prospect of rising in time to the situation of officers, and of continuing so, in case our power should remain unimpaired. In addition to this, pensions being given to them after wounds, and settlement of lands after long service, will make them, while we respect their opinions and religion, as much to be relied on as our European soldiers.

The impossibility of overcoming prejudices and customs was early proved, by the violence of M. Lally's temper at the siege of Madras, in 1758. He had just arrived from Europe, full of ideas engendered in that quarter of the globe; and, with the besotted obstinacy of ignorance, attempted, abruptly and violently, to break through their habits. He wished to have made the Sepoys work in the trenches, which being the duty of the lower castes, was contrary to every feeling of the higher, and the soldiers at that time enrolled amongst the French Sepoys would rather have perished than have dug a trench to cover them from a musket ball. He even attempted to make others, besides the Koolies, carry burthens, which is a service appointed to this caste, who are, like the rest of the Hindoos, so rivetted to their manners, that they will not carry any thing on their shoulders, but on their head alone. This violence towards the French Sepoys not only caused great desertion from the army, but the accounts of it spread with such celerity, that a reinforcement about to join was considerably diminished on the road, from a dread of the unusual services to which they heard those in camp were exposed.

So great a change has taken place, since the time of M. Lally, by allowing time and forbearance to work their own way in the British service, that the highest caste man looks upon it to be as much his duty and will fill a gabion with as much readiness, as a grenadier in a king's regiment. The introduction of our system, and the regular behaviour and conduct we insist upon, has, in a great degree, altered for the better the military classes in India; and will no doubt, in a few years, entirely supplant the disgraceful and obnoxious *condottieri*, who have arisen since Aurungzebe's death. That this is now taking place every day must be evident, from the increase of our subsidiary forces in the countries of the native powers, which renders a reduction of their unorganized troops necessary. Indeed as far back as thirty years ago the irregular soldiery felt the difference occasioned by the introduction of our mode of warfare; and we learn from the Seir Mutagherin that they complained at that period of the loss of employment from this cause. How much more must they now feel it, when our empire, or the system under our influence, that of subsidising, has extended over about three-fourths of India!

CHAPTER XIX.

Quit Sooné—Painful reflections—Pindarries—Instance of their turpitude—Arrive at Seroor—Size of cantonments in India—Auxiliary horse—Poonah subsidiary force—Orders from General Smith—Difficulties in continuing the march—Accounts of the Peishwah's army—Determined to proceed—Arrangements—Sepoys disguised—Salee Mehumed Khan—Milk plant—Accounts from Poonah—Still determined to proceed—Phoolsheer—Quit Seroor—Bengal cavalry—Camel-drivers desert—Precautions—Sepoy hircarrahs—Arrive at Corry Gaum—Account of the late action in the village—Anecdote—River Beemah—A European in the service of the Peishwah—Pass the river—Arrive at Wargolly in safety—Suspicious rencontre—Approach Poonah—Its appearance—Intelligence of the Peishwah—Visit the position to cover the corps at Poonah—Cantonments burnt—Sungum, the residence of Mr. Elphinstone—His valuable papers destroyed—Gossains or devotees take advantage of the disturbances—Peishwah's intended palace—Flag-staff—Kirkee—Field of battle—Account of the action—Mora Dikshut—Alarm of the Peishwah—Excavation—City of Poonah—The Peishwah's palaces—Marquis Wellesley's picture—That of Sir Barry Close—Globes—Sacred chamber—Idol with an elephant's head—Annual fête—English clock—Orrery—Peishwah's palace—Bed—Nana Fernavez—Attempts to induce our Sepoys to desert—Accounts of the Peishwah—Comparison of the Mharatta empire and that of Germany—Sevajee—Fall of the house of Timor—Invasion of Nadir Shah—Disorganization of Hindoostan—Invaded by the Mharattas—The various generals become sovereigns—Battle of Panniput—Scindiah—Defeats in 1803, 4, and 5—The Rajahs of Satarrah compared to the *Rois fainéans* of France—The Rajah with the Peishwah—The present Peishwah—His eloquence—Unpopularity—Treasury—Goklah—Southern Jagheerdars—Ghun Put Rao—Colonel Deacon and Captain Davis—Leave the Bengal cavalry—Trimbuckjee—Reduction of the Pindarries.

Seroor, 29th January, 1818.

AT daylight this morning we found ourselves about ten miles from this place, having beat the drum at half-past one o'clock, and moved off our old ground before three, after taking leave of Mr. Hamilton, who returned to Ahmednuggur.

This country was the scene of the violent devastations committed by the Pindarries, and the whole of it was plundered by them. A hill, about twelve miles from hence, was pointed out to me as being the position taken up by two officers with a small guard, not amounting to ten men, who defended themselves, though with the loss of several lives, against these robbers, killing many of them, till a relief from Seroor arrived. A circumstance was also mentioned to me which puts the turpitude of these lawless defiers of all institutions, human and divine, in its proper light. A surgeon was travelling in his palanquin in the vicinity of Seroor, with an English boy about ten years old, his servant riding a horse by his side, when a party of the same wretches approached them. The surgeon got out of his palanquin, and desiring the boy to dismount, galloped off, not doubting but his youth would save the child. But he had miscalculated in supposing these villains had any commiseration for age or sex, as Captain Wilson informed me he found the boy speared to death. But when the tender and weak frame even of females did not check their bloody hands, little better could have been expected.

As we approached this place, its magnitude surprised me, extending for above a mile along the foot of a hill lately fortified, and only inferior in size to Khanpoor, or Futty Ghur, under the Bengal presidency. Persons in Europe will be astonished to hear that the former of these places stretches five miles along the banks of the Ganges, and contains above two hundred and fifty well built European houses, with good and roomy offices, each surrounded by a garden. It boasts a bungalow for a chapel, theatre, custom-house, barracks, large artillery ground, and, on the outside, an excellent race-course.

As we entered the cantonment, we passed the encampment of the Poonah auxiliary horse; who it appears suffered most severely at Corry Gaum.

This cantonment was formed here for the Poonah subsidiary force, being forty miles from that capital, thus making the reliefs easy, as one or more battalions were always at that city. I waited on Colonel Fitz-Simmons of the 65th regiment, who informed me that he had received orders from General Smith not to permit me to proceed on to Poonah, should the Peishwah have marched to the northward. He stated that by the intelligence received this morning his highness was understood to have done so, and recommended me not to go on. He at the same time advised me to consult Captain Betts, who commanded the cantonment, and who, from his knowledge of the language of the country, had charge of the intelligence department, to obtain information from him, and to make my report in the course of the day. I accordingly went to Captain Betts, in whose house I met Captain Staunton, who commanded at the action at Corry Gaum, Captain Swanston, who commanded the Poonah auxiliary horse, and many others.

It appeared that the Peishwah had been obliged to turn to the north, and, if moving only with cavalry, it was thought he might be near Corry Gaum, or Phoolsheer on the river Beemah, by this night; the former of which places lies on the direct road from hence to Poonah. All reports agree that he has left his guns and infantry in Nepaunee, a fort subject to him, belonging to one of the southern jaghirdars. In his former route to the northward he passed by these two places along the banks of the Beemah, the immense body of cavalry he had with him rendering it absolutely necessary that he should move in the vicinity of some considerable stream; it is therefore probable he will again attempt the same road.

After many arguments on both sides, whether to go, or wait for more certain intelligence, I made up my mind, unless some certain news arrives of its being impracticable, to quit this at six o'clock in the evening, and to take along with me my regular cavalry, the

Nizam's horse, all the Poonah auxiliary horse I could procure, and 200 fresh infantry, with 100 rounds of ball cartridge for each man, to be carried on the camels belonging to the regular cavalry, leaving their grain and baggage at this place; for should we reach Poonah, we shall get plenty there. Some hircarrahs have been sent out to the southward, as well as some horsemen, to inquire if any rumours announce the proximity of the Peishwah's army; and two Mharatta Sepoys in our service have disguised themselves, and gone on to Corry Gaum, with orders to remain in that town if all is safe, but in case of the enemy's appearance to come back and meet me.

On my going down to the camp to inform the jemidar of the Nizam's horse of my intention to move on at six o'clock (this allowing them above eight hours rest), he alleged the impossibility of undertaking a further advance of forty miles, after so long and fatiguing a continuation of marches as they had had from Nagpoor. As I concluded the enterprise and dash would have stimulated all in a similar manner to myself, this refusal made me extremely angry; but as I am fully aware that the troops I have with me could not be saved from destruction if we fell in with the whole army, and that the 200 infantry are sufficient, if posted in a village, to keep off any bodies of hostile cavalry, I have not pressed the matter. They, however, said they would go with me on foot, but this I conceived to be, and treated as, a *façon de parler*.

Some ladies, who had fled hither for shelter from the storm his highness the Peishwah had raised against us at Poonah, wished to accompany me this evening; but as I felt they would be rather out of their element should we have to defend the already bloody spot of Corry Gaum, I have determined they shall not proceed with me, and also refused a piece of artillery which was offered me. The latter would only encumber us, and the happy termination of our enterprise entirely depends upon the suddenness and celerity of our movements.

The hedges around the houses here are formed of what they call the milk plant. It is a sort of creeper, and on a branch being broke off a white liquid exudes of a very caustic nature, so as to injure the hands. It acts also as a very strong cement, and is so highly poisonous that it is frequently employed to render the wells useless.

Three o'clock.

A letter has been received from Mr. Coates at Poonah, advising me not to venture on, and stating that Colonel Boles has moved from the Little Bhore Ghaut to the eastward to head his highness. If he arrives there before the Peishwah, he will be between him and us, and I have still determined to attempt the march, though it is a little hazardous. But were I to remain here any longer, it is possible that the road might be rendered unsafe for several days. This is the only instance of a serious nature in which I have had to judge between rashness and want of enterprise, and my journey through this disturbed country drawing to a close, I feel that I do not too much offend against prudence in endeavouring to proceed. I have consequently sent off four of the Poonah auxiliary horse to patrole, and not to return till they see an enemy.

I have made myself master of the ground between this and Poonah, with the situation and position of the villages; and find the road is entirely across a plain as far as Wargoly, about two miles on the other side of Corry Gaum, and ten miles from Poonah; from thence that it undulates, and is very defensible, and that Wargoly itself is walled, and a good position. The only dangerous part appears to me to be the plain, that extends from Corry Gaum on the Beemah to about two miles beyond that town, being in the vicinity of the favourite city of the Peishwah, called Phoolsheer, or the City of Flowers, where he has many adherents. This city was, a very few years ago, a village; but, by his highness's numerous donations and additions, it is increased very considerably. The whole distance from Seroor to Poonah is not above forty miles; and I hope, by leaving this at six o'clock this evening, to pass the worst of the way before daylight to-morrow morning. The village of Corry Gaum is on this side of the river Beemah, about twenty-eight miles from hence. To be prepared against all events, we are to take a surgeon with us.

Poonah, 31st January, 1818.

After much difficulty, we left Seroor about half past six, on the evening of the 29th; all there very anxious to hear of our safe arrival at Poonah, and ourselves big with the chance we had of another affair of Corry Gaum. Captain Hicks, who had seen me so far, although his destination was Seroor, determined to accompany me quite to this city. I had about 100 of the Poonah auxiliary horse, and 200 infantry, besides my little band of Bengal cavalry, who had been my companions for so long a march without leaving a man or horse behind, and the three right-hand men of the front rank having carried the three captured standards all the way. The camel-drivers, or sirwans, as they are called, thought it so desperate a business, that they attempted to drop behind the first half hour; and on my representing to them the certainty of their destruction if they separated from us, as many bodies of the enemy's cavalry were around, they fairly loosened the ropes of the camels, which ran off the road, with these rascals after them, and I have no doubt made the best of their way back to Seroor; at least, I never saw or heard any thing more of them.

We continued moving as compactly as possible; and I sent forward the jemidar of the auxiliary horse with six men to discover the situation of the village of Corry Gaum, and of the small party which had quitted Seroor three hours before us. I halted about five minutes every hour, and found we had made twenty miles by three in the morning. I patroled all the villages we passed, both through and around them; and, as we had a fine moon, the march was pleasant. When within four miles of Corry Gaum, I was put on the alert, by meeting one of the Sepoy hircarrahs, whom I had sent on in the morning, with orders not to return unless the enemy were in the neighbourhood. I of course expected, the moment he made his appearance, to hear some news of them that would stop our march; but he declared that all was quiet in the place, although I am of opinion he never had been there.

As we approached the sanguinary town of Corry Gaum, I was again thrown upon the *qui vive* by the flash of a gun or pistol in that direction; but, from no report reaching me, I was convinced it had originated in that most unsoldierlike trick so common among the native cavalry in India, of flashing in the pan of their pistols to light their pipe. This is not the first time I have looked with anxiety to the advanced guard after one of these flashes, until the continued stillness has assured me the trigger was not pulled in earnest.

When on the high ground, over the village of Corry Gaum, I observed some fires in the direction of Poolsheer; but was soon satisfied the town of Corry Gaum was safe, as the jemidar in advance sent me word it was totally deserted. We skirted its ruined houses; and I should have been extremely happy to have passed it a mile to windward, as the horrid and corrupt smell from the half-buried bodies of men and horses rendered it most offensive. The enemy's cavalry seem to have been very bold, for vast numbers of their horses lay close to the inclosures; and the usual quantity of old clothes, scraps of cloth, and rags, denoting a field of battle, covered the ground. The jemidar of the auxiliary horse pointed out the house in which our wounded were placed. The fate of Mr. Wingate, a surgeon who was wounded, after distinguishing himself in leading troops to the

N N

charge, is remarkable. He had, I was informed, with the other officers in the same situation, been placed in a small pagoda or temple, of which the Arabs, in one period of the action, took possession. This gentleman was wounded in the arm, and, to stop the effusion of blood, had screwed a tourniquet on. The Arabs, thirsting for plunder, attempted to take it off, conceiving it to be a Tusveez, or charm, such as the Mahometans wear, and, when able, enrich with the precious metals. This, for a reason obvious to us, Mr. Wingate attempted to keep; and the enemy, more convinced, from his unwillingness to part with it, that it must be of great value, in order to secure it, buried their daggers in his body. I have reason to believe that the whole of this inhuman party were bayonetted, as Captain Staunton, aware of the situation of these officers, rushed in, and saved the rest, Mr. Wingate alone falling a victim to Arab rapacity.

This gentleman was not the only medical person who distinguished himself on the occasion, as Mr. Wylie, of the Poonah subsidiary force, led the Sepoys on several times to successful charges with the bayonet.

At the present season of the year almost all the rivers are much diminished, and above two-thirds of their beds are dry sand-banks. Very unfortunately, the Beemah, which runs near the town of Corry Gaum, had withdrawn its waters close under the opposite bank, which is very high, where the Peishwah was posted on his elephant; and, during the whole action, our troops could not procure a drop of water, so that they were situated as if they had been in the deserts of Arabia. The enemy, on the contrary, had plenty of this indispensable necessary of life.

An European is stated to have been seen very active in the army of the Peishwah during the action, and is supposed to be a deserter from one of our corps; though this cannot be accounted for satisfactorily, unless a report be true which we heard, that some Europeans were with the Pindarries, and may have subsequently joined the Peishwah.

After crossing the river Beemah I halted, and found the infantry very much fatigued and straggling; and it became necessary, though in the most dangerous place, and the morning breaking, to remain above half an hour, until nearly all had joined us. I then moved on, and in half an hour more crossed the plain, gained the strong ground, and was satisfied we were in safety. At seven we halted at Wargolly, and permitted the Sepoys, half the number at one time, to bathe in a fine tank. The villagers informed us that the road was quite free to Poonah. One of the natives took me aside, with a great deal of mystery, and showed me under his sleeve, tied round his wrist, a sort of brass medal, very thin, with the letters P. P. on it, and informed me he was of the Poonah Police. This man having corroborated the statement of the villagers as to the absence of all danger on the road, Captain Hicks and myself, after some consultation, determined to push on to Poonah, and to take the Bengal cavalry with us, leaving the infantry and auxiliary horse to come on more leisurely, as many of the former were reported absent.

On our road towards Poonah, as we ascended from the bed of a small river, we suddenly met about thirty horsemen, who instantaneously stopped, seemed to hesitate, and then turned short out of the road, as if to avoid us. One of my men, however, rode up to them, and they resumed the road, *salammed* to me; and, on being asked to whom they belonged, named one of our officers who commanded a corps of irregulars. We accordingly passed on, and never thought more of them.

The plains, in the approach to Poonah, are extensive; and we descried the tents of the troops, which, on a nearer view, we found were pitched in the grounds of the old cantonments, plundered and burnt by our vindictive enemy. The tents, surrounded by hedges of the prickly pear and milk plant, had a very curious appearance.

The city, seen at a distance through an immense grove of mango trees, was about a mile behind the camp, having a back ground of strongly marked mountains, with Sone Ghur, one of the forts given up to us by the treaty of June last, on their summit.

An officer galloped out to meet and conduct us to the tent of Colonel Burr; and, as we passed Major Ford's battalion, several scores of the Sepoys crowded round Captain Hicks to welcome him home, all appearing delighted to see him. It was most gratifying to witness a friend thus cordially received.

I dismounted at Colonel Burr's tent, where I found that officer and Colonel Osborne; and I am now the guest of the former, who is all I could ever wish my most generous host to be.

I was dreadfully fatigued, having travelled at a foot's pace above sixty-five miles on the same horse in less than thirty-six hours, and my mind nearly as much exhausted as my body; but, being now within 100 miles of Bombay, I have reason to trust that my fatigues are nearly at an end. I found the Peishwah was moving to the north, and that no action of consequence had taken place between his highness and General Smith's force; but a great deal of useless skirmishing, and both parties much worn out with marching and countermarching.

It seems the road between this and Bombay is far from secure; and Colonel Osborne, who is anxious to quit this place, to take a command lately conferred on him in Guzaraut, is waiting for the protection of my escort. I therefore settled to leave this to-night, and he is gone on to Tally Gaum with one hundred men, who are to relieve the same number who will accompany me. I thus hope to reach Bombay in thirty-six hours.

I was yesterday informed that 200 of the enemy's cavalry were in Poolsheer when I passed it, and there are about the same number round the neighbourhood of this city. On my stating that we had met a party of irregular cavalry, Colonel Burr assured me they belonged to the enemy, as all our auxiliary horse are armed with English weapons. I thought, at the time they quitted the road in the sudden manner they did, that it was very unaccountable; but I must do justice to their presence of mind, though Colonel Burr says that the same trick has of late been frequently and successfully played off against us. A vast number of the Mharattas received leave to quit our ranks on the breaking out of the war; and, thus knowing the name of our officers, have often resorted to this *ruse de guerre* to escape.

This morning Mr. Coates met me at breakfast, and I promised to call upon him when I returned from viewing the present position occupied by the troops, and the field of battle, between Gunish Kundee and Kirkee, the site of the action of the 5th of November, where my host had commanded. I found that Mr. Coates had taken possession of one of the Peishwah's palaces.

About ten o'clock I mounted a very fine but vicious horse of Major Ford's, and accompanied Colonel Burr along the position which General Smith has pointed out, and ordered him to defend, should the Peishwah attack him during his absence. It is strong, has several works with heavy guns mounted, and the flank and rear strengthened by an abattis and breastworks. The length of its front is about 1000 yards. From the back of the position to the city extends a grove of mango trees in rows, and in every part round the city are similar orchards. They were planted by the order and at the expense of the Peishwah, and their number, we were told, exceeded 300,000.

The same scene of desolation presented itself here, throughout the cantonments, as at Nagpoor, and from the same cause, having been destroyed by the enemy. Every where tents had taken the place of houses, in what in India is called the *compound*, or inclosure round the residence. This is, I have understood, derived from a Chinese word *compong*, an inclosure.

We afterwards proceeded (though the sun was very hot) towards the village of Kirkee, leaving the city on our left, and passed through the grounds of the Sungum, formerly the abode of Mr. Elphinstone, our resident. It must at one period have been a very beautiful spot, consisting of a number of detached houses and cottages, dispersed over a very extensive and well laid out garden; but there is hardly one stone left upon another, and the banqueting-room was as completely in ruins as the rest. Great part of Mr. Elphinstone's valuable collection of papers and manuscripts was lost, and the rage and ungenerous feelings of the enemy were carried so far as to destroy the English fruit-trees, which had been introduced; though their ignorance fortunately saved the most valuable peach-trees, those grafted being in appearance not worth the trouble of extirpating. Immediately opposite the Sungum was a holy spot, inhabited by some Gossains, a most horrid set of Hindoo fanatics. On the flight of the Peishwah's army, our troops being much exasperated, entered this sacred spot, and found these devotees had removed some sofas, tables, &c. to their own quarters from the Sungum; and glasses and several bottles of claret were found *emptied* on the table.

Before we arrived at the Sungum, a piece of level ground was pointed out to me as having been the intended situation of a magnificent palace for the Peishwah, to be erected at the expense of 150,000*l.* by English architects: this project had gone so far that the site was sanctified, by being spread over with cow-dung, and the ground-plan marked out. The Bramins did every thing in their power to prevent its being carried into effect, and I was told gave out that the English intended to bury a living child under the foundation of each column; and the sudden disappearance of some children, doubtless taken off by these wretches, induced his most superstitious highness to give up the idea, although considerable quantities of stone had arrived on the spot.

We then passed the flag-staff near the residency, which used to bear our colours. This they had surrounded with the furniture from the houses, and converted into one vast fire.

The village of Kirkee is strengthened by a river, which runs on three sides of it; but its localities were only of use to secure our baggage, sick, and stores; as the force under Colonel Burr moved forward. I was much delighted with his account of the affair on the very spot. The ground was perfectly open, and with the overwhelming force of cavalry against us, stated to have been not less than 15,000, I am surprised how our little force escaped annihilation. The colonel was shot through the hat, in the only attack of infantry the enemy made, I believe by one of Goklah's battalions; but they never came within fifty yards, though their cavalry cut at our troops in the ranks with their swords. In this charge of cavalry Mora Dikshut was killed. He was a great friend of the English, particularly of Major Ford's, whom he had informed of the Peishwah's intention to overwhelm our force, and offered to save him and his family; stating at the same time, though disapproving totally the Peishwah's conduct, that he was his servant, and would stand by him, and follow his orders to the last. Mr. Elphinstone, and all who knew him, regretted his death. The remains of horses and men marked the scene of this charge, the failure of which was the loss of the battle, as the Mharattas withdrew their guns to the other side of the town after their discomfiture; and his highness was so alarmed, that it was with the greatest difficulty Goklah could keep him from flying to Punderpoor on the night after the action.

We proceeded, after we had seen the ground, and heard all these particulars, towards the city, taking in our way a curious excavation made in the rocks to the west of it. This cave is different from any other I have seen, being dug into the strata of rock, below the level of the surface, and consisting of a square opening about eighty feet in each face, nearly twenty-five feet deep; and having in the centre of the area a small coarse temple, not unlike a great table, supported by plain pillars, and the roof flat. Within, immediately under the centre, the bull Nundee has originally stood; but he has been split in two, and his halves lie on each side of the temple, which I suppose is about sixteen feet in diameter, its summit nearly level with the surface, and immediately in the middle of the area. On the north side the excavation is continued above sixty feet under the ground, which is supported by several ranges of plain square columns, and there are in it no figures whatever. The centre table-like temple has a very druidical appearance.

To reach the city we crossed the river at a ford below the commencement of a stone bridge, begun by some former Peishwah, but, according to the absurd reasoning of this country, not continued by the present.

Many of the houses in Poonah have a very striking resemblance to those in Spain. The place was much depopulated, and a general stillness prevailed around, such as might naturally be expected in a conquered city; although in Nagpoor they seemed to have recovered more in three weeks than the good people here in three months. Besides the old palace, where Mr. Coates resided, there are two others in the city, which Mr. Elphinstone had ordered not to be entered by any one; Mr. Coates had, however, taken inventories of every thing within them, having first pulled off his shoes, to treat the royal residences with due respect. The old palace is surrounded with a wall and circular bastions, having an open space in its front. The walls of an inner court are miserably daubed with the Hindoo mythology, elephants, and horsemen. His highness made but little use of this abode except on public occasions, though it contained the temple or room for the yearly fête, in honour of his protecting deity Gunish Kundee.

I found Mr. Coates in a deep veranda in one of the small courts, crowded with trees and shrubs, and he was so good as to shew us round the palace. The great quadrangle is more handsome than that at Nagpoor, has sculptured wood pillars and cornices, which are very splendid, and the whole palace is glazed throughout. A very fine room, with dark-coloured wooden pillars, and carpeted with red cloth stuffed with cotton, displayed a full-length picture of the Marquis Wellesley, which had been found neglected in a small adjacent apartment; and near the likeness of this great statesman was a miniature of Sir Barry Close, also found in the palace, let into the wall in the plaster. There were also two very large well-finished globes, with the names in the Latin language, and the false horizons of silver. These, it was supposed, had been a present from the King of England to a former Peishwah, previous to the year 1788. From the top of the palace I had a most extensive view of the city, camp, mango groves, the ruins of the Sungum, and holy hill of Parbutty, to the south-east of the city. Poonah, not having any suburb like Nagpoor, is inferior in population, and covers less ground.

We now proceeded to the holy chamber, dedicated to a deity who could boast of an elephant's head and trunk, and who, to complete the interest he excited, was painted blue. He was sitting cross-legged, but we did not find this sapient gentleman ready to receive us, for after rummaging about he was discovered put by in a cupboard, to keep him from the dirt and flies. The room is vaulted, and about fifty feet long, and very high, with a gallery which runs round it, like our music galleries in ball-rooms. It is one mass of mirrors intermixed with green foil, inlaid with gilt wooden partitions, and numbers of English cut-glass chandeliers. The decorations were covered, to save them as well as their master. To the fête in honour of this tutelary divinity the resident was always invited, and the Peishwah did not himself do the honours, as he was also a visitor to his long-nosed patron. I saw here an English clock, which was found going well, in the palace; several large English books of fine engravings, and the remains of a very large orrery nearly destroyed. There was, besides, a native map, but I imagine Goklah must have a better one, to have so long escaped our pursuing army.

After procuring all the intelligence and papers I required, Mr. Coates shewed me the Peishwah's sleeping room, hung round with very large mirrors, and lighted with English glass shades. His bed, which was of orange velvet, hung like a swing from the ceiling. A picture of Nana Fernavez, the greatest statesman of his day, who presided many years over the councils of this court, seated by the side of a former Peishwah, who about thirty years ago threw himself from the top of the palace, were also pointed out to me.

On my return to the camp, I passed a man hanging, guarded by a small detachment, and learnt that he was one of those emissaries who had attempted to decoy our Sepoys from their duty. He was the second who had suffered, and as above fourteen others were in confinement, it was supposed one or more examples would be added to these. The attempt to seduce our Sepoys to quit their colours was the first and leading point in the Peishwah's policy. Almost in every instance, the soldier came and reported that he had been tampered with; and when the enemy saw that bribes would not tempt them from their duty, he resorted to the most cowardly means. The southern Concan furnishes to our Bombay army a large portion of its Sepoys, and belongs to the Peishwah. They are certainly his subjects, and he declared he would persecute their wives and children, if they remained firmly attached to us. But even this threat failed; not one soldier of our regular troops went over, and not above seventy men of Major Ford's battalion, who were recruited in the name of his highness, and were to all intents and purposes his troops; yet they felt more affection for their European officers than for the sovereign who paid them, and fought for our cause in preference to his. On regaining my tent I found it absolutely necessary to remain another day, as I had not the papers I required, and in consequence sent to Colonel Osborne, at Tally Gaum, to inform him of this circumstance, and that I should leave this to-morrow night.

Poonah, 1st February, 1818.

I dined yesterday with Colonel Burr, and this morning after breakfast proceeded into the town, and heard various reports respecting the approach of the Peishwah's army, which was stated to be moving in this direction. It was added that his advance of cavalry, consisting of 7000, had arrived on the Beemah the same day I passed it, and that my escort could not return, on account of their having stopped the road. It is certain that the Peishwah, instead of having taken refuge in a hill fort with the Rajah of Satarah, as was originally believed, had returned to the north, and is, without doubt, to-day within twenty miles of this city above the Ghauts.

The comparison I am about to make between the military constitution of the Mharatta confederation and that of the Germanic empire will not be deemed uninteresting, and I shall, at the same time, give a rapid sketch of the rise of this power.

It is well known that the power of the Mharattas originated in the talents and success of their great founder Sevajee, who was little better than a powerful landholder. The strong forts he possessed along the western Ghauts, and his predatory and abominable system of warfare, subsequently confirmed that authority which he founded by illegitimate means. That power being unchecked, in consequence of the weakness of the successors of Aurungzebe, became still more enlarged and consolidated. This monarch, who possessed by far the most extensive dominions of any sovereign of the house of Timour, dying in 1707, left the succession disputed, and the empire, for the next thirty years, became a prey to the most horrid and violent convulsions and revolutions, which prevented the power of the kings of Delhi from being felt in the Dekhun, and the whole of it was at times overrun and plundered by this rising power.

"That a house divided against itself cannot stand" was fully exemplified in the family of Timour, which might be said to have fallen to pieces by its own weight; and the different competitors for empire, rising one against the other, facilitated the subjugation of Hindoostan by Nadir Shah, in 1739. On this conqueror's withdrawing, the country relapsed into the same internal miseries; but it was not until the reign of Mehumed Shah, the possessor of the Mogul throne (whose ministers were very supine and inefficient, and every department of the state disorganised by the conquest of the Persians), that the Mharattas, finding the field open and undisputed, spread themselves by violent encroachments over Hindoostan. Few countries of India have since that period escaped being either annexed to their dominions, or plundered by them. Oude, being defended by the Ganges, is one of those not subject to their inroads; also Lahore, Multan, and Tatta, from their great distance from the Mharatta territories.

This confederacy continued greatly on the increase; the various generals of the Mharatta armies subjugated a fourth of India; and these chiefs having followed the example set them by the rajah's minister the Peishwah, had become sovereigns in the persons of the Gwykwar, the Bhoonslahs, Scindiah, and Holkar, who, still holding nominal appointments from the head of the Mharatta empire, looked up to him, and were bound to join him with their troops, should he be engaged in war. They thus held their kingdoms on a kind of military tenure, exhibiting a constitution not unlike the Germanic empire.

The crisis of this power happened in 1761, when in the neighbourhood of Delhi, meeting the Abdallis from the northwest, they were totally defeated in one of the most signal and sanguinary conflicts recorded in history, decided on the plain of Panniput, 80 miles north of Delhi. There were said to be 200,000 men on each side. This overthrow checked for some years their aspiring and usurping views; and Rennell even affirms, that on this occasion they received their death-blow. Scindiah, however, through the assistance of French officers, had, before the commencement of the present century, again become very powerful, having possession of all the north of Hindoostan, including the Doab*, besides Malwa, with the imperial city of Delhi, and the person of the sovereign. The losses they sustained in quarrels with each other, particularly Scindiah and Holkar, and the several defeats they met with from Lord Lake and the Duke of Wellington in 1803, 4, and 5, reduced them to a low ebb, and the Pindarries began to rise on their ruins. A state of peace from the year 1805 to 1817, had, however, somewhat re-established them all; and they were thus equal to the daring acts of hostility which this last autumn has produced, and which has ended in their total and complete reduction.

The first usurping Peishwah (in Persian, Guide) was the religious adviser of the Sow Rājah, and taking advantage of his incapacity, placed his master in confinement. It will readily occur to those versed in the early history of France, how much this usurped authority resembles the reigns of the *rois faineans* of France, with their *mâires du palais*. In both cases the son of the usurper, being a man of equal abilities to his father, continued to exercise the functions of government, till by degrees the people became accustomed to the rule of an imprisoned monarch, whose authority was exercised by the minister. But the farce of appearing to act under the orders of the Rajah of Satarah, a descendant of the family of Sevajee, has been always

* The Mesopotamia of the Ganges and Jumna.

kept up; the new Peishwah nominally receiving from the rajah the khelaut, or dress of honour, appointing him to the situation.

This shadow of a sovereign continued in a state of the utmost obscurity and inefficiency, and known to our officers only by name. After the Peishwah's flight from Poonah, Goklah was sent with a large body of horse to bring him from Satarah, and he has ever since accompanied the army.

The present Peishwah is about 45 years old, and a man of education and abilities, but without firmness to carry through what his mind would otherwise direct with judgment, being totally deficient in point of political courage. He was thought at one time by those who best knew him to be a very superior man; and General Malcolm, I was told, reported that his eloquence surpassed all he had ever heard. He is far from being popular amongst his subjects, as the murder in 1815 of the Shastry, a Bramin, the minister of the Gwykwar, by Trimbucjee Dinglia, and without doubt with the connivance of his highness, shocked all devout Hindoos. He has also the character, and I believe not without reason, of being dreadfully dissolute and depraved.

His territory was one of the finest in India, returning richly to his treasury, and it is supposed that he had about 300 forts, of which some are very strong. I have understood that he has now with him above a million of pounds sterling, principally in gold ingots, and as long as this lasts he may command a number of men. He is particularly attached to a quiet life, with all his comforts around him, and detests with all his heart being led about the country by his head adviser Goklah, incessantly pursued by our army. This chief was one of the first of the southern jaghirdars who joined the Duke of Wellington in 1803, and his attachment to our cause was most useful at that time; I believe he distinguished himself personally against the enemy. Of late he became dissatisfied with us, and has done all he possibly could to alienate the Peishwah's mind, and exasperate the other jaghirdars into hostile measures; the latter of whom bring into the field 12,000 horse, and it is to their disaffection that we anxiously look for the fall of the Peishwah's army. It has been intimated to them, that those who do not immediately quit the army of his highness will be severely dealt with; but that no kindness will be shown to Goklah, whose territory has already been seized by Colonel Monroe, or rather received at the hands of the ryots, who delivered up the jaghire with the utmost readiness and delight, having themselves, as I was told, expelled the Mharatta authorities.

The attachment of the southern jaghirdars to their master has been highly creditable to them, as previous to the breaking out of the war, it was with the greatest difficulty that the British government could keep the Peishwah from encroaching on them, and had it not been for our interference, they would have fallen under his powerful arm; yet the moment they were called on for their military services against us, they were ready to support their sovereign, and act against those who were lately their protectors.

I find that Trimbucjee Dinglia joined the Peishwah about the latter end of December, and that he has remained with him ever since. It only required this to complete his highness's unjustifiable and depraved conduct, thus classing himself with a murderer.

News has been received of the Peishwah's being at Fultun, half-way between this place and Punderpoor, on the 29th, and that General Smith and Colonel Boles were in pursuit of him. In the direction in which he is now proceeding, he will fall in with Gunput Rao. But Colonel Deacon is moving down upon him from Jaulna, by Monghy Puttun, and Captain Davies from Khandeish, by Toka.

I here part with my detachment of Bengal cavalry, and not without regret. The jemidar has received from me the highest testimonials of his excellent conduct, and my orderly, who wished to accompany me on to Misr (Egypt), has also been recommended for promotion. I have further written letters to Captain Sydenham, requesting that Salle Mahumed Khan may be noticed in any way he may think fit. My escort was to have attempted to return this day to Seroor, having halted yesterday owing to the insecurity of the road, but the same cause has prevented their departure this morning. It is my intention after dinner to take leave of Colonel Burr, whose kindness and attention I shall always reflect upon with pleasure. He has ordered 50 of the irregular horse to accompany me, besides 100 infantry, and the governor of Bombay's body guard, consisting of about 20 men, who had been sent up here on the news of the first action.

I shall feel much regret at taking leave of Captain Hicks, who has travelled so far with me, and from whom I have received so much attention and kindness, particularly as I have so little chance of ever seeing him again. It is the most painful circumstance which arises from the profession of a soldier, after forming familiar and dear friendships, to be torn from them at the end of three or four years, only to form others to be again broken off at the end of as short a period.

I have received letters from Captain Sydenham, stating that Colonel Adams's cavalry had cut to pieces 1000 of the Pindarries; that the individuals were selling their horses, and about to apply to more peaceable employments, but that their guns, families, and baggage, had fallen into our hands.

CHAPTER XX.

NARRATIVE OF EVENTS AT POONAH.

The Peishwah's preparations for hostilities—The smothered embers threaten to blaze out —The natives look upon war as certain—Unfounded reports respecting our situation in Hindoostan—Our Sepoys stated to be treacherous—This causes much uneasiness —Jemidar tampered with—Turpitude of the Mharattas—The resident evinces much confidence in the Peishwah's durbar—Bad situation of the cantonments—Difficulty of moving the troops—More decided symptoms of hostility—The Peishwah's troops encroach on our camp—Assurances of a friendly nature to his highness—Arrival of the Bombay European regiment—The brigade moves to Kirkee—Cantonments plundered —Hostile language—Resident's remonstrance—General Smith concentrates—Light battalion—Complaints of the Peishwah's minister—The light battalion ordered in from Seroor—Communication with the Peishwah—Dictatorial language—The resident's answer and remonstrance on the 5th of November—Threatening language of Wittogee Naik to the resident—Negotiation—The Peishwah joins his army—Hostile movements of the enemy—Troops withdrawn from the Sungum—Residency burnt—The brigade advance from Kirkee—Mharatta army—Dhaporree battalion—Enemy open a cannonade—Attack of infantry—Of cavalry—Enemy retreat and withdraw their guns—Loss of the enemy—The Peishwah and his army in the utmost consternation—Arrival of the light battalion from Seroor—Horrid act of barbarity of the enemy—Extraordinary powers of Goklah—Fidelity of our Sepoys—General Smith arrives at Poonah on the 15th of November—Enemy's position—Arrangements for attack—Skirmish—Retreat of the enemy—Flight of the Peishwah—Arrangements for saving Poonah—British standard hoisted on the palace—Forty-seven pieces of cannon fall into our hands.

DURING* the last fortnight in October, the intrigues of the Peishwah with other native courts, his eager collection of troops, his calls on his various feudatories to repair to Poonah, his profuse expenditure, and his undisguised attempts to seduce our Sepoys from their duty, betrayed his impatience to throw off our yoke. From these various indications and preparations, it was impossible not to infer that the irritability and aversion of his highness to the

* Principally taken from papers laid before parliament.

British government were such as were likely to burst into a flame; and our resident, from a desire to prevent this result, was obliged to temporize, and affect a confidence, which the court of Poonah little deserved. His highness also prepared his forts for defence, and entrusted some of them to his chiefs, who were desired to defend them to the utmost in time of need. The natives looked upon these measures as the prelude to a war between us and the Peishwah, and many inhabitants of different ranks moved their families from Poonah in October.

His highness was so successful in fostering sentiments of antipathy against us, that all rumours to our disadvantage, however false, particularly such as spoke of the disaffection of our troops, and of combinations against us in Hindoostan, were received with the greatest pleasure in his capital. Efforts were made on our part to show the durbar the true state of affairs in Hindoostan; but it became evident that war would ensue, and several of the chiefs stated decidedly that such was the Peishwah's intention. We were even warned that no reliance could be placed on our Sepoys, whose minds were asserted to be totally alienated; and this corroborated the reports in circulation some months before, of endeavours to win them to betray their officers. In the middle of October, some of the Sepoys of Major Ford's battalion deserted, and the Peishwah's attempts to deter them from serving us created much alarm. This system of sowing disaffection among our troops appears, as before stated, to have been the leading feature of his plan.

A few days subsequent to the period mentioned, intelligence was received which fully established the fact; as a jemidar of our Sepoys, being tampered with, disclosed the affair to his officers, and was desired to encourage the invitation. After some interviews with inferior agents, he was, on the night of the 3d of November, introduced to the Peishwah and Goklah, in the palace in the city, and was pressed to desert, with as many men as he could bring over, at the moment of attack, was promised a large sum of money and still further advantages, and on the morning of the 5th was sent for, and informed that the attack was to commence that day. Previous to this, one of our Sepoys, passing through the Mharatta camp, was taken to the tent of Goklah, where several of the principal officers persuaded him to desert with his arms. It is to be remarked, that all these plots against us, affecting the very existence of our army, were carried on, not only in the time of the closest friendship and alliance, and of profound peace, but were accompanied by the warmest professions of friendship.

Nothing can more strongly demonstrate the general turpitude of Indian politics than the three instances of the Mharatta powers who have gone to war with us; as they have all evinced more or less treachery, and justified, by their want of fidelity, both in a political and moral point of view, the punishment that has fallen upon them.

As it was very desirable that the secret enmity of the court of Poonah should be restrained from openly bursting forth, and more particularly till the treaty with Scindiah should be signed, a general appearance of confidence was shown towards the Peishwah's durbar, though a strict eye was kept on their proceedings. About the period that the decisive terms were proposed to Scindiah, the affairs at the Peishwah's capital had become so alarming, that it would have been imprudent to continue this semblance any longer, as the hostility towards us was the general talk of the country.

The principal danger which threatened us was from the corruption of the loyalty of our Sepoys. To avoid this, no other means appeared so likely as the removal of the brigade from their cantonments in the immediate neighbourhood of the city; but the same reason that had obliged us to pass over his highness's late conduct without remonstrance rendered this measure difficult, as the alteration might afford grounds for our enemies to calculate on the probability of a rupture, and give hopes to the disaffected throughout India.

But, in addition to this cause of alarm, the cantonments, which were always badly situated, from one of their flanks absolutely resting on the city, had of late been nearly surrounded by the Peishwah's increasing army; and it was impossible but that the movement of our troops would at once disclose to him our distrust. It was also thought probable that this movement might even bring on a crisis, and it was therefore postponed, not only to assist the negotiations in Hindoostan, but to admit of the arrival of the Bombay European regiment, which was expected to arrive on the second of November.

Previous to this, however, the preparations of the Peishwah had advanced so far, that he appeared little desirous of concealing his intentions, and it became evident that the time for action could not be far distant. Our resident, under this impression, determined no longer to expose the brigade, in its hazardous situation, to the danger of a surprise, particularly as every appearance intimated a design to attack it before the junction of the European regiment. The Peishwah's intrigues with our Sepoys had at this time become more open, and his troops crowded much upon the cantonments; those in Poonah were ordered to move out of the city, and an effort was made to encamp a body of them close to our magazine, which had, according to the information received, been pointed out as an object of great solicitude in case of attack. This presumptuous attempt was checked by the officer commanding (Colonel Burr); but the numerous indications of attack had begun to make an impression on our troops, and the general conversation in Poonah and the cantonments was directed to the Peishwah's design of surprising our lines.

In consequence of this state of affairs, on the 29th October orders were sent to Colonel Wilson, who commanded the European regiment, to hasten his march so as to arrive the next day, and the brigade was ordered to be upon the alert. At the same time our resident sent a message to the Peishwah, stating that this was only a mere military precaution, as the continuance of a state of security was essential to disciplined troops, in the immediate neighbourhood of another army. His highness received assurances at the same time that with us no inimical design existed, as he might be satisfied that we had no demands against him, and had not at that time any discussions of consequence with his durbar, excepting those relating to our common operations against the Pindarries. It was further recommended to his highness to withdraw his troops that were nearest ours.

This message was received with displeasure. His ministers complained that his highness could not keep what troops he pleased at his own capital, but declared that his purposes were quite friendly, and that there was no occasion for our vigilance. The next day the European regiment marched in, and those troops of the Peishwah which pressed most on our lines were reluctantly withdrawn a few hundred yards.

On the 31st we began to move our stores and provisions to the neighbourhood of a village three miles from Poonah, called Kirkee, which, from the river winding round part of it, was the best defensive position in the neighbourhood. On the 1st of November the brigade moved to this ground, though the Peishwah had previously desired that it might be allowed to remain. This was however evaded by his highness being informed that the troops were marching by orders from Sir Thomas Hislop. The consequence of our withdrawing from the cantonments was their being plundered by the Peishwah's people, without any obstruction from their government; and an European officer was robbed and wounded in open day about two miles from the residency, while the language of the Peishwah's ministers became that of utter estrangement. It was announced, as if in defiance, that their troops meant to form a camp between our old cantonments and our new position, and 1500 horse moved down for that purpose. Upon this, Mr. Elphinstone sent a message, begging that the motives of our removal might not be misunderstood, and desiring that the Peishwah would forbid these aggressions; at the same time, with a firmness now become necessary, declaring that if any troops attempted to press on us, as in our old position, they would be treated as enemies. In answer to this, a promise was given that the Peishwah would restrain his troops.

On receiving the first intelligence of the intended removal to Kirkee, General Smith, who was posted at Bysapore, to the north of the Godavery, with detachments towards the ghauts, and who was prepared to act in case of a rupture with the Peishwah, concentrated his force at Fooltomba, to the south of the river; recalling his advanced troops, and ordering his light battalion, which was on its route from Seroor to join him, to return to that place, in order to be nearer Poonah.

Notwithstanding the assurance given, the troops of the Peishwah still threatened to advance; and their conduct was not only decidedly hostile, but had such an effect on the common people, that it was not safe for British officers to ride out on the roads. The remonstrance of our resident brought forth many complaints from Ballaba, one of his highness's principal advisers; amongst others, that we had infringed the treaty of June, and that if we wished to conciliate the Peishwah, we must renounce the cessions made to us by that treaty, and allow Trimbuckjee to be restored to favour. Major Ford, to whom this extraordinary message was delivered, pointed out its impropriety, and one more civil was substituted.

The crisis was now evidently at hand, and Mr. Elphinstone, on the 4th of November, wrote to order in the light battalion and the 1000 auxiliary horse that were at Seroor. They had made one forced march, when their approach became known to the Peishwah on the morning of the 5th, and his highness hastened to get all in readiness in the city. As these agitations, however, had not been uncommon for ten days before, the resident merely sent a message to inquire the cause, without taking any corresponding measures. A vaqueel of the Peishwah brought back the reply, that our line at Kirkee had been under arms from sunrise, and that his highness was resorting to a similar preparation. He however went back with an assurance that no precautions for defence had been taken at the residency.

In the course of the day a battalion of Goklah's marched down near the residency; and, after some time, the vaqueel again returned with a confidential servant of the Peishwah's, who stated that his master had heard of the approach of General Smith, and the near arrival of the battalion from Seroor; that this was the third time we had assembled troops at Poonah, and that the last time we had surrounded the city; that therefore his highness was determined to bring matters to an immediate settlement. The message now assumed a highly dictatorial language, for it demanded the removal of the European regiment from the brigade, that the latter should be reduced to its usual strength, that our cantonments should be taken to a place to be pointed out by his highness; but that the residency might remain; and on these terms his highness would continue his friendship with the British government: otherwise, that he was actually mounted, and would retire some distance from Poonah, to which place he would never return until his terms were complied with.

Mr. Elphinstone replied, that he believed General Smith was still at Fooltomba, that the battalion was certainly coming in, and that the great assemblage of troops by his highness, and the position they occupied, were sufficient reasons for strengthening the brigade; but that he could assure his highness there was no aggressive intention, and he must do him the justice to own, that not one of the former proceedings against his highness, of which he had complained, were undertaken without full notice; that it was out of his power to withdraw our troops; and that his highness was not entitled by any engagement to demand it; that on the contrary he had promised to send his troops to the frontier, and that he ought to fulfil his promise, which would remove every ground of disagreement.

He was answered by Wittojee Naik, the servant of the Peishwah before mentioned, who, in a style of complaint and menace, adverted to the former disputes, in which he said the Peishwah had given way, merely from friendship to our government, and asked Mr. Elphinstone if he imagined his highness was not a match for us, on the day Poonah was surrounded. He then repeated his message, and desired a categorical answer. This was replied to as before, and the resident put the question to him, if he was to consider his highness at war with us; but he said he had no instructions on that head, and that his highness would regulate his actions by ours. He was afterwards much more distinct, for he repeated his demand, declaring that if not complied with, the friendship between us would not last, and even warned our resident of the bad effects of a rupture. He was again assured of our wish for peace; and Mr. Elphinstone further stated, that if his highness moved to his army, he would withdraw to the camp, but if he remained quiet, we should still consider him as a friend, and he (Mr. Elphinstone) should be careful not to cross the river which separated our camp from the city; adding, that if his troops advanced towards ours, we should be obliged to attack them.

As soon as Wittojee Naik returned to the city, the Peishwah left Poonah, and withdrew to the Parbutty Hill; and within an hour after, large bodies of troops began to move in the direction of our camp, in such a manner as to threaten to cut off the residency from it. On the receipt of Wittojee Naik's message, the company of native infantry left in the cantonments, and the de-

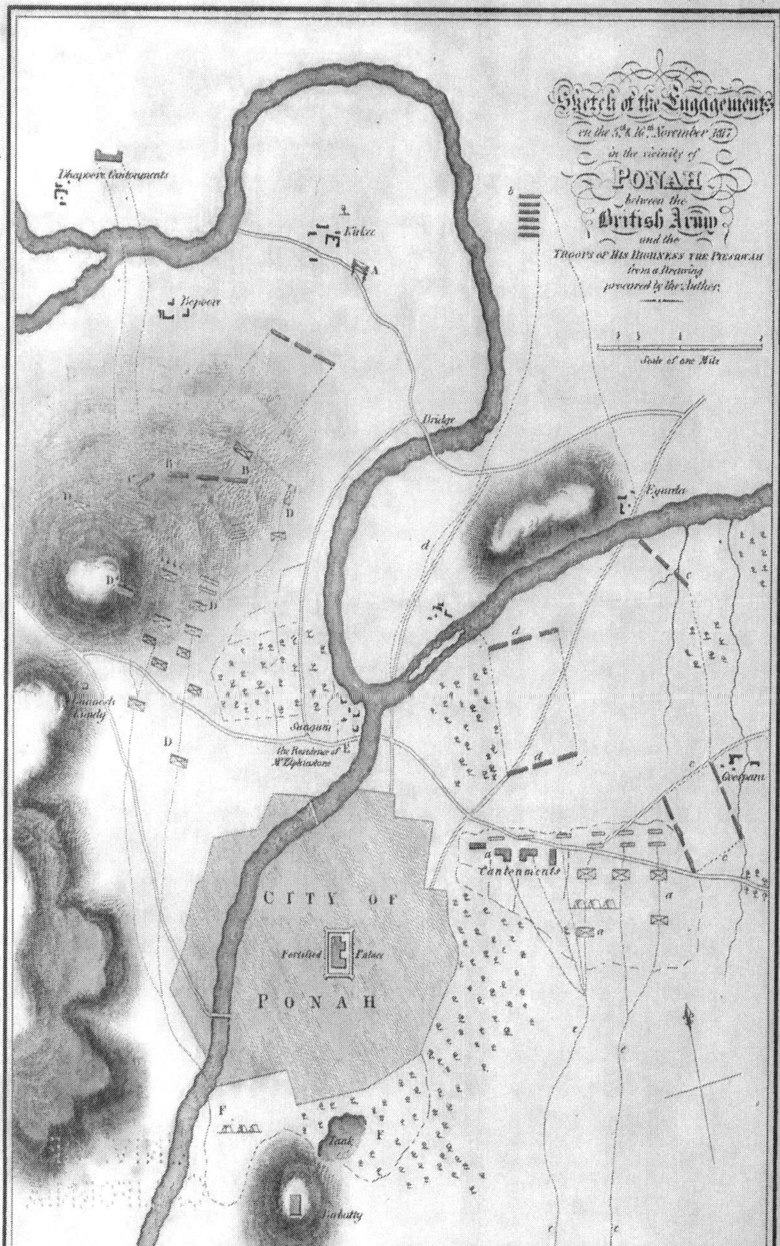

G. Fitz-Clarence delt.

Published as the Act directs 2d Feby 1819 by John Murray Albemarle Street London

J. Walker Sculpt.

REFERENCES TO THE ENGAGEMENTS NEAR POONAH.

The British troops are coloured red—the enemy's yellow.

Action of the 5th of November.

A. Baggage, recruits, &c. with two 12-pounders.

B. British line.

C. Dhapoore battalion.

D. The Peishwah's army.

E. The British residency.

F. Camp the enemy occupied for some days after the action.

Action of the 16th, and the disposition made by General Smith for a general attack on the 17th of November, 1817.

a. Enemy's camp.

b. Ground the British troops moved from.

c. Colonel Miles's column.

d. General Smith.

e. Flight of the enemy's army.

tachment at the residency were withdrawn, and marched towards the camp; and on the probability of the communication of the residency being endangered, Mr. Elphinstone quitted it, which was a signal for its being plundered and burnt.

Colonel Burr, on receiving the news of this hostile measure, put the brigade under arms, and being joined by Mr. Elphinstone, pushed forward from the village of Kirkee, leaving a detachment and two twelve-pounders to defend the camp, baggage, and non-effectives. About a mile in advance he halted, to await the junction of the Dahporee battalion under Major Ford.

The Mharatta army, with their left on a strong knoll in front of Gunish Kundee, and their right towards the Moota river, appeared in heavy masses amounting to 15,000 horse and 8000 infantry, as if ready to crush the small force opposed to them, which did not exceed 1800 men. On the approach of the Dahporee battalion, the corps in the pay of the Peishwah, officered by Europeans, and whose affection it was supposed his highness might have alienated, had he succeeded in his views, was looked to with anxiety; and the line having been joined by the detachments from the cantonments and the residency, advanced towards the enemy, who opened a cannonade upon them, while his cavalry attempted to turn both their flanks, and succeeded in getting into their rear. A body of Goklah's infantry made an attack on the left of the line, which was repulsed by the 7th native infantry. This attack was supported by a body of horse, which charged the 7th native infantry so effectually that they were with difficulty extricated from their perilous situation, having become insulated by a forward movement. At length, by ordering the European regiment to their assistance, the enemy's cavalry were repulsed, leaving many men and horses on the ground. They fell back to a distance, and never afterwards hazarded a repetition of their charge. By this time Major Ford's battalion had joined, and behaved throughout with the utmost steadiness and fidelity. The line continued to advance, and the enemy gradually withdrew their guns and troops to the city; and left us undisputed masters of the field of battle. Our brigade returned at dark to the camp, without having sustained considerable loss, the whole being under 100 men, and only one European officer (Lieutenant Falconer, 2d battalion, 1st regiment) wounded. On the part of the enemy 500 men were killed and wounded, and several sirdars of the highest rank were sufferers. Mora Dickshut, to whom the British were much attached, and a Pithan sirdar, were killed; and some others, including a relation of Goklah's, and a brother of Mora Dickshut, were wounded.

The whole of the enemy's army was in the utmost consternation and confusion during the night after the action: the Peishwah himself was about to set off for Porunder, and was with the greatest difficulty prevailed on to remain in camp by Goklah, who declared that his flight would be followed by the dispersion of his army, which was much disheartened, and continued on the side of the city farthest from our camp. Our brigade remained in its position, being augmented on the morning of the 6th November by the junction of the flank battalion and 1000 auxiliary horse from Seroor. The Peishwah meanwhile employed himself in encouraging his sirdars, paying for horses that were killed, and bestowing presents and distinctions on such men as had been wounded.

On the 10th of November he removed his army from behind the city, and encamped to the east of our cantonments, about four miles from Kirkee. Various attempts were made to cut off our supplies, and to shut up the roads, which naturally succeeded from our total want of cavalry; and two cornets, of the names of Hunter and Morrison, were taken prisoners within twenty miles of Poonah. These gentlemen were well treated, having fallen into the hands of a Major Pinto, a Portuguese; but were subsequently moved to a fort of Goklah's. Two other gentlemen of the name of Vaughan, one a major in the army of the Madras presidency, were not so fortunate. They were on their way from Bombay to Poonah, and were seized at Tally Gaum; and though they made no resistance, but remonstrated with their inhuman captors, pointing out to them the consequent retaliation, and offering to ransom themselves, they were in cold blood hanged to a tree by the side of the road. The Peishwah, it is true, acted himself in a more civilized manner, having permitted a conductor and the moonshee of the resident, when taken, to be sent into the camp. The latter had an interview with Goklah before he quitted the city, when this chief produced a paper under the Peishwah's seal, investing him with all the powers of government. On this occasion the Peishwah appears to have made over to Goklah the whole of his authority, and to have given him the same powers as that of the vaqueel Moutulluck, who on particular occasions was appointed by the kings of Delhi.

The moonshee also learnt from Wittojee Naik, that the cantonments were burnt by the Peishwah's orders. Some skirmishing took place in consequence of an effort to bring in some stores, but, with the exception of an attempt to throw rockets into the camp, all remained quiet till the arrival of General Smith. Numbers of the Mharattas in our auxiliary horse were, from the change of circumstances, paid up and allowed to quit our side, but, as I have elsewhere stated, not a single Sepoy deserted from our regular troops.

General Smith, who collected his troops on the 3d of November at Fooltomba, in consequence of the very unpleasant aspect of affairs at Poonah, had proceeded on his march, and arrived on the 8th at Ahmednuggur, where he seized the pettah, which had been ceded by the late treaty to us, though not given up. From this place he took his battering train, which had remained in the fort, (the garrison of which consisted of the 4th native infantry), and large supplies of grain and stores, which he procured for his own troops and those at Poonah. On his route, between Ahmednuggur and Seroor, he heard from the reports of the country of the actual breaking out of hostilities; and his march from Seroor was performed with extreme difficulty, as the enemy's horse hovered all round, and he had no cavalry, though the 2d native regiment was on its march to join him. He was consequently obliged to shorten his marches and preserve close order, and did not reach Poonah till the 13th. He did not however lose any baggage, and had killed many of the enemy, particularly in a very gallant charge made by Captain Spiller, with 400 of the auxiliary horse, in which the son of the Rajah of Akulcote, with a number of men, were slain on the side of the Peishwah, whose loss made a very strong sensation in their camp.

General Smith, on his arrival at Poonah, found the enemy in position on the opposite side of the Moutee Moula river, occupying the ground of the old cantonment, having his right on a mangoe grove, with a steep nullah (or stream) crossing its extremity, and his left along the enclosures of the north front of the officer's lines of houses towards the suburbs of the city. He had eleven guns in battery on his left, and a few more scattered along his front and right. It was the general's intention to have attacked him on the 14th, but he was disappointed in finding a ford. On the evening of the 16th, however, the disposable corps, after providing for the safety of the camp and position of Kirkee, were formed into three divisions of attack. The first, under his own orders, consisted of

The horse artillery,
His Majesty's 65th regiment of infantry,
Light battalion,
1 Battalion 2d regiment native infantry,
1 Battalion 3d regiment native infantry.

The second, under the command of Lieutenant Colonel Miles, consisted of

Detachment foot artillery,
Bombay European regiment,
One battalion 7th regiment native infantry,
Residency guard.

The third, under the command of Major Thatcher, consisted of

One company of Europeans,
2d Battalion 9th regiment native infantry, and
Two guns.

The first was destined for the attack of the enemy's left, and to cross the river at the residency. The second, under Colonel Miles, was directed to act upon the enemy's right, and to cross the river by the yellow ford before sunset. The third was ordered to precede the first division by a different route, to prevent the enemy opposing its passage. The whole three columns were to move at daylight on the 17th to the attack of the enemy's position.

The division under Colonel Miles was opposed, but without checking its advance; and in the course of the night the Peishwah drew off the largest part of his army, and the rest under Goklah retired on the advance of General Smith, on the morning of the 17th, leaving great part of their camp standing. The Peishwah was supposed to have fled at two o'clock in the morning, and passed on to Saporee, where, on being joined by Goklah, they continued their flight to Maholy; Goklah being sent to Satarah to bring out the rajah, in order to have the pageant of the government in their custody. They remained some time at Maholy, waiting for Appa Dessaye, one of the southern jaghirdars. Only one gun was found in the camp, and pursuit was impracticable from the want of cavalry. The loss of Colonel Miles's division was small,—only sixteen killed, and one European officer and seventy-six men wounded.

The general, in conjunction with Mr. Elphinstone, made every arrangement to save Poonah from the destruction which threatened it; the troops being very much exasperated at the perfidious conduct of the enemy, in burning the residency and cantonments, and murdering the two Mr. Vaughans. Some of the Sepoys' wives who had fallen into his hands were also massacred, and a Sepoy who had strayed from General Smith's line of march was mutilated, which atrocities our soldiery would have retaliated by plundering and burning the capital. But fortunately his army took a different direction, leaving only a few Arabs for its defence, and they were prevailed on to withdraw, so that we obtained quiet possession of it, with a train of forty-six pieces of cannon; the British standard was hoisted on the palace under a royal salute; and through the prudent conduct of those high in command, no excesses were committed.

It was ascertained that the attack on the 5th of November was principally owing to the persuasion of Goklah, and that after the Peishwah had given the order he took alarm, and even sent to stop Goklah from commencing hostilities. The latter, hearing of the approach of this message, anticipated its arrival by beginning the cannonade, and Mora Dickshut was intrusted with the zerric puttah, (the standard of the Mharatta empire), though it was known he was very averse to the war, and was even accused by Goklah of intrigues with us. Goklah told the vaqueel of Appa Dessaye before the action, that his principal hope of success was in the disaffection of our Sepoys.

CHAPTER XXI.

NARRATIVE OF EVENTS AT POONAH.

Various intelligence on taking possession of Poonah—Arrangements—Death of Lieutenant Ennis—Remonstrance of the resident—Letter on the murder of the Messrs. Vaughans—2d Madras cavalry join the army—Eighteen guns fall into our hands—Various marches of the Peishwah and General Smith from the 22d November to the 29th December—The general disposes his force in two divisions—Cause of the action at Corry Gaum—Brilliant achievement—Gallantry of the British troops—Immense superiority of the enemy—Repulse and retreat of the enemy—Retreat of the British detachment to Seroor—Our severe loss—Feeling of the Peishwah's army after this defeat—Retreat of the Peishwah—Marches from the 3d to the 10th of January—Colonel Boles takes post on the 8th at the top of the little Bhore Ghaut—General Smith on the 12th at Fultun—Peishwah on the 13th at Conjuljee—General Smith at Islampoor on the 14th—On the 16th General Pritsler near Gokauk—The Peishwah the same day at Yedhully—On the 17th skirmish—On the 18th the Peishwah marches to Gulgully—General Pritsler on the 18th at Maulwounchee—Other movements to the 28th—The Peishwah descends the Salpee Ghaut on the 29th—His highness marches to the Moria pass—Ghun Put Rao's movements—General Smith and Colonel Boles on the 31st at Lonud—Colonel Deacon and Captain Davis's detachments.

AS it was probable the army would have to follow up the success of the 17th, it was necessary to appoint proper officers for the police of the town; and Captain Robertson, the Persian interpreter to the general, and Mr. Coates, the surgeon of the residency, were left. The enemy were not so successful as at first, in cutting off our supplies; but Lieutenant Ennis of the Bombay engineers was surrounded while surveying near Sakoor Mandava, and shot by some of the adherents of Trimbuckjee, who had not up to this period joined the Peishwah. In consequence of the murder of the two Mr. Vaughans, Mr. Elphinstone addressed a letter of remonstrance, both to Goklah and the Peishwah. To the former it was explicitly declared, that any individual, however high his rank, who ordered the death of a British officer, should answer for the crime in person; but to the latter it was only stated in general terms, that any repetition of such barbarity should be punished by retaliation.

On the 18th of November, the 2d Madras cavalry joined the camp, but much reduced by the very long and continued marches they had made. On the 18th or 19th, General Smith sent a detachment to seize several of the enemy's guns which had been withdrawn upon their evacuation of their camp towards the hill fort of Soneghur, and 18 pieces of cannon fell into our hands after a trifling resistance, during which two officers of horse artillery, Lieutenants Willock and Johnson, were severely burnt by an explosion of some gunpowder. These guns, added to the 46 found in the arsenals at Poonah, and one in battery, made together a train of 65 pieces of cannon. The Peishwah, who had fled to the southward with his army, taking the Rajah of Satarah with him, gave out that it was his intention to return to the capital, but it was supposed he only held this out to encourage his troops; and General Smith, accompanied by Mr. Elphinstone, moved with the army on the 22d of November from that city. On the 23d the general, having his heavy train with him, had a most difficult task in ascending the little Bhore Ghaut, and it was not accomplished till late in the night. Fortunately the enemy did not attempt to defend the pass, or it might have cost us two or three days, and many lives. The divisions halted on the following day.

On the 25th, while on the march near Jeejoory, the enemy showed from 4000 to 5000 horse on both flanks of the column, but the 2d cavalry pursued and dispersed about 2000, though with little effect; the regiment being completely broken down and almost useless, from its incessant forced marches. The army encamped on the banks of the Neerah, after passing it by the bridge, and on the 26th marched to the foot of the Salpee Ghaut. Intelligence being received that the enemy intended to oppose us in this pass, the general halted on the 27th.

On the 28th, the troops mounted the ghaut totally unmolested till they reached the top, where the enemy displayed about 600 horse and threw a few rockets, but the advance soon drove him back. As we proceeded, the enemy retired, gathering strength on his way, and in the evening threatened us with from 3000 to 4000 horse in front, and the same number in the rear. He, however, suffered much during the day from our gallopers. Up to this period our loss was too trifling to be mentioned.

On the 29th, on the march to Julygaum, a large body of several thousand horse appeared as usual, and laid themselves open to a similar loss. The army would have been much distressed had the villages been destroyed; but even as it was, some want of grain was felt by the followers. The Peishwah was supposed to have moved in the direction of Meritch, where it was the general's intention to follow him, hoping that Brigadier General Munroe, who had received orders to check him, should he advance to the southward, would oblige his highness to take refuge in a hill fort, in which he might be blockaded.

My accounts are very imperfect from this day to the 6th of December, nor do I even know by what route the general moved, but the enemy did not press the line of march. On the 7th, during the march of the division to Punderpoor, he again showed from 6000 to 7000 horse, and even seemed inclined to attack, but afterwards kept in a very dispersed order, and only some slight skirmishing ensued. The general was very desirous to leave his heavy guns behind, and to pursue the Peishwah with a light division; but having halted the 8th and 9th at Punderpoor, he received intelligence of the enemy having again turned towards the ghauts, probably with the intention of flying to one of his hill forts; and it was not deemed advisable to part with them, till the result of this was ascertained. General Smith, about this period, received orders to place himself under Mr. Elphinstone's orders, and was informed that General Pritsler was on his route to join him. The general, however, found the Peishwah was moving north, and a corresponding movement was made by the division, which arrived on the 11th of December at Andoos, on the Neera. The following day it reached Neemgong, on the Beemah, and encamped near Seroor on the 17th.

The Peishwah in the meantime reached Wutloor, near Joonere, where it is believed he was joined from Sungumneer by Trimbuckjee, with about 1000 Arab and Bheel infantry. From Wutloor he moved up the Log Ghaut to Baumunwarra about ten miles, and thence to Lingdeo about nine miles. Between these three places his highness spent the time from the 17th to the 27th. The route the Peishwah had taken was very difficult for guns; and General Smith pursued him by the Nimba Dewra Ghaut. He left Seroor on the 22d December, arrived near Ahmednuggur on the 24th, and reached on the 26th Hunwut Gong, nearly in the direct road from Ahmednuggur to Coper Gaum. The general made a long march to Sungumneer, and on the 27th to Toogong or Talgong, and on the 28th to Akowla, on the Paira river. This brought the division to the northward of the Peishwah's army within the ghauts; and his highness, who was about to proceed on a religious ceremony to Nassuk, and calculated on the general's moving towards Coper Gaum, sent his tents on the 27th to the Wassiera pass, as if he intended to cross the valley of the Paira near Akolah, and advance by the great road to Nassuk; but on hearing of General Smith's approach, he changed his route, and retreated to Cootal on the western road through Rajoora. On General Smith's reaching Toogong, his highness seemed to have thought he could not pass to the northward, without the risk of being entangled in the hills, and overtaken by our troops; he therefore retraced his steps on the 28th of December, and arrived on the same day at Wutloor, a distance of nearly 20 miles.

From this place he proceeded by Chaukien, about 40 miles in two marches. At Chaukien is a little fort, from which he drove out a party of our peons or police officers, and leaving 100 Arabs for a garrison, marched to Phoolshur on the 31st of December: General Smith altered his direction of march on the Peishwah's returning to the south, and moved on the 29th with great difficulty up the Wassera Ghaut, as the several passes had been barricaded and entrenched by the enemy. The guns could only be dragged by great labour of the troops, and the rear guard did not reach camp till next day. The general, finding that the Peishwah continued his flight, now formed his army into two corps, proceeding himself on the 30th in direct pursuit with the horse artillery, the 2d Madras cavalry, his majesty's 65th regiment, and the 1st battalion 2d Bombay native infantry; while Lieutenant Colonel Boles of the Madras establishment, with the foot artillery, the Bombay European regiment, and two battalions with the battering guns, descended the ghaut, and made parallel marches to prevent the Peishwah's escape towards Khandeish.

On the approach of the latter to the southward, Colonel Burr, who commanded at Poonah, uneasy at the proximity of his army to that city, ordered in from Seroor a detachment, which, marching on the night of the 31st, reached Corry Gaum on the Beemah river, about two or three miles from Phoolshur, at the very time the enemy assembled at the latter place.

This gave rise to one of the most brilliant affairs ever achieved by any army; European and native officers and soldiers displaying the most noble devotion and most romantic bravery, under the pressure of thirst and hunger almost beyond human endurance, and opposed to an immensely superior force.

This detachment consisted of about 500 men of the 2d battalion 1st Bombay native infantry, two six-pounders, and about 250 auxiliary horse, the latter under the command of Lieutenant Swanston, and the whole under Captain Staunton. It left Seroor at half past eight P. M. on the 31st December, and having proceeded towards Poonah, after a long night's march of twenty-eight miles, arrived at ten in the morning of the 1st of January at Corry Gaum. Here its further progress was arrested by the appearance (according to information then obtained) of the Peishwah with a very large army, supposed to be 20,000 horse, 8000 Arab infantry, and two heavy guns, the whole formed on the opposite side of the river, which was fordable. Captain Staunton took post in the village of Corry Gaum, and selected commanding positions for his two guns.

Corry Gaum is composed of a number of stone houses, with stone walls round the gardens, and is a very defensible position. The enemy, perceiving Captain Staunton's intention, sent three different bodies of Arabs, consisting of about 1000 each, under cover of their guns, and supported by large bodies of horse, to prevent his taking post; and in some measure, from their superior force and the nature of the village, succeeded in obtaining possession of the strongest post in it, from which they were not dislodged during the day. The detachment continued incessantly engaged till nine o'clock at night, when the enemy were repulsed. The action was of the warmest and most sanguinary description. The Arabs, sword in hand, supported by their cavalry, charged several times to the very muzzles of our guns, and were only pushed back by the bayonet. The Peishwah's army, which had lost many men, refrained from attacking on the following day, perhaps hoping to starve the heroic band; as the river being nearly dry, and its small stream running on the farthest side of the bed, they had little or no water. On the morning of the 2d January it took possession of the post the enemy had occupied the day before in the village, and Captain Staunton remained sole master of the long disputed spot. In the evening, despairing of being able to make his way to Poonah, his men having been forty-eight hours without food, and no prospect of procuring any in the deserted village where he was posted, Captain Staunton determined upon attempting to retire on Seroor; and having collected the whole of the wounded, and secured the guns and one tumbril, the detachment commenced its retreat at seven P. M. being under the necessity of destroying one empty tumbril, and leaving the camp equipage. It succeeded in reaching Seroor on the morning of the 3d of January.

The loss, as may naturally be supposed, was very heavy. Lieutenant Chisholm of the Madras artillery, Assistant Surgeon Wingate, 2d battalion 1st regiment native infantry, and 50 men, were killed. Lieutenant Connellan, Lieutenant Pattison, Lieutenant Swanston, and 113 men, wounded. This is exclusive of the auxiliary horse, who suffered very much, having 96 men and nearly all their horses killed, wounded, or missing. Lieutenant Pattison is since dead.

It is impossible to describe in adequate terms the gallantry of all engaged; and after this affair, to use the language of the Peishwah's army, they looked upon 1000 of our troops as being equal in action to 20,000 of theirs.

The Peishwah, informed of General Smith's approach, continued his march to the southward by the Little Bhore Ghaut on the 2d, and was followed by the whole of his army in the course of the night; having lost above 500 men in these unsuccessful attacks. General Smith arrived at Chaun on the 3d of January, and hearing of the affair at Corry Gaum, pushed on to that place, and saved several of the wounded men. He halted on the 4th of January, having marched continually for a fortnight, and passed over 200 miles of country.

On the 7th the general encamped near Seroor, and was on the 10th at Pangaum, and Colonel Boles took post at the top of the Little Bhore Ghaut, it is believed, on the 8th of January. On the 12th General Smith was at Fultun, and the Peishwah on the following day at Conjuljee. General Smith was at Islampoor on the 14th. General Pritsler, whose division consisted of

Two squadrons 22d dragoons,
Seventh regiment native cavalry,
Eight companies European flank battalion,
Three companies of rifles,
Eight companies 2d battalion native infantry,

with a detachment of artillery, and had not absolutely joined General Smith's division, though acting in concert with it, was on the 16th twenty-five miles north of Gocauk, and the Peishwah at Yedhully.

On the 17th a very considerable body of the enemy in two divisions, supposed to amount to about 10,000 horse, approached General Pritsler's camp for the purpose of reconnoitring. The cavalry picquets were ordered out, and were afterwards supported by the remainder of the cavalry under Major Doveton, who followed the enemy about four miles from camp, and successively charged and put to flight both divisions. They, however, gave the major an opportunity of charging them a third time, when they fled in all directions, leaving 40 men killed and wounded. Our casualties were one man wounded, and two horses killed. The total loss of the enemy was estimated at 100 men. On the 18th the Peishwah having sent his guns and Arabs into the fort of Nepaunee, marched towards Gul Gully, and encamped on the banks of the Krishna or Kistnah river; and General Pritsler was at Maulwounchee on the right bank of the Gutpurber, near Gocauk. General Smith was on the 20th of January at Arrewarrie, thirty-five miles north-east of Meritch, marching on Hubney. On the same day General Pritsler was at Yedda warrah, twenty-five miles from Gocauk. On the 21st January

General Smith was at Kalegaura, and on the following day marched towards Meritch in order to intercept the Peishwah, who had arrived at Utnee on his return to the northward; but when informed of the general's approach, his highness moved in a westerly direction towards Emvir, giving out that he was marching on Nepaunee—a report which was generally credited in the country. General Smith, on hearing of his change of route, immediately moved on Augur, and arrived there by twelve o'clock, after a march of twenty-eight miles.

Early on the morning of the 23d he learnt that the Peishwah had made a shew of pitching tents at Anor, where he halted a few hours; but suddenly struck his camp, changed his route to the north, and marched to Konnandwer, still giving out that he had gone to Nepaunee. The general again moved in the direction of Meritch, and arrived at Tenklee (fifteen miles) by two o'clock P. M. The enemy suddenly made their appearance on the morning of the 23d, while the division was on the march, and destroyed some of the followers. On the 24th the division marched to Tesgaum, having been pressed in an unusual manner, the Mharattas behaving somewhat better than on any other occasion, and obliging us to take up ground to cover the baggage, though our artillery did much execution. A few men were wounded, and Ensign Newhouse of the 65th regiment slightly hurt. On the 22d General Pritsler was at Jamcundy, remained there two days after, and then continued to move northward after the Peishwah. On the 26th General Smith was at Dangally or Cheerapoor, and arrived at Pousasully on the 27th. The Peishwah was at Kurah on the 24th, and Mehowlee on the 28th, where General Smith approximated so nearly that his highness marched on the following night, and came down the Salpee Ghaut on the 29th, intending to march on the Neera bridge; but finding Colonel Boles had arrived there, he turned off near Fultun, and after resting a few hours marched towards the Moria pass, which leads directly on Punderpoor. The direction which the Peishwah had now taken, it was supposed, was with a view to join Gunput Rao, who, crossing the Nizam's territory, had arrived on the 22d of January at Peeplegaum, and at Boreghaum on the 23d, passing on without molesting the inhabitants to the Godavery river.

On the 31st General Smith and Colonel Boles were at Lonud. Gunput Rao had been closely followed by Colonel Deacon's division from the neighbourhood of Jaulna, consisting of

Two squadrons Madras cavalry with gallopers,
1000 Nizam's horse,
500 Salabat Khan's horse,
17th Madras light infantry,
500 Nizam's infantry,
1000 Salabat Khan's infantry, and four guns;

and was at Peepree, fifteen miles from Jaulna, on the morning of the 24th, moving on Munghy Puttun. This officer was afterwards ordered to join General Smith; and a corps under Captain Davies, consisting of 2000 reformed horse, and a Nizam's battalion, which had been posted on the frontier of Khandeish, was directed to act in a similar manner. The latter was moving by Toka, and they were to join at Rasheston.

CHAPTER XXII.

Quit Poonah—Escort—Road from Poonah to Bombay—Bheels—Reflections—Arrive at Tally Gaum, a village belonging to Scindiah—Low Ghur—Carli—Post—Visit the cave of Carli—Description of the cave—Pillars—Mahometan tomb—Statues of elephants—Arched roof—Tomb-like mass—Canopy—Cave of Bhudism—Inscription—Wooden rafters—Other excavations—Cisterns—Proceed to join my escort—Alarm—Jemidar of the escort—Bhore Ghaut—Valleys—Fine scenery—Condallah—Post—The road down the Ghaut—Chain of western Ghauts—Similarity of the Andes and Western Ghauts—Hummauls—Arrive at Panwell—Harbour of Bombay—Elephanta—Serjeant in charge of the cave—The Trimurti—Fanaticism of the Portuguese and Mahometans—Approach Bombay—Ships at anchor—Sea breeze—Parsees—Portuguese militia—Meet his honour the governor—Dinner.

Bombay, February 4th, 1818.

ABOUT twelve o'clock on the night of the 1st of February, accompanied by Mr. Elliott, I quitted Poonah, after taking leave of Captain Hicks. My escort consisted of 20 regular horse, 100 infantry, and 50 auxiliary horse commanded by an European officer. The road to this place had been at the beginning of the disturbances covered with the enemy's horse, but communications have of late been interrupted by the Bheels alone; and so little did they act from a motive of duty or affection towards the Peishwah, that many supplies had arrived from Bombay under their charge, as they were not only contented to let them pass on receiving a per centage, but willing to guard them themselves. How very similar are the human race in all parts of the world! Some years ago a traveller in Italy was securely conducted through the most dangerous spots for robbers by guards of the same class received into the police, who were paid for it, and who would sometimes entertain the persons under their care with accounts of the nefarious actions they had committed at such and such places as they passed on the road; many of which tales were heightened by murder having attended spoliation. It is the same thing in the desert between Aleppo and Bagdad; a sum of money secures you a convoy of the very Arabs who would have plundered you.

We continued on our route till daylight of the 2d, when we arrived at Tally Gaum, where another European officer and 100 fresh infantry were posted to relieve those I brought with me. I learnt that Colonel Osborne had pushed on the day before, and was well satisfied that he had not been obliged to stop for me. I got some fine and most refreshing fruit, which Colonel Burr had ordered to be placed in one of the dhoolies. This village was the fatal spot where a sirdar of Goklah's cavalry murdered Major Vaughan, of the Madras native infantry, and his brother. Their graves, side by side, were not twenty yards off the road. The village belongs to Scindiah, and the inhabitants were in great alarm lest, acting with the blind revenge so common amongst themselves, we should rase their houses to the ground. I attempted to quiet their fears, and then continued to walk on with the officer commanding the relief; and passing along a valley watered by a small river, about twelve o'clock saw Low Ghur, a very strong hill fort, apparently three miles off, to the left of the road, garrisoned by several hundred Arabs in the Peishwah's interest. We soon after arrived at the village of Carli, where we had a small post of 100 infantry and 50 auxiliary horse, under the command of an European officer. I found here two officers who were anxious to go on to Poonah with my return escort. They had arrived from the top of the Great Bhore Ghaut, which is only eight miles distant, and informed us that the road was quite open below the ghauts, as Colonel Proctor was in the neighbourhood, employed in reducing some forts. The fortress in the vicinity, and overlooking the village of Carli, consists of two table lands separated by a deep valley, and the faces of each scarped. They have the names of Low Ghur and Issa Ghur.

I had always determined to see the cave of Carli, about two miles from the village of that name; and the officer stationed there and one of those I had met proposed to accompany me, taking twelve men as a protection against the Arabs, who sometimes come over from the fortress, to collect the revenues of the sacred spot. I mounted a horse of my escort, and we set out, after I had requested Mr. Elliott, with my palanquin and escort, to proceed on the road, as I intended to ride across the country after them. At the foot of the range of hills, similar in appearance and character to those at Ellora, we dismounted, and began to scramble up the mountain by a very bad and narrow path, little better than a water-course, and all suffering much from the heat. We soon reached a narrow terrace on a level with the cave, where we were well repaid for our exertion. This cave, like those at Ellora, also faces the west, but is in other respects different from them. The entrance is much more handsome than any at Ellora, having been ornamented with two obelisks in the style of that at Indra Sabha. One of these pillars, of which both are crowned with lions, has been broken down, and the whole very much defaced. A plain Mahometan tomb, evidently a modern work, is built immediately in front. The height of the entrance appears to be sixty feet. After passing the remaining pillar, we entered a sort of vestibule, about thirty feet wide, and extending along the face of the rock about thirty yards. The ends have figures of elephants projecting from the walls, similar to those at Ellora, and above them many and various ornaments. On crossing the vestibule we advanced into the cave, which is about eighty or ninety feet long and thirty broad, supported by thirty-eight square stone pillars, with a passage round, between them and the rock. These pillars have very curious capitals, consisting of two elephants, with a male and female figure on the back of each. All these appear pressed down by the incumbent weight, the elephants being nearly upon their knees. The roof is arched to a considerable height above the pillars, which may be, with their capitals, rather more than twenty feet high. At the farther end is a large round mass of rock, like a tomb, about twelve feet high, rather more in diameter, and terminating at the top in a cupola, about twenty feet in all; and over the centre of it, suspended from the top, hangs what appeared to me to be an imitation of the shell of an immense tortoise, about ten feet long, resembling a canopy to the tomb-like mass below. I could pass round to the back of this, the wall of rock being pared off to admit a person behind it; but to save trouble, time, or expense, the colonnades on each side are not continued behind the tomb-like mass, though this is not perceived by a spectator standing at the entrance, or a little way within the hall. This cave is considered to be one of pure Bhudism, and that which appears to me similar to a tortoise-shell is stated to be the expanded hood of the deadly *cobra capella.* On the remaining pillar on the outside, and round the doorway, is an inscription in a very extraordinary character, which I regret I had not time to copy.

What must strike the most inattentive visitor in this cave is the vaulted roof, which looks as if supported by arched rafters of wood, and he is not mistaken as to the material. The roof has been compared to a ship in her timbers inverted, and without decks, and certainly strongly resembles it; but the rafters are not strong enough to support any considerable weight, as they are of a very singular shape, not being above two or three inches thick, though about sixteen or eighteen deep, and disposed very close to each other. They appear in very good condition, but why they are placed here will, I believe, puzzle the wisest heads, unless they were intended to fasten draperies or festoons to during religious festivals. It is a curious circumstance, that the only vaulted cave at Ellora should have arched rafters cut out of the rock (and not of wood), somewhat similar to those at Carli; and as I mentioned, in describing the great temple of Keylas, that the rock is sculptured in imitation of beams resting upon the pillars. The rafters at the arched cave at Ellora, however, appear equal to the support of the roof, but at Carli they resemble broad planks more than beams.

We proceeded, after examining this, to some other excavations, which were in all probability the habitations of the priests. They have all been much damaged intentionally; and the staircase, by which we ascended to a suite of rooms, hangs from the rock to which it was attached, the first three or four steps, which reached to the terrace foundation, being broken off. We mounted by two flights of stone steps and a ladder to a large low room, about thirty feet square, and having, on the three sides towards the rock, a number of small cells off it, about eight feet square, with common sized doorways leading into them. This was well lighted from a sort of gallery, with windows cut on the outside of it.

The officer who accompanied me fired off one of the Sepoy's musquets in the chamber, and the violent echo and long continued reverberation, now at a distance, now returning with increased violence, and thrilling through the enormous mass over head,—the noise surpassing thunder, but of a more hollow tone, was the most awful and overpowering sound I ever remember to have heard. I almost hoped, after the second return of the deep aggravated roar, that it was the last; but I was mistaken, and peal after peal followed in quick succession, and lasted several minutes, giving one the idea that the rock, indignant at its stillness being broken in upon, expressed its displeasure previous to closing the disturbers in its embrace for ever. So wonderful and indescribable a noise would, I think, try the nerves of a very strong-minded woman; and I felt a chill creep through my frame which I never recollect having experienced in any former instance; so much so, that if it had been proposed to fire a second musquet, the impression made upon me would have caused me to object to it.

Large subterraneous cisterns, full of water, are cut out of the rock, as at Ellora. Some Bramins had taken possession of the rooms, and a little colony was established in the great cave, their clothes being hung to dry upon ropes, fastened from one pillar to another. There is another cave, but the route is so difficult, and the precipice, near which you pass, so dangerous, that I did not attempt it, especially as I was tired with having travelled all night, and anxious to reach this place. The whole work has been evidently much injured, and, as usual, the blame is laid to the Portuguese; but it is still more likely to have been done by the Mahometans, as we have seen at Ellora; and there is reason to believe that the Portuguese never came up the great Bhore Ghaut.

I took leave of my two companions, and could but just perceive the shining of the arms of my escort, two miles on the road, from which I was about a mile to the north. I struck across the country to head it, galloping pretty fast, and at the foot of a little hill saw to my surprise, from a direction whence I could not expect friends, a native horseman, armed with a spear, coming towards me at speed. I concluded he was one of the enemy, and my alarm and consternation on discovering my situation will never be erased from my memory. I found I was totally helpless, having, without thought, most imprudently thrown myself on the first horse I met with, and left my sword in my palanquin: the pistols in the holsters were unloaded, and I had no ammunition. He fortunately turned out to be one of my own escort, which was resting under some trees off the road until I arrived; but the surprise will be a lesson to me for the future never to leave off my sword again on any account.

We proceeded towards the top of the Ghaut, and I found the jemidar of the auxiliary horse, who had relieved the others at Carli, was a man from Khorisan, and that he had been all over Persia, Cabul, and the countries to the east of the Caspian. He spoke

Persian, and I had a long conversation with him. He told me that Mr. Elphinstone spoke Persian better than any Englishman he ever met. Balk, he asserted, was as large a city as Delhi.

As we approached the limits of the great table-land of India south of the Nerbuddah, the country became less cultivated and more romantic; and within a mile of this termination, the views became every instant more magnificent. The bare points of the rocks and hills appeared above the trees and verdure; and the immense mountain to the south of the pass, which overhangs the plain, is seen threatening all below. The vast chasms, and perpendicular walled valleys, many hundred feet beneath the level of the land on which I stood, were finer than any thing I had ever beheld; and the numerous forts on the different pinnacles of the mountains, some near, others more distant, added to the sublimity of the scene. I wished for a glimpse of the sea, and since I have arrived here have been told that from one particular spot this can be obtained, though my longing eyes were disappointed in viewing that which an Englishman feels to be next neighbour to his native country.

I found a large detachment at the top of the ghaut, near the village of Condallah, and many officers waiting for escorts to go to Poonah. After I had taken some refreshment, leaving Mr. Elliott, who was much tired, I continued, with the officer who commanded my fresh escort, to walk down the ghaut. The post at the top is entrenched, a large working party being at this time employed to make the road passable for guns, which the Peishwah previous to the war had always refused to permit, as he conceived it would, if rendered safe and good, be a point of access from which we might invade his territory; though he might at the same time have recollected that the Dekhun was full of our troops, and his dominions open to the Madras army from all quarters. The road has been made well about half-way down, but is even now very steep.

The number of beautiful views which continually presented themselves were delightful. I never in any part of Spain or Portugal saw finer scenery. One valley, bounded with mural sides, was so deep, that I could not perceive the bottom, except from the very brink of the precipice; and, being covered with trees and shrubs of the most charming foliage, added much to its other beauties. We found it tolerably easy to descend that part on which our pioneers had been employed, but the remainder was extremely difficult; and it took us till twenty minutes after six (near one hour and a half) before we overtook the escort and my palanquin below in the plains of the Concan. But magnificent and stupendous as the scenery is around, it does not, I am told, in any degree equal the ghauts to the southward. The extreme steepness of this pass, which I conceive to be five miles by the path from the bottom to the village of Condallah on the summit of the table-land, is so great, that it was usual for the convoys of bullocks to be several days in passing it.

The chain of western ghauts extends from the province of Khandeish, on the banks of the Taptee, to Cape Comorin, never being more than fifty, and not often less than thirty miles from the sea. In their whole extent they are stated to have but few passes, but when they become better known, I have no doubt many will be discovered, as was the case in the Pyrenees when occupied by our army.

The geographical structure of the peninsula of India strikingly resembles that of the South American continent; the vast chain of the Andes on the west being sixty miles from the Pacific Ocean, to which it presents a precipitous face, and slopes by a gradual and gentle declivity to the Atlantic, into which the Amazon, Plata, and other rivers which have their source near the Pacific run. In this peninsula, in the same manner, the great rivers, the Godavery, Krishnah, Cauvery, and other streams which fall into the bay of Bengal, take their rise near the sea on the Malabar coast. The Nerbuddah and Taptee, however, passing westward to the north of the range of ghauts, fall into the gulf of Cutch.

I had gone through so much fatigue and personal exertion, that I was quite unwell when I reached the bottom; and, lying down in my palanquin, was taken up by the *hummalls* (the Persian word) as they here call the bearers of Calcutta, the cahars of Hindoostan, and the bhoeys of Madras and the Dekhun, and never opened my eyes till called by Colonel Osborne in a little hovel dignified by the name of an inn, at Panwell, the village at which officers generally land from Bombay on their route to the Dekhun.

I found a boat belonging to the superintendant of the marine ready for me, and that the tide would answer at nine; and having dressed, and partaken of a splendid breakfast, I walked to the boat, which was very comfortable, and larger than the row boats on the Ganges. Panwell is situated on an inlet of the sea, which takes its name from the town; and, after a passage down of about ten miles, I reached the open harbour, of which the view was beautiful.

The harbour of Bombay extends many miles up, the road where the ships lie being off the town, which is on an island nearly the most western point on the coast. I ordered the boatmen to proceed to the island of Elephanta, which is situated in the harbour, and about two o'clock we brought-to off that celebrated spot. I was put on shore on the side opposite to that where parties generally land, and did not see the statue of the elephant near the landing place. The island from the water appears to be formed of two hills, joined below, and covered with trees and some cultivation. A bank of mud rendered it necessary that we should be carried on shore. We soon found volunteer guides to show us the road to the cave, and after ascending about half-way towards the summit, descried the habitation of a serjeant of veterans who had been placed here by government in a snug cottage, to take charge of it and the figures. Familiar as I was with such curious excavations, I was much damped in my expectations from the interior, by finding a white-washed wall built across the cave, with a door and padlock, for the key of which I had to wait. At length, the key being brought, we entered, and I am well pleased to have seen the cave of Elephanta; though the only extraordinary thing, after those I had previously visited, was the famous three-headed figure or tri-murti, supposed to be of Brahma, Vishnu, and Seva, at the farther end. It is a very gigantic bust, and the ornaments, &c. beautifully carved, though now damaged by age or malice. The cave had at one time three faces, of which the centre only was supported by pillars; the other two are much destroyed, it is said by the Portuguese, as I was told at Carli. The poor subjects of his most faithful majesty were certainly in that instance calumniated; and it should be recollected that the Mahometans were just as desperate fanatics as our good allies. If, as is stated, the Portuguese fired cannon upon this cave, I cannot help thinking it curious they should only destroy the sides, and not the principal temple; and I firmly believe no such thing ever happened. I conceive the sacrilegious hands of the Portuguese have been less active than is supposed, notwithstanding the character they have got from Knox, as destroyers of the remains of idolatry in Ceylon. I asked the serjeant if any change had taken place in the pillars or what few figures there are, during the time he had been in charge. He answered that for the last six years only one small piece of stone had fallen from one of the pillars. This cave is certainly well worth seeing, but greatly inferior to any of those at Ellora, or that of Carli.

We returned to our boat, and after a few tacks, about four approached the town of Bombay, or the buildings which extend along the water-side to Massagong. The shipping, fort, and dock-yard, were in sight, with the steeple of the church and top of the government house; the whole presenting a view so European, that it delighted me, and I felt I was approaching my long destined haven. We passed through the vessels at anchor, and landed at the new bunder, or mole, which runs out from the esplanade. I found the palanquin of Mr. Warden, the chief secretary to government, and a note from him to say, that the moment I arrived he would take me out to the governor's country house at Parell, being some distance from the town. I walked across to his temporary bungalow, built on the glacis, where many of the gentlemen live. These buildings are removed during the south-west monsoon. The sea breeze was delightful and refreshing, and I felt each respiration give new life and vigour. I did not find Mr. Warden, the principal secretary, at home, but was carried into the fort to his office, where I was kindly received by him, and getting into his carriage, proceeded towards Parell.

As we proceeded, I observed the Parsees taking their station to pay their last devoirs to the departing sun, seated facing the west on the grass of the glacis. I saw large bodies of unarmed men at drill, and heard that the presidency had been so totally without troops after the breaking out of the war, that the governor had raised the Portuguese militia from the residents in Bombay and adjacent villages. After we had passed the limits of the glacis, we entered a long straggling street, with many good houses, principally of wood, which I was informed belonged to the Parsees.

I think the native women whom I saw carrying water in large copper vessels better looking than any I had previously noticed any where in India. The Parsees, who have kept their blood pure, are very white; but the Portuguese, who have pursued a quite contrary course, are even darker than the natives. This last circumstance I cannot account for.

I learnt from Mr. Warden, that the governor was to dine at six o'clock with one of the members of council, and that he had no doubt I should accompany him. I was much fatigued, and should have been better pleased to go to bed; but ere we reached Sir Evan Nepean's house, we met him in his carriage, accompanied by Mr. Thomson, who had been previously Lord Hastings' private secretary, and who had one year before quitted Calcutta in an Arab ship to go to England by way of Egypt. He had been taken ill on the Malabar coast, had remained at Cochin several months, and had been two months in Bombay.

Sir Evan received me most kindly, and I got into the carriage, and accompanied his honour, for so he is here called, to the dinner party; and to my great relief, being quite overcome with fatigue, returned early to his residence. This morning, after a good night's rest, we proceeded about ten o'clock into the town to the government house, where I have now my habitation. Mr. Thomson intends to accompany me through Egypt, and tells me that Captain Blast, the officer who commands the Mercury, the Company's cruiser, under orders to carry me to Suez, affirms that we should not lose a day, as the best time of the year for this voyage is already past. I have in consequence settled that we shall sail from hence on the 7th instant, as I hope by that time to have all the papers and information I require. Parell, the governor's country seat, is about four miles from the town, and has been a Portuguese chapel, but, with the addition of an upper story, makes a very good house. Sir Evan lives in a very private manner, which, from the situation of Bombay, is of small consequence, as there is comparatively but little communication with the natives; and it does not require that they should judge of our power, or form their political ideas from our imposing appearance, as in Hindoostan. I learn that the government of this presidency sent home, *via* Egypt, an officer, Captain Moore, with the accounts of the late events at Poonah, and who must reach England long before the accounts of which I am bearer.

The docks, which I am to visit this evening, have furnished the navy with some of the finest ships; and I shall of course see the celebrated Parsee builder, who has had the entire management of them since the death of his brother. His name is Jumpsetjee Bomajee. The houses at this presidency are inferior to those at Calcutta or Madras; but I think they are better furnished, the rooms at the other two cities being almost bare, as all kinds of draperies and furniture harbour musquitoes.

CHAPTER XXIII.

Visit the docks—Their history—Formerly at Surat—Malabar pirates—Lowjee, a Parsee —Hereditary virtue—Manseckjee and Bomajee—Framjee Manseckjee, and Jumpsetjee Bomajee—Cornwallis, a frigate built for the Company—Ships built for the Royal Navy —List of ships built in the yard—Vessel for the Imaum of Muscat—Steam-engine used in the docks—Teak wood—Church—Tombs—Bombay like a Portuguese city—Accounts of Egypt—Caves in Salsette—Parsee servant—Infamous proposal of the Peishwah—Fête at the government house—Rooms of the Literary Society of Bombay —Zodiac — Moulah Feruz—Dussateer — Its translation — George Namah — Fire temple—Burial-place—Arrangements for sailing.

Bombay, 5th February, 1818.

YESTERDAY about four o'clock I accompanied Captain Meriton, the superintendant of the marine, over the dock-yard. The docks are of granite, all dovetailed, and are three in number. Their history is curious. Previous to 1735 there were no docks at this place, the principal building station being at Surat. The Company had, as early as 1673, been obliged to build ships of war, to defend their trade against the Malabar pirates.

In 1735, on a vessel being built at Surat for the Company, the agent who was sent there was so much pleased with the foreman, a Parsee, of the name of Lowjee Nassarwanjee, that he tried to persuade him to come to Bombay, the government being desirous to establish a yard on that island. The attachment and fidelity of this Parsee to his master would not yield to the advantageous offer made until his permission was procured. A short time after this period, Lowjee, with a few artificers, arrived at Bombay, and selected for the docks part of the ground on which they now stand. Being a thoroughfare, however, they were not very advantageously situated. The scarcity of timber obliged government, the following year, to send Lowjee to the north, to negotiate for a supply from the natives in the forests, and on his return he brought his family, and settled them at Bombay.

Indeed, the history of this dock-yard is that (and a most pleasing one it is) of the rise of a respectable, honest, and hard-working family, as through several generations the chief builder has been a descendant from the first settler Lowjee: and so incorruptly and disinterestedly have they all acted in the discharge of their duty, that none of them ever attained to affluence. The frequent use of the dock-yard, particularly by the king's ships, which had formerly to be hove down at Hog Island, rendered it necessary to increase the size of the yard, which was carried into execution after 1767. In the year 1771 Lowjee introduced into the yard his two grandsons, Framjee Manseckjee and Jumpsetjee Bomajee, but, determining they should learn their profession practically, he made them work as carpenters at twelve rupees a month.

In 1774 Lowjee Nassarwanjee died, leaving nothing but a house and a sum of money under 3000*l.* He, however, bequeathed the remembrance of his integrity to his grandsons, Mansackjee, who succeeded him as master-builder, and Bomajee as his assistant, and they carried on the business with as much success and credit as the founder of the yard. In 1776 the docks had acquired great reputation, and during the subsequent war in India, and the severe actions between Sir Edward Hughes and Admiral Sufrein, our vessels were docked here: and these two worthy successors of Lowjee built two ships of 900 tons.

Bomajee died in 1790, and Manseckjee in 1792; the former in debt, and the latter leaving but a small provision for his family. They were succeeded by their sons, Framjee Manseckjee and Jumpsetjee Bomajee. The success which attended the exertions of the last in building the Cornwallis, a frigate for the East India Company, in 1802, determined the admiralty to order men of war for the king's navy to be constructed at this spot. They intended to have sent out a European builder, but the merits of Jumpsetjee being made known to their lordships, they ordered him to continue as master-builder, without the intervention of European direction or aid. The excellent construction of two frigates and a line-of-battle ship spread the fame of this worthy Parsee over England. Never have the orders or expectations of government been misplaced or disappointed.

In 1805 the dock-yard was enlarged and shut up, the thoroughfare being discontinued. Two more docks have since been added, and, for the service of the royal navy alone, the following ships have been constructed at this port: four 74's, two 38's, two 36's, two 18's, and two 10's. And at present I saw the Malabar 74, and a 38-gun frigate building; the latter is to be named the Saranga Pataum, (Seringapatam). Besides these, since the dock-yard was established they have built nine ships above 1000 tons, five above 800 tons, six above 700 tons, five above 600 tons, and thirty-five others of a smaller tonnage.

The sons and grandsons of Jumpsetjee are now in the dock-yard. Thus five generations have followed each other; and I am happy to say, his son promises as well as any of his ancestors.

The Imaum of Muscat, one of our allies on the coast of Arabia, has a vessel of 60 guns building for him at the present time, of a particular construction, as he always takes his women to sea with him. He is almost continually in the personal command of his fleet, as his neighbourhood is infested with the Whehabbee pirates, and his ambition leads him to attempt the reduction of several islands in the Persian Gulf.

The dock-yards have lately had a steam-engine added to them, which has greatly facilitated the work in the docks, as the water is pumped out by it in a few hours. Three or more vessels can be taken in during the springs, while formerly one, or at most two, was the number inspected or repaired in each month. It would be advantageous if the power of the engine could be increased so as to draw large masses of timber from the shore into the yard.

Beside these docks, there is a building slip near them; and at Massagong, and at Colabah, in the neighbourhood of Bombay, are others.

The expense of building the Cornwallis, of 74 guns and 1767 tons, including lower masts and bowsprit, was 60,762*l*., and that of the Wellesley, 74 guns and 1745 tons, 56,003*l*. On board the former of these vessels I came out to India, and she is a ship of very fine qualities. The teak timber, of which they are constructed, lasts much longer than any other wood. The worm will not eat it; and it is supposed to be from the same cause that the iron bars do not corrode in it; an oil remaining in the timber, the smell and taste of which the former do not like, while it prevents the rust of iron.

I was much delighted with the appearance of the venerable Jumpsetjee Bomajee, and had a long conversation with him. I made the veteran builder promise to give me his picture. He is to call on me to-morrow, and to bring with him a piece of plate the Board of Admiralty presented to him on the arrival in England of the Minden, 74, built in this dock-yard. Captain Meriton shewed me a model of that vessel, which was built piecemeal and at the same time as the vessel itself, and every timber was added as the shipwright placed them on the vessel in the building dock.

After I had viewed all I wished, I walked round the outside of the walls of the fort, and entering by a different gate, visited the church, which was open; but I saw the interior to great disadvantage, as it was almost dark. It appears very neat, and two of the monuments, those of the late governor, Mr. Duncan, and Captain Hardinge of the navy, both of white marble, are extremely handsome. The town is fortified, and presents to the eye a complete Portuguese city. The green within the walls, where the troops once used to exercise when alarmed by the power of the neighbouring states, is now crowded with bales of merchandise, a finer field being open to the troops in the plains of the Dekhun and Guzaraut. I dined with Sir A. Anstruther, the recorder, and in the evening returned to Parell.

This morning at breakfast I met the archdeacon, Dr. Barnes, whom I had the happiness of knowing previously at Calcutta. He has arranged to accompany me to-morrow to see the Parsee high-priest, and then to a garden in the neighbourhood, to view a small fire temple, and the outside of one of their burial-places.

On the evening on which I arrived at this place I met a gentleman of the name of Briggs, belonging to a mercantile house at Alexandria and Cairo, who has lately come from Egypt. He is now employed in opening a trade between Egypt and India, and has given both Mr. Thomson and myself letters to his house at Cairo and Alexandria, and much valuable information. He tells me it will be impossible to procure letters of pratique, and that I must undergo a quarantine of forty days on entering Europe.

Mr. Briggs has also brought a sword from the Pacha of Egypt to Lord Hastings; but the difficulty of communication with head-quarters is at present so great that it must be sent round by sea. The intelligence he has given me concerning Egypt is most satisfactory; and should the season be too late for a good passage up the Red Sea as far as Suez, I can with ease land at Cossier, and, by traversing the desert, reach the Nile below Thebes. If I should find time to visit the ruins of this city, it is possible I may meet Mr. Salt, as he is actively employed in searching for antiquities in the city of One Hundred Gates.

I have heard, since my arrival here, that the caves in the island of Salsette are better worth seeing than that of Elephanta, but that the difficulty of reaching them prevents their being generally visited or known; and that they are so distant from any road that it would require a day to get to them, and the same time to return. Jumpsetjee called upon me this morning, having brought with him his urn, a present from the admiralty. It is a handsome piece of plate, but not very massy, with an inscription; and the handle on the top is the exact model of the Minden without her masts, and has her name in very minute characters on the stern. Upon the whole it did not seem to me worthy either of the dignity of the donors or the merit of the donee. He presented me with an engraving of himself, a strong resemblance, which I will carry to England with me, as he is a character I highly respect. I hired a servant to wait on me here, who is a Parsee, and to my astonishment last night refused to put out my candle, but called another person to do it. This originated in the reverence of that sect for the element of fire. I should be curious to know what they would do if their houses were in flames. These gentlemen would make very bad firemen to any of the insurance offices. They are all well educated, and generally speak and even write our language perfectly. They are in their complexion much fairer than the natives, though not quite so fair as the British.

I have heard to-day a report of a most nefarious proposition of his highness the Peishwah to our government at Bombay, in which he offers to poison his adviser, Goklah, if we will make peace with him. This is quite consistent with his treachery towards us, and will meet with its due punishment.

Bombay, 6th February, 1818.

After dining yesterday with Sir Miles Nightingale, we returned to the government-house by nine o'clock, and soon after about three hundred people assembled in the ball-room in honour of the queen's birth-day. I had a very long and interesting conversation with Mr. Erskine, a gentleman distinguished for his talents and oriental learning. He has studied the Hindoo mythology at its source, in the sacred language, and has sent home, for publication in the first volume of the Researches of the Bombay Literary Society, an account of the cave of Elephanta. He was delighted to hear that I had made interest for the removal of the white wall, door, and padlock, in front of the cave; or, as I had also suggested, the removal of it below the terrace, so as not to be seen. I think I have raised his curiosity so far that he will make a point of seeing Carli and Ellora, and, with his great knowledge and study, he owes it to the world to give his opinions and remarks on these extraordinary places.

The officers of the newly raised regiments of cavalry were in great numbers in the room, and I did not much admire their uniforms, one of which is red and white and gold, the other red and white and silver. As I had arranged to sail to-morrow, I have been much employed all day; but snatched an hour to proceed with Dr. Barnes to see Moulah Feruz, the Parsee priest, and the garden of a rich man of the same persuasion, in which is a fire temple and a burial-place. We first, however, went to the rooms belonging to the Literary Society, and looked over the library and some of the curiosities; among which I was particularly pleased with the small zodiac brought from some place on the coast of Malabar. Taurus is represented as the Indian bull, with a hump on his shoulders; and the alligator was in the place of one of the other signs, but which I forget. We then proceeded to the house of Moulah Feruz, who received me very civilly; and I conversed with him respecting the book his father brought with him from Ispahan, which Mr. Duncan previous to his death was himself about to translate and publish, and which is now finishing by Mr. Erskine. I was anxious to procure one copy of the translation as far as they had gone, and one in the Persian as far as it had been printed, which he has promised to give me to-morrow. The original is in a language different from Persian, and the majority of the words are from the Sanskrit, but written in the Persian character, and numerous notes in the modern language. It is called the Dussateer.

Moulah Feruz shewed me a translation he had made into Persian from the English of Orme's History of the Wars in India, and stated that it was in the same verse as the Shah Nama of Ferdauzi. He is anxious to receive from England the history of India between the period where Orme's leaves off and the accounts of the wars of Tippoo, if any such exist; being desirous to complete this his history of our power in India, which he entitles *George Namah*, or the History of the Georges. I fear there is no book of the kind in print, though from the Seir Mutaghrein and the Annual Register much may be collected.

We next went on by the road to Malabar point, where the governor has another house, and about half-way to it stopped at the garden. The fire temple is a small building, about eight feet long and five broad, with a pent roof, small iron grated windows, and a door strongly padlocked. The smoke had no other means of escaping but through the windows. The fire, which is kept constantly burning, has for fuel the best and sweetest woods, and it is a crime to throw any impure substances into it. Herodotus tells us that the ancient Persians did not burn their dead bodies, as they thought it profane to feed the divinity with human carcases.

I did not go very close to the burial-place, but I have been assured, by those who have ascertained the fact, that the body is not permitted to be destroyed by vultures, as is generally supposed. On the contrary, it has an iron grating over it to preserve it from their voracious appetites. The Parsees are particularly anxious that the eyes of the profane should not see the interior of these cemeteries. The view of Bombay from this garden was beautiful, and the road from it, shaded by innumerable cocoa-nut trees, delightful.

Sir Evan Nepean intends we should dine on board his yacht to-morrow, and from that vessel take leave, and go on board the Mercury. I have received from Mr. Warden, the chief secretary to government, twelve hundred dollars for any expenses I may find necessary in Egypt.

CHAPTER XXIV.

Moulah Feruz—Accompany the governor on board his yacht—Arrive on board the Mercury—Reflections—Accounts received at Bombay from the armies—Arrival of our resident at Holkar's camp—Sir Thomas Hislop returns to the southward—Killidar of Assier Ghur—The operations of General Munro in the south of the Peishwah's dominions—Various petty affairs—Reduction of the forts in the Concan—Reflections on India—Our position at the time I quitted it—The Mercury—Crew—Guns.

On board the Honourable Company's cruizer, Mercury,
February 8th, 1818.

EARLY yesterday morning Moulah Feruz called on me, and brought with him an entire copy of the *Dussateer*, in Persian, and all the sheets of the translation which had been printed. It appears to me to be a collection of incoherent sentences, the style not unlike the Khoraun, and I was disappointed in not procuring Mr. Erskine's preface. About two o'clock I accompanied Sir Evan Nepean and Mr. Meriton on board the yacht, having previously sent all my baggage and cot to the Mercury. A servant, who spoke Persian and Arabic, whom I had hired, absented himself on our quitting the shore, and did not rejoin us.

We found on board the yacht Sir Miles Nightingale and his family, and I received from his excellency the latest military news from Sir William Kier's force. We continued sailing about the harbour, and having partaken of a cold dinner, Mr. Thomson and myself took leave, and at five o'clock came on board this ship. After Captain Blast had received his orders, we got the anchor up, and with a fine breeze put out to sea; and the darkness soon shut from us the shores of the most interesting country I shall in all probability ever see in the world.

Thus, after a journey of considerable difficulty and interest of above one thousand miles, I am safely on board a vessel, looking forward to the journey through Egypt.

The intelligence received from the army of Sir Thomas Hislop, and of Sir William Kier's division, subsequent to the treaty of peace with Holkar, and other information which I received at Bombay, is as follows:

In consequence of the treaty, Major Agnew, who was appointed resident at the court of the Maha Rajah Mulharao Holkar, arrived in his camp at Boughur on the 10th of January, attended by a strong escort of 250 infantry, 100 cavalry, and two pieces of cannon. He was most favourably received, and a very general appearance of gladness was evinced by all ranks at the conclusion of the peace. A body of 2000 horse quitted Holkar's service on the 9th, under their commander Ram Deen, who is averse to the treaty. They were at Ratchrode on the 10th, and it is conjectured that some of them will try to join the Peishwah; others go to Scindiah, where they have connexions; and some return to their homes. This very desirable arrangement being completed, Sir Thomas Hislop intended, on the 13th of January, to proceed to the southward by Onail, and had ordered the battering train of the Bombay army to join him, as the siege of Assier Ghur is now become an object of the first importance. The killidar has, there is reason to believe, received a lack of rupees in gold from the Peishwah to hold out to the last, and was busily employed in repairing and provisioning his fort, which is one of the strongest in India, and garrisoned by many Arabs and good troops.

I have now only to state, that General Munro had moved into the southern jaghires, and took a fort on the 5th of January, named Gunduck; on the 9th Dummul surrendered after a few hours battering. The general had seized the whole of Goklah's jaghire, and taken the following forts: Rana Bednour, Bunkapoor, Old Hoobly, Nowdgood, Muncotta, or Murrerecotta, Sawanbutty, Adore, Angel, and several others; and conquered the greatest part of the Peishwah's territory south of the Mulpurbar with the aid of the inhabitants of the country, who had expelled the Mharattas. A detachment of cavalry from this force had, on the 21st of January, cut up a party of 400 Pindarries, who had penetrated by the ceded districts, and were returning from Chitteldroog.

A body of Goklah's horse had also been cut to pieces. Colonel Prother had taken Kurnalla and, it is believed, Boput Ghur, the former in the Lower Concan, and was proceeding to reduce the several lines of forts on the ghauts, on the plains, and on the sea-side. Five companies of the 89th king's regiment were ordered up from Quilon to join this latter force. Sir Evan Nepean had sent a battalion to the Lower Concan, to secure the wives and families of our Sepoys from the ungenerous treatment they were suffering from the Peishwah's officers.

As I have now quitted India, it will I think be right, after the account I have given of the various occurrences which have taken place in that country within the last year, and their very important results, to view our empire as it now stands in February, and contrast it with what it was at the beginning of the cold weather. We were at that time at peace with all the states of India, and an easy conquest of the Pindarries appeared not only probable, but in all human calculation certain. Before I enter upon that topic I intend to devote a few pages to the consideration of some points respecting our empire, and its situation, both moral and political, first adverting to the great or rather total difference between European and Indian manners and sentiments.

Perhaps I may for a time dishearten my reader, by stating that it is absolutely necessary to reside some time in the country to become fully informed respecting it. Many, who have previously conceived themselves entirely masters of the subject, have acknowledged, before they have been long in India, that unless they had quitted Europe they would never have thoroughly understood it. It is far from my wish to make those in Europe despair of becoming acquainted with our Indian empire; but the difficulty of inducing them to shake off their prejudices, look with kindness and tolerance, if not with respect, on those of the natives, is so great, that I fear they cannot be overcome without visiting a country which is almost like another world. The peculiarities which are presented to us, in reviewing the political state of our Indian empire, will not admit of the application of European principle: never, from so small a beginning, has dominion swelled to such a magnitude, or advanced with so rapid a course. Within the last eighty years it has grown from an emporium of commerce to a mighty empire, the most populous in the world, China alone excepted.

When we reflect on the deep-laid plan of the jesuits for the formation of an empire in Paraguay, and have seen these subtile politicians, with their established forms of government, and their settled rules of subjugation, entirely unsuccessful; and when we look on the other side, and trace a company of merchants settling on the coast of India, solely with mercantile views, without guile or insidious projects, (for no one will be so hardy as to say, an idea of conquest ever entered the heads of the first establishment of the Company) becoming so powerful, as to be sole masters of a country as large as two-thirds of Europe, we must admit that all human foresight or calculation availeth nought, and bow the knee to overpowering influences.

It is curious to observe how early it was remarked by an historian, who, adding vast information to great talents, and having witnessed the infantine attempts of the two great rival nations on the coast of Coromandel, and the state of the native powers, formed a correct judgment of the future destinies of this vast country, so as in the following sentence to become absolutely prophetic, that "The interests of the Indian princes and Moorish governors perpetually clashing with one another, and with the interests of the Mogul, will perhaps always prevent the empire of Hindoostan from coercing the ambitious attempts of any powerful European nation when not opposed by another of equal force, much less will any particular principality in India be able to withstand such an invader." The destruction of the French power by the fall of Pondicherry, in 1761*, from which it never recovered, though this nation subsequently gained a footing at the courts of the Nizam, Tippoo, and Scindiah, all of which fell under the excellent policy of the present governor-general's great predecessor, placed India in exactly the same predicament which had been thus speculated upon, and the transfer of the empire of Hindoostan into our hands has completed Mr. Orme's prediction. It has, ever since that period, been our policy not to suffer the introduction of "another European nation of equal force," and thus this great field (which it has ever been) for adventurers, has been now shut up against them, whether they appear under national banners or as individuals.

Had Albuquerque, Dupleix, or Lally, or their governments at home, ever supposed it was possible for a European nation to rule two-thirds of the dominions of the Mogul, and even hold him personally as a pensioner on their bounty, what would have been their exertions, to have realized such hopes for themselves? Indeed the efforts of the French to introduce their power into the further peninsula a short time before the revolution, and their subsequent attempts at the native courts which I have before mentioned, show how desirous they were of making India, in a future war, the theatre of contest, and proves how deeply they regretted the loss they had sustained on the coast of Coromandel. They had just been tantalized by a

* It is remarkable that in little more than fifty years the principal seats of the French power in Europe, Asia, and America, have fallen under the ascendency of British arms; and, if we include their baffled aspirings in Egypt, this remark will apply to the four quarters of the globe. The places alluded to are Paris, Pondicherry, Quebec, and Cairo or Alexandria.

prospect of further acquisitions, having tasted the delights of sway in the fine provinces and splendid revenue they possessed; and their brilliant, though short, career in India rendered their downfal the more mortifying. We now see, in an undisputed sovereignty, both of Hindoostan and the Dekhun, those who were first taught, on the coast of Coromandel, by the French nation, to aid the native powers, and to follow the examples of their rivals in acquiring territorial possession.

But if the French had established themselves in the Dekhun, and had not been thwarted in the prospect by the jealousy of their commanders, would they have been able even in that case to erect so great a structure as the British have done? May it not be affirmed (without being charged with an overweening national partiality) that it is to our possessing a higher degree of probity and honour, and to the parliamentary control over those who acquired that distant dominion, that we are indebted to our having attained, and maintained, the high ground on which we stand. And do we not now hold our eastern empire from having established an opinion of our superior justice, as well as power? I do not mean to say that the French are so much our inferiors, as to suppose their failure would have flowed wholly from this cause; but having no check like our parliament, they would not have had so great a fear of detection and counteraction in the path of ambition and extortion. But their revolution having brought forward so many worthless characters, it is likely that they would, in the time of terror, have been happy to seek an asylum in the East, and doubtless would not have added to the stock of either probity or honour in their settlements; and it is probable that tyranny and oppression would have been exercised by them over the natives, and have ended in discontents, rebellion, and expulsion. This is presumable from the conduct of those employed in the early part of our eastern rule, which will not, I fear, bear much inquiry. But for the last fifty or sixty years our administration of government has been gradually becoming more perfect, the servants of the Company most respectable and trust-worthy, and from them collectively as many men of first-rate abilities in their different lines, and, I will venture to say, of correct morality, drawn, as from any other class of society under the British empire.

The natives under our protection have, for fifty or sixty years, with the exception of Tippoo's ravaging the Carnatic, Holkar the Doab, and the incursions of the Pindarries, felt the advantage of living under our rule, and the security from violent inroads, which had almost annually devastated their homes for a long period preceding the establishment of our government. The province of Bengal, which was plundered continually, (almost every year) has been free from these miseries for the last sixty years. I trust the fall of the Pindarries will ensure a similar quiet to the whole of our dominions, and those of our allies, for a still longer period to come. These advantages, added to the excellency of our regulations, to the mitigation of the sanguinary parts of the Mahometan laws, and the introduction of seasonable and well digested additions, and to the impartial and equitable administration of them, with the security of living under the greatest power in India, will make the population of our provinces happy, and, putting all political consideration out of the question, our increase of territory a blessing to millions. It has already been remarked, that one of the chief causes of our ascendancy over the natives of India has been our military science, consisting in our superior engineering, discipline, and tactics, agreeably to what was said by a great philosopher, that "knowledge is power:" may we not with truth assign as another cause of that ascendancy, and of our future prospects of permanency, our superior good faith and honour, agreeably to the common adage, that "honesty is the best policy?"

It is not from speculation or hearsay, but from the conviction, arising out of actual observation, that I have thus ventured to advance what I have stated, and I cannot bring a stronger proof of it than what I am about to mention. The population of our territory annually increases by the emigration of thousands, from under bad rule, to that of our more paternal government; and no one will contend that a fairer criterion than this can be adduced. But in further confirmation, I have been assured, that when the governor-general visited the provinces under the dominion of the Newab Vizier, in 1814, many of the inhabitants asked with anxiety, which shewed their wish for the change, and a hope of its confirmation, if we intended to introduce our officers and government; and in very decided terms proved they had compared the two systems together, and not to the advantage of their own sovereign. This superior security, being actually experienced by the natives of our own provinces, will make them dread any change in their rulers; and if we continue to have men of talents and honesty at the head of affairs, able and willing to shield them from danger, and to ensure them the blessings of mild and just legislation, may we not, I ask, create a sentiment, which they never entertained towards their native rulers, of attachment and gratitude towards us?

The reader will perceive how much this statement of facts militates against some of the favourite prejudices of Englishmen. It is in our nature to indulge, and invite as it were, feelings of commiseration, and to view political subjects on the darkest side. It has been already admitted that there was too much reason for this in the early part of our Indian administration; and the mind of the nation was exasperated by their errors being exposed by the unexampled eloquence of Mr. Burke, in his invective against one of our greatest Eastern statesmen; the deep impression of which has not even yet worn off. I have been told that it is a common question, but half in jest, on the return of a person from India, " How many newabs have you plundered, and what rajah's jewels have you carried off?" and although an attempt is made to show that the accumulation of fortune in India is, as in other countries, only the reward of a long residence, and, as our government is constituted, of a strict and honourable attendance to business and duty, an idea still remains as unfavourable, as false, of its mode of acquisition: so difficult it is to remove early impressions. Instead of these gloomy and unfavourable views of British domination in India, I should be disposed to assert, that an enthusiastic mind would be justified in picturing to itself, that Providence, fatigued with the continued sight of misrule and crime, had, by a long chain of events, brought the British power, with those concomitants of justice, honour, and good government, which we are collectively and individually taught by our invaluable constitution, to better the state of existence of one hundred millions of people, by staying the hand of oppression.

Another most mistaken opinion held by many in England is, that the wars undertaken by our local government spring principally, if not solely, from ambitious views.

All our wars, subsequent to the period at which Lord Cornwallis went out to India, will bear a very strict and severe scrutiny into the motives in which they originated, except that of his lordship's first war with Tippoo, which was fairly challengeable, from an article in the treaty with the Nizam. With this exception they will be found to have been entered upon from sound reasoning, justice, and policy. Perhaps, until Lord Cornwallis became governor-general, it is not right to view India as a national concern, excepting with respect to its commerce; for though the Parliament had interfered long before, and made efforts for its improvement, yet the subject was so little understood, and the arrangements for its government so crude and ill adapted to their object, that our Eastern dominion could hardly be regarded as a component part of the British empire till a governor-general was appointed, who was to be considered as the delegate of the nation, and not of the India Company.

In all occurrences, like those which I have endeavoured to narrate, the British government has been successful in every part of India, and the hostility of our faithless enemies has only served to draw down merited punishment on themselves, and tend to the aggrandizement of our empire. Even Scindiah, our ally, had not strength of mind, or sufficient political faith and wisdom, to enter heartily into the execution of his offensive and defensive treaty with us, so as to compensate for the wreck of reputation he sustained in submitting to our terms. His troops had lost confidence in him and his government, and the little command he had over them had vanished. His dominions were surrounded by our subsidiary troops, or by territories under our controlling interest. He was, in short, but a little higher in political importance than Holkar before the war, and had comparatively dwindled into insignificance; standing alone, in India the only wretched remains of the once overpowering Mharatta confederacy, whose conquests, by the anarchy they had once occasioned, laid open the field to us, and who now fell under our far-spreading power.

Scindiah had by his lukewarm policy, and, in a great degree, neutral character, rendered our government dissatisfied with him; and his commanders and officers had on many occasions laid themselves open to our most severe reproof.

By the treaties with Kerrowley and Boondie and Kottah, a strong barrier had been formed to the north of his country, secured by our guarantee. The Newab of Bopaul was reinstated in his neighbourhood as an efficient Mahometan prince, and it is with the most gratifying feelings that we now see this state, which had so long ago assisted General Goddard, in his almost unexampled march across the peninsula to Surat, requited for its many sufferings.

Holkar was united as intimately and as strongly as a treaty, a resident at his court, and a subsidiary force, could bind him. The various Rajahpoot states have implored, with expressions of the strongest anxiety, to be taken under our protection, which, if they should procure, would for the future shield them from the miseries they have endured for so many years.

Two-thirds of the Pindarries are dispersed or destroyed, and the remainder only supported and kept together by hopes from the Peishwah; who, totally stripped of his dominions, having forfeited them by his treachery, holds nothing but the ground he covers, and some forts, which we are rapidly reducing one after another. His several sirdars are but confederated by some secret magnet, which must lose its power daily. His capital, Poonah, is in our possession, and he has become little better than a Pindarry himself. Thus the conduct of the native princes has constrained us to be the only great power in India, the dominion of which is only bounded (including the states under our influence) by the snowy mountains, the Indus, and the sea.

Thus the British government, at the commencement of the year 1818, possesses an empire little inferior to that of Alexander, of the Romans, the Kaliphat, Timourlung, or Ghingis Khan; an empire which is likely to be of longer duration than any of them, for its rise has not depended on the talents and fortunes of one man, but on the grand principles of our physical, moral, and intellectual superiority. We may thus, with the character worthy of our nation, continue to make our sovereign and uncontrolled sway (which it must still remain, as the natives are unable to feel the happy effects of a free government,) the most benign despotism that ever existed; and apply with the hand of a parental monarch, to those who are our subjects, the happy rules of equity and moderation which we are taught from our own constitution.

By our commanding political situation, which gives us the most unlimited power over the native courts, we can insure permanent tranquillity, and induce them to look on us alone as the keystone of India. Thus it will be our policy to place ourselves at the head of a commonwealth of nations, and making ourselves the arbiter of all misunderstandings among them, eradicate the ruinous and fallacious policy of short-sighted imbecile princes and profligate ministers.

The vessel on board of which I now am is very small, being only of 180 tons burthen, and the cabin confined, though built with a poop on the quarter-deck. She has a large complement of men, consisting of a captain, two lieutenants, a surgeon, three midshipmen, a gunner, thirty English sailors, twenty-eight Sepoys of the marine battalion, and thirty Lascars, or Indian seamen. She carries twelve carronades, and two long nine-pounders, and observes the same discipline on board as a king's ship. Great pains seem to have been taken to ornament the quarter-deck, and above the wheel are the Company's arms, and on the boards, to cover the ends of the spars on the booms, are painted their crest. Much of the rope used on board is made from the filaments of the husk of the cocoa-nut, which lasts well, and is less expensive than rope made from hemp.

Mr. Thomson has taken up his quarters on one side, and my cot is slung opposite.

CHAPTER XXV.

The island of Socotra—When discovered—Overrun by Albuquerque—Company's marine a bad service—Number of ships—Treaty with Cutch—Imaum of Muscat—Pirates—Whchabbee pirates—Mode of fighting—Cruelties—Desperate gallantry—Arden—Straits of Babelmandeb—Want of water in the Red Sea—Arrive at Mocha—Boat upset—Arabs—Their song—Quit Mocha—Foul winds and calms—Long passage—Navigation of the Red Sea—Daos—North-west winds—Determine to put into Cossier—Reflections on the communication from India to England by the Red Sea and Egypt—Abyssinian sheep—Sepoys and Lascars—Mode of living.

On board the Honourable Company's cruiser, Mercury, 16th Feb. 1818.
Lat. 13°. 6″. N. Long. 53°. 35″. E.

OUR passage hitherto has been very good, and we this day made the island of Socotra, which lies off the African coast. This island is famous for its aloes, and is thinly inhabited. Vasco de Gama passed it without seeing it, and it was first discovered to Europeans by Fernandez Pereyra in 1506; it was subsequently overrun by Albuquerque. Marco Polo tells us that the inhabitants at the end of the thirteenth century were Christians, having a bishop; and Sir Thomas Rowe, when on his embassy to Jehan Ghuir, put into this island. It was then governed by a Mahometan prince, but Sir Thomas was convinced that the former inhabitants must have been Christians, as some images and crucifixes were found in one of the churches.

Our latitudes and longitudes up to this day have been as follows, viz.

	Latitude.	Longitude.
February 9th . .	16° 51″ N. . .	67° 33″ E.
10th . .	16 41 . .	64 37
11th . .	15 26 . .	61 57
12th . .	14 20 . .	59 45
13th . .	14 07 . .	57 50
14th . .	13 53 . .	56 07
15th . .	13 33 . .	54 20

The captain, however, informs me, that the length of our passage after we get to the north of nineteen degrees in the Red Sea will, in all probability, *malgré* our present good fortune, make our voyage a long one.

I have had some conversation with this officer respecting the Company's marine, which appears to me to be a very bad service. He has been twenty-one years in it, and has not long been made a captain. All the large ships are given over to the king's navy; and such ships of war as are in the Company's employment are treated only as merchant vessels, which any king's officers of the navy may command. The Company at one period had several frigates, but at present their marine consists of the following vessels:

		Tons.	Guns.
Teignmouth	Ship	250	16
Benares	——	250	16
Ternate	——	250	16
Aurora	——	217	14
Mercury	——	185	14
Nautilus	Brig	185	14
Antelope	——	185	14
Thetis	——	185	14
Psyche	——	180	12
Vestal	——	160	12
Arid	——	159	12
Prince of Wales	Ship	148	12
Sylph	Brig	78	6
Rodney	Ketch	148	6
Ernaud	Timber Ship	550	

The annual expense of the foregoing vessels, exclusive of the timber ship, is about 425,826 rupees, or about 50,000*l.*; that of the Ernaud 36,000 rupees. This latter vessel is employed in carrying timber from the forests of the same name on the Malabar coast to Bombay. The other vessels are made use of as packets, between the Persian Gulf, the Red Sea, and Bombay; and to convoy merchant vessels along the dangerous piratical coast of Cutch. By our late treaty with Cutch, however, the Rao has become responsible for any losses we may sustain from pirates fitted out from his ports, and has been obliged to promise to return to the owners all shipwrecked property. Previous to this, a misfortune of that kind was a source of emolument to the inhabitants on the sea coast, as formerly in Cornwall.

One of the cruisers, the Aurora, is to convoy the trading vessels from Surat to the Red Sea in March; but there is reason to believe that no pirates are on the coast of Arabia, outside the Persian Gulf. The Imaum of Muscat, our ally, is at open war with all the pirates, but his ambition leads him to very unjustifiable acts. His invasion of the island of Bhareen met with the success it deserved, and he was repulsed last year with the loss of 2000 men, and one of his brothers killed.

The coast of Malabar, and of Cutch, have been notorious from the earliest period for harbouring pirates, and the desperate and successful actions they fought with the Portuguese and English prove how powerful they must have been; since both nations were obliged to have several large men of war to secure their merchant ships from their grasp. It was only in their very haunts, like the Pindarries, that they could be exterminated; and the fall of Severndroog, about 60 years ago, crushed this pest, which, according to historical accounts, had endured for 2000 years, and was, in all probability, coeval with the trade carried on between Egypt, Yemen, and India.

The present society of this description most formidable to the west of India is the Whehabbee pirates, certain Mahometan sectaries extending along the southern coast of the Persian Gulf; and though within the last ten years they have been severely checked, their vessels and houses burnt, and their forts destroyed by an expedition from Bombay, they have of late rallied, and having increased considerably in numbers and strength, have again drawn on them the attention of our government. Their principal settlement is at *Ras Ul Kymer.* They can collect a body of 16,000 men in vessels of several hundred tons, which are propelled both by sails and oars. By their sweeps and great numbers of men, they have during calms the greatest advantages over other vessels. Their ships are built very high out of the water, far overtopping the bulwark even of a frigate; and as it is their mode of fighting to board with the utmost intrepidity, throwing at once a whole crew of perhaps several hundred men on board their opponent's ship, they are generally successful. They have commonly a large gun on the quarter-deck which traverses in every direction, besides two long pieces of cannon in the prow close to the water. They are cruel to a degree, and often sacrifice their prisoners in the name of God, cutting their throats with ceremonies similar to what they use when they kill an animal for food. They avoid our men of war, only looking out for vessels that will reward them with plunder. On their settlements on the coast being attacked, they fly up the country, but soon return and repair the damages.

The Mercury is furnished with boarding nets, which fasten very high up in the shrouds to repel their assaults. Their principal enemy is the Imaum of Muscat. He has had some most desperate engagements with them, and on more than one occasion has, by boarding, been beat off his quarter-deck; and, I believe, in the last instance, he gave all over for lost, and ordered the vessel to be blown up, but fortunately a gun on the poop, loaded with grape, drove the assailants overboard.

It is possible we may see Arden, a large town outside the Straits of Babelmandeb, once in possession of the Portuguese. It at present belongs to an independent chief, or at most a sort of dependent on the Sultan of Senai, a country in the interior.

On board the Honourable Company's cruiser Mercury, March 16th, 1818.
Lat. 21°. 59′. N. Long. 38°. 26′. E.

The distressing intelligence which met us at Mocha on the 21st ultimo was so unexpected, and of so painful a nature, that I have not written since that period. After the 16th instant off Socotra, we had unsettled weather and light winds, and it was not until the morning of the 20th that we came in sight of the high land to the north of the Straits of Babelmandeb, vulgarly called Babelmandel. About noon we passed through this strait by the largest passage, leaving the island of Perim to our right. I think I never saw a more inhospitable looking place; not a tree or shrub was visible, and I pitied the troops who had been encamped here during the Egyptian expedition. For several months there is not a drop of fresh water on the island, and they were obliged to be furnished with this necessary of life from the ships. Captain Blast informed me that it was so scarce at Cossier, where the Indian division landed, that ships were freighted with water alone from Bombay to that port, and the troops were under the necessity of taking sufficient from the vessels for the first two days march into the desert.

Mocha is at no very great distance from the Straits. We anchored off it before dark, and found the Honourable Company's brig Vestal, which had returned from Suez, having carried Captain Moore to that port. The captain sent a boat on board of us, and the officer, in the most abrupt manner, informed us of the loss all had sustained by the death of the Princess Charlotte. I was invited on shore by the governor, but I did not land; and as fate would have it, the boat had not left the ship ten minutes after my refusal before she was upset by a violent squall; and we were for some time in considerable alarm, as we could not, with our glasses, discern either the lieutenant or midshipman. The first lieutenant, however, soon got another boat hoisted out, and rowed to their assistance; and in half an hour returned for a bucket to bail the boat out, and relieved us from our fears on account of those we thought lost, as all were hanging on to the bottom of the boat, but not in imminent danger. Captain Faithful, who commanded the Vestal, came on board in the course of the morning, and brought the Maltese newspapers with him. He stated that Captain Moore had found no difficulty in leaving Suez, which he did on a camel, two hours after he landed, and that he had arrived the next day at Cairo. We sent for various articles of provision from the shore: the Arabs, who brought them off, were much blacker than the Indians, and had full as slender bodies. Whilst they were carrying the wood for fuel from the boat into the ship, they continued to sing a continual humming song, similar to that used in India, when a number of men are employed in raising a weight or an anchor. It is a repetition of *alla-alla-yè-la*; this they accompanied by clapping their hands.

On the 21st we sailed at two o'clock, with a fine breeze from the southward, and were in latitude 14°. 29′. N. long. 42°. 28′. E. at noon on the 22d. On the 23d we had light baffling winds from the northward, having lost our favourable breeze; and since that period it has continually blown from the north-west, or we have been detained by calms. So long has our passage been, that at one period Captain Blast intended to put into Juddah for water: had he done so, I would have attempted to cross by land from that city to Suez on a dromedary; but a good south wind this morning has done some good, and our commander has determined to proceed at least as far as Cossier. I had hoped to have been at Suez by this time, but the continual winds from the north-west, which blow nearly all the year round, have disappointed all my wishes and expectations. I am convinced the only good passages which can be made in this sea should be undertaken in November or December, and I might, if I had reflected before I came into the Red Sea, have concluded, from the scanty traffic on the outside of the shoals, that some good cause existed for its being so little frequented. The prevalence of these north-west winds impedes the navigation, and renders it, for more than nine months in the year, almost a hopeless task to beat up against them in the open sea. In all probability it was the same at the earliest periods; as in the time of Marco Polo the large ships which came from India were unladen at the port of Arden, outside the Strait of Babelmandeb, and the merchandise placed in smaller boats, which he calls djerms, the word used to this day. These vessels, it may be presumed, sailed, as they do now, between the shoals and the coast of Arabia, taking advantage of the land breeze in the morning, which we have had but once in the open sea. The djerms anchor every night, and whenever we were near enough the shore, we saw them taking advantage of or waiting for this slant of wind.

Mocha is now the intermediate port between Egypt and India. I could not help feeling interested in sailing up this sea, which, from time immemorial, was the channel of communication with the latter country, until the discovery of the Cape of Good Hope.

The author of the Periplus of the Red Sea states, that he went down in the open sea. If this was the general custom at all times of the year, there must have been a great assemblage of vessels in the ports of Yemen during nine months; for it is only during November and December, and part of March and April, or a little later, when the south-west winds prevail, that ships of any considerable size can return. At other times I conceive the traffic was carried on, as at the present day, within the shoals. At present the djerms only venture into the open sea, when they stretch across from one shore to the other; and from the extreme unfitness of the vessel and every thing on board, they attempt it with the greatest anxiety. The daos are stupendous boats, of from 4 to 500 tons, with one large mast, immense lattine sails of the thickest cotton, and every part of them of the most unwieldy description. They are, however, well calculated to carry vast quantities of merchandise, and many of them come across the open sea in July and August to Bombay. I saw one in that harbour which had been coppered, measuring 450 tons, and carrying above 550 tons of rice and other grain: her mast was one piece, as large as the main-mast of a 74.

They are numerously manned, and do every thing by main force, accompanied by the whole crew yelling in chorus. We have not seen a single ship except the Vestal since we entered the Red Sea.

On board the Honourable Company's cruizer, Mercury, March 23d, 1818.
Lat. 25° 53′ N. Long. 35° 55′ E.

Since the 16th instant we have had but one good day's run, and we must, it is thought, unavoidably put into Cossier, where I hope to find means of crossing the desert.

I have considered the route over-land from India to England, by this sea and Egypt, and I am satisfied it is not a good way for an officer to return home, if despatch be required, except in the months of November and December; and the quarantine laws on entering Europe would even then greatly impede him. By the establishment of Arabs with dromedaries from Arden to Mocha and Juddah, by way of Suez to Cairo, and from that capital on to Alexandria, I think letters might reach England in less than seventy-five days from Bombay during the north-east monsoon.

All our fresh provisions are nearly out; the fine Abyssinian sheep we took on board at Mocha being all expended. They are of a peculiar breed, and very handsome, being of the purest white, with black heads and feet, and their tails very large. Diodorus Siculus speaks of the sheep in Arabia with large tails. The sailors have been on a short allowance of water for some days; and were it not that the ship has tanks for it, she would not, from her want of room, be able to carry above a month's provision of this necessary. Her orders are to call upon some small independent states outside of the Straits of Babelmandeb, and then to proceed to the Persian Gulf; and Captain Blast does not expect to return to Bombay for fifteen or sixteen months. He is consequently obliged to carry as much salt provisions as she can stow. The Sepoys and Lascars on board live upon rice and salt fish, and the English on the usual ship's provisions. One half of the galley is for the use of the latter, and the Mahometans, who will not eat off any dish used by the soldiers, have the other side to themselves. They only eat twice a day, having no meal like the mid-day dinner of the Europeans. During the time I passed on board I was once amused by their congratulating the captain on the first appearance of the new moon; the seranj and many of the sailors coming aft on purpose to salam to him.

CHAPTER XXVI.

The Mercury makes the Brothers, two small islands off Cossier—Gale of wind—Egyptian coast—Hopes of landing—Inhospitable shore—Cossier—Arrangements—Inquiries to be made of the governor of Cossier—Polacre—Depth of water off the town—Lieutenant goes on shore—Pilgrimages—Camels—Good intelligence—Salute—Land—Natives—Their dress—Governor's house—Governor—A Greek—Captain of the polacre—Arrangements for leaving Cossier to cross the desert—Interpreter—A Turkish soldier to act as escort—Coffee—Salutation—The governor visits the Mercury—The author quits the ship—Leave the standards behind—Takes leave of the governor—Mount the camel—Quit Cossier—Conversation with Mehumed—Pain arising from the motion of the camel—The road—Rocks—Rest—Reflections—Camels—Continue the route—Desert—Rains—The author's attendants—Dress of the Turkish soldiers—Their arms and ammunition—Dress of the soldiers in India—Robbers—Birds and lizards—Water—Hadjees—Pilgrimage—Position of the Mahometans in prayer—Accident—Conversation with Mehumed—Heat—Camels—Watering place.

Off How, a village on the Nile, March 30th, 1818.

THE last four days I have travelled with great fatigue; and from the mode of crossing the desert, having no opportunity, it has been out of my power to write regularly; but being at last on board a boat on this celebrated and classical river, and having slept a few hours last night, I will collect my thoughts, and, if possible, recall all that has occurred to me, and the many interesting scenes I have witnessed since I left the cruiser on the 26th.

On the evening of the 25th the Mercury made the Brothers, two small islands in 26° 19′ north: they are to the northward of Cossier, but in a latitude which it is recommended to reach before attempting to enter that port; for the prevailing winds in this sea being from that quarter, vessels can run down to the port, with a free wind, between the shoals and the shore. We were becalmed the same evening after nine o'clock, and continued so till about one o'clock on the morning of the 26th, when a violent wind from the

N. W. drove us off the Brothers, and continuing to increase, we were obliged to leave our two landmarks, and attempt, by tacking, not to lose ground, and we run in for the Egyptian shore,—these islands being about thirty miles from that coast. But from the tempestuousness of the gale, we gave up all hope of reaching our port that day, a high-running sea and the violence of the wind carrying us to leeward. However as we approached the shore, both moderated, and by six o'clock we saw the whole line of coast, and now relied as confidently on landing in the course of the day as we had concluded to the contrary two hours before.

Still the town was to be discovered; for it is difficult to be seen, owing to the houses being of the same colour as the sand on which they are built. The steril and desolate appearance of the shore, the emerald mountains and broken ground, a description applying to all the country, presented a combination of all the horrid accounts of the most inhospitable shores that ever hero of romance landed on. We were under greater disadvantage than those adventurous characters; for should the governor of Cossier be unable to assist us by mortal means, we could not expect any help from a friendly magician to cross that part of the country between it and Khenne on the Nile, so forbiddingly filled up in D'Anville's map, as the "Great Desert." This rugged shore afforded us a specimen of what we were to expect; and with the prospect of 120 miles of this kind of country before me, I wished myself well over it. I had, when at a distance, observed some spots more dark than the rest, differing considerably from the several shades of the brown, sandy, and thirsty colour which predominated; and had hoped on approach they would have proved to have been patches of verdure. But, alas! they were only cavities deeper than others; and I conceive the aborigines could not have had any word for the colour, the return of which adds the greatest beauty to the most pleasant of our northern seasons. The difficulty of discovering the town was happily obviated by our descrying a three-masted ship in shore at anchor to the southward of the course we were steering, which at once put at rest our apprehensions of having been blown to the south without seeing the houses, as there is no other port where vessels can lie safely on this part of the coast, but that of our destination. About twelve o'clock no doubt could be entertained of our landing in the course of the day.

As in duty bound, I prepared every thing to quit the vessel the moment she anchored; and stated my wish to the captain to have a boat with an officer to go on shore with me to wait upon the governor, in order to expedite my departure, if it were practicable; but he recommended me to permit the officer to go first alone, and not to appear too anxious about it, and assured me if I failed at Cossier, he would, after taking in water, prosecute his voyage, and land me at Suez in fifteen days. Believing, however, that I should gain time by the route of the desert, I determined to prefer it. Disregarding, as I ought when employed on a duty requiring expedition, all personal inconvenience, I was most anxious to know if it was possible for an individual with but little baggage to pass from Cossier to Khenne, on the Nile, in a day or two, or less. If this was answered in the affirmative, I wished to know the manner of crossing the desert, and was desirous of hiring some one who could, with Arabic, speak either English, French, or Spanish, Portuguese, Persian, or Hindoostanee, and who would accompany me to Alexandria. I also requested the officer to ask if the road across the desert was safe. In the event of the first of these questions not being answered in a satisfactory manner, and its being found impracticable to proceed with the necessary despatch, inquiry was to be made in what time two persons could pass, forming, with guards, a little caravan; and similar questions that naturally arose from this, as in the first question. I was also desirous of knowing where Mehumed Ali, Pacha of Egypt, was, being most anxious to see him; and the governor was further to be informed that I had letters from our government to his highness, Sir Evan Nepean having given me one for him.

Mr. Melsom, the second lieutenant, was ordered on this duty; and the boatswain's mate, a man, I believe, from some part of the Barbary coast, and who spoke Turkish and Arabic, with English, accompanied him, as well as a Lascar, who spoke Arabic and Hindoostanee.

About two o'clock, having passed round the head of the shoal, we steered south, and ran along the shore towards the town and the three-masted ship. The former appeared to promise but little, though the number of persons collected to see us come in was very considerable, particularly when it is recollected that but few could be women. The sea broke on a sandy beach to the north of the town, the houses being built on the sand, which extends some distance from the bold shore, and appears to have been formed and thrown up by the sea; and I almost despaired, from the wall of rock at the back of the town, of finding an opening to pass into the interior. The three-masted vessel hoisted a crimson flag, and on approach proved to be a polacre, a vessel well known in the Mediterranean, the masts consisting of one piece, but with yards across, and square rigged. A smaller vessel hoisted similar colours, but the fort none. There were several daos in the harbour.

After we had passed the polacre and some part of the town, we continued sailing, in all appearance, to run on the sands, yet the man heaving the lead in the chains did not find bottom, the anchoring ground being so very steep and sudden. When within a quarter of a mile of the beach we found ourselves in seven fathoms water, the throw of the lead the last cast finding no bottom. The next gave us five, when the anchor was let go, and the ship swung into three fathoms and a half, and I saw plainly the sand and weeds under the vessel's bottom before they warped her into deeper water.

It was just three o'clock when we anchored. The captain hoisted out the jolly-boat, and Mr. Melsom, with his little suite, left the ship for the shore with my best hopes for success, as I was aware that the time I had lost by my long passage from Bombay, and the difficulties which had retarded my journey across India, I ought to make up for when in Egypt. I followed him with my eyes, and saw him land amongst the crowd which closed on him, and had I not heard of the rank of a Turk being shown, by his attendants beating his inferiors, I should have fancied he was being well thrashed; for the uplifted sticks, and showers of blows distributed on all sides amongst the crowd, gave it the appearance of a cudgelling match.

The town appeared miserable. The houses entirely of mud, built round a small fort mounting towards the sea two guns, with its walls and towers loopholed. This is the port whence the corn and other provisions are embarked for the Arabian coast; as Mecca, Juddah, and indeed all western Arabia, depend on the exports of Egypt for their sustenance. It is also to Egypt and the states of Barbary what Surat is to India, the port whence pilgrims embark on their way to Mecca. Multitudes of devotees, however, go by the caravan from Cairo to Suez, and on to Mecca along the eastern shore of the Red Sea. I observed several tombs of the Mahometans, with small white domes, similar to those in India. Great numbers of camels appeared in all directions, and many asses: large piles of bales of merchandize lay upon the sands, and I thought a caravan might be on the point of departure across the desert.

However anxious I might be for the return of Mr. Melsom, I could not but, on its being announced, go to dinner, as in all probability it was the last civilized meal I should take for some time. About the middle of it, one gun was fired from the fort. I thought my ambassador stayed an unconscionable long time on shore; but just after dinner he returned, and set every doubt and fear at rest. He stated that every thing was so satisfactory, that he had not even written an answer to my questions; and that on inquiring about the safety of the road, the governor replied, "wherever Mehumed Ali governed, gold might be placed on the road, and none would touch it." I immediately put on my red coat and sword, and accompanied the lieutenant on shore with the interpreter; and as the captain had been informed the gun we had heard was a compliment to us, we returned it with three, which were to be explained to the governor, as one to Ali Pacha, one to himself, and one for me.

The tide was out when we approached the shore, and some men brought a sort of hammock of net, slung between two poles, for each of us to be carried through the mud to the land. We then walked through the crowd to the house of the governor, and I was much struck, as I passed along, with the difference of the countenances and dress of the natives from those of India. Their features are larger and coarser, their stature taller than the people of the Dekhun and Bengal, and their dress Turkish, and most unbecoming; nor did I see a naked person amongst them. Their turbans differed from those of India in being more bulky. The houses were mere huts. That of the governor was very miserable: some coarse mats were spread on the ground of the passage that led to the room where he was, and as I had ascertained the mode of salutation by putting the right hand to the breast, I acted my part famously.

The governor was seated in the alcove formed by the window, which looked out on the harbour, supported by cushions of different colours, with several small carpets, and smoking a sort of hookah, greatly inferior to those we use in India. He was a man of about thirty, uncommonly handsome, his beard shaved, and only wearing mustachios, though habited *à la Turque*. Two chairs with straw bottoms were placed for us; where they got them I do not know. All the rest were seated on the ground. The room was very mean, nothing but plain white walls, and the roof of coarse rafters, filled in with the leaves of the date tree. On one side was a drawing of a ship, in, I think, pen and ink. About ten or a dozen turbaned soldiers waited opposite the governor, whose dress was very picturesque, and several Turks were sitting round him on the ground. One man was as white as any person I ever saw, with red mustachios, and I have since learned that he was a Greek, and the treasurer. The captain of the polacre was present, a very fine looking fellow, whose rich laced dress, turban, bare legs and slippers, with his pistols in his girdle, dagger and sword, made him resemble a perfect Rinaldo Rinaldini. The civility of the effendi, which I found was his title, was very great: he stated that I might arrive at Khenne in two days, if I left Cossier that night; that he could reach that place the day after he quitted the sea-side on a dromedary, but that I must expect to be longer, as I could not be accustomed to travelling on the back of a camel, which was totally different from the motion of a horse. I answered that I had been used to riding and fatigue, and felt equal to attempting it, and that I only wished to return on board to fetch some few things, and should then be ready to start. He answered that the camels were gone two hours journey to water, but that they should be ready the next morning. I was, however, firm to my purpose, and he promised all should be ready at seven o'clock, with a guard, water, &c.; and that he would write to the effendi at Khenne to accelerate my progress, by procuring me a boat to go down the Nile to Cairo, and he only regretted he had not time to prepare bread and other refreshments for me.

My next most desirable object was to procure some person who could act as my interpreter, and the captain of the ship sent for a man he had on board named Mehumed, who soon made his appearance. He was a well looking stout fellow of about forty, appeared very good humoured, and a great favourite of all those assembled around. He said he spoke English, Spanish, Italian, and Arabic, and asked forty dollars to go down to Alexandria, and twenty more to pay his captain who had advanced him that sum. I consented to this, and informed him I was to quit Cossier in three or four hours. He spoke a little English, and Spanish fluently, and between these two I hoped to get on very well. A Turkish soldier, named Mustapha, was also ordered to prepare himself to accompany me: he was a short fat man of about sixty years old, and did not seem to relish the idea of his trip. The governor asked me how the captain had brought the ship into the harbour, and seemed surprised when I told him we had maps of the port on board.

The plague was reported not to be at Alexandria, which they call Ischander and Iskanderia. He inquired if there was no shorter road from Hind (Hindoostan) to England than through Cossier, and some other questions of no importance. Coffee was twice brought us in small china gilt cups without the stand; it was excellent, but without sugar or milk, and some sediment remained at the bottom of the cup. I also mentioned that Mr. Thomson wished to start next morning, as I was aware he would not undertake so rapid a journey as I speculated upon; and the effendi promised that all should be ready, as well as a person who understood some European languages and Arabic. The interpreter spoke Turkish to the governor, but many present only spoke Arabic, which is the language of the country, the Turkish being that of the latest conquerors, like the Persian in Hindoostan before the fall of the house of Timour.

I observed several persons come in during the time I was before the governor, and those who were his inferiors saluted him in a very curious manner. He held out his hand, and when they bent down to touch it with theirs and attempted to kiss it, he snatched it away as soon as their hand reached his, and the person retired after kissing his own hand.

When I rose to depart for the vessel, his excellency offered to accompany me on board. We proceeded to the sea-side, and he entered the jolly boat, his attendants being in another boat belonging to the shore. We found the captain and Mr. Thomson ready to receive us on board, and they had some little conversation. I stated my doubt to the captain of the polacre whether my newly engaged interpreter would not run away, but he answered, if he did the pacha would cut off the effendi's head. They took some coffee, and returned on shore; and I prepared for my journey.

I asked the officers to assist me with light portmanteaus, and the surgeon, Mr. Nimmo, was so kind as to give me a basket with a lock and key, and a small leather portmanteau. These, with my three despatch boxes, my bottle case filled with brandy, pistols, sword, and cloak, were all I determined to carry, with some pens, ink, and paper, six changes of linen, and 300 dollars, which I had received at Bombay.

About eight o'clock I was ready, and after shaking hands with all on board, and finding my baggage increased by a little box from the captain's steward, containing something to eat, I left the ship; and having rowed on shore, went to the effendi's house, where he was seated in the same room as in the morning, employed in dictating and making up letters for me to carry, and sealing them with his own seal. He had an immense lantern of five sides on a small stool before him, and a pair of tin snuffers. I found I had left the standards we had taken at Jubbulpoor behind me, and having brought them so far I was unwilling to lose them, and sent to the vessel for them. The governor asked me what intelligence I was carrying to England, and said he supposed the armies of the eastern nations were not disciplined like our armies in Europe. (A Turk talking of disciplined armies was excellent.) He also wished to know if we had any merchandize on board the vessel.

About nine, the standards having arrived, and Mustapha having given notice that the camels were all ready, and my several boxes on their backs, I took leave of Mehumed Effendi, after presenting him with my Dollond telescope, very much against my will, as I had brought it from England with me, but I saw he expected something. He cautioned me to be careful not to fall off when the camel rose from his recumbent posture. We then proceeded to the yard of the house, where I found seven camels; one for myself, one for Mustapha, one for Mehumed, my interpreter, with my clothes, two for the other Turkish soldiers, one for water, and another for an Arab, with a negro to mount occasionally. I placed my cloak and silk levadah* on the saddle of my camel, tied a cord to the pummel of it, so as to hang in two loops to receive my feet on each side in place of stirrups, and mounted, taking fast hold of the handles of the saddle before and behind. It is impossible to conceive the awkward and unpleasant situation and posture I was thrown into, on the camel rising, as they are all at a very early age taught to lie down to receive their loads. But they are at all times so unruly as to render it necessary to tie the thigh and leg together when bent under them. The animal on rising throws the body of the rider into a horizontal position, the head forward, then in a like position backward, and the different contortions he is shaken into are very painful and dangerous. I however, by holding very fast, got safe from the ground with the camel.

I now wished Mr. Melsom adieu, gave presents to the rapacious servants of the effendi, and turning my back on the ship, skirted the town, crossed the sand, and found myself in a few minutes sur-

* A wide silken quilted wrapper.

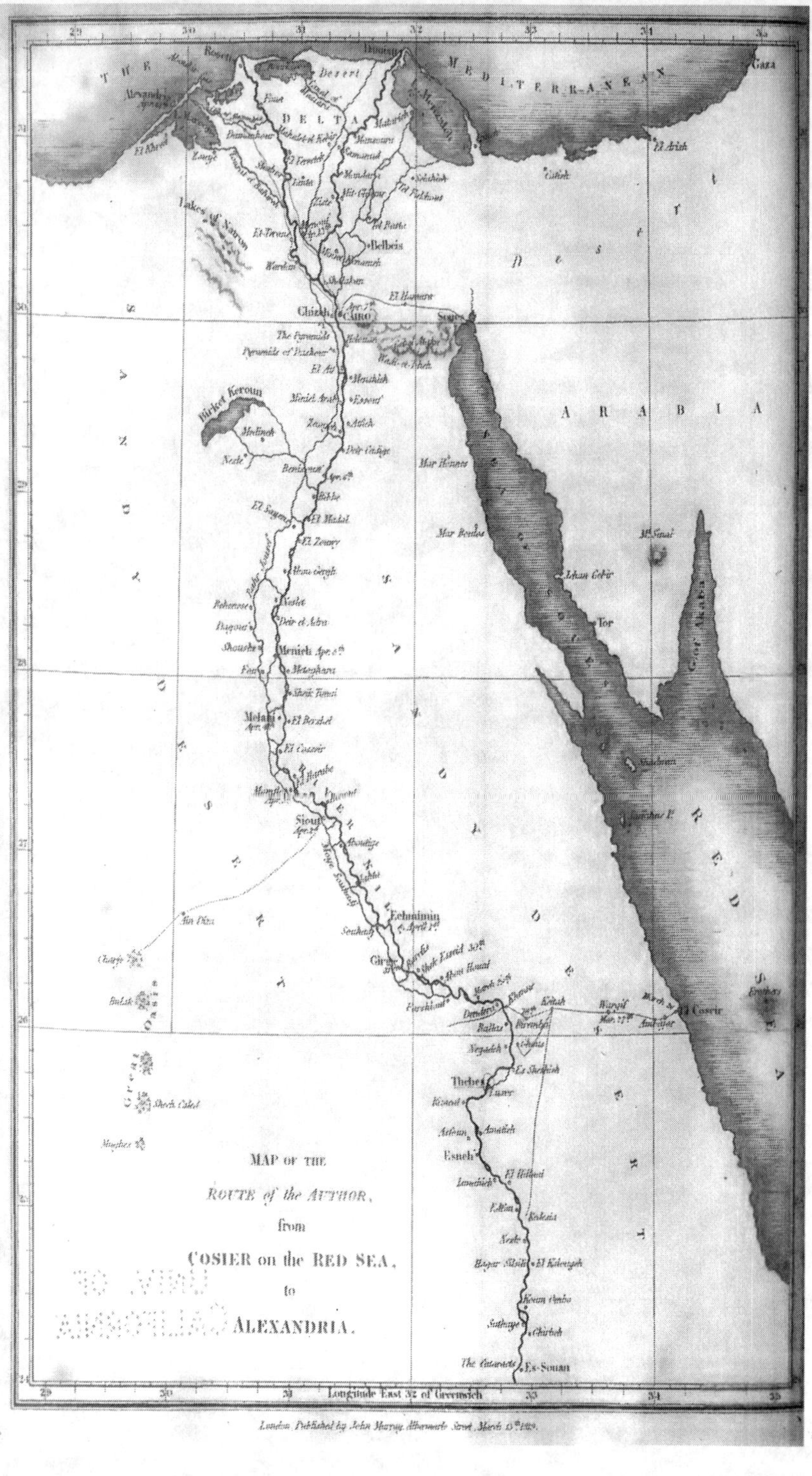

London Published by John Murray Albemarle Street, March 13th 1829.

rounded by rocks on all sides, and felt as forlorn as when I quitted the camp of the governor-general. I had the rope of the camel's head in my hand, and I found the motion unpleasant, as is that of all animals which move two legs on the same side at one time. I did not know what to make of my fellow travellers, but Mustapha offered me his pipe: I smoked very comfortably, and soon became more used to the movement. I talked with Mehumed, who stated that he had been in England, France, and Spain. He knew all the seaports in the Mediterranean, and I promised myself great amusement in his conversation on the dreary road. I learnt that we were to proceed at a foot's pace the whole way; and after two hours travelling was much alarmed with respect to the motion of the animal, for about that time I felt a most violent pain in my side and back, and this continued to increase, so that I was obliged to dismount and walk. The road was hardened by the track of the caravans, so that I got on well, though very tired, having been on deck all the night before during the gale.

About twelve o'clock we arrived at the first watering place, called Ambojar, about nine or ten miles from Cossier; and the moon soon after arose, and showed me the barrenness around. The road in general was shut in on both sides by walls of rocks, except where little plains of sand extended, dotted with large stones, and behind those on the sides, others more distant reared their heads above in the wildest confusion, and most fantastic shapes, and different colours. Avenue after avenue, thus bounded, continued to present themselves. I again mounted my camel, and became more easy when upon its back; and my desire to get over my journey made me bear up against what inconveniency remained. About two o'clock my guards complained of being tired, and wished to lie down, but I was resolved, and did not stop till about an hour after, when the return of pain obliged me to rest, and we all dismounted, tied the camels' legs, and those who accompanied me soon fell asleep. But, though I was very much exhausted, the new situation in which I was placed prevented me from sleeping. The comparison with even the night before was great; then on board a small vessel riding out a gale; now wrapped in my cloak, lying on the ground amidst the stillness of the desert, surrounded by camels, Turkish soldiers, and Arabs asleep. It is on such occasions I feel repaid for all fatigues and difficulties: then I reflect upon the novel and curious circumstances of my position, and contemplate the difference between the manners and feeling of countries more or less civilized and those most refined. The camels did not attempt to rise, but lay on their sides to rub themselves; the saddles on their back, which cover the sides of their hump, not permitting them to roll over. The moon was beautiful, and just as I had dropped asleep, a large company of persons, with camels, &c. passed close to us; and, turning to the east, I saw the first streaks of daylight. Having called my drowsy companions, we mounted and proceeded on our road, and when day broke I could view this most singular desert at my leisure, as we moved through the rocks.

I had always understood that this desert consisted of a great expanse of sand, but it was masses of irregular rock, of all shapes and heights, from twenty to 100 feet perpendicular; and where they are low enough to see beyond them on the road sides, all appears alike, dreary and frightful. Large cliffs, of many tons weight, frowned from the slanting sides, and appeared to require only a touch or a breath to precipitate them into the road. Some formed perfect cones, and the stone was generally of a red colour. We often passed small open spots, from about 100 yards to a mile square. The sharp edges of the rock in many places shewed through the sand, and the whole was bounded by masses on masses of rocks, piled on each other in the most splendid wildness,—doubtless the most unfinished of all nature's works. To my surprise, though there is hardly any water to be found on the route, I saw many water-courses and deep fissures in the earth, and on inquiry found there used to be very heavy rains in the desert; but for the last four years they have almost totally failed, as there has been only twenty-four hours rain, and that five months ago. The road runs between the rocks, and does not, in a single instance, pass over the smallest elevation.

I had, when in broad daylight, a very good view of my companions, and we formed a most singular group, only requiring a sandy-haired Scot to have made all the different gradations of colour, from the fairest to the darkest of mankind. Of this strange assemblage I was the most white; Mustapha, a native of Constantinople, next; then came one of the soldiers, a native of St. Jean d'Acre; another from Alexandria; Mehumed was from Tangiers, one an Arab of Egypt, each successively darker than the preceding; and, to complete the whole, the negro with curled hair, thick lips, flat nose, and ebony complexion. The dress of the Turkish soldiers is very handsome. The turban is large, being a piece of muslin bound in many folds round a small scarlet cap, with a blue tassel at the top: a vest generally of silk under a cloth embroidered jacket, not unlike the jacket of the Spanish peasants, the sleeves cut open from the shoulder: a large red sash round the body, and the pistols and dagger stuck into an embroidered belt over it. Sometimes a white petticoat from under the sash as low as the knees; others wear loose white trowsers; some Turkish cloth breeches of an uncommon size; and below the knee to the ancle, which is left bare, the leg is covered with a sort of gaiter of different colours, ornamented with gold or silver lace. Red slippers are generally used for the feet.

The sword is worn by a cord which passes over the shoulder and round the body, and the gun is generally carried on the shoulder. The pistols and other fire-arms are all foreign, being from London and several other cities of Europe; and the flint is in most cases secured by a silver plate fastened to the cock, to prevent its falling out. Their ammunition is also carried in the belt. Each of the soldiers with me had a large pair of saddle-bags on the camel, well filled with clothes, and his pipe and tobacco—the first stuck in his belt with his pistols, the latter in a little bag hanging from his sash.

The dress of the Mahometan and Hindoo soldiers, in India, is totally different from this. It consists of a long vest from the neck to the ancles, with sleeves open half-way from the bottom on the sides, with this dissimilarity, that they button their vest across the breast on opposite sides according to their religions. They have a sash, small turban, and are armed with a matchlock, sword and dagger, a peculiar shaped powder-horn, a small bag of balls, and a shield of a round form, with several bosses, usually hung on the back: sometimes shoes or sandals. The dress of the Arabs is nothing but a large, loose, brown sackcloth gown with immense sleeves, and extending to the feet; a little skullcap, and always the pipe and tobacco. The lower classes in India are naked, excepting a small cloth round their loins; and so partial are the Sepoys to this unshackled costume, that the uniform is taken off as soon as they get off parade.

As we proceeded, Mustapha pointed out to me a spot where he had last year rescued, from the hands of some robbers, a number of travellers. These freebooters did not appear, by the account I received from the interpreter, to be Bedouin Arabs, but a robber, with about fifteen followers whom he had collected. This road was at one period almost impassable for the Bedouins; but Mehomed Ali has, by his vigorous administration, totally destroyed their predatory expeditions. In the midst of this desolate situation I saw some birds which I believe to be partridges, and some sand larks, as well as a small lizard. I conclude from this that there must be water in the neighbourhood, perhaps only in the holes of the rock. Near two hours after daylight we met nearly 100 camels laden with wheat and dates, escorted by about ten Arabs armed with short spears; and during the rest of the journey, almost every half hour we fell in with small caravans of asses and camels. The good water used at Cossier is brought on asses from a distance of above forty-five miles on this road, that in the neighbourhood of the town being very bad. What a misery must it be to live in a place without this blessing! indeed, were it not the great port for the exportation of corn, &c. to Mecca and Juddah, and for the embarkation of pilgrims to the former of these towns, it would doubtless be deserted. Mehumed and Mustapha are both hadjees, this title being given to all Mahometans who have gone to the holy city. It is one of the most orthodox rites of their religion to undertake this pilgrimage, and indeed all ought once in the course of their lives to do so; but of late years they have decreased very much in numbers, though those who have accomplished the duty are still very much respected. At a great distance from Mecca, where the visiting it becomes a serious undertaking, it is extraordinary what credit they gain by this journey. When I was at Delhi in 1815, a servant of the officer who had charge of the palace had gone on this holy excursion, and the king and whole court treated him in consequence with the greatest familiarity; and his majesty on his return sent for him, and the fellow, I believe, thought himself a saint.

It is curious, that in the course of my route I have found the Mahometans change their position in prayer. They are obliged to turn their faces towards Mecca while thus devoutly employed; and in India, all turn to the westward and south-west. In this country, all turn to the east, and at Alexandria, I suppose, I shall find them facing to the south-east. As to the Lascars on board the Mercury, they were not aware of the change after we had entered the Straits of Babelmandeb, and with the greatest innocence still faced the west, but would have been much shocked had I told them that they turned their backs on Mecca.

About ten o'clock we were overtaken by two soldiers on camels, who had left Cossier a few hours after us. They were carrying money to Khenné, and as they had no water, they pushed on to the spot where it was to be found, which was stated to be about three hours distant.

About eleven o'clock we entered the longest avenue, or lane of mountainous walls on each side, I had seen: it could not have extended less than three miles. It was covered with little yellow prickly bushes, which the camels eat with great relish, and we saw several parties of camels and asses feeding on it. My guards procured a lettuce for me from some of those who had arrived from the banks of the Nile, which refreshed me much; and they offered me some pieces of sugar-cane, but I was afraid it would, by the clammy juice it contained, only add to my thirst.

Fortunately, Mehumed amused me much by his remarks. He stated that he had been on board the Sultan, one of our line of battle ships. In the course of our conversation he asked if I knew King George, who, he supposed, must be 100 years old. He said that he never drank any intoxicating liquors while on board our man of war, and in half an hour after mentioned the price of gin, rum, and beer, in England, and of wine in France and Spain, and of the date brandy in Egypt; and since we have become better acquainted, last night, to his own share, drank above two thirds of a bottle of that liquor. I asked him how he avoided eating pork on board a ship, as the Mahometans, following entirely the Jewish law in this respect, do not permit the use of hog's flesh; but he answered, with the most ingenious casuistry, "*pork board a ship, all the same as mutton.*" He declared there were some very fine cities in England, mentioning as specimens Portsmouth and Plymouth. The English fought well at sea, he said, but badly on land; and he appeared to have been on the coast of Catalonia when our force was besieging Tarragona. He evidently had learnt English on board a man of war, from the knowledge he had of our *vulgar tongue*, but this did very well in the desert.

Towards mid-day the weather became very sultry, the heat being reflected from the rocks on each side; and had it not been for the gusts of wind which sometimes swept down the valleys as we passed, it would have been dreadful. I have been told that the Sepoys who marched from Cossier to Khenné under Sir David Baird, during the time we occupied this country, could not bear the intense heat thus reverberated, and complained of it as worse than India. I found very little difference between the camels of this country and the dromedaries of India; though I believe I never saw one of the former during the whole time I was in that country, as I have understood there are not many in it, although we call them all indiscriminately camels. The dromedary will trot from six to ten miles an hour, but the camel only travels at a foot pace. In India, a small piece of stick, with little knobs at the ends, is passed through the gristle of the dromedary's nose, but the camel here has on a rope head-stall.

It is curious to observe the dromedary, when taking water, throw up from his stomach, out of his mouth, on one side, a blood-coloured bladder, accompanied with a violent bubbling noise, which gradually decreasing, from the water and air being drawn from it, he again sucks in and swallows. The gait of a dromedary, with its long legs, when going at its greatest pace, is very similar to that of a deer. I made inquiry how long a camel could exist without water, and was informed that if they were fed on green forage, they could live many days without it; but that they could go five days without any thing to drink and but little to eat, and they would fail at the end of eight days altogether if they had no water, though ever so regularly fed. These, they said, were extremes, but I had no opportunity to prove them, and only relate what they told me. Camels are formed for a dry country. The long broad foot is only of use in sandy hard roads, and they are absolutely useless and inefficient in rainy or swampy weather. The poor animals slip their hind legs, which spread open outwards, and never recover themselves. The expense to the officers of the army of the Dekhun, who moved up during the rains, was in this respect excessive. Many hundreds of these animals fell victims to the slippery ground.

CHAPTER XXVII.

Watering-place in the desert—Cisterns—Beer—Coffee—Wargiff—Bedouin Arabs—Caravans attacked—Trees—Oases—Rest—Sandy desert—Mountains on the Nile—Cave—Wells at Keitah—Sick people—Turkish soldiers—Carelessness of the Turkish soldiers—Mirage—Water of the Nile—Arrive at the cultivation on the Nile—Reflections—Benhut—Rest—Illness—Proceed to Khenné—Mode of raising water—Egyptian village—Mahometan tombs—Causeway—Khenné—Coffee-house—The effendi—Require a boat—Unpleasant situation—European gentleman—Intelligence of Mr. Salt—Send a letter to the consul—Mr. Anderson—Wish to visit Dendera—Proceed to Dendera—Turkish soldiers—Tents—Boats—Ferry—Copts—Distant view of Dendera—North gate—The great temple—Mahometan fanaticism—The back of the temple—Anxious to visit Thebes—The religions of Egypt and India—Return from Dendera—The plague at Alexandria—Mehumed Ali's family—Whehabbees—War between them and the Turks—Camels used in war—Rosary—Rencontre with an Albanian—Bad discipline of the Turks—Barracks—Mr. Anderson's house—Austrian botanist—Proceed to the boat—Buckshes—Miserable boat—How, a village on the Nile—Crocodiles—Alligators—two kinds on the Ganges—Cummere—Gurial—Commencement of a bridge—Gibel Mokuttum—Cultivation—Villages on the Nile—Oars—Turkish soldiers ill use the Arabs—Reflections on military despotism—On our Indian army—On England.

THE watering-place did not appear, though it was near one o'clock, and I became almost exhausted; but a little after that hour we at last reached it. It is called Aumur, but the disappointment I met with was great, as the only water to be procured, and that in very small quantities, was what dripped from the rocks, and was found in the hollow. The persons who frequented the desert have formed two sorts of cisterns about eight feet deep, by scraping away the sand until they come to the solid rock, and hollow out in it, about eight inches deep, a hole, which on being emptied, as it does not contain above a gallon of water, replenishes itself in a short time. I am confident that at the expense of a little gunpowder, wells might be excavated, and a certain and plentiful resource of water be always preserved in this part of the desert. I determined to remain in this spot for three hours, and remembering the small box that the captain's steward had put up for me, I opened it with avidity, and found it contained, perhaps, the only meat I could not have eat; but I could hardly have supposed I should have had such bad luck as to find my stock of provisions, in the middle of a desert where there was a great scarcity of water, a piece of ship's salt beef. There were, however, some biscuits in the box, and searching lower, I discovered to my astonishment, of all things the most unexpected and the most welcome, a bottle of English beer. Had it been of adamant, I would have forced it open; and had vast sums been placed at my feet, I should, at the moment, have refused them rather than forego the draught of delicious malt and hops. I ate some biscuits, lay down under a shelving rock, and soon fell fast asleep.

About half-past three Mehumed awoke me, and proposed to resume our march; and I asked for some coffee, in hopes it would keep me awake. A collection of camel's dung was immediately got together, and being lighted by a flint and steel, used for smoking, Mustapha made some excellent and strong coffee. As we were about to mount our camels, some persons passed having their animals laden with clarified buffalo's butter, and all my attendants having procured some of it, (not unlike in smell to train oil) crumbled two loaves of brown bread upon the inside of a sheep's skin, poured the butter upon it, and one of them, tucking up his sleeves, stirred this agreeable mess with both his hands, and called the remainder, who ate it with their fingers. Such a pottage I never saw before, and hope never to see again.

We at length mounted, and about five o'clock entered the pass of Wargiff, where Mustapha told me the French were posted on the landing of our troops at Cossier, and I think I never saw a stronger pass. It is almost impossible to describe these most singular cliffs; and the road between them was twice as deep and more narrow than the worst streets in London. I do not know how any troops could force or turn it. This spot was one of the worst when the road was infested with the Bedouin Arabs; and Mustapha, who gave me this information, mentioned that these Pindarries of Egypt had at times defeated caravans of 2000 soldiers, and seized the camels they guarded.

These robbers, however, are now nearly subdued, perhaps totally so, by the all-powerful Pacha. Some distance from this celebrated pass, Mustapha pointed out the head of two small valleys which opened into the road, nearly opposite each other, where within the last two years a large caravan had been attacked and carried off. At the mouth of one of the valleys, two Turkish soldiers defended themselves until one had received seven musket balls. I had the curiosity to count the trees in this day's journey, (the 27th) and I found that six was the number. I learnt afterwards at Khenné that there are several small oases in the desert, containing trees, grass, &c.; but I have no doubt if they have not more rain, these will also perish. Our course was nearly west, but I observed when we turned to avoid rocks which lay in our front, we generally turned south. I suffered very much from the motion of the camel, but could and would have continued on all night, had not the soldiers complained that they were tired; and after nearly quarrelling with them, I was obliged, at twelve at night, to give way to their importunities, and we rested about two hours, when I again made them mount, and proceeded. At daylight, I found we had entered a totally different country from that we had passed through before, it being entirely of sand, all the rocks and stones having disappeared, and the only rise above the sand being not unlike the sides of a gravel-pit. The view around was very extensive, and all being of a sand colour, had the look of a heavy fall of dirty-coloured snow;

I mean that it formed one uniform expanse, as when the ground is covered with snow in England. Mustapha directed my eye to the mountains (just visible) on this side the Nile, and I almost despaired of ever reaching them. When we had traversed this barren wild for four hours after daylight, the soil again changed to a hard gravel, with loose flat stones dispersed upon the surface—and the heat became dreadful. We passed what at a distance appeared to me to be the mouth of a cave, not far from the road; but though I had a great desire to view it, I was so fatigued that I could not muster up strength to do so. Here I must take blame to myself for a gross piece of indolence and forgetfulness. I now recollect, perfectly, this very cave being mentioned in some book published in England, where it is stated not to have been entered; and I think the reviewers express a hope that some traveller will make a point of examining it; and in so unfrequented a road, no traveller may again pass for years. However, this is the first time I have to regret my bodily exhaustion having overcome my spirit of research.

I saw several antelopes, or animals of the deer species, in the desert. About 12 o'clock we reached the wells at Keitah, where there are some small mud buildings with domes. These were full of sick persons, and there being in Egypt a disease supposed to be contagious, called the plague, I would not permit myself to take the rest I required, and determined to proceed. We however dismounted and made coffee, and I smoked two or three pipes, and had the camels fed, having brought us so well from Cossier with only the halts I have mentioned. We heard that a large force of Turkish soldiers had arrived at Khenné, on their way to Mecca from Cairo, and I hoped to find some good fast-rowing boat which had brought them up the river, to take me down. The wells were full of water, but of different qualities; one excellent, the other bad. From this point there are three roads to Wargiff, where they all unite, that is to say, the one we came, and two others, one on each side of it.

Many beggars descended from the houses, and the soldiers were very liberal in relieving them with my biscuit. They also amused themselves by firing at crows and vultures, and with their firelocks cocked, and holding the muzzles very low, jumped about the baggage without any care. Had they fallen, some camel, or perhaps man, would have been killed or wounded. I had often heard and read of the very great carelessness of the Turks with their fire-arms, and here I saw it fully exemplified. This may be accounted for from the taint of fatalism influencing more or less every action of their lives. This place is forty miles from Khenné, which I hoped to reach by midnight.

We continued our route, meeting many camels, asses, and a few dromedaries. I saw at a distance, though very imperfectly, the pillars of sand of which Bruce gives so tremendous an account. These are only what in England we call whirlwinds, which take up leaves, &c.; but here the light sand is raised in great quantities, and kept in the air as long as the column does not encounter obstacles to break it, which are rarely met with in this sea of sand. I did not perceive in the desert the optical deception which the French call "mirage," though in the extensive plains of India I have often witnessed it. The Persians call it "Surab," and the Hindoos, in the desert of Jesselmere and Biccaneer, "Chit-traum."

About five o'clock I met those persons who had quitted the banks of the Nile in the morning, who gave me plenty of water, which was most refreshing. I must own I felt a pleasure in thus quaffing the water of this classical river, and remember well when crossing the Ganges, opposite Benares, in 1815, after having been only fifteen days in India, and travelling 500 miles, that I experienced the same satisfaction in filling my horn cup from that sacred stream. About six o'clock we were overtaken by an Arab on a dromedary, and who, I hoped, might have brought my dressing-case, which I had left behind by mistake; but I found he had been sent after us by the effendi with his watch, which was broke, and he wished Mustapha to take it to Cairo to be mended. He had quitted Cossier on the morning of the 27th. Just before sun-set, I descried the smoke of the villages on the cultivated ground watered by the Nile, and soon after came in sight of the beautiful fields of green barley. I felt a strong desire to dismount and run into it; and the number of date trees, the houses, lowing of cattle, barking of dogs, and hum of voices, united with the pleasant vegetable smell, awaking the joyful association of civilized life, made the contrast with the desert so forcible, that the sensation I experienced cannot be described. I felt in a new world; and the delight of having crossed the desert, and reached the habitations of man, and the banks of the Nile, gave me new vigour—I forgot my fatigues. My mind, thus exalted, took a hurried view of the many historical events which had in my infancy made the river Nile as familiar to me as the Tiber and the Thames; and I recollected that in this country, in all probability, our arts and sciences had their origin; that the most civilized nations had borrowed their ideas from it; and that at this moment, in it the noblest remains of antiquity existed, towering in their magnitude over the puny works of later ages. It was gratifying to know that it was in a state of the greatest tranquillity, and that I could pass, with facility and ease, through a region, which, a few years ago, was most dangerous to a visitor.

We left the large and straggling village of Benhut on our left, and skirted the cultivation, which extends to the very foot of the hills, or rise of the desert, as far as the level of the river will permit its water to inundate; and thus there is no gradation, but a sharp line which bounds the most fertile and the most barren districts on earth. Our camels passed slowly over the fissures made by the heat of the sun on the mud, which the river leaves on its return to its usual bounds.

The Arabs, to whom the camels belonged, begged me not to take them into Khenné at night, as the troops would seize them to transport their baggage and water; and as I was very tired, and had arrived within six miles of that place, where I was aware I could not do any thing at night, I agreed to sleep by the side of the road, and rising early, reach the town by the time the effendi was in his court. We continued on, however, to a small village at some little distance on the road, where I observed the cattle to be very similar to those in Europe, and the children outside the houses playing in security, with an air of the greatest tranquillity around. We dismounted, and, to my surprise, on attempting to stand, I staggered several paces and fell, and it was only by degrees that I overcame the giddiness which had seized me. I was obliged to be held up for several minutes before I could stand alone, and after a short time, a violent headach came on, and I found I had exerted myself almost too much. I however lay down, wrapped myself up warm, and screening my head with the clothes of the camel, tried to sleep; but my ideas wandered in so distressing a manner, though much exhausted, it was very long after my companions had gone to rest that I fell asleep. This will not be thought surprising when it is considered that I had travelled 120 miles in 45 hours, on the same camel, with such rough riding as horsemen cannot conceive; and had, besides suffering other privations, scarcely allowed myself any repose.

I passed a very restless night, and called my companions before daylight, when, having mounted our camels, we proceeded towards Khenné. As the day broke I found we were still skirting the edge of the desert. The fields of green corn on the left hand principally consisted of barley or bearded wheat, and some sugar-cane; and almost as soon as it was light enough to work by, I beheld the peasants raising water to irrigate their lands. I was much amused at the manner in which they managed it. On the part nearest the desert, where the ground was highest, a deep well was dug, I suppose to the level of the Nile, and the water was raised from this by a leather bag at one end of the lever, by one man, to the height of perhaps ten or twelve feet, and emptied into a small reservoir, where another lever and attendant, like the lower one, raised the water above him; and by a continuation of the same means it was hoisted until it reached the surface of the field. I have, since I have been on the river, seen no fewer than six of these stages to raise the water from the Nile. The counterpoise on the other end of the lever consists of a mass of straw and mud made into a great ball.

We passed several petty villages, and as they all appeared alike to me, I will describe one of them. The houses are small, and of mud, and generally built so as to form a square. Part of the house is raised like an overgrown chimney, a little ornamented, and the windows appear hardly capable of giving any light to the interior. A considerable number of date trees are planted near and around the habitations, and are almost the only trees I have yet seen. The Mahometan tombs are here unlike those in India, which are very neat, but these are only banks of mud, about three feet high, ten long, and five broad: a few are of brick.

As we approached Khenné we observed a high causeway of brick, which leads to the Nile through the cultivated land. It is about twelve feet high, and of use during the early and latter period of the inundation to reach the true bed of that river. About half a mile from the town the road conducted us through the fields, and we finally turned our backs on the desert. We here overtook one of the sheep I had so often heard of, with their prodigious tails, and immense quantity of wool. On entering the town, which appeared to have been once surrounded by a wall, we went through some miserable mud houses of several stories high, with very small windows in general projecting from them. We passed under a cloth, which stretched across from the tops of the houses, and found it was a coffee-house, where many Turkish soldiers were sitting smoking, and drinking coffee; the whole appearance of the place was mean, being built of brick baked in the sun.

We proceeded to the house of the effendi, and, ascending some stairs, I found him seated in a large alcove, with a window at the back looking out upon the Nile, which ran under the walls, and did not appear above 300 yards across. He was sitting on a part of the floor raised above the rest, covered with carpets and supported by cushions. His secretary was busily employed near him, and several other persons were in the room. I stood waiting to be asked to sit down; but Mustapha was so long in finding my credentials, which he carried from the effendi at Cossier, that I seated myself on part of the carpet. On my letter being read, the effendi asked me to sit down by him near the window, ordered coffee, and gave me his pipe. I stated, through Mehumed, that I wished for a boat immediately, and asked if any person in the town or neighbourhood could speak English or French. The first request was answered by informing me that they had sent for the *capitaine de port*, and the latter, that they had sent for an Englishman who lived at Khenné. I was well pleased to hear this, though much surprised at the intelligence. A general tumultuous conversation then commenced among all who were present, Mehumed taking the lead. First my hat was noticed, then my sword and dress; and I found it totally impossible to get Mehumed to attend to me, for he had, by dint of strength of lungs, become the spokesman. I sat for about a quarter of an hour without being able to obtain his services, while all the inhabitants of Khenné had crowded to see me: I then almost fancied that my interpreter and the effendi had entered into a partnership to show me for the lucre of gain; and, in my own defence, began to take hold and admire the swords, pistols, &c. of my neighbours, calling them all "tieb," a word which I had learned in the desert, and which being translated means "good." Many asked me questions, and seemed totally unaware that I neither knew Turkish nor Arabic, although I frequently caught words I was acquainted with in Persian and Hindoostanee. In short, I never passed a more unpleasant time, but was much relieved by my pipe, which was four feet long. At last a gentleman, very fair, and well dressed, like a Turk, came in, and addressing me in French, said he was glad to see me. To him I stated that I was in want of a boat, and, in as few words as possible, my business. He answered that he was sorry Mr. Salt had only quitted Khenné the day before, having passed by from Thebes, where he had been for the last five months; that the arrival of an English ship at Suez had required his presence at Cairo, and that he had left his secretary, Mr. Beechy, among the interesting ruins of that great city. I immediately asked if it was possible I could send a despatch after him, so as to overtake and stop him, which my new friend said he could do; and I wrote immediately a letter while they sent for a man and dromedary. I was told that Mr. Salt had determined to stop at a town called Sciout, about 100 miles down the river, with a chief named Mehumed Bey, and that there was no doubt I should overtake him. I had conversed some minutes with the gentleman who spoke French, and cast many an anxious look at the door for my countryman: I at last asked of my new friend where he was, at the same time stating that I was an Englishman. He answered that he was *Anglois* also, and I addressed him in consequence in English; but he informed me he did not speak the language, having been born at Constantinople, and that his name was Robert Anderson. I mentioned my wish to see the celebrated ruins of the Temple of Isis at Dendera, and he, with great good nature, offered to take me, as it was directly opposite; but remarked that he was fearful there was no good boat, with a cabin and rowers, ready for me, and that I could only expect a small one. To this I made no difficulties, only desired it to be prepared before noon; and after despatching the dromedary, by which I sent a letter to Mr. Salt, stating that I had arrived from India, that I had letters from Lord Hastings to him, and that if the business which called him to Cairo was not very pressing, I should take it as a favour if he would wait for me, and that I intended to leave Khenné as soon as the boat was ready, we went from the effendi's to the house of the captain of the port, who expressed his regret at having no other boat than the one he had ordered for me. My new friend, Mr. Anderson, had got from his house some bread and butter, and coffee, of which I partook; and a bottle of brandy of the country, made from dates, being introduced, every one present, Turks and all, took a small wine glass of it with the utmost *sang froid;* nor was the *capitaine de port,* as Mehumed called him, contented with one glass. I found my despatches and clothes had been carried up to Mr. Anderson's house; but as it was out of the way, he had directed breakfast to be brought for me to the house I was in. I was now ready to accompany him, and, to my astonishment, found the two donkeys saddled and bridled at the door. *Malgré* the miserable descent from the back of a camel eight feet high, to that of so humble a beast, but just high enough to prevent my feet trailing on the ground, I mounted, and found him a most agreeable little animal; though after the motion of the camel, it was some time before I could sit with ease or safety.

We proceeded along the banks of the river to the northward, and met many of the Turkish soldiers who were encamped on the sands of the river, about a mile below the town. These were fine young men, in their becoming dress, with their pistols and swords, and I observed they had generally light hair. As we passed this camp, we occasionally heard the reports of their muskets; and what renders it dangerous to be in their vicinity, is that they have no idea of blank cartridges, and even at their reviews fire ball, without any kind of precaution, in all directions. The soldiers appeared much surprised at my dress; and only in one instance I perceived signs of an intention to insult, but even of this I was not certain. I learnt from Mr. Anderson that the force consisted of 400 men, and that 300 were to march the next day, and the remainder the day after. I was astonished to find their tents, &c. precisely the same as those we use in India; and the officer's tent was what we call a single pole tent, but with this difference, that it was painted green with red ornaments. I am not surprised at want of discipline, if 400 uncivilized soldiers have but one officer. The boats, with large lattine sails, which had brought them up from Cairo, lay off the sand, and I did not observe any guards or sentries. We crossed the sands of the river, below the tents, to a ferry, where the asses readily leapt the side of the boat; and the Charon of this stream was, I think, the most powerful man I ever beheld, and seemed very good-humoured. We had several Copts on board, who, Mr. Anderson informed me, were Christians, being obliged to wear blue turbans, as a distinguishing mark; and, perhaps with too little thought, I asked him, seeing that he wore a white turban, if he was a Christian; which he answered rather sharply by *pourquoi non?*

We crossed a well cultivated plain, and I soon began to make out one of the gates at the southern end of the ruins, and a few pillars on the other extremity. The former then appeared, like the stones at Stone Henge, two large upright blocks with one placed across. I felt not precisely disappointed, but I own I was doubtful how the most perfect ruins in Egypt could be conjured out of what seemed to me, on approach, to be an immense heap of rubbish, broken tiles, and half-mouldering bricks. We passed round to the north, and observed some awkward pillars, which certainly do not seem to be either of the same era or architecture. I had some difficulty in guiding my patient little animal through the number of pits which had been dug by the neighbouring Arabs, in search of treasure or antiquities to sell to Europeans. In short, these pits render the ground almost impassable, and some which I with care avoided must have been twenty-five feet deep, being laid bare for four or five series of bricks, which I believe to have been foundations of houses at different periods; and the whole gave me an idea of a village in ruins, which had been the theatre of hostile demolition, as the walls of houses, formed of mud, and, in some places, high walls with battlements, appeared to shut me in. My kind guide informed me that the Arabs had, from a wish to avoid the inundation of the Nile, and from the security of the spot, raised a village on and about the temple; but I saw no person in the ruins. After we had passed through about 200 yards of this dangerous ground, in a southern direction, we came in front of the north gateway, which is formed of immense blocks of stone, covered within and without with hieroglyphics. Its magnitude and simplicity are most striking, and the gate I had observed to the south must have been of the same kind, though I did not see others to face the east and west. Like many of the ancient Egyptian remains, the sides inclined inwards gradually towards the top, and were crossed by, I think, three stones of great magnitude, one of which had fallen, though the sides and other transverse blocks appeared completely firm; and I was truly delighted to find on both fronts, on the cornices, the orb with expanded wings, and two serpents supporting that well known and celebrated symbol so common throughout Egypt.

I have, in one instance, in India seen the same style of building, namely, that with the inclination inwards of the side walls. This was in the tomb of Touglick, about ten miles from Delhi, in the valley between the two fortresses, called Toughlickabad; which is a most surprising work of human labour and perseverance. The tomb is in form of a pyramid, truncated about a third part of its base. This base is about thirty yards square, surmounted by a handsome dome; which kind of construction gives an idea of great strength. It is possible the Mahometan sovereign may have had some architect with him, who had seen the Egyptian architecture on the spot; for within five hundred years after Mahomet, the frequency of pilgrimages to Mecca must doubtless have led some persons to Cairo, and even to Upper Egypt.

The figures on this gateway at Dendera are not so large as life, and all in basso relievo, except the globes and fish, which appeared to me to be in alto. The fall of one of the three large stones, which covered the top of the gateway, I cannot account for, since the two others are in their places, unless we suppose that some spirit of fanaticism, which has damaged the other parts of the building, should have made the Mahometans lay their sacrilegious hands on it. Through this gateway I had a perfect view directly before me of the portico of the great temple, which did not seem to me to be very striking; and it was not until I had observed the great disadvantage under which I saw the building, that I was aware of the magnitude of the work. The heat was excessive, and I was far from well; but I knew that the opportunity of finding myself in the ruins of an Egyptian temple was not to be again seized, and though my time was very much limited, I tried to see every thing.

After leaving this gate, which is covered I suppose above half its height with rubbish, I turned to the west, passing over heaps of ruins to a smaller temple. The gateway and front were buried about two thirds of their height. This gateway was similar to the first, and the cross stone at the summit was the largest hewn block I ever beheld. I had not time to measure it, but guessed it to be twenty feet long, six broad, and from four to five thick. All these gates are of white calcareous stone, but this small temple was lined with a much darker stone, and uniformly sculptured in figures and hieroglyphics. The interior near the back wall was not so much filled with earth, and I descended about twenty feet, though not near the bottom. The blocks of stone which formed the roof were of a size well calculated to raise our opinion of the knowledge which these indefatigable Egyptians had of mechanics. The vicinity of the mountains of calcareous stone on the east of Khenné afforded them materials within a few miles; but the darker stone, which is granite, must have been brought from beyond the cataracts. I walked round the south of the building, and found on that side a colonnade, so hid by the accumulated debris of ages, that I stood under the ceiling of it between the roof and the cornice, by the side of one of the capitals. These appear, from one which had been cleared of the surrounding rubbish, to be human figures, with the lotus on their heads; and their depth in the ground may be judged, when I state that the capitals were from four to five feet square. I am convinced, from the immense quantity of earth raised on the side opposite to this building, that another similar to it exists, and from being thus buried, is probably in better preservation; and I had no doubt that the first gate I had entered led originally (and would do so now, if the encroaching rubbish and sand were cleared away) into a court, of which the portico of the great temple formed the south side, and these temples the sides on the east and west; but how they were connected, I do not know.

We then proceeded to the great portico, built with white stone, and presenting a long façade, stated to measure 132 feet in length, and I should think from fifty to sixty feet in height above the ground. The side walls incline inwards gradually to the top, but so buried is the whole in rubbish, that I touched with ease, from whence I stood, the piece of granite introduced to receive the posts of the door, being of harder stone than the calcareous.

About half way up the front row of pillars there is a wall built along, connecting them, to within thirty or forty feet of the top, with the door in the centre, and above it the range is open admitting the light, so that from the exterior I saw the roof, supported by the massy pillars. The outside is one continued work of hieroglyphics, and the winged orb and serpents are above the door. On entering, the eye hardly knows where to rest; the ceiling supported by twenty-four gigantic pillars in four rows, twelve on each side the door, of proportions truly wonderful, the colossal heads forming the capitals. There are innumerable figures on the walls, and immediately opposite the entrance, a large door, where, through the gloom, other massy columns appear, and seem to invite the visitors to further investigation. The depth of the vestibule is, I think, about seventy feet, and the pillars are above twenty feet in circumference, their capitals representing the faces of women on each side the square, separated by folds of drapery at the four corners; these, being larger than the columns, are at least eight feet square, and the features of the heads are evidently African, or rather those of the negro. The ceiling is perfectly complete, and consists of enormous masses. It is highly painted, and the colours are as vivid as the first day they were laid on. I had to regret my not having taken notice of the celebrated zodiac, but I was unfortunately at this time ignorant of its existence, having, till lately, supposed it was in the ruins of Thebes. The whole of the columns, walls, cornices, and ceilings are covered with figures and hieroglyphics; but that same destroying zeal so much to be regretted in the caves of Ellora in India has vented itself on these striking and majestic buildings. The introduction of the second commandment into the religion founded by Mahomet, and his rigid construction of it, has destroyed more valuable traces of the fine arts than can ever be replaced; and the conquest of Egypt within twenty years after his death, in the khaliphat of Omar, when enthusiasm was at its height, rendered every thing that was represented by a graven image an object of destruction to religious and fanatic rage. The faces on the capitals, and the figures within reach, have been much mutilated; but their numbers, which made Savigni despair of a draftsman being able to copy them in many years, should he even be stationed on the spot, appear to have overcome the patience of the Mahometans, and their fiery zeal seems to have evaporated before a hundredth part of these sculptures were damaged. The ceiling is carved, and painted of a most beautiful blue and yellow, which has stood the test of several thousand years, and in some places still actually preserves a brilliant and glossy appearance. At the west end, in the interior of the portico, I discovered the top of a door just above the surface, leading, no doubt, into other apartments; and had my time permitted, I should in all probability have found a corresponding door on the east side. This satisfies me that if the walls of these buildings were cleared, it would be discovered that there is a court-yard in front of this vestibule, surrounded by buildings. The earth on the outside of the east and west ends is higher than the top of the doors I have described; and I am convinced, that by digging three or four feet, they would come upon the roof of these apartments.

It is to be hoped that some public spirited society of antiquaries in England or on the continent will, in these "piping times of peace," take advantage of the tranquillity which Egypt enjoys under the Pacha Mehumed Ali, and send some person, well qualified for the undertaking, to clear the most perfect of ancient temples, and restore to the light the whole of this singular work. The expense would be very small, the price of labour being cheap, and 1000*l.* would be sufficient for the whole undertaking.

But to return to the inner chamber of dark stone; opposite to the entrance of the vestibule: It is supported by pillars of a similar magnitude to those of the latter, but the capitals are of the flower lotus, so sacred among the ancient Egyptians and the Hindoos; but the darkness of the interior prevented me from seeing the extent on the sides. This chamber was about forty feet across, and led by a doorway, so choked up with earth that I was obliged to crouch to pass under it, into a plain chamber lighted from the sides by windows, and having on the right a small door, which Mr. Anderson informed me I should explore, when lights from the neighbouring Arab village arrived. I returned through the dark chamber and vestibule to the front, and am persuaded that the accumulation of rubbish in the dark chamber could not have been formed from the refuse of villagers, but I rather think that some Mahometan conqueror, despairing of levelling it to the ground from its strength, had actually formed the idea of covering it over. We then walked round the west side of the building, and I found, to my surprise, that I had not penetrated into it above half its depth, which Savigni reported to be 252 feet. The earth on the sides gradually ascends to the back of the temple, where in some parts it nearly covers the wall. The sides are ornamented with hieroglyphics, and the spouts for carrying off the water from the summit are lions couchant, as large as life, projecting on stands from the roof. The back is buried to within about 30 feet, and in addition to the usual mysterious symbols are several gigantic figures.

Turning this part, we came to the east side, where the earth was so high that I gained the top of the temple, which I found covered with huts of mud; but this village was totally deserted, as well as that below. I observed the manner in which they contrived to throw light in upon the rooms below from the roof, and how they closed up these apertures. It was on the same plan as an embrasure, narrow at one end and becoming wider by degrees, and there were large pieces of stone to fit, and close them if necessary. The roof of the vestibule is higher than that of the other part, and a small stone flight of steps once led to it; but these have been lately much damaged, so that it was difficult to ascend. I walked on to the edge of the vestibule over the door, and discovered several names, but I had not my pencil to copy them; I however recollect there were several of the names of French officers cut in the stone. We then returned to the front of the temple, and rested.

Mr. Anderson informed me, that at Thebes there were several halls formed on a similar principle to this, but on a much larger scale, and with above one hundred columns; but stated that the roof of the greatest was imperfect, and had fallen down in some places. I am aware that this is supposed to be the most perfect temple in Egypt of the age in which it was constructed. While I listened to Mr. Anderson's account of the wonders of Thebes, how the desire grew on me to visit them! and when I considered the short distance they were from me, and the improbability of my ever being in their vicinity again, it made me almost wish to play truant, and loiter on my way: it would only have taken me three days to have visited them and returned to Dendera; but a sense of duty made me relinquish the idea almost as soon as it was formed.

After waiting some time, I became impatient for the arrival of the person who had been despatched for the lights, as it was near one o'clock; at last, however, he made his appearance with some wisps of straw and a little fire. We followed him through the vestibule and dark chamber, and entering with difficulty the small door I before mentioned to the right, turned back down a narrow passage, where I passed several openings into inner chambers; and, after a few minutes, began to ascend a flight of stairs of dark-coloured stone of the most gentle ascent. I am sure that one step was not more than two inches above another. These stairs turned at right angles, at every ten or fifteen steps, and we ascended by them to a considerable height. The light was admitted by loop-holes, admitting but little, and yet the workmanship expended on the walls on each side and roof was as elaborate as where most exposed to view. I concluded that these steps would carry me into the back part of the temple, to which I had not seen any door, and which covered an area above one hundred and fifty feet long, and one hundred broad, and must doubtless contain many chambers and curiosities; but they ended on the summit of the building, and I found, to my regret, that Mr. Anderson did not appear to know what was contained in this mysterious spot. Though these ruins have been described by others, I could not help imparting to my readers some idea of objects so stupendous and unique, well meriting notice, though even at the risk of repetition, and which filled my mind with such astonishment and delight. I found, however, some consolation in not having seen Thebes, when I reflected that Denon mentions this temple in the following terms, after having seen the splendid remains at that city. He was delighted, he said, to find, on his second visit to it, that his enthusiastic admiration of the great temple was not an illusion produced by the novelty of its appearance; since after having seen all the other Egyptian monuments, this still appeared the most perfect in its execution, and constructed at the happiest period of the arts and sciences.

The striking similarity of some points in the ancient religion of Egypt, and the present one of India, has been frequently remarked, and in many instances there is a singular coincidence; but still does this carry with it conviction of their being more nearly related? Man has, in every country on the face of the globe, certain objects presented to him, which, from the same causes, have become more or less venerated; and the priests have ever, by adding mystery and obscurity to popular superstition, exalted their sublimity under a variety of imposing appearances. It is true that the attachment of the Egyptians to the sacred bull, and of the Hindoos to that animal, was the same in both countries; but this may have originated from its usefulness in agriculture. We have all heard of the sacredness of the stork throughout Europe, on account of its utility in destroying vermin, and to this day in Portugal the laws forbid the killing of calves, except for the sick. From the same motive, I have supposed, was originally engendered the worship of this animal. This early state of feeling may have grown, by the assistance of crafty priests, into veneration and devotion. The worship of the lingam and phallos, common to both nations, certainly affords the most forcible idea and emblem of the universal creative and generative power.

The lotus was alike sacred to both, as was an idea of the metempsychosis. The Egyptians have the serpent as a favourite symbol as well as the Hindoos; but that of the latter is the deadly cobra capella, and is by analogy placed by them in the hands of Seva, the destroying power, as is represented in the famous trimurti in the cave of Elephanta, in the harbour of Bombay. It is worthy of remark, that the snake used in the Egyptian mythology should be represented with a thick neck, which has never been accounted for. The cobra capella, when in a state of irritability, has a wonderful expansion of the back of the head and throat. In this striking similarity between the Hindoo religion and that of the ancient Egyptians, I have felt most anxious to trace a closer connexion throughout; yet I have been obliged, though very unwillingly, to give up the idea, and I do not think that their common origin can be established, so as to build on it any secure hypothesis. The division of caste, common to both, was equally so to the Hebrews. I made every attempt my time would permit to discover the celebrated figure which caused the Hindoos, with the Indian contingent, to find fault with the natives of this country for allowing a temple of Vishnu to fall to ruin, but did not succeed. This would, I think, prove much; and I greatly regret my not knowing where to find it.

But should it be established that this affinity does exist in a very strong degree, so as to convince some of their common origin, the boasted antiquity of the laws and sciences of Egypt must give way to the stern obstinacy of the Bramins, since it was impossible these sages could have travelled to Egypt, as they could not have passed the Indus, or Attock, which mean the forbidden; nor would they, from their known dislike to the sea, and from the almost utter impossibility of securing their food and water from contamination, have taken that route. It is supposed, therefore, that if such connexion did exist, the Egyptians visited India, like the philosophers of Greece, to acquire knowledge. We have, from numerous authorities, many proofs that the East was always looked upon as the seat of wisdom and learning, even so as to become proverbial: and we have no accounts of individuals travelling west for instruction; on the contrary, all our information tends to prove that it was the reverse. The appellation of the "Wise men of the East" is too well known to require comment; and the Greek authors speak of the Indians as the wisest people in the world. It is true, however, from the account I have received of an excavation at Yusambal, in Nubia, which Mr. Anderson mentioned to me, that it bears a similar character to those I have seen in India; and supposing, as has been before conjectured, that there was some early and intimate connexion between the Ethiopians or Abyssinians and the Hindoos, it would follow that the arts and sciences, and even religion, originally from India, may have passed through Ethiopia and Nubia, and descended the Nile into Egypt, whence being fostered, they have spread, by the advantage of the Mediterranean and intercourse with the Levant, over Europe, and thus have given the latter country the credit of being the first possessor of them.

I had been anxious to return, as I found the day fleeting fast away; and in addition to my wish to move through Egypt with celerity, I thought any unnecessary delay, after requesting Mr. Salt to wait for me, would not be correct: but I discovered that my host intended I should dine first, and, mounting our donkeys, we set out towards the boat. After we had lost our way, and blundered about in a most absurd manner, on the little plain we had to cross, we reached the boat, where there were many passengers to go with us, and some large baskets of camels' dung for fuel, wood being scarce. I have not seen any trees but dates, and the few of a kind I am not acquainted with, in the desert. There is very little timber in the country; and when the Venetians succeeded in inducing the Turks to oppose the Portuguese, the timber to build the fleet of the soldan of the Mamelukes was cut down in Dalmatia, from whence it was carried to Alexandria, and thence across the desert to Suez.

I learnt from Mr. Anderson that the plague was at Alexandria, which will, I fear, retard my arrival in England, as the only hope I had of reaching in time, to anticipate the despatches by sea, was my receiving letters of pratique from that city, so as to land in Europe, and travel as fast as post horses would carry me. He informed me that Lord and Lady Belmore, his Lordship's brother and two sons, with their surgeon and chaplain, had lately gone up as far as the cataracts in two large boats, and had returned to Cairo, which they were preparing to quit; and that several other English gentlemen had lately visited this interesting country. Mr. Anderson had lived here three years, and had no intention of removing.

I found Mohamed Ali was on his return from Alexandria, and might be expected at Cairo in a short time. His family did consist of five sons; but last year, his favourite, Tousson Pacha, who was a bashaw with three tails, had caught the plague of a Constantinopolitan slave, and was carried off by this dreadful malady. He has two in Arabia, one his own son, Ibrahim Pacha, commanding against the Wehabees, and a son-in-law in Yemen, also in command of some troops. Two more sons were at Cairo. Ibrahim

Pacha has lately gained great advantages over the reformers, and was, when the last accounts came away, within forty miles of their capital city called Deyriah, and only waited for reinforcements on the march to join him from Yambo to attack the place.

The Wehabees are a sect of puritans of the Mahometans, taking their name from their founder, Abdul Wehub, who lived about 70 years ago. They had at one time extended themselves across from one sea to the other, and were in possession of Mecca: this brought on a war between them and the Turks, which still continues. They have been driven into the interior; and all the coast of the Red Sea, including Mecca, is in the hands of the Turks. They fight on camels, one man facing to the front, and another to the rear, and are armed with muskets. Diodorus Siculus mentions that the Arabs were, in his time, armed with bows and arrows, and went to war in a similar manner. The custom of fighting on camels has been very general throughout the East. The ancient armies of the Tartars made use of them. Camels, in Dara's army, in 1658, when it was opposed to that of Aurungzebe, had small swivels on their backs. The rajah of Biccaneer, in the deserts of India, has a similar corps. The French, when in Egypt, formed a corps mounted on these animals; and in India we have a dromedary corps, the camels carrying a small howitzer, which throws a shell as large as an orange.

The expense of the war in Arabia, I was informed, was extremely burthensome, every thing being carried from Egypt across the Red Sea to Juddah or Yambo, from Cossier or Suez. I inquired if the plague ever shewed itself in the villages and towns above Cairo, and learnt that when it did so it was most particularly destructive.

Observing that Mr. Anderson had a rosary in his hand, I asked him what use he made of it. He answered that he only carried it for amusement; but that the Mahometans, on dropping a bead, called on one of the attributes of God. A Mahometan rosary consists of 101 beads: Catholics will doubtless be surprised to hear, that in all probability the custom was borrowed from the East, as the Hindoos use them; but their string consists of 108 beads.

Before we arrived on the other side of the river it was three o'clock. I felt much annoyed at having lost so much time; and to add to my vexation, my donkey, in attempting to jump out of the boat, fell into the river over head and ears, and after being dragged out, was in a state unfit to be mounted, so that I was obliged to walk, though very far from being well. As soon as the sun had dried the saddle, I again rode, and met many of the Turkish soldiers returning from the town with large round cakes, having holes in the middle, strung upon a cord. A very narrow pathway ran along the bank, and I of course, considering the pre-eminence of my donkey, rode upon it; but a half drunk soldier differing from me in opinion, came impudently straight up to meet me, and was surprised and enraged when my animal fairly ran him down. He unslung his musquet, all the time abusing me, and I began to repent the audacity of my charger, when Mr. Anderson spoke to, and quieted him. We met two soldiers as we entered the town, wounded; one so badly, that he was supported on an ass, and the other much hurt: If I had seen these maimed gentry before I jostled the Albanian, I think I should have guided my donkey out of the way. Mr. Anderson informed me, that under any other Turkish pacha, the excesses which they would have committed in Khenné would have been great, but that the vigorous arm of the present ruler shielded persons and property from their rapacious gripe. We passed by several streets, and observed the soldiers preparing their arms, &c. for the next day's march; and a large new raised building was shewn, as the barracks for the troops.

Mr. Anderson's house was a mean, irregular abode; but it contained a good room in the interior. I found my baggage and despatches, and a table spread with knives, forks, spoons, glasses, and napkins in the European manner; but I was so feverish, that I could only drink water, which was delightfully cool, from earthenware jars of a very porous quality, manufactured at Khenné. I noticed his bed, formed of a great many small pieces of wicker wood, not close together, but sufficiently strong to bear his weight; and he told me this was to prevent the scorpions from harbouring about the furniture, as it is easy to be removed and washed. Before we sat down to dinner, a Greek gentleman, whom I had seen at the house of the captain of the port, came in, and stopped to partake of our fare, and I observed that he brought a servant with him completely armed. From Mr. Anderson I learnt that he was the banker or cashier belonging to government. I had previously sent to inquire whether the boat was ready, and had despatched Mustapha and Mehumed to it with my baggage. When dinner was nearly over, the arrival of two Englishmen was announced, and two Europeans entered the room; but from their reception being in Italian, and from their appearance, I was convinced they were not Englishmen. Mr. Anderson introduced one of them to me, as Monsieur Sieber, a botanist, travelling under the orders of the Austrian government; and I found him to be a very well informed man. The other person appeared to be his servant. M. Sieber was very inquisitive about India, which he had a strong inclination to visit. He seemed, as far as I was a judge, to be generally well versed in natural history. He told me he had collected a large variety of new plants never before known, in number near 400, and that his boat was absolutely crowded with cases containing specimens of subjects in natural history. He had heard of the gentleman who at present has charge of the botanical garden at Calcutta, but he had forgot his name. He happens to be a friend of mine, a Danish gentleman, Dr. Wallack; and I promised to leave for Mr. Sieber, at Cairo, at the house of our consul, a letter to introduce him, and thus commence a correspondence. Of this he highly approved, and thanked me much. He asked me my name, and seemed grateful for my attention. He stated that he was born at Prague; and remarked that it was one of the very few cities on the continent which Buonaparte had not entered as an enemy, and I think he even said it was not entered by any of the French armies.

It was now near six o'clock, and I took leave of my kind host and the German botanist; and mounting my donkey, went down to the boat, which was placed just above the Turkish camp. The Turkish soldiers who had come with me from Cossier accompanied me, and asked for buckshes, or presents; the same word used throughout India, and without doubt that from which we derive our word Christmas-box. I gave them some money, and in return they fired their muskets over the boat. I found all the servants of Mr. Anderson importunate for buckshes, and I was obliged to give every one a trifle. A large basket of bread, with two or three bottles of date brandy, and some baked fowls, were in the boat, which was very miserable, only covered with a coarse cloth, and hardly room enough for Mustapha, Mehumed, and the two rowers. We glided gently down the Nile, passing the Turkish encampment; and I made Mehumed tell the rowers I should expect them to row all night, as I was desirous of reaching Sciout. To this they answered, that they intended to go only as far as Girgé; but I paid little regard to this. I was, after the fatigues of the preceding day, most happy to lie down, and spreading my cloak and putting on my serada, I soon fell fast asleep. On awaking in the night, I found the boat fastened to the shore, and the men belonging to it asleep; but I soon roused them, and made them commence pulling at their oars, and Mehumed, and the man who steered, occasionally relieved the others. This morning I landed at a small village, and procured some coffee; after which continued our voyage, till, by D'Anville's map, and the account of the Arabs, off the village of How, from whence I have dated this part of my Journal.

I have seen several crocodiles, and fired at one, and Mustapha at more, though I think with but little execution. The largest was about eighteen feet long, and the rotundity of the belly continued all the way along to the tail, whereas the alligator is flat, and the nose of the crocodile is much longer than that of the latter. We have two kinds of alligators in India; one, the Cummere, with a sharp long nose, is harmless; but the Gurial, with a round snout, is dreadfully rapacious, and will often carry off persons bathing in the Ganges. When I was at Patna last year, I was informed that in three years two men of his Majesty's 24th regiment had thus met their death. I observed on the other side of a village which we passed this morning the commencement of a bridge, two of the buttresses being above the water, and some very large blocks of stone near the water's edge. The mountain, called Gibel Mokuttum, to the east of the Nile, has had its base washed by the river in several places; and in others, the winding of the stream leaves it several miles. These mountains are the never-failing mines of stone which have been used in Dendera and the other vast remains in this country: they are of calcareous stone, and from the appearance of being scarped, have, without doubt, received their name, that of the "Hewn Mountains." The view from the boat has been, since morning, the same, with only the difference of being more or less distant from Mokuttum; the cultivation uniformly extends to the desert, and the villages are all alike, and built in small groves of date trees. The richness of the country, clear of the desert, cannot be equalled in any part of the world. In consequence of the river being so low at this time of the year, the course it runs is very meandering, and I conceive I must pass over a third more space than D'Anville represents in his map. I fear I shall not arrive even at

Girgé to-night, nor reach Sciout till the day after to-morrow. I find they use here the same kind of oar as in Europe, being totally different from those of India, which are very like the instruments bakers employ to put bread into or take it out from an oven. I observe, when there is not any wind up the river, they track up with ropes; and I have just seen a large boat full of soldiers thus drawn by many Arabs who were guarded, and, with the greatest tyranny, continually thrashed by soldiers. Oppression is always hateful in every point of view; but when one of the profession of arms, feeling himself warranted by the weapon he carries at his side, acts unjustly and cruelly, he at once disgraces it, and must heighten the disgust.

In this instance, we have an example how the best institutions may become perverted; and most painful is the contrast between the first freemen who drew swords at the call of their country to resist attack, and face danger, to those I now speak of, who, from habit and the despotic rule of their master, have become a scourge to the people they were originally intended to protect. This country is governed by the most severe and unrelenting military despotism; and the profession of arms being almost the only one of profit or honour, the fellah appears solely to exist for the support of the soldiery.

Those under our dominion in India are more fortunate: there the civil power is always paramount to the military; and the latter only acts from motives originating in a government which is ever anxious in extending protection to the people under its charge. Far from our army being a curse to the ryots, it defends them from attacks, suppresses banditti, and, as we have lately seen, is employed for their advantage, and the increase of their security, who, relying upon the duty we have imposed on ourselves in becoming their protectors as well as governors, are peaceably engaged in tilling the ground, or other useful ccupations. An Englishman travelling in foreign countries, whether for pleasure or business, should never forget that the most instructive lesson he can receive arises out of the comparison he makes between his own country and others; and of the innumerable blessings and advantages we enjoy, feeling that not one is more conspicuous, not one more to be cherished and valued than our freedom from military insolence and oppression. Our insular situation has, at all times, rendered those enormous military establishments which overwhelm continental countries unnecessary; and the free spirit of the nation has never failed to display a salutary jealousy of large standing armies. From these and other causes, we are exempted from the abuses of military power, so observable not only in the barbarous and despotic governments of Asia and Africa, but in the more moderate governments of Christendom. Such were the reflections that crowded on my mind, when I beheld the unfeeling and wanton exercise of authority by the Turkish soldiers over the Arabs; and I blessed my lot which was cast in a country, where the like painful spectacles of cruelty and degradation can never meet the eye.

CHAPTER XXVIII.

Find it necessary to procure a khanja—Strong winds—Difficulty of making way down the river—Alligators—Boats—Lattine sails—Date brandy—Gibel Dogan—Tobacco—Sand irritates the eyes—Girgé—Minarets—Gun-boat—Difficulties and delay—Ophthalmia—Blind persons—Coffee-house—Turkish soldiers—Effendi—Bad boat—Require a khanja—Succeed in procuring one—Idiot—Dread of the plague—Songs of the boatmen—Drum and flageolet—Nile has no tributary stream after entering Egypt—No crocodiles below Girgé—Scorpions—Recipe for the bite of a scorpion—Disagreeable rencontre with some Turkish soldiers—Caves in the Mokuttum.

To the south of Girgé, on the Nile, 1st April, 1818.

ON the 30th, I continued to glide gently down the river with the assistance of oars, as the stream does not run fast at this time of the year; and despaired of reaching Cairo for many days, since by the map of D'Anville, which Sir Evan Nepean gave me, I found that I had made but little way. I now learnt from Mehumed, that the proper boat to procure would be a khanja with twelve oars. At any rate I was determined to change that I was in wherever I could, as it was not only inconvenient, but very slow. I counted seven crocodiles in the course of the 30th. Towards evening, a very strong wind from the north blew up the river, and not only made it very uncomfortable, but as the boatmen said dangerous, the waves running very high. They wished to come to an anchor near the banks; but as I did not see any great chance of being upset, and the worst that could happen, would be taking in a little water, I would not permit it, though we made hardly any way. The rowers at last got out, and hauled the boat along shore by a rope; and several times, from the shallow state of the river, they were obliged to wade through the water and deep mud, which they did without any appearance of dreading the crocodiles. I have observed the same want of precaution in India among the Dandys or boatmen on the Ganges; and on one occasion, my boatmen had one of these gigantic reptiles amongst them. I am surprised that more persons are not carried off in that river, as all the Hindoos on its banks are obliged to bathe daily; but when an alligator is killed and opened, many bangles or metal bracelets of women and children are generally found in the stomach, and I believe that corpses are invariably divested of these ornaments before they are thrown into the river.

Many large boats with large lattine sails, taking advantage of the fine wind, passed very fast up the river. I tried to procure some dates, but they are not in season till much later than this period. I found several bottles of the brandy made from this fruit on board; and when diluted with water it is very pleasant, but as I have heard very unwholesome. However, Mehumed, to my astonishment, despatched a bottle of it in the course of the night, and I expected to see him become intoxicated, but I was mistaken; and he at last overcame the rigid scruples of Mustapha, who drank about half a pint, and between every sip turned to me, rubbing his stomach, saying, to my infinite amusement, *bono bono*, doubly delightful certainly from its being forbidden.

Smoking was very refreshing, but I was under much alarm lest the sparks, &c. should fall on the clothes and burn the boat. I observed in D'Anville's map a mountain named Gibel Dogan, or the mountain of tobacco, and supposed from this that the Arabs had a word for tobacco, though I had always conceived that this herb was introduced only from America, and bore the same name all over the world*. In India they have no other name for it but tumbacco, and in Persia the same. I have however learnt from Mehumed that dogan means smoke, as we say smoking tobacco. May not this mountain, mentioned by D'Anville, have been formerly a volcano?

* Tobacco is the word used for this herb in the Loochoo Islands.

The banks were covered with very fine cultivation, but the prospect was always bounded on the east side by the Mokuttum, and to the west by the sand hills of the desert. The north wind, which blew with very great violence, carried great quantities of sand in the air with it as it crossed the dry part of the river, and the eyes became very sore from it; but I recollected that Ali Bey el Abassi supposes he saved himself from the ophthalmia by never rubbing them, and though the irritation invited it much, I was determined to follow his example, but washed them every hour. The sand appeared in great clouds, and absolutely darkened in some degree the sun's light, while it lodged in every fold of the clothes and cover of the boat. The night was dreadfully cold and the wind very cutting, and I was obliged to permit the boatmen to rest some time; but Mehumed prescribed date brandy to them, and towards morning they set to the oars again.

About twelve o'clock we saw Girgé at a distance, situated on a high bank on a point to the west of the river, round which the stream runs with some rapidity. The Mokuttum comes down almost to the opposite side of the river. The town has several minarets; and the houses, intermixed with date trees, appeared to be several stories high. The wind was constantly against me, and I was very happy when I reached the place.

Mehumed informed me that at every large town on the Nile there was a gun-boat, and a naval officer; and seeing the gun-boat under the town, I landed, and went up to it. I found an old sailor seated on the bank, on a straw-bottomed chair, who told me the effendi, the captain of the port, and all the officers of Girgé, were gone with Mehumed Bey to quell some petty insurrection in the country, and that they would be back at night. This was two disappointments at once: one from its appearing very improbable that I should get a boat, and the other from Mehumed Bey, who I ascertained was the governor of this part of Egypt, having come from Sciout, and being undoubtedly the person Mr. Salt was to have remained with at that place, so that I had very much to fear I should not find him there. I was in a most desperate dilemma; but asking if there was any person to whom I could apply, they said there was an inferior agent, who could do nothing, but that I had better walk up to see him. I in consequence entered the town, and passing through some very narrow streets, which did not appear much frequented, arrived at a large building, with a small square in front of it; and after much talking and disputing, while I was surrounded at the door by many children and idle spectators, I was told to return in an hour, as the person whom I was to see would then be out of his haram. My patience had been very nearly all evaporated during the discussion, but on receiving this message I forgot all my good resolution as to keeping my temper, and desired Mehumed to inform them that I insisted on seeing the important personage who wished me to wait for an hour. I gained nothing, however, by my anger, of which they made very light, and had the mortification of being obliged to wait for half an hour, to be gazed at by blear-eyed children. About thirty assembled around me, and not one of them without the ophthalmia. I was in great alarm lest I should catch it, as multitudes of flies were buzzing round the heads of all those afflicted with it, and alighting on the corners of the eyes, when driven from one they flew to another, thus without doubt communicating the disease. I moved my handkerchief continually round my head, but did not succeed in keeping it quite clear. I suppose that children are more subject to the disorder from the impossibility of making them understand the bad effects of rubbing the eyes. The number of blind people was very distressing, and I observed many who walked by themselves without difficulty.

Mustapha, whom I could not allow to quit me, asked me to go to a coffee-house with him, to which I assented, and found a small stove with coffee on the side of the street, which was covered over from the tops of the houses with a coarse cloth. Here many Turkish soldiers were seated, smoking, drinking coffee and sherbet, and playing at chess and drafts. Some of them were superbly dressed, and a small stool being brought me, I sat down in the middle of them, drank my coffee, and smoked a pipe which one of them lent me: they were very civil. I have learnt, from my previous dumb interview at Khenné, what to do on these occasions; and I admired their pistols and swords, as they did my arms, and we were good friends immediately.

We had not been here above half an hour when I was informed the gentleman was ready to see me; and as I went away from these fierce-looking fellows, one of them for fun, or perhaps with an intention to insult, called out pretty loud "Jon," to the amusement of the by-standers. I took no notice of it, but proceeded to the house where I had been before, and ascended a large flight of steps into a room, where I found, on a raised platform, a young man plainly dressed; and near him two boys of fifteen or sixteen, uncommonly handsome, one dressed like a military man, and the other in the common dress of the Turks. I explained to him that I wanted a boat to continue my way to Cairo, which he agreed to procure. After coffee, pipes, &c. and taking notice of swords and difference of dress, I looked at the room, which must have been originally very handsome, but is now divided off by wooden partitions. The walls and roof were inscribed with Arabic sentences, in gold letters on a painted ground.

I then took leave, and returned to the water side, and on inquiring for my boat, one was shewn me, if possible, worse than that in which I had come from Khenné. Through Mehumed, I declared to the soldier who accompanied me that I would not go in it, and now mentioned a khanja, which I had forgot to do before. One was pointed out to me round the neck of land which ran into the river, but I was told I could not have it. I however despatched Mehumed and Mustapha to procure it for me, and after some argument this was effected. This boat was above thirty feet long, with a low cabin, about twelve feet by five, only calculated for the sedentary habits of the Turks, as it was not above four feet high. The windows were trellised, and the inside neatly painted with wreaths of flowers, &c. There were places for fourteen rowers.

This morning I was obliged to land at a village to procure more rowers. While I was there, an idiot came into the room half naked, very muscular, and about thirty years of age; and I think I never saw a more horrible figure. He was much noticed; almost every body gave him a little money, and I followed their example. It is remarkable that in almost every part of the world there is something connected with these unfortunate beings considered sacred and auspicious, which is very happy for them, as it ensures their kind treatment.

In the continual intercourse I was under the necessity of having with the people of the country, I must own the idea of the plague often presented itself, and I regretted I had been so inquisitive with respect to it, as Mr. Anderson's information had made me very uneasy. At Girgé, yesterday, I saw some very *plaguy*-looking people, but did not ask any questions: I tried to avoid touching them as much as possible, but it was hopeless in a crowd.

I have been much amused with the songs of the boatmen. The master of the boat, or one of the rowers, sings a short verse, which is repeated by the whole in chorus, and is far from being disagreeable. They also join in a sort of cry, of two or more words to some of the songs, and are accompanied by a small drum, beat by the hand, and a boy playing on two reeds tied together, like a double flageolet. We have a very fine wind from the south, and have hoisted a large lattine sail. The boat I am in is not unlike the morg punkah of the Ganges, but not so long. From what I have seen, I think the boats on the Ganges are much more numerous than on this river; but many other rivers run into the former, while this has not one tributary stream after its entering Egypt. I have not seen a single crocodile since I passed Girgé. Mr. Anderson told me there were none below that place.

On opening my basket of clothes this morning, I found in one of the folds of a shirt a young scorpion, about half an inch long, of a light colour, almost transparent: how he got there I cannot conceive. I however committed him to the Nile, and shall be careful to search if any more are among my effects. According to Mr. Anderson, this is not the time of year in which they are dangerous. I mentioned to him the application which gives much relief to the person stung by one of these reptiles. The pain is in general excessive, and where deaths have ensued, they have been too readily attributed to the poison; whereas I believe they have been caused by fever brought on by the very great pain. The remedy to which I allude is pounded ipecacuanha, made into a paste, and applied to the wound itself. I carried some with me, as well as some eau de luce, which is very efficacious for the bite of snakes. A gallant general, who fell in the Nepaul war, was once saved by the latter, being insensible from the bite of a snake, but recovered in consequence of taking it. The natives of India are aware of its good qualities, and anxious to procure it, calling it *sefait dewi*, or white medicine.

Five o'clock in the evening.

I little thought, when I put down my pen this morning, that I should have met with an adventure which has delayed me more than two hours, and at one time threatened to be very unpleasant. I was reading some of the papers I had with me, when I heard a violent dispute between some persons on the shore and the boatmen, as we passed under the bank; and on coming out of the cabin to inquire into the cause, heard the report of a musket. A ball whistled over my head, and I saw a party of Turkish soldiers running along the bank with their muskets in their hands, calling to us to stop. I desired the boat to be steered to the other side, but the water was too shallow; and as we were obliged to pass close under a point of land where these ruffians had taken post, I was obliged to put in to the shore, when four of the soldiers rushed in a most tumultuous manner into the boat. I could not get either Mehumed or Mustapha to attend to me; the latter had thrown himself on his face in the bottom of the boat the moment the shot passed over, crying out most lustily for Alla and Mahomet, and it was ten minutes before I could make out whence this violent proceeding had originated.

It appeared that there was a detachment of 60 soldiers at a village about two miles from the river, who were going to Sciout, and had no boats, and the effendi, or, as Mehumed called him, general, had ordered the men who had thus captured my boat to wait on the banks, and to stop any vessels that might be passing to take them down. . Mustapha, who had now recovered himself, told them who I was, and they gave me one of their comrades to go to the village, for they would not quit the boat. I therefore put on my sword, and set out with Mehumed, Mustapha, and the soldier.

The village was at a considerable distance: after a long walk in the middle of the day, I reached it, and met a respectable man who spoke Italian, who having heard my story, told the soldier he had acted wrong, and I now desired to be taken to the effendi. I found him at his prayers, and he could not be interrupted; but as soon as he had finished, I stated how I had been treated and fired at, insisted on redress, and called for the soldier who had accompanied me, but he had disappeared, finding things going against him. I then represented that as I had been thus taken out of my boat by the effendi's orders, I demanded that he should come back with me the two miles to the bank of the river, and reinstate me in due possession. This seemed to stagger all present, and

Mehumed said I did not know to whom I was speaking. I again repeated my demand, and the Turk who spoke Italian said the effendi was sorry I should have been thus ill used, but that it was not his fault. I was, however, determined to show that a red coat was not to be insulted with impunity, and made Mehumed understand, that if my wish was not complied with, I would not stir; that the despatches I carried were of great consequence; that if they did not arrive, my government would call upon Ali Pacha to account for it, and that the blame must fall upon the effendi's shoulders; and to show I was determined, I got up, and with apparent unconcern examined some very beautiful muskets hung at the bottom of the room.

After some discussion, in which I took no part, though Mehumed protested he had seen many Englishmen, but none like me, I was informed that two asses were sent for, and that the effendi intended to accompany me. This being arranged, I took some coffee; and having refused the invitation of the gentleman I had first met to stay a day with him, we mounted, and proceeded to the river. When we came in sight of it, to my great amusement I saw the rude soldiers who had rushed into my boat with the utmost violence drawing off across the fields, and avoiding us; and I took possession under flying colours, and have just got under way again. Thus ended this very unpleasant business, which at first appeared to threaten serious consequences. Just before this occurred, I passed under the Mokuttum which came close to the river, and saw halfway up some caves hewn in the mountains, but I was unable to visit them, being anxious not to detain Mr. Salt, if I should overtake him at Sciout.

CHAPTER XXIX.

Cold night—Violent north wind—Arrive at Sciout—Accounts of Mr. Salt having gone down the river—Ibrahim Pacha—Covered streets—Shops—European carriage—Effendi—No hopes of overtaking Mr. Salt—Appointment—The Pacha monopolizes every thing in Egypt—Italian medical gentleman—Conversation with him—Immense wealth of the Pacha—His tyranny—Comparison between the natives of India and Egypt—Plague—Europeans in the service of the Pacha—Account of the death of Sheik Ibrahim—Account of Belzoni—Arrive at Mr. Meroka's house—Female slaves—Tattooing—Slaves throughout the East—Take leave—Arrive at Monflot—History of Mehumed.

On the Nile, between Sciout and Monflot, April 3d, 1818.

ON the evening of the 1st instant the wind became again unfavourable, and blew the whole night in a violent manner from the north; and the cabin not being made for bad weather, the cold was severe, the wind finding its way through the trellis-worked windows. The boat was obliged to be moored to the shore the greater part of the night, as it was impossible to make any way.

On the morning of yesterday the wind continued equally adverse, and we did not reach Sciout till eleven o'clock in the day, when it blew almost a hurricane. The town of Sciout is at some distance from the river; but the moment we reached the shore, I proceeded to it. We learnt, on the road, that the British consul had gone forward, which disappointed me much, but I still hoped to find it false on arriving in town.

This place is the seat of the governor of Upper Egypt. He is absent, being in command of the army opposed to the Whehabees in Arabia. He is son of Mehumed Ali Pacha, and his name Ibrahim Pacha. We saw his palace at a distance, which is a fine, well-built house, surrounded with a wall and gardens. The town is built on a hill, and makes a showy appearance, having many mosques and minarets. We proceeded through some streets entirely covered at the top, with small apertures to admit the light, and some neat shops beneath for the sale of slippers, pipes, clothes, &c. and reached the house of the acting effendi. In a court-yard we saw a European carriage standing, evidently out of repair and disregarded.

My bad fortune always brings me to the house of these Turks when at prayers or asleep, and I was told that this gentleman could not be seen; but on pointing out the necessity of his admitting me, I was, after waiting a few minutes, ushered into his room. He was lying on the floor surrounded with pillows, evidently very ill, and fanned by several slaves. He asked me to sit down, and upon Mehumed informing him that I wanted a boat, he sent for the captain of the port. I inquired if he had heard of the British consul, to which he answered in the negative; nor had he heard of the man on the dromedary I had sent with my letter. I therefore fear I shall not see Mr. Salt, unless the messenger has had the sense to follow him down the river. It is possible, however, that I may find him to-night at Monflot. I should have been well pleased had I overtaken him, as he would have given me much information concerning this country and its antiquities. The room this sick person lay in was far from comfortable, having only small holes about a foot square in the walls near the ceiling; and the strong wind blew about the oiled paper which had once filled them up. The cause of the room being thus imperfectly lighted is to be found in their jealousy of their women.

After some difficulty it was settled that I should continue in the old boat I had brought with me from Girgé, and an order was given me to procure more rowers. I asked if any person in the city or neighbourhood spoke any of the European languages, and was answered in the negative. I then took leave, and returned through the town with the deputy of the captain of the port, to procure more men to row. I found considerable difference here as well as at Girgé in the manner I was treated by the effendi, after having been used to have the population of the villages and towns in India come out to meet me, with offers of their services and supplies.

We proceeded, on donkeys procured by my companion, the deputy, back to the boat. I found the wind as strong as when I quitted it, blowing a perfect hurricane; and the sand, which was carried with velocity through the air, covered every thing, and precluded looking to windward. Mehumed informed me that Ali Pacha had made a monopoly of butter and tobacco, as of almost every thing that would bring money; and added, by way of explaining the matter, "that none but generals" (the term he used to any one in office) "*in Egypt sold butter or tobacco.*"

The gale continued so violent that the boatmen could not quit the shore, and at dark I gave up all hopes of its force abating, and was about to lie down, stuffing my clothes, linen, &c. into the numerous holes, to try to keep out the wind; when, to my surprise, I saw a European, mounted on a donkey, coming towards the boat. I at first thought it might be Mr. Salt, but on his alighting, he addressed me in Italian, and I found he spoke French also. He said that his name was Meroka; that he was a surgeon, and an Italian by birth, and lived in Sciout. I made him acquainted in a few words with my business. I walked up and down the shore with him, regretting that I had not known of his being in the town, but the effendi had informed me there was no European within reach. He stated that Mr. Salt had passed in his way down two nights before, and that he would not stop, as it was his wish to get speedily to Cairo. I learnt that Ali Pacha was returning, or had arrived at Cairo from Alexandria; and that of all despotisms ever known, this government was the most decided. My visitor was only surprised how it was continued, since all ranks, soldiers and husbandmen, were equally in thraldom. He stated that the sums of money which the Pacha drew every year from the country, and the sale of its produce, was inconceivable, and that he would never permit any one to grow rich but himself. He seizes the grain, tobacco, butter, cloth, and in short every production of the country, and pays for them what he thinks fit, only allowing the Arabs and Copts enough to exist on, thus rendering himself abhorred by the cultivator of the ground; while by having taken into his hands the whole of the commerce of Egypt, he has made the merchant destitute. All the exports are derived from his granaries or warehouses. How debased is human nature when thus trod under foot by a fellow-creature, who, in these eastern countries, can hardly boast of any intellectual advantage over him who earns his bread by daily labour! Here the pacha, with the strong unbending arm of power, converts all the produce of Egypt, and the industry of its inhabitants, to his own use; and although property is secured from robbery by the vigour of the police, yet the all-powerful government is their worst plunderer.

How long a period will it be before these eastern despots prove, by the introduction of a more liberal policy, the great advantages of a general affluence throughout their dominions, instead of thus sweeping all into their own coffers, and by cramping industry, and destroying all stimulus to improvement, act in a manner equally impolitic as it is unjust and oppressive. Every show of capital, or earnest of speculation, excites jealousy and mistrust, and monopoly crushes ambition and exertion. How truly delighted I shall be to reach that country, where all are free as the air they breathe, where all are equal in the eyes of the protecting laws, which are formed as exigencies arise, to increase the prosperity of all, and where person and property are shielded alike from the violation of the prince or the subject. When a Briton considers the happiness of those under British rule in India, contrasted with the state of these slaves, he will feel his country rise higher than ever in his estimation. I have, during the short time I was at Calcutta, witnessed the extraordinary and increasing confidence which daily shewed itself. The rich natives have overcome the feeling of distrust which existed under their own rulers, and now, by building palaces and enclosing gardens, prove the reliance they place in our established power and justice, which enables them to bring their capital into the light of day, secure against all domestic oppression and foreign violence*.

Mr. Meroka told me that the pacha last year fed all the south of Europe with grain, clearing several hundred per cent. on what he expended, or rather gave to the fellahs, for he seems to think that every thing belongs to him in the country, and treats Egypt as a planter does his West India estate. All the produce as well as his slaves, from whose labour it is derived, belong to him; and even the soldiers fear rather than love him, except those about his person, for in his personal intercourse he is extremely mild and conciliating. Thus having taken to himself the property of the commercial and agricultural classes of the community, he does not, like other despots, permit his army to partake of his power, but has tamed them, which I believe was never done before with Turkish soldiers, and holds them, as Mr. Meroka says, "*comme des enfans.*"

After we had walked an hour, and he had corroborated what Mr. Anderson told me respecting the plague being at Alexandria, with the addition of its being also at Rosetta, the wind not decreasing, he wished me to accompany him to his house, to which I consented. We continued in conversation, and he informed me

* I have been assured since my arrival in England, by persons who accompanied the governor-general from Calcutta in July, 1817, and who have since returned to that city, on their way home, that they had seen in every direction the most astonishing improvements and additions, both useful and ornamental, carried into effect by the rich natives.

that on his first arrival in the country he was seized with the plague, as were also his wife and child. Mr. Meroka, it appeared, was surgeon to the governor of Upper Egypt, Ibrahim Pacha, now absent. He told me farther, that he was recommended to him by curing him of a wound he had received in the fleshy part of the shoulder, at a grand review given at Cairo, in honour of the retaking of Mecca. It was occasioned by one of those accidents so common among the Turks at their military spectacles: they fire with ball in all directions, and appear to have no idea of blank cartridge, so that casualties often occur. He states that there are generally about twenty Europeans about the person of the pacha, and about eighty in his service. Several Italians are now with the army in Arabia, but, as far as I could learn, none of them hold any military appointment whatever.

Among other news, I was informed of the death of Sheik Ibrahim, whose having penetrated to Tombuctoo I had been led by one of the Reviews to consider certain. This was a piece of intelligence at which I was truly sorry, as no person was ever better qualified, by talents, and the knowledge he had gained in a six years' residence in Egypt, for accomplishing that interesting object. He was a Swiss, of the name of Burckhardt. A caravan had arrived at Sciout from Senar, a country in the interior of Africa, within the last few days. I also learnt that Mr. Salt had made some very wonderful discoveries in Upper Egypt; and that an Italian gentleman, of the name of Belzoni, had within the last month opened the second pyramid. Mr. Meroka recommended me to stop in my way down at the house of a Mr. Brine, an Englishman, who had charge of a sugar manufactory at a place called Rodomon, near Melani.

The servant had been despatched on the donkey to order supper, and we walked into the town some way to my companion's residence, on entering which I found it comfortable, and a good table laid out in the European manner. He introduced me to his wife, who also spoke French, and the table was soon covered with an excellent supper, and some good wine, including a bottle of claret. They were both truly kind, and I was not a little pleased with the change, from a miserable boat on a sandy bank, to the comforts of civilised society. In the course of the conversation it appeared that he was, like every European in Egypt, infected with a love of antiquities, and that it was his intention to send his wife in a short time to find the Oasis, containing the temple of Jupiter Ammon, which he said was only a few days' journey in the desert. The lady too was anxious to go, and sanguine of success, as the natives respect a veiled woman, and she would meet with no insult or difficulties.

As it grew late, I wished to return, and my entertainer sent for donkeys for us. While they were preparing, he shewed me nine female slaves he had bought within the last few days. They had all the appearance of the negro, but the hair, though woolly, was in long ringlets, and their teeth were filed away to a sharp point. One of them was burned, by way of ornament, down the front of her person, and it made me shudder to reflect upon the pain it must have given her to undergo the operation. It was more severe in length and breadth than the firing of a horse. They seemed cheerful, and were certainly what he called "*des esclaves superbes.*" It is curious to observe how extensive this custom of tattooing is. The ancient Britons were formidable to their enemies from being thus marked, and it is even now common amongst our sea-faring people. The women in the neighbourhood of Patna, in India, are all tattooed; and Symes tells us that it is common in Birmah: and here again we find it in the interior of Africa; and it extends across this vast continent, as all the African negroes in our West India islands are marked in a similar manner. The negroes on the western coast of Africa, those of the eastern, bordering on Egypt, and probably throughout the interior of that continent, are all alike in their characteristic of jet black complexion, broad noses, thick lips, and woolly hair, similar to those I saw at Rio Janeiro, from the coast of Guinea, and those I now speak of. Egypt and Turkey will in a few years be almost the only countries in the whole world where this traffic will be carried on, for it has long been abolished in our Indian territories; and this adds something, in a mere humane point of view, to prove the advantages which have arisen from our eastern rule, as the trade in slaves from Africa to India was carried on at an early period.

It is a part of the state of the court of Delhi to have Abyssinian slaves, as well as negroes. The first are called Hubshee, from Hubeish, the name used by the Mahometans for Abyssinia; and the latter are distinguished under the comprehensive term of Caffre, or infidel, from which we have derived our word Caffre, which proves that our earliest navigators, on the eastern coast of Africa, fell in with the Mahometans in their first voyages. The Turks and Arabs are very much attached to female negro slaves, and all the people of fortune have several of them in their harams; and I heard of a son by a negro woman, at Moccha or Juddah, I forget which, who was, with all the marks of his origin, received on equal terms with the rest of his children by his father, the leading man of the city.

On our return to the boat the wind was still so violent, that it could not proceed down the river. This morning, the gale having abated, I have made some progress, and hope to reach Monflot by the evening.

On the Nile, between Monflot and Rhodomon, 4th April, 1818.

I continued my voyage yesterday, in hopes of my letter having been carried to Monflot, as the man on the dromedary had not made his appearance at Sciout; and in the evening, as we approached it, we met a boat, the people in which answered to our qnestions that the British consul was there. As the night drew on, when about a mile or perhaps more from the place, on the right bank of the Nile, I observed a tower and ruins, but could not gain any information from the boatmen concerning it. Monflot, situated on the left bank of the river, appeared a good town; and about dusk I pulled into the shore, and amongst a number of boats and khanjas, made inquiries without success for the consul Inglaize. I at last despatched Mehumed and Mustapha to the captain of the port to know where he was, and was informed he was at Rhodomon, the sugar manufactory. I was in consequence most anxious to proceed, but found that some of the boatmen had taken advantage of my being near the shore to desert, and on my proposing to go on, I found a general mutiny, in which Mehumed took part. I however insisted on their putting off, though reduced to eight men, and succeeded. A glass of date brandy brought the surly barbarian Mehumed to order, and he and Mustapha having drunk a bottle between them, the former became very communicative, and gave me some of his history. He told me how he had fled from Tangiers to Ceuta, and joined the Spaniards: then entered our navy, and was made prisoner on the coast of Catalonia by the French. He remained four years and a half at Verdun; and on his return received 450 dollars, as pay due to him. He had afterwards gone back to Spain; then proceeded to Alexandria and Rosetta, where he had become a soldier, and served Ali Pacha, but getting into debt, had sold all at Mecca or Juddah, and for subsistence turned sailor on board the polacre in which I found him. In reply to my wish to know why he did not revisit his own country, he said he was poor, and did not wish to be seen by those who had known him formerly; and there appeared a sort of mystery about the early part of his story: upon questioning him, he at last told me he had shot a man, and was obliged to fly to save his life.

CHAPTER XXX.

Arrive at the sugar manufactory—Rhodomon—Received by several Europeans—Mr. Brine—Mr. Salt gone forward—Sugar manufactory—Coppers—Rum—Probability of underselling the West India produce—Garden—French mameluke—The Turkish army in Egypt—The Pacha not cruel—Improvements he has made—Bchar Josef—Dinner—French officer of the imperial guard—Take leave of Mr. Brine—Ruins below Rhodomon—Ruins of Antinoe—Corinthian pillars—Arrive at Meniet—Find Mr. Brine's secretary at a Greek doctor's—Interview with the Bey—Importunity of his servants—Nautch women, or almes, at the Greek doctor's—House—Dinner—Confusion and departure.

On the Nile, between Meniet and Biniswief, April 6th, 1818.

I WAS fortunate enough to reach Rhodomon about four o'clock, and at a considerable distance perceived the fires and smoke from the chimneys of the manufactory. Having landed, I proceeded to the house, through a large grove of date trees. In my way I passed a spacious garden, containing all the English vegetables, and bespeaking the vicinity of a civilised community. The building was extensive, and on entering a court-yard and inquiring for Mr. Brine, I was shewn up stairs to a sort of covered veranda, where several Europeans advanced to meet me. One I addressed in a modification of Spanish, and then in an attempt at Italian, having been questioned in the latter language; and after a very awkward conversation on my part for a few minutes, we discovered, to our great amusement, that we were both English. I expressed a wish to see Mr. Brine, who soon made his appearance, having been hurried down from his room by a message that a Russian gentleman wanted to speak to him. He was very kind, and informed me that Mr. Salt had been wind-bound until that morning, and had quitted Rhodomon about ten o'clock. Here I was again disappointed; but Mr.

Brine obligingly despatched his secretary to overtake and stop him, if possible; and I agreed to remain all night. I stated to him in general terms the news I had brought with me, which seemed to give him satisfaction; and his appearance was that of a thorough right feeling Englishman, and a hearty well-wisher to his country.

After some conversation, he acquiesced in my proposition to visit the manufactory. It appears that he is in partnership with the pacha; that is to say, he has made an agreement to share the three first years' profit with his highness, on condition of teaching a certain number of Turks how to make both rum and sugar at his expense. On inquiry how, in such a despotic country, he had secured this agreement, I learned that he had taken the precaution to place the signed and sealed document in the British consul's office; I however think his tenure but an insecure one. He informed me he had once been a captain of a merchant vessel, and did not know much how to make sugar when he commenced; yet he had, by industry and perseverance, succeeded. I went through the several apartments and stores, and found the work was on a very extensive scale; insomuch that it would be able to send fifty tons of sugar to Europe in the spring.

The improvements under contemplation were very considerable, and the whole manufactory had an appearance of success. Mr. Brine told me he got his coppers principally from Trieste, but had several English. He also gave me a glass of his rum intended for the European market, for the pacha is more a money-making man than a Mahometan, and has no objection to compound intoxicating liquors for us infidels, if we pay well for them. It was very excellent; equal to any rum I ever tasted. I met many Europeans in every part of the manufactory, and learnt that there were no fewer than forty, principally Italians. Sanguine hopes were entertained of underselling our West India markets in the Mediterranean, and furnishing the coasts of the Black Sea, Greece, Dalmatia, and Italy, with sugar and spirits of a superior kind, at a very reasonable price. Should this system be carried on to any large extent, which I think highly probable if the present pacha lives, as his comprehensive mind must perceive the advantages of it, I have no doubt it will make a serious change in the vent of our West India produce. This great man, with his extraordinary talents and foresight, will make Egypt as valuable to himself, as was ever projected by the French in their ill-fated expedition. Mr. Brine had a great number of labourers employed in the building, and I suppose must have a *carte blanche:* I was proud to see my countryman alone deemed worthy of such high trust. It appeared that the men in office around him (Turks) were all jealous of him, but he had carried most of his points against them. After inspecting the manufactory, he took me into his garden, well stocked with vegetables; but the potatoes had not succeeded well. I have no doubt, however, that the pine apple and mango, if introduced, would thrive; and think it a pity they have not yet found their way to this fine country. A French mameluke, attached to the establishment, joined us, dressed in the Turkish costume, and entered into conversation. I must say I pitied him; though, considering the changes his unfortunate country has lately undergone, he has perhaps prolonged his life, and been well out of it. I mentioned the pacha to Mr. Brine, who gave me some information respecting him. It appears that the military force under his command is great, and that he cannot have fewer than 30,000 men in Egypt, not only subservient, but even attached to him; and Mr. Brine thinks that no European power, including the Turks, could make any impression on him. It is only of late years that he has named himself pacha, having been the last twelve years, step by step, gaining the ascendency at which he has now arrived. He is not represented as cruel, though obliged, from his very peculiar situation, to be severe in his punishments; and, like other despots, finds himself compelled to govern by fear.

He is so tyrannical, that his son dared not write to him, and was under the necessity of allowing any communication to pass through the usual channels of business. He appears, however, to pay the utmost attention to the general good of the country, by the means drawn from it; and though the lower classes, ever blind to prospective advantages, may grumble, yet he is a better sovereign by such wise expenditure of his revenue than the Pharouns, as the Arabs to this day call them, who raised the pyramids, or the temple of Dendera. He has restored the road between Rosetta and Alexandria, which was destroyed by the British army in 1800, and allowed the sea to flow into the Lake Mariotis; and he has lately opened, or rather begun to re-open, the *Behar Josef*, a fine canal which runs parallel to the Nile a little way above Rhodomon, and waters a fine district containing 40 villages in the desert. He has now 30,000 men employed upon it, and as soon as the harvest is in, intends to employ at least 100,000 to be ready for the rising of the Nile, as it is his wish that it should not only be open, but navigable all the year round. He has even an intention of carrying it to Alexandria. I think it is a curious thing that two such men should have arisen together as Ali Pacha of Albania, and Mehumed Ali Pacha of Egypt. The Turkish government is too much afraid of men of talent to allow such things to occur, except in rare instances. I have no doubt, should the son of this present pacha be as great a man as his father, that Egypt will be separated from Turkey for ever.

At seven o'clock we sat down to a plain and plentiful foreign dinner, seasoned with welcome and good humour, which was most acceptable to me. At table I met a French officer of the late emperor's imperial guard. His name was Balle, and he had fled from France after the battle of Waterloo. He was a very handsome man, and had been in the Spanish war, so that we fought our battles over again. He denied that the imperial guards were engaged at Fuentes d'Honore, when with their red feathers they ran in a most

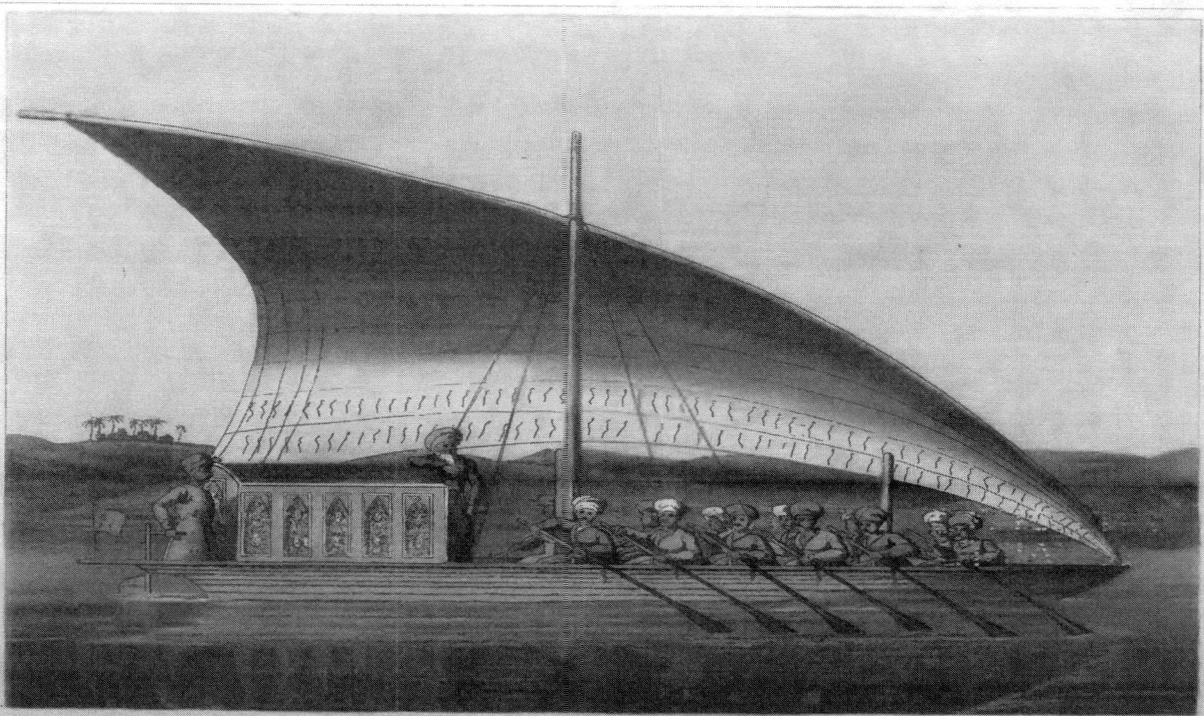

G. Fitz-Clarence del.t

Engraved by R. Havell & Son

A KHANGA ON THE RIVER NILE.

London, Published [illegible] by John Murray, Albemarle Street

active manner before the 79th regiment; and affirmed that the imperial guard was not engaged at Waterloo: but considering all this as natural in the quarter whence it came, I made due allowance. He was anxious to go to America; the further the better, he said, from France. I could not but pity the cruel dilemma in which he appeared to be. He told me he was of the *legion d'honneur*, and had hoped to have risen high in the service. His is a sad fall, from basking in the beam of imperial favour to becoming almost an object of charity to a sugar manufacturer. We talked so much, and so late, that more wine was drank than was desirable, and I took up my quarters in Mr. Rossi's room. This morning, having received on board sufficient men to carry me to Meniet, I hope to overtake Mr. Salt at that place. I took leave of Mr. Brine, and very much fear I shall not often find so worthy a man as he approved himself in our brief intercourse.

I had heard of some curious ruins about three miles below Rhodomon, and fully intended to see them as I passed; but so numerous are the remains throughout this country, that I landed at a wrong spot, the site of the ancient city Antinöe, where I much admired some magnificent Corinthian pillars. There had been six, I think, to a ground portico, but only three were standing. The massive cornices, and entablatures of beautiful workmanship, lay on all sides.

The whole country was covered with bricks and stones; and I saw about a mile distant on the desert other pillars, similar, I conceive, to those I have mentioned. There were also the remains of a flight of steps down to the river.

I observed a great number of wells, from which the water was raised differently from those I have formerly mentioned. What I now saw consisted of wheels turned by oxen, having cords and numberless earthenware pots attached to them, which pots were emptied into a cistern. The wind became dreadfully violent, and prevented my making much way; but about six o'clock in the evening I reached Meniet, which had the appearance of a large town. I did not, however, see any khanja; and we were soon hailed by a boy from the shore, informing us that Mr. Rossi was at the house of a Greek doctor, and that Mr. Salt must either have passed before he was set on duty, or had not yet arrived, as he had been ordered to watch by the side of the river, and mine was the first khanja he had seen.

I landed, and walked with our guide to the house of the Greek doctor, where I was much chagrined at not meeting our consul. However, after some discussion, we repaired to the house of the bey, who was a man of very high rank. We found him seated in a small court-yard smoking, but removed to his room of business, well fitted up with cushions, &c. and the windows of painted glass. I made the Greek our interpreter, and it may be easily conceived how long a question was in reaching the bey;—longer than a telegraphical communication would take to go from London to Portsmouth, and by as many intermediate stations. I spoke French to Mr. Rossi, he spoke in Italian to the Greek, and the latter in Turkish to the bey. The latter was inquisitive about India, and said he came from a country near it; but this proved to be Damascus, so little do they know of geography. I persuaded him to allow me a man on horseback to go to Beniswief, in the hope of finding Mr. Salt. I then brought forward my principal want, that of men, as those of the "fabrique," as every body called the manufactory at Rhodomon, were to return, and to this also he assented. After coffee, &c. and pipes, we took our leave, and were absolutely mobbed for buckshes by the servants of this great man, before we were out of his presence, and I was obliged to be very liberal to make them quit me. This is not the first time I have met with this really disgraceful kind of begging, which adds greatly to a traveller's expense, and procures little or no thanks for his liberality. It reminded me of the custom I have heard of, of giving vails in

England, happily abolished about fifty years ago. I found it was the intention of my new friend, the Greek doctor, and Mr. Rossi, to give me a dinner, and that the former had ordered a party of nautch girls, or as they are called here *almés*, to dance before me; and though very impatient to be gone, I could not decline the well meant treat. These *almés* are, in comparison with the nautch girls of India, very inferior performers, and by no means so graceful. I was surprised to see vast quantities of spirits drank by all around me. The bottle of date brandy on the table, containing a pint or two, was more than once replenished before dinner. The Greek brought out a number of ancient coins, and insisted on my acceptance of them, as well as of two little Egyptian figures of blue clay. The horrid noise of the instruments on which they played during the dancing of the *almés* was deafening, and I was truly happy to get rid of them. About eight o'clock a cloth was spread on the table, with plates and forks, but only one knife. A Turk and a Copt, two dirty persons, were, I discovered, to be of our dinner party, and nearly all were drunk with the quantity of brandy they had swallowed. We had no wine, and it was impossible for me to take the fiery spirit they were gulping in bumpers. I felt some curiosity to see what sort of a dinner we should have, and was not sorry when anchovies and water-cresses were put on the table; but the same forks which they put to their mouths were repeatedly plunged into the salad, and the anchovies were hauled out of the dish with their fingers. The remove to these consisted of a whole sheep roasted on a square tin; and the fellow who brought it seized the knife, and taking hold of a leg, with his hand wrapped in rags, began to carve it, while the surrounding guests with their fingers pulled off the brown outside and eat it. This took away what little appetite I previously had; and the Greek doctor, perceiving that I did not eat, began very good-naturedly to whimper, and make all sorts of faces at having nothing better to offer me. The brandy produced a very evident effect on his senses; and quitting the room, he appeared, on his return, dressed in a lieutenant's coat of one of our regiments of infantry over his native dress. Where he got it I do not know. The repeated draughts from the brandy bottle had now completed the general intoxication: the Turk became exceedingly familiar, and the doctor began to talk Arabic to Rossi, and Italian to the Turk; while Mehumed, to complete the scene, was heard in the back ground swearing violently in all the languages he knew—now appealing to me in Spanish and English, then to Rossi in Italian, and in Arabic and Turkish to the Mahometans, having quarrelled with the "*capitaine de port*" about the wages for the men who were to go as far as Cairo. I made a vain attempt to quiet this modern Babel, and finally quitted the scene. I was met in the street by a marriage, which appears similar to those I have seen in India; the bridegroom being carried round the city with various attendants, &c. I was well pleased to get on board my boat about eleven o'clock, after having paid treble for my entertainment, to satisfy the pressing demands for money by all around.

CHAPTER XXXI.

Pass Beniswief—Slaves—Old Cairo—Bolac—Giza—Immense numbers of boats—Consul's house—Janissary—Enter a house—Surprise the inhabitants—Mutual alarm—Wears off—Explanation—No accounts of our consul-general—Take leave—Proceed to Cairo—Dogs—Narrow streets—Gates—Arrive at Mr. Salt's house—Kind reception by Mr. Salt—Belzoni—The pyramids—Day settled to visit them—Pacha—Discoveries at Thebes—Levé—Interesting conversation—Box of curiosities—Papyrus—Wax figures—Sculpture—Linen—Mummies—Leather—Gilding—Scarabeus—Sarcophagus—Statues of black granite—Wooden figures—Intelligence from Alexandria—Of the Tagus frigate—Curious coincidence—Plague—Visit the pacha—His person—Conversation—Anecdotes of the pacha—Scotchman—Caves in the Mokuttum.

Cairo, April 8, 1818.

I REACHED this far-famed city so late last night, that I have as yet had no opportunity of seeing it, it having been several hours dark before I entered the hospitable house of our consul-general, who received me with all that attention and kindness which can only be truly valued when distant from our own country and friends. But to resume the thread of my narrative.

I passed Beniswief during the night of the 6th: the exertions of the boatmen were very great; they never ceased pulling all the following day, being still in hopes of overtaking Mr. Salt. We passed a large number of boats, or rather rafts, filled with female slaves for the market at Cairo. About six o'clock we arrived off Old Cairo, a sort of suburb, which extends along the banks of the Nile, at some distance to the south of the present city. I was desirous of landing here and walking across; but Mustapha opposed it, alleging that many half drunk Turkish soldiers were strolling about, and that should they, by any chance, have become irritated by loss of money from gambling or otherwise, they would not feel much compunction in venting their rage or disappointment by shooting a Christian. He, however, informed us that the British Consul lived at a village between Cairo and the old city, called Bolac, and that we should reach it in half an hour.

We passed close under the town of Giza, situated on the left bank of the river; but it was too late for me to catch a glimpse of the "wonders of the world," the pyramids, at a distance, though I strained my eyeballs to see them. It was quite dark by the time we had passed this town, and after rowing an hour and a half more, we found ourselves at last at the mouth of a small creek. We entered it, and observed the whole shore along the village of Bolac entirely covered with boats; so crowded that it was with very considerable difficulty we could find a vacant place to approach it. Mustapha, who said he was confident of knowing the road to the *Consul Inglaisé*'s house, was to accompany me; and leaving Mehumed in charge of my clothes, &c. I took my sword and pistols, with my despatches, and landed, to proceed to the long wished for termination of all my toils. The bank was steep, and I followed my guide for about half a mile to a house which he said was that of our Consul. After a little demur, a heavy door admitted us into a court-yard, and we discovered that the gentleman we wanted did not live there; and a Turkish soldier, who was the janissary of the house, explained to me, as I understood him, that it was the residence of the *Consul Rousse*. As I could not make myself understood either by Mustapha or the janissary that I wished to speak to the consul, and as this sturdy fellow would not permit me to enter the house, I was obliged to shew some determination and obstinacy, and a violent altercation took place, in which I joined with all my strength of voice, in hopes of attracting the attention of the family; but this proving fruitless, I pushed by him into the house, and, after some little difficulty, making out the staircase, I ascended, not knowing whither it led, only hoping it might by chance reach the first story.

After groping my way, I at last caught a glimmer of a distant light, and found myself in the first of a suite of rooms, one of which was lighted. I pushed on, and threw the company into the greatest confusion; and when I consider my dress, with a long beard, which I had not shaved from the time of my accident at Jubbulpoor, four months before, my sword, pistols, and red jacket, I am not surprised at their amazement, as certainly they had never before met with so rude an intrusion. The room was fitted up in the European manner: there were only three persons in it, and they were dressed as Turks. This destroyed all my hopes, and I began to think I had intruded upon the haram of, perhaps, some jealous Turk, who would have me decapitated on the spot. After our mutual surprise had in some degree subsided, and I did not see any mutes with scimitars rush in to seize their victim, I attempted, in French, to address the frightened inmates. To my delight, I was answered by one of them in the same language; and I forthwith made all the excuses I could, stating that I was an officer from India, and that my wish to reach Alexandria on my way to England, and anxiety to find the British Consul, had impelled me to become an intruder. This had a good effect, and I was desired to sit down. One of these persons now proved to be a lady, who addressed me in her native Italian; and the third person was also an Italian. They informed me that the Consul could not have arrived, unless within the last two hours, and offered me a bed; but I felt satisfied that I should find him. The house in which I was belonged to the Austrian Consul, an Italian of the name of Rossi, and not the *Russian*, as I had imagined. He appeared to be a very old feeble man, but had evidently the remains of a fine person: the lady was his wife. After a short delay, a servant appeared with a large paper lantern, and announced the borico or donkey being ready, and I took leave of them. The night was very dark, and the streets of Bolac all closed at each end by a heavy wooden gate, which on a signal was opened, and we were permitted to pass after the janissary was recognized. The houses on each side appeared to be of stone, with heavy wooden jalousies protruding into the street, and the celebrated crowds of dogs gave notice by violent howling of the untimely arrival of a stranger. After a ride of above two miles, and crossing a sort of open place surrounded with houses, I entered the city of Cairo, and envied the people who were comfortably situated on all sides of me, for I knew it was possible I might encounter a new difficulty in establishing myself in Mr. Salt's house, should he not have arrived. The streets narrowed very much in the city, and there was the same precaution of closing the ends of the streets as in Bolac. I hardly met more than a single person in the streets, but was surrounded with hundreds of yelping dogs. I observed great quantities of glass used in the windows, and the whole appearance of the city was that of a civilized capital, not only from the fineness of the houses, but the excellence of the police. At last we reached the door of the house I was in search of, and learned, with pleasure, that its owner was at home. I jumped off my donkey, and passing through a narrow passage, entered a court-yard of small dimensions; and from the extraordinary figures against the walls around me, should have fancied I was in the catacombs, had I not recollected that I was in the sanctum sanctorum of an inveterate and most successful antiquarian. The lantern illuminated the massy figures around, and having the prospect of viewing them the next morning, I went on with the hope of entering when supper was on the table; but before I could attain the desired object, I had to pass two large wooden figures, like porters, at the door, from the tombs of the kings of Thebes.

Mr. Salt was seated at table, having just finished his meal. He had only arrived half an hour, and had not received any of my despatches. I presented him with a letter from Lord Hastings. While at supper, Mr. Belzoni, of whom I had heard so much, made his appearance, and I was greatly struck with his person, being in the Turkish costume. He was the handsomest man I ever saw, was above six feet six inches high, and his commanding figure set off by a long beard. He spoke English perfectly, and the subject which had engrossed his thoughts so long, that of opening the second pyramid, was brought on the tapis. As I wished to proceed to Alexandria without loss of time, we fixed the earliest day possible for viewing the adjacent wonders, which is arranged for to-morrow, and I look forward with the greatest pleasure to what will always form an epoch in my life. I also intimated to Mr. Salt my desire to see the pacha, and his interpreter was directed to inquire this morning when it would be most agreeable to receive us.

Mr. Salt spoke in raptures of his late discoveries at Thebes, and said that he intended to return, the moment he could, to Upper Egypt. He had many letters from Alexandria, but had not looked over them, and could not inform me what prospect I had of quitting that port. It was, however, necessary to give buckshes to the janissary belonging to Mr. Rossi, before I could retire in peace; and I passed a most refreshing night after my fatigues.

About eight this morning we met at breakfast, and I found that Mr. Belzoni lived in the house, and was not only a resident with, but in the pay of Mr. Salt. I had much conversation with Mr. Salt and Signior Belzoni respecting the late discoveries in and near the ruins of Thebes, which seem to surpass every thing in the world, except Ellora. The tomb lately opened by Mr. Salt was discovered by Mr. Belzoni, by what he calls a certain *index*, which has guided him in opening the second pyramid: what this index is, I know not; but certainly he has been most successful, and cherishes the intention, if supported by our government, of doing much more. In my opinion he is too valuable a man for us to permit to labour for any other nation. Fame appears to be the object for which he is most anxious, though he has nothing to live on but the produce of a few statues sold to the Comte de Forbin, (who has been in this country, travelling for the French government,) to replace those various niches in the Louvre now vacant by our having forced them to deliver back divers works of art to their original possessors.

Mr. Salt, after breakfast, produced a box, which contained a great variety of curious and interesting objects, which he had collected during his absence from Cairo. He shewed me some beautiful specimens of papyrus which he had himself taken out of the mummy wrappers. They all appeared to have at the top of the roll a representation of religious worship, and the figures were painted in more than one colour. He pointed out some small wax figures; one with the head of a woman, one with an eagle's head, one with a monkey's, and another with that of a ram: these were uniformly found in the better sort of mummies. To prove that sculpture had been carried to very great perfection amongst the ancient Egyptians, he shewed me a small leg and thigh made of wood, about 10 inches long, most correctly carved, and equal to, if not surpassing any thing I had previously seen. He shewed me also a piece of linen covered with hieroglyphics, which appeared exactly as if it had been printed. Several mummies which he had opened had down the front of their person broad pieces of leather, gilt, as fres has the day they were made; and I have understood that gilding has, in several instances, been proved to be well known to the Egyptians. Mr. Salt further produced a most curious and valuable scarabeus. It is about two inches and a half in length, and near two inches broad. The flat side is entirely covered with beautifully executed hieroglyphics. I procured two of these, much smaller than that above mentioned, one of which I intend for the British Museum.

Mr. Salt mentioned to me that he had of late found a great quantity of dried fruits at Thebes, and whole dresses formed of a kind of bugle. Both he and Belzoni were enraptured with the sarcophagus they had discovered, and when I fully comprehended its beauty and value, my feelings were congenial with theirs, without having seen it. A piece of alabaster, nine feet three inches long, would in itself be a curiosity; but when it is considered that so much pains have been used in the elaborate carving of so fragile a material, it almost surpasses belief. It is made something in the form of a human body, but the sides of it are not above two inches or two inches and a half thick, all deeply carved in minute figures representing triumphs, processions, sacrifices, &c. All these figures are stained of the deepest blue; and when a light is placed inside, the alabaster being transparent, they appear upon a pellucid ground. This sarcophagus is doubtless unique, and will, I trust, under the auspicious exertions of Mr. Salt and Belzoni, find its way to the British Museum. It was found in what Belzoni supposes to be a tomb of the god Apis, and was most unaccountably placed across the top of a hollow passage, which leads 300 feet beyond into the solid rock, and has not yet been explored to the utmost. The sarcophagus was placed across this passage, with not above one inch resting on one of the sides, so that had it slipped, it would have fallen and been shattered to pieces. We visited the court-yard which I mentioned having passed through last night, and surveyed four statues of black granite as large as life, with women's bodies and heads of lions. They were in a sitting posture, with the emblematical key of the Nile in one of their hands. Belzoni discovered these, in company with above thirty others, deep under the sand. They had been deposited there without regularity, as if to be concealed. Two of these he had sold to the Comte de Forbin for the French Museum. Mr. Salt next drew my attention to two wooden figures as large as life, found at Thebes in a standing position: they were covered with a sort of varnish, and had their eyes and part of their bodies inlaid with some metal.

Mr. Salt having read his letters from Alexandria, informed me that the Glasgow frigate, having a gentleman on board negotiating for a supply of grain for Malta, had been some days off that port, but would only communicate by letter, and without having any intercourse; as it was to return to the Ionian Islands to take Sir Thomas Maitland from Corfu to Malta, and the orders were positive to avoid incurring the necessity of placing the general in quarantine. This destroyed all my hopes of a passage in her. Fortunately, an accumulation of letters proved the possibility of there being another of a later date; and, on further perusal, I found, to my delight and surprise, that the Tagus frigate, Captain Dundas, was expected daily to arrive, having been ordered to take the two young princes of Morocco from Alexandria to Tangiers, on their return from their pilgrimage to Mecca. There are some incidents in the actual course of human life which make probable the most singular coincidences we have ever read of in fiction. In 1815, on my way to India, when at the island of Madeira, I fell in with a squadron of frigates which had come from the coast of America in chase of a hostile squadron, and put into that island for water, &c. On board of one of these frigates I found a brother, at that time serving as a midshipman: now, on my return, I shall in all likelihood meet him again at Alexandria, as he is on board the Tagus.

The plague is stated to be at Rosetta, and many accidents happen daily; but at Alexandria, up to the present time, they have had only a few. This expression of accident, applied to so mortal a disease, is rather incongruous. As it is as well to avoid the plague when it is in one's power, I have determined to go across by land, on dromedaries or horses, from hence to Alexandria, and not by the usual passage down the Nile to Rosetta.

It was announced that the pacha would receive us at three o'clock. About a quarter of an hour before the time appointed we mounted our horses, and proceeded through the city to his house. Mr. Salt's janissary, on horseback, carried a large silver stick before us; and two syees (the same word we use in India) or grooms cleared the way with sticks twenty feet long, these being a mark of authority. In front of the pacha's residence was a large detachment of cavalry and infantry. We passed into a court-yard separated from the street only by a wall. Here we met many Europeans habited in the Turkish costume, who, we understood, were in the pacha's service. We were shown into a room having its walls gaudily painted with miserable landscapes, surrounded with sofas, and lighted by large glazed windows, as in Europe. The pacha, we were informed, was in his haram.

After we had remained about ten minutes, he made his appearance, and I observed his numerous attendants salamed to him in the same manner as is the custom throughout India. His highness was plainly dressed. He is not above five feet nine inches high, but of a most pleasing and open countenance, without any indications whatever of age; on the contrary, he does not seem to be above thirty-nine or forty, though he is older. He sat down with his legs under him on a sofa, with a large pillow to support his back, and seemed particularly glad to see Mr. Salt, who, it appears, has established a feeling of respect for the British name and character throughout Egypt, so strong that individuals of a rival European nation when on the Nile, being challenged from the shore by the police, have been known to call out that they were *Inglaize.* The pacha asked me a variety of questions; amongst others, the cause of our having stopped merchant vessels from Surat, bound to the Red Sea. I answered that it was from an anxiety for their safety, as the Whehabee pirates had overrun the Indian Sea, and that we meant to send a vessel of war to protect them. I told him it was our intention to attack them by sea, and asked him if he would assist us by land. He seemed very much pleased with the idea, and informed us his son had defeated the army of the Whehabees, and was within 40 miles of their capital, Deyria, which city he expected would soon fall into his hands.

It may be noticed, to show how little he was acquainted with the situation of our possessions in India, though our successes have, I understand, made him exceedingly jealous of us in that quarter, that he asked me how far I had been in the interior from Bombay. There was some difficulty in explaining this to him, as they do not understand lineal measure, having nothing like the English mile, Persian pharasang, or Indian coss, and measure distances by so many munzils, or days' journey; I however stated that I was two months, or sixty days' march, before I reached the port from whence I sailed.

He now, with a degree of cunning for which he is celebrated, after I had satisfied him as to the heads of our late victories, asked if our governor-general of India had not been changed within the last year. This question was founded on a hope and suspicion that our government might act towards unsuccessful chiefs, as is the case amongst the Turks, by an almost invariable and immediate removal; and was doubtless intended to shake the faith of all that had been said before the crowd of sycophants standing around. I was at a loss, and simply answered in the negative; but Mr. Salt, perceiving at the instant the drift of his question, overset his whole hypothesis, and confirmed what I had previously asserted, by explaining that Lord Moira had been created Lord Hastings, being a grade higher, for his great, successful, and eminent services. This was beating the pacha upon his own ground. He then inquired into the number of our troops, which staggered him; but in all probability he did not believe that our force was so considerable. Coffee was presented to us twice during our visit. He smoked during the whole time; his pipe being splendidly ornamented with jewels. He had several rings on, one with a single diamond of very large size. His manner was delightful; soft, mild, and courtly, such as would bear a comparison with the most polished European prince.

All the while we were in his company, we reclined upon the

sofas with the utmost familiarity, which towards Europeans he rather encourages, no doubt for the reason he assigned to Mr. Salt, that they were the only people from whom he got information. A French gentleman who spoke Arabic, and had been long settled in Cairo, acted as our interpreter. We took our leave, after he had promised me an order for the use of the horses of his tattars, communicating between Alexandria and Cairo.

It is believed that the pacha would declare himself independent, if any naval power would take charge of his commerce and shipping; and I have no doubt, should any such power quarrel with the Porte, this would be a successful stroke of policy. He, however, keeps up a show of obedience and respect to the head of the Turkish government, and by valuable presents maintains his interests at Constantinople. Let us hope, for the happiness of Egypt, that he will live to establish his power, and found a dynasty, as even his despotism is better than the dreadful state of anarchy to which it was previously subjected. The admirable order established in Egypt by the pacha formed a very striking contrast to the accounts of murders and robberies in the various countries of Europe, which were read of in the French and Frankfort papers. Here we could travel with the utmost safety of person and property, which fully corroborated what Mr. Salt had written to Lord Hastings. The pacha has been anxious, from a spirit of enterprize, to send a vessel round the Cape of Good Hope, but has not, to my knowledge, carried his purpose into execution. He has made application to the government of Bombay to build him two frigates, but as no means of payment were stipulated, they had not been commenced.

On returning home, I found a Scotchman who had been a private soldier in our army, and made prisoner at the unfortunate expedition to Rosetta. He was very young at that time, and was not informed of the general deliverance of the prisoners. During the time he remained in slavery he turned Mahometan, and having made himself master of some common rules of physic, and the use of a few drugs, has become a successful medical practitioner. At the time of the expedition against Algiers, Mr. Salt took advantage of the feeling of the moment, and pointed out to the pacha that Osmond (the name he took on his change of faith) was the only British slave perhaps in the world. This had the desired effect; and since he has obtained his freedom and formed connexions at Cairo, together with being fortunate in his practice, he is determined to remain here, and continue in his adopted religion. He was a great friend of Mr. Burckhardt, or Sheik Ibrahim, the name by which he is more generally known, who bequeathed him the little property of 12,000 piasters he had with him. He told me that Sheik Ibrahim died of a dysentery, of long duration, brought on by poor living, to which he had attempted to accustom himself for several years, in order to encounter the privations he expected to meet with in the interior of Africa.

I mentioned to Mr. Salt the caves which I remarked in the Mokuttum, and which I had not time to examine. He says they are remarkably beautiful, which adds greatly to my regret at not having seen them. Mr. Salt has given me a very correct idea of the figure supposed to be that of Vishnu, seated on the lotus in the temple of Dendera, which certainly bears the strongest possible similarity to the Indian deity.

To-morrow we are to visit the pyramids.

CHAPTER XXXII.

Set out to view the pyramids—French mamelukes—English mamelukes—Aqueduct—Khaliz—Canal of Trajan—First view of the pyramids—Approach them—Division of the desert and cultivation—Situation of these vast piles—Sphinx—Caves—Late discoveries in uncovering the sphinx and pyramids—Third pyramid—Mr. Salt—Captain Caviglia—Removal of the sand which covered the sphinx—Back of the sphinx—Portico in front of the second pyramid—Triangular stones—Second pyramid—Causeways—Entrance to the second pyramid—Want of research among the Turks—Formerly opened by the Arabs—Tablets of hieroglyphics—Forced passage—Danger to the workmen—True entrance—Egyptian priests not to be confided in—Belzoni's account—Enter the pyramid—Portcullis—Forced passages—Subterranean chamber—Passage leading to the principal chamber—Crystals—Principal chamber—Sarcophagus—Bones—Iron mallet—Arabic inscription—Return to daylight—Proceed to the buildings in the neighbourhood of the great pyramid—Paintings—Proceed to the great pyramid—Ascend the pyramid—Difficulties—View from the summit—Pyramids of Sacarrah—Causeways—Descent from the pyramid—Interior of the great pyramid—Captain Caviglia—Davidson's chamber—Well—Captain Caviglia's enterprise—Subterranean chamber under the base of the great pyramid—Names on the outside of the pyramid—Cave in the face of the calcareous rock—Return to Cairo—Reflections—Accounts from Abyssinia—Abyssinian—Account of Belzoni—Visits—Levantine lady—Dress of the Egyptian women—Dress of the Turks—Fort—Hall of Joseph—Elephant—Artillery—Rain—Pacha's palace—Mosques—City of Cairo—Its population, &c.—Khamsien—Signior Rossi—Head of Orus—Arm—French stone.

Cairo, March 10, 1818.

YESTERDAY, Mr. Salt, Belzoni, and myself, started early. In our way to the place where we were to cross the Nile, we passed the saltpetre manufactory belonging to the pacha, and there saw one of the French soldiers of Buonaparte, who had become a mameluke of the name of Selim; many of the French deserters having assumed this character. I made inquiry whether there were more of them, and learnt that they were reduced to twenty-five, of whom several were in Nubia with the rest of the mamelukes. There were at one period, it appears, three English mamelukes, worthless drunkards, who, for the honour of their country, are fortunately dead. We proceeded by the aqueduct which supplies the city with water when the river is low, and the Kaliz or canal, understood to be that of Trajan, which conveys the Nile water, when at its height, through the city of Cairo. It is at this time quite dry, and much choked with rubbish, but is annually cleared out previous to the Nile reaching its greatest elevation. It was not until we reached the banks of the Nile to embark, above the island on which is the Nilometer, that I caught the first view of the pyramids with the sun shining on them, and my sensations were similar to those I experienced when advancing to view the caves of Ellora.

On landing on the opposite side at Giza, we mounted our donkeys, which were excellent, and approached the pyramids, passing between the green fields of corn. I know not the reason, but they are not the striking objects I should have supposed, nor have I been so much transported by them at any time as when I stood in the area of Keylas. They are, I am told, called by the Arabs *Gebel Pharoun*, or the Mountains of Pharaoh; and also, *Ul Haram*, or the Forbidden. Every thing in Egypt, the ruins of which are large and their era unknown, are stated by the Mahometans to have been built in the time of Pharoun, with whom they were acquainted from the history of the Old Testament, one of the pillars of their faith.

As we neared the pyramids, they gradually shewed the ranges of steps, losing the exact pyramidal shape, and their apex becoming flattened. The second pyramid looks, from afar, higher than the largest, its base being upon a more elevated level, though in reality it is twenty feet lower than that generally known as the great pyramid of Egypt. The third pyramid is evidently considerably smaller. The separation between the desert and the cultivated ground is a sharp line on a bank, one side of which is green, and the other sand.

The pyramids stand upon a calcareous rock, about 40 or 50 feet above the level of the cultivation, and the three greatest are placed with respect to each other, to use a military term, in echelon, the largest being most to the northward and eastward. It has often been remarked that the four faces exactly correspond with the cardinal points. The immediate vicinity of the pyramids appears to have been a favourite spot for interment, there being several minor pyramids of 40 or 50 feet in height at the foot of the eastern side of the great pyramid, and to the west some large piles of masonry, each containing several small rooms.

The sphinx, of which the head and breast only are above the sand, is directly south of the great pyramid, about eight or nine hundred yards; and to the south-east of this figure, in the calcareous rock, are some small caves. The sand from the Lybian desert is most painful and fatiguing to pedestrians, and yet we were obliged to quit our asses and walk to the sphinx. I was much disappointed with it, after the fine excavations I had seen in India; though at present it should be recollected above 40 feet are under the sand, the whole altitude 70 from its base to the top of the head.

I have been most fortunate in travelling through Egypt during a period of tranquillity and security which has, within the last two years, permitted inquisitive and persevering Europeans to elucidate many points, and even make fresh discoveries. All the great objects which were now before me, the sphinx, and the greater and second pyramid, have been successfully visited, much having been already added to our former knowledge of them. At a distance were Arabs employed on the third pyramid, by Belzoni; and certainly, if we may judge from his former success at Thebes and the second pyramid, it is to be hoped he will not labour in vain.

The bust of the sphinx has been often described, and I will therefore only repeat what I was told upon the spot, by those who witnessed the removal of the sand, which has for ages hid the lower part of this colossal figure. I shall, however, enter upon it with deference, as Mr. Salt, I have reason to believe, is about to present the world with a detailed account of the whole of these interesting wonders, and no one, from his talents and acquirements, is more capable of doing them justice; but his various publications, and zeal for inquiry, are too well known to require any further encomiums.

In the course of last year, an Italian gentleman of the name of Caviglia, a captain of a merchant vessel sailing under British colours, arrived at Cairo. At the same time that he was successful in his discoveries in the great pyramid, of which more hereafter, he and Mr. Salt undertook to remove the sand which enveloped the sphinx. This was only to be accomplished by carrying it away in baskets, which, to any others than these persevering gentlemen, would have been looked upon as an endless work. They at last, however, cleared it sufficiently away to disclose the base of the front, the left arm and paw, and the avenue or approach which led to the front of the figures. They discovered, in the avenue, which is cut out of the calcareous rock on which the pyramids stand, two flights of steps, with an intermediate terrace, descending towards the sphinx, on which were two small Grecian buildings, erected for two of the Roman emperors to witness the ceremonies of worship. Between the paws of the sphinx was a small temple or altar, which amongst many ornaments had a most beautiful stone tablet, covered with hieroglyphics, which is in the possession of Mr. Salt at his house in Cairo.

Imperfect as this account may seem, when Mr. Salt's publication shall appear, I trust it will be recollected that I only visited this place once, when I wished to remain for weeks, nay months, to clear away every atom of sand or rubbish from so classical a spot, by the labour of hundreds of Arabs; but I had not come through Egypt purposely to visit the country, or make antiquarian researches. The back of the sphinx, which extends about one hundred feet to the westward, is just perceptible above the sand, and resembles the well trod path or limits of a sentry's walk. The sphinx must thus stand in an area, like that which surrounds the second pyramid.

To this pyramid we next proceeded, with difficulty passing over the ground between it and the sphinx, where the sand has been blown into small undulating banks or ridges. The second pyramid was the great object of Mr. Salt's present visit, as heretofore he had thought he was well acquainted with every part of the neighbourhood, having (I think he told me) remained at one time three weeks in tents, while the sphinx was uncovering.

As for myself, all was equally new and interesting, and I only desired to be spared as much from extra exertion as possible, as Belzoni had threatened me with extreme fatigue, it being at all times a good day's work to enter all the passages and chambers, and mount the summit of the great pyramid. But with the addition of his great discoveries, it was now a still more severe undertaking.

We first proceeded to the remains of what is supposed to have been a portico, about 200 yards to the east of the second pyramid: this building has had three entrances, one to the east, one to the north, and, I think, another to the south; but at the moment this was so secondary an object, in comparison with the wonder of the world before me, that I did not pay so much attention to it as I have since wished I had done. It is absolutely a horizontally built Stone Henge. Some of the blocks of calcareous stone are of an immense size; and two which were particularly pointed out to me, one upon the other, on the east side, forming part of the north-east angle, Belzoni told me were 24 feet long, eight in breadth, and the same in thickness. From age, they are perfectly honeycombed, and positively united together, though their original separation is distinctly seen from the sharp edges being rounded by time. The walls of this portico are not above twice, or at the utmost thrice, the breadth of these stones in height.

What may be under ground I know not; but it appears to me that it has either never been completed, or the finish of the building must have been of much lighter and less lasting materials than what is left. Belzoni now took us to a spot where he had opened the ground between this portico and the pyramid, having dug down several feet, till he met with a pavement of large blocks of well-hewn, flat, calcareous stones: as it was much covered in, I cannot be a competent judge of all the attendant circumstances, but in one part there seemed to be a wall of no great height, formed of calcareous stones upon the pavement.

The whole ground in the neighbourhood of the pyramids is strewed with small pieces of granite, which are supposed to have been placed at the angles to prevent the effects of time; for the soft calcareous stone of which the main bodies of these stupendous buildings are constructed, or the plaster with which they were covered, would have early crumbled into dust at their most exposed parts. In passing the north-east angle of the second pyramid, Mr. Salt showed me two triangular stones of a dark colour, about six feet on each side, level with the face of the ground, certainly not calcareous, and I think not granite. Mr. Salt had often remarked them before. We left some Arabs to dig down to see if their sides were hewn, similar to that presented to the surface.

From this point I had a good view of the pyramid. It is placed in a vast area, cut about 40 feet deep out of the rock, thus leaving an open space between the face of the scarped rock and the pyramid of I should think 200 feet on the north, west, and south sides, so that the base of the pyramid is below the real level of the ground; and the architect, as will eventually be seen, has taken advantage of this, and though the hewn stones on the outside commence from its base, yet a mound of rock was undoubtedly left in the centre. I conceive that the stones dug out to form this area were made use of in building the pyramid, although it is evident that the greater part of the materials was brought from the other side of the Nile, from the mountain Mokuttum, by the two celebrated causeways which Herodotus states were works almost equal to the pyramids themselves. However long these vast masses may have been in constructing, yet had not these two communications between the pyramids and the quarries been opened, so that during the whole year, even at the time of the inundation, they could procure stones from them (being above the level of the rise of the Nile), it would have required a period of time one third longer. In this case, during one third of the year, the country would have been impassable, not when the river overflowed its banks, for then, by water carriage, the blocks might have been transported; but when it left the earth a black, heavy, unctuous mud. When I passed over it off the paths or roads, the ground was very unsafe and rotten, and it was with difficulty we could keep our asses on their legs. To the north of the pyramid, in the area, are several grave-like looking holes of a regular figure. These may have been the matrices of great stones used in the buildings. This pyramid has evidently been faced with a slate-coloured plaster, of which about 100 feet from the top remains, and round its base are heaps of rubbish and dust, which have in time fallen down its face. It was with great trouble that Arabs scrambled over this coating to place the lines for Belzoni's measurements: I was anxious to have ascended the face of the pyramid to where the plaster commences, but my time would not permit it.

It was particularly interesting to hear, on the spot, the remarks of one gentleman who had deeply studied the subject, and of the other who had immortalized himself by discovering the entrance to the chambers contained in the enormous mass before us. In the area under the opening, which is on the north side, at the foot of the rubbish are many large stones which had been removed by this enterprising Italian, and afforded us an idea of the vast difficulties he had surmounted. He had made, through the crumbling rubbish, a firm footing with large stones to reach the openings. He had previously informed us that when he first determined on attempting to open the pyramid, he had deemed it necessary to ask permission of the Kaiya Bey. This leave was granted. The rulers of Egypt themselves never entertain a feeling for such researches. They despise our curiosity, or conceive that we are digging from an interested motive of finding treasure. Belzoni was obliged to make use of a little *ruse de guerre* to prevent a knowledge of his work becoming generally spread, and attracting troublesome and inquisitive visitors. He began his operations on the 10th of February on the north side, employing many Arabs in cutting through the stones and rubbish which had accumulated for ages from the upper parts of the pyramid. He worked for many days unsuccessfully, but determining to persevere, and on the 17th fell in with the forced entrance (1).

There had always been Arabic written accounts of this pyramid having been opened by the Arabs with the hope of gain; and from them we learn that in the sarcophagus were found the bones of a man, and some small gold tablets, covered with hieroglyphics, which, from the same sordid motive as led to the investigation, were put into the crucible, and divided amongst the sacrilegious spoilers. They are stated to have been but of little intrinsic value; but what a loss was sustained to the lovers of antiquity by this barbarous and avaricious outrage! The hieroglyphics, both from the value of the metal on which they were wrought, and the history which they were doubtless intended to communicate, it may naturally be supposed, must have been executed in the highest perfection of the art, and in every point of view invaluable.

This entrance, discovered on the 17th, Belzoni was satisfied was a forced passage, and not the real one. On the following day he got in about five feet, when the stones and rubbish began to fall from above, and though constantly cleared away for some days, continued to descend in great quantities, till at last an upper forced entrance (2) was discovered, communicating from above with that which entered horizontally into the pyramid. He then perceived another entrance (3) which was evidently a continuation of the first passage (1). This passage was cleared from its numerous obstructions, and extended above 100 feet into the centre of the pyramid. About half way from the entrance another forced descending passage was discovered, 40 feet in length. Though the work in the horizontal passage was continued to the length I have stated, it ended abruptly. The workmen had been exposed to the danger of being crushed by the hanging stones over their heads, which had been loosened by their operations, and for myself I felt anxious to change my position every instant, as some stones, of several tons weight, appeared to threaten our destruction.

To those who value actions by the motive which occasioned them it will be satisfactory to learn, that the Arabs, who first attempted to open the pyramid for the "lucre of gain," met with many more difficulties than their successor Belzoni encountered; and in search of the right passage, their obstacles must have been almost incredible, as the stones were in all probability broken piecemeal with mallets. The dangers were equally great after the removal of a stone, until the safety of the foremost workmen was proved, by another dependant on it for support not falling and crushing the "*enfant perdu;*" and all must have been in imminent peril.

We next proceeded to the real entrance, and I cannot understand by what indication Belzoni dug so directly down upon it, for it was no less than thirty feet to the eastward of the forced passage. I have tried without success to account for the clue which led him to the immediate spot, though in all probability it was similar to that which guided the Arabs, and thus the antiquary was the gainer by their former labours proving it a hopeless task to reach the centre of the pyramid by force. This sagacity is the more remarkable when it is considered that in his great discoveries at the tombs of the kings of Thebes he dug down immediately on the entrance, though it had in the course of time been covered by a cascade, or stream of water falling over the entrance, and yet his index was equally successful. After many days' hard work, on the 28th of February, Belzoni discovered the corner of a block of granite in an inclined direction, towards the centre of the pyramid; and was convinced, from the inclination being the same as that of the first pyramid, and doubtless from granite having been used in the interior of it, that the object he desired was near being accomplished; and subsequent discovery of other large blocks on the 1st of March, although they materially retarded his approach, yet gave him almost certain hopes of succeeding.

On the 2d of March he opened the true entrance to the pyramid of Cephrenes. It had been generally believed that this pyramid contained no chambers, but this was contradicted by the account of the Arabs having opened it. The authority of Herodotus would indeed have led us to suppose that there were no interior chambers, had it not been contrary to common sense that such a mass of building should have been erected without an intention of containing something. But Herodotus obtained his intelligence on this point from the Egyptian priests, who, it would thus appear, knew very little about the matter; and it is evident from the late discovery that the pyramids themselves were, in the time of Herodotus, of so great an age, that the real circumstances of the second pyramid, if not of the others, were forgotten, and much shakes the confidence placed in their traditional information.

From having seen this pyramid within five weeks after it was opened, and being accompanied by the projector and accomplisher of this unique exploit (for the great pyramid has been open from time immemorial), I accompany what I saw with his account of the proceeding, and his remarks upon it. I have done this as I conceive it will enhance the interest of the narrative.

The four blocks of granite, forming the entrance to the passage, which is an opening four feet high, and three feet and a half wide, are well hewn stones; and there is a continuation of them slanting downwards, at the same inclination as that of the pyramid of Cheops' namely, an angle of twenty-six degrees with the horizon. The length of this first passage is 104 feet five inches, lined the whole way with granite, and it can therefore boast of a superiority in this particular over the passage of the great pyramid, which is only of calcareous stone, though it has been supposed by some travellers that it is lined with white marble; but by the use of passengers, in placing both hands on each side in ascending and descending, it has altered its appearance, and at first deceived me.

After having satisfied our minds as to the inclination of the passage, in which we found Belzoni was correct, we took off every thing but our shirts, and the lower parts of our dress, leaving them in charge of our janissaries. We each received a piece of wax candle. The extreme hardness of the granite floor to the passage will render it a work of time to make steps, or rather resting-places for the feet, as in the calcareous flooring of the passage of the great pyramid, to prevent slipping down; as it was, I risked very nearly breaking my neck. A strong bar of wood, about five feet long, was placed resting across the outside granite blocks, with a rope from the centre of the length of the passage. This greatly facilitated our descent. Belzoni, proud of shewing us his discovery, went first as our guide, Mr. Salt went next, and I followed. This passage (5 and 4) on its discovery was full of large stones, which it required very considerable force to draw forth, as it was literally up-hill work, and the accumulation was greater below towards the portcullis (6), or door of granite, which is fitted into a niche above, so as to have fallen and entirely blocked up the passage. This moveable piece of granite Belzoni found supported by small stones within eight inches of the floor, and in consequence of the narrowness of the place, it took up the whole of that day and part of the next to raise it sufficiently to afford an entrance. It is one foot three inches thick, and together with the work of the niche, occupies six feet eleven inches where the granite work ends. To pass this (the stone not having been raised above a foot higher than it was originally found) it was necessary to creep upon the belly. Belzoni, having gone through, assured me, from the other side of the stone, that he had placed two pieces of granite to support it, and thus confident, I with some difficulty passed under it. We relighted the candles, which had been extinguished, and prepared for further progress. We were now able to stand up; and after walking along the passage (7), cut in the rock, twenty-two feet seven inches long, came to a perpendicular descent of fifteen feet. Before arriving at this, however, to the left, is a small forced passage (9), cut in the rock, and also above on the right is another forced passage (8), which runs upwards. It is evident that this forced passage was made to ascertain if there was another in conformity to that of the pyramid of Cheops. The perpendicular descent was made easy by a number of stones being formed into a rude flight of steps. These were placed here by Belzoni.

We now turned down the passage running to the north (12), which is much blocked up with stones and rubbish; but Belzoni, as might naturally have been expected, proceeded, on the first discovery, along the passage (10) towards the centre of the pyramid. The inclination of the passage (12) is the same as that by which we at first descended. After proceeding forty-eight feet six inches, we came to a horizontal passage (13), and continued advancing about thirty feet, where the passage widens or forms a recess eleven feet deep. We then turned to the left into a passage (15) twenty feet long, which brought us to a chamber (16) thirty-two feet long, and nine feet nine inches wide, and eight feet in the centre and six feet on the sides in height, with a pent roof. A number of calcareous stones, about eighteen inches long, eight wide, and six high, were piled against the wall. Belzoni informed me, that when he first entered it there were some inscriptions formed by the smoke of a candle on the roof, which he fancied were Coptic; but as several visitors have since taken similar means to commemorate their curiosity, they have become so blended, that nothing is to be clearly distinguished. We returned to the passage (13), which runs north about thirty feet more, at the end of which is a niche to receive a portcullis similar to that before mentioned (17). This had evidently been of granite, and fragments of it lay about. We then ascended the passage (18) which runs in the same inclination, and I followed Mr. Salt up to the place where the passage is filled with large blocks of hewn calcareous stone (19), at forty-seven feet six inches from the niche. This passage issues out precisely at the base of the pyramid.

Our next investigation was directed to the passage leading to the centre and chamber . This passage is almost entirely cut out of the living rock; but about half way there are some stones introduced, as Belzoni supposes, to fill up fissures in the stratum. In many parts the walls are encrusted with fine crystals, frequently resembling a fleece, and sparkling beautifully with the reflection of our candles. This passage is five feet eleven inches high, three feet six inches wide, and the whole length, from the perpendicular to the great chamber (11), is 158 feet eight inches. We now entered the great chamber, which is, according to Belzoni, forty-six feet three inches long, sixteen feet three inches wide, and twenty feet six inches high. The architect has taken advantage of a large mass of native rock to fill up the centre of the pyramid, as almost the whole of this chamber is cut out of it, excepting a part of the roof towards the western end, which is of masonry, perhaps introduced for the same reason as that I before mentioned in explaining the passage. The floor of this chamber is exactly level with the base of the pyramid: the roof is also of a pent-house form. On the wall, immediately opposite where we entered, Belzoni[1] has inscribed, in the Italian language, in large letters, which extend from one end to the other, his name and the date of his discovery. In the west end of the chamber, a sarcophagus of granite is buried in the ground to the level of the floor, and placed due north and south. This sarcophagus is eight feet long, three feet six inches wide, and two feet three inches deep inside, surrounded by large blocks of granite, placed there in all probability to prevent its removal; but Belzoni has determined upon that measure, though it must be attended with much labour. The lid is placed diagonally across it. Belzoni, however, found in it the bones of a human skeleton, which are in all probability, if one of the accounts of Herodotus be correct, the bones of King Cephrenes, who is supposed to have built this pyramid. He presented me with three or four pieces, and on learning it was my intention to deposit them in the British Museum, he added others, making in all seven pieces. The floor of the chamber has been forced up in several places, doubtless in search of treasure. Under one of these stones he found a piece of metal, evidently the head of an iron mallet or hatchet. This, which he was so good as to give me, I also intend for the British Museum. Very high up in the centre of the wall there are two small square holes, about a foot in diameter, one to the north, and the other to the south. They are of considerable depth, like those in the great chamber of the first pyramid, and I cannot conjecture what can possibly have been their use.

On the wall of the western side of the chamber is an Arabic inscription, which declares, "This pyramid was opened by the masters Mehomed El Aghar and Otman, and inspected in the presence of the Sultan Ali Mehomed the 1st Yugluck." Belzoni stated that

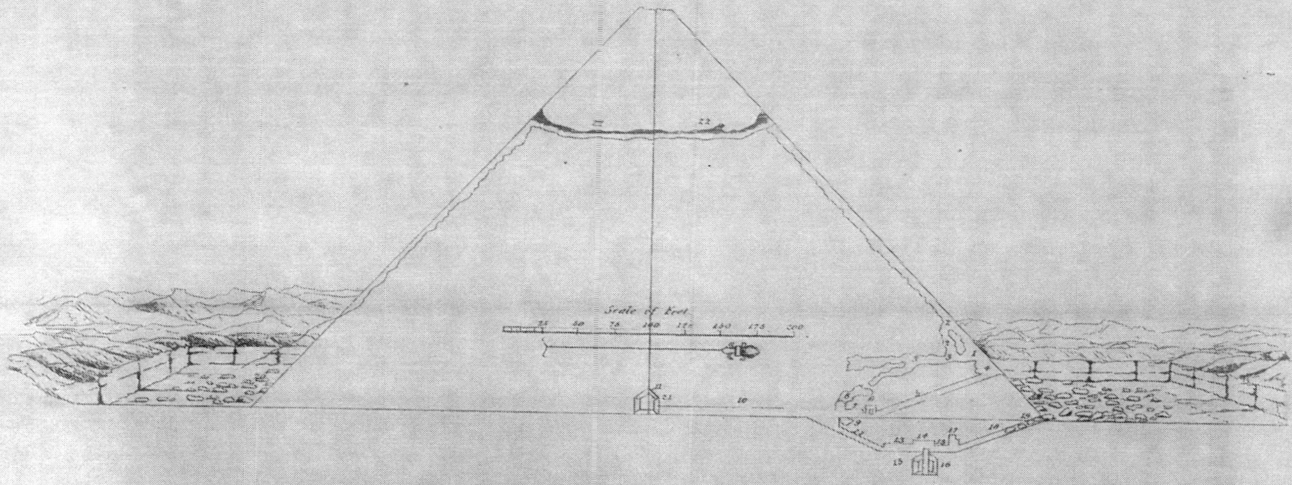

THE SECOND PYRAMID OF EGYPT,

With the late Discoveries by Sign.^r Belzoni in 1818.

there were several inscriptions on the walls, but I was not satisfied as to the character in which they were written. The crystals on the walls had formed most beautiful shapes, and so hard that it was with great difficulty I broke some off to keep as relics of my interesting excursion. On the left hand side of the passage, on returning, a few feet from the great chamber, two Arabic inscriptions give the names of two men who had visited this pyramid, the last thing worthy of note which I remarked in the interior of this stupendous fabric; issuing from which, we revisited the light of day.

I cannot help thinking that this pyramid must contain more chambers, which it is possible may yet be discovered. I should conceive that at whatever period it may have been opened, it was immediately closed again, as the state of the granite passage, the whiteness of the calcareous walls throughout, and the very small number of inscriptions, prove that only few persons had entered it On the block of granite across the entrance on the outside, Belzoni has also cut his name—and certainly no one has a better claim to be indulged in this innocent vanity.

Having dressed ourselves, we proceeded, attended by a whole troop of Arabs, to the buildings of masonry situated to the west of the great pyramid. The paintings in the interior of one of these are particularly curious, representing, among other things, the mode by which large stones were transported both by land and by water. In the former of these the stone is placed on a sledge drawn by bullocks with collars, which at the present period are not used in the country. Figures of persons ploughing, driving herds of cattle, fishing, in several instances cooking immense quantities of provisions, and in one design, an uncommonly spirited fight in boats, in which the weapon made use of is a spear, and the figures are particularly slender and black. They appeared to me to represent persons similar to the Arabs I saw at Mocha, or the slight forms of the inhabitants of the southern parts of India. They did not strike me as having the features of the negro.

I now determined to ascend the great pyramid, and we walked together to the entrance, which is on the north side, where, leaving Mr. Salt and Belzoni, I started with a few Arabs, to undertake the difficult task. It was by the north-east angle that I climbed up, for the stones which form the steps are from three to four feet high; but after mounting a considerable way, I was completely fatigued, and, added to this, a violent north wind blew the sand from the desert continually over me. If I looked down, I was affected with sickness, and I had no companion to stimulate me by emulation: but my perseverance, which was about to take its flight, rallied afresh on my recollecting the regret I should feel, did I not overcome the difficulties; and after many halts to rest, and a good deal of assistance from the Arabs, whom I caused to take hold of each arm, I at last gained the summit.

This pyramid has been proved, by geometrical measurement, to be 577 feet in height, from its base to its summit. This is somewhat more than if the Monument were placed on the highest summit of St. Paul's: and when an inhabitant of London is told that the area on which it stands is about the extent of Lincoln's Inn Fields, he will form a fair and adequate conception of the sort of object which it exhibits. About two thirds up the north-east angle of the pyramid, there is a small cave or hole about twelve feet deep and high, which appears to have been formed by removing several large stones. The view from the top is extraordinary; and far from this building ending in a point, which it appears to do at a distance, there is a space of at least 20 feet square. It looks, indeed, as if it had never been finished. I observed the pyramids of Sacarrah at a distance, towards the south-east, and think there must be more than twenty of them, of which I understand the greater number have

CHAMBER & SARCOPHAGUS, *in the 2nd Pyramid.*

THE REAL & FORCED ENTRANCES TO THE 2nd PYRAMID,

Re-opened by Sig.r Belzoni, 1818.

not been opened. The two causeways spoken of by Herodotus take a direction from the pyramids, one to the north-east, and the other considerably to the eastward of south-east, and are astonishing works. I followed them with my eye towards the Mokuttum mountain, till lost in the distance.

The line which bounds the cultivation and the desert is seen most perceptibly from this height, and the crop of green corn is not two yards from the burning sand; thus marking the utmost extent of the yearly inundation. The desert extends to the westward, till, in the horizon, it is blended with the sky. As it has been customary for travellers to inscribe their names on the summit, I chose a place for mine on the same stone on which Lord Belmore had inscribed his, that of his lady, and that of his lordship's brother, Captain Corry. There was also the name of Rosa on the stone, which I concluded was that of some enterprising damsel, and gave her all due credit for her successful attempt; but have since learnt that it was the cognomen of her ladyship's lap-dog. The calcareous stone is very soft, and I found great facility in carving mine, though a very long one. I looked for the names of the various persons who had previously visited it,—I found that of Lord Hutchinson, with the date, 1801. Several French names with the date, An. 9, of the republic. I also saw that of Chateaubriand, and somebody has taken the pains to engrave under "*il n'étoit pas ici,*" which I was assured is really the fact. It was my wish to have dated some letters I intended for India, from the top of the great pyramid; but I found the Arabs had only brought up my memorandum book and pencil.

In descending, which I much dreaded, being always affected with giddiness in looking down from a height, I found it extremely easy; the reason I know not, except my being aware that the alternative was to remain the rest of my days upon the top of the pyramid, or of continually looking down during my descent; and I had no return of my usual complaint. I found my companions at the entrance, and after resting a short time, was accompanied by Belzoni through the interior, which is a most distressing and fatiguing perambulation. So much has been said by all travellers of this pyramid, that I should have wholly passed it over, had it not been for the late discovery of Captain Caviglia. The extreme heat of the interior is not to be described; and what with climbing, scrambling, and advancing up the steep passage, particularly after my previous fatigue, I do not recollect ever being so distressed.

I am happy to have it in my power to vindicate the character of a British officer in the campaign of 1801, who has been accused of being the first defacer of the sarcophagus in this pyramid; for it is stated by Tavernier, who visited Egypt 100 years before any English soldier set his foot here, that it was customary for travellers to break off pieces and carry them away. He adds, "the stone, &c. of which it is formed is very hard, and very neat when polished, which induces many to break off pieces to make seals of; but it requires a strong arm and good hammer to knock off a bit." The individual above alluded to was a gallant officer of highlanders, who has been loaded with the epithets Goth, Vandal, sacrilegious destroyer, for having broke off a piece of this monument, and when I viewed the injury I felt equally ready to disapprove of his violation; but having met this passage in Tavernier, I think it right to do away a false impression.

There is a small chamber above the king's, as it is called, to distinguish it from the room beneath, which is designated the queen's. This small chamber, although discovered as early as 1764, by an Englishman of the name of Davidson, is but seldom spoken of by travellers, perhaps on account of its being impossible to get into it without a rope ladder. Belzoni informed me it was not above five feet high, and had for its floor the seven great stones which formed the roof of the king's chamber, having only the depth of the stones between them. He had, to try if it was possible, entered the pyramid without a light, and felt his way through the passages to the sarcophagus in its centre, and back again, and fully succeeded.

As we returned from the queen's chamber, we stopped at the celebrated mysterious well which has drawn forth so many conjectures from antiquaries; but has now considerably lost its interest, from having been completely explored. In the course of last year, Captain Caviglia attempted to dig to the bottom of it, and succeeded gradually in increasing its depth, until the want of air extinguished the candles, and it was said forced blood from the noses and eyes of the workmen, and compelled him to give up the undertaking in despair.

We next retraced our way to the end of the first passage, which inclines downwards towards the base of the pyramid, immediately under the three great granite stones which were forced down from the interior in the original construction, in order to block up the passage to the king and queen's chambers at the angle formed by the ascending and descending passages, where the forced passage has been made to get round the blocks of granite.

Caviglia, from a motive of good nature, having workmen on the spot, began to clear away the stones and rubbish to make this part of the passage more easy to future visitors. A great accumulation of stones, dirt, and sand had formed in this angle, as the declivity of the passage propels every thing towards it, and the north wind continually blows into the entrance of the pyramid the sand from the desert, which gradually finds its way to this spot. The workmen continued to remove the rubbish, and by degrees discovered that they had entered a passage, which giving them fresh hopes, they continued clearing out about two hundred feet or more. I cannot speak with great exactness, for when at Cairo, Mr. Salt shewed me all the drawings and measurements of his interesting work on the pyramids, which he is (I believe) about to publish; and I should have been guilty of a great want of delicacy if I had asked for copies of them, or what is worse, of a breach of confidence, if I had attempted to recollect them. I only state what I saw, and the account of the discovery. This passage, which the workmen had broken in upon, Denon supposes, (for it was partly explored in his time, and he gives us a drawing of it), was first opened when the great granite blocks, which stopped the passage, were found.

After clearing out the passage to the distance I have mentioned, although for many days they carried away vast quantities of stones and rubbish, the work seemed to grow upon their hands, and a vast heap of rubbish accumulated on the outside of the pyramid. Though they wrought with great exertion and perseverance, they did not appear to advance, and there was no sensible diminution of the mass which arrested their progress. After many days hard work, the rubbish was discovered to fall from above, and to Caviglia's astonishment and delight, proved in course of time to be the outlet and bottom of the mysterious well, which had baffled all preceding conjectures. What had been collected for so many centuries from various causes, amongst others, the custom of travellers throwing down stones, some of whom (if I recollect right) affirm they heard them fall into water, had rendered so much labour necessary. The well had now emptied itself of the rubbish downwards as fast as that below was cleared away. The line of the well (falsely so called) is about 150 feet from the gallery leading to the queen's chamber into that beneath. Belzoni, Mr. Salt, all the Arabs and visitors, had been both up and down it, there being small holes cut for the feet and hands; but Belzoni, who is not so stout as myself, had great difficulty in squeezing himself through certain parts of it, and my spirit of perseverance and research was fast giving way to fatigue and heat; the whole of this passage being so low and choked up, that we were obliged to creep upon our hands and knees, and in many places crawl quite flat on the ground. The minute particles of dust irritated the eyes and lungs, and, added to the heat,

G. Fitz Clarence. del.

Engraved by R. Havell & Son.

INTERIOR of the CHAMBER cut in the Rock at the Base of the GREAT PYRAMID of EGYPT.

discovered by Captain Caviglia in 1807

London, Published April 1819, by John Murray, Albemarle Street.

brought on a painful difficulty of breathing. After Caviglia had ascertained the interesting fact respecting the well, he still continued to clear the passage, and further ascertained that it continued sloping downwards about thirty feet, became horizontal towards the centre of the pyramid, and led him at last into a chamber cut into the rock immediately at the base, and under the centre of the pyramid. This chamber is, I should think, about sixty feet long, twenty broad, and eight feet high*. It is only half finished, if indeed any judgment can be formed of the design, as on the western end the rock has not been cut down so low as on the eastern, leaving a sort of platform, with two coarse hewn pillars, as if supporting the roof: two or three rough steps lead between them by a narrow passage to the farthest end, amidst the unfinished mass of uncleared rock. In the south-east angle they have dug deep. This excavation is irregular, and descends lower in some places than in others, and the whole is evidently left incomplete. In all probability, whenever the work was broken off by the death of the founder, or on the closing of the pyramid, the designers were in search of the level of the Nile. Herodotus, in speaking of them, mentions that a period of time was employed in forming "the vaults of the hill upon which the pyramids are erected." It is possible he may here have alluded to the two chambers and passages lately discovered, and not to the small and inconsiderable caves in the face of the calcareous rock to the east and south of the sphinx.

We now returned along the horizontal passage with similar difficulty to that we had encountered on entering; but in the ascending passage our difficulties increased; for the Arabs in front of us loosened large stones, which in our descent had only bruised our back and legs, but now our faces and heads were exposed to them, and I avoided some awkward blows reserved for Belzoni, who was behind me, and

* Sixty-six feet long by twenty-seven broad.—Vide Quarterly Review, No. 33.

liable every instant to some severe hurt. This part of my enterprise was very painful. The little glimmering of light which appeared through the entrance into the pyramid, by the distance contracted perspectively into a very small hole, made me almost despair of reaching it; and I was so exhausted that I threw the wax candle away, requiring both hands to assist me in my advance. We rested for some minutes at the angle of the two passages, and were much refreshed by some water brought us by the Arabs. After recovering a little from our fatigue, we ascended the remainder of the passage, and reached the outside of the pyramid, more completely worn out than can be described.

In taking leave of these stupendous works of human ingenuity and labour, the sentiments expressed at the caves of Ellora obtruded still more strongly on my mind. Religious enthusiasm shews human nature at once in its highest exaltation and lowest debasement. While our hearts swell with pride in reflecting that we belong to the same species of beings to whose sublime conceptions, profound science, invincible and persevering labour, these structures are indebted for their existence, how are we humiliated by feeling the degradation of reason betrayed in the grovelling superstition which formed the object of these everlasting piles, if they are to be considered as temples, or the still more fruitless purpose, if they are to be regarded as sepulchres; and we are compelled to acquiesce in the justness of that apostrophe of the poet, which pronounces Man to be,

> "Sole judge of truth, in endless error hurl'd,
> The glory, jest, and riddle of the world!"

I found I had satisfied my curiosity, at the expense of the greater part of my few remaining clothes, which my journey across India, and the frequency of sleeping in them, both in that country and in this, had previously rendered threadbare. On the large stones above the entrance of the pyramid, are the names of many persons who had visited this spot. Amongst others, I observed those of Major General Ludlow, G. Drummond, 8th Regiment, Castiglione, Clementi, Brivanali, 1586, Davidson, 1764. Just outside the king's chamber, in the interior of the pyramid, is the name of J. Coke, 1624.

After putting on the clothes we had left on the outside, we returned towards the sphinx, passing by the triangular stones we had ordered the Arabs to uncover. They had dug down the sides of one of them two feet deep, which proved them to be hewn on their sides, as well as on the exterior part in view, and of a prismatic shape. Belzoni wished us to visit the work he had commenced on the third pyramid, which, there is reason to believe, has never been opened.

I picked up, in the neighbourhood of the pyramids, several pieces of granite and calcareous stone, and found encrusted in the latter many shells, several of which, resembling those of muscles, though smaller, being an inch long, but considerably thicker in proportion than the shells of this fish in Europe, I broke out of the mass. All these various substances I intend to keep as memorials of this interesting day.

In one of the small excavations in the face of the calcareous rock, which fronts the east, about 400 yards south-east of the sphinx, we partook of some cold meat and Madeira, and after this necessary refreshment inspected the interior of the cave. Let not the reader fancy this was similar to those I have seen and described in India: it is inferior to the commonest excavated cistern for water, either at Ellora or Carli, not only in size but materials. Here the soft calcareous stone is hollowed out; but in India it is the compact, and I may almost say, adamantine granite. One side of this cave is covered by a group of, I think, seven figures, one of which is much smaller than the rest,

They have been all much defaced, through the fanatic zeal of the followers of Mahomet. It is melancholy to find this illiberal and absurd enthusiasm spread over so large a portion of the world. This cave having been once the residence of a sheik or holy Mahometan recluse, he would have thought it unfit for his habitation, had he not thus destroyed these monuments of idolatry. Two or three small chambers led to a room nearly filled with rubbish, in which, almost buried and out of an upright position, is a fine sarcophagus of red granite without a lid. In one of these small chambers, on a border cut in stone, is a well executed hippopotamus.

We at last mounted our asses, distributed some piastres amongst the Arabs, and returned towards Cairo, my mind being as much delighted as my body was fatigued with the excursion.

The vastness of these works, including the large stones in the portico eastward of the second pyramid, added to the immensity of the Egyptian obelisks, and the great size of Druidical stones, makes it probable that in an early and barbarous age, when the tasteful beauties of architecture and sculpture, and the symmetry of building afterwards exemplified in Greece, were imperfectly known, magnitude was the object aimed at, as the most imposing and noble species of record. Denon states that he has convinced himself, that the mode of building by the Egyptians was first to erect masses, on which they afterwards bestowed the labour of ages in the particulars of the decoration, beginning their work with shaping the architectural lines, proceeding next to the sculpture of the hieroglyphics, and concluding with the stucco and painting. The portico to the east of the second pyramid, in the size of its stones, will not yield to any other remains in Egypt; and from its great antiquity, and its being destitute of sculpture, (supposing this theory of Denon to be correct) it is possible that the ornamenting anew these immense masses, long after their first construction, may have been not only the addition of a subsequent age, but even a subsequent improvement growing out of the invention of the sciences.

I was informed that there were no hieroglyphics in any part of the pyramids, but there are a few on the north face of the scarped rock round the area of the second, though I did not see them.

As we returned to Cairo, Mr. Salt showed me some fine red granite pillars which had belonged to a temple dedicated to Trajan.

This morning after breakfast he informed me, that he had within the last few days received a packet containing a long letter, and a variety of specimens of plants and of birds, from the Englishman of the name of Pearce, settled in Abyssinia, of whom he speaks in his travels in that country.

Abyssinia is represented to be in a most dreadful state of internal commotion. He sent for the native who had been the bearer of this communication, and on his entering the room, I should have fancied he had been a Bengalee, both from his dress and appearance. This is curious, when we consider that the other inhabitants of Africa, except those in the districts washed by the Mediterranean and those of the Cape of Good Hope, are negroes. It is not unlikely, therefore, that one may have been a colony from the other.

I have had a long conversation with Belzoni. He professes that his great anxiety is to become known to the various antiquaries of Europe, and to be taken by the hand by them. Although he is very far from being in even a state of mediocrity with respect to fortune, he is ambitious of fame, and of becoming celebrated for his discoveries. He said he looked upon it as a fortunate circumstance I had passed through Egypt, and trusted I should be able to speak of him in England, so as to bring his merits before a nation to which he declares himself to be most devotedly attached. He had sent an account of the opening of the pyramid to Lord Aberdeen; but feared, from the possibility of his lordship's being upon the continent, it might not obtain publicity.

I suggested to him, therefore, the propriety of drawing up an account of the opening of the second pyramid, and offered to take it for him to England, and attend to its publication. He expressed his gratitude for this, and assented to it, and he is now busily employed in making a drawing of the pyramid, its chambers, and several openings. He is to write the account of it in Italian, and Mr. Salt has undertaken to translate it into English; but as it is my intention to start to-morrow night, I fear he will hardly have time sufficient to complete it. I am truly happy thus to have an opportunity of being of use to so able and enterprizing a person.

A great nation like England should not miss the opportunity of making their own a man of such superior talents. He possesses, to an astonishing degree, the secret of conciliating the Arabs, and literally makes them do what he chooses. His commanding figure, amazing strength and height, which ever have in barbarous countries a great effect, as we learn from the travels of Bruce, aid him much in his enterprizes. Mr. Salt tells me, that in moving the head of the young Memnon which has been sent to the British Museum, and the bulk of which made the French despair of carrying it away, he had nothing to assist him but what he found upon the spot. He projects some most extraordinary researches, and every success is to be expected from his genius; but he intends, previously, to return once more to Thebes, and bring down the alabaster sarcophagus. He at the same time means to complete a work he has undertaken, which will be the first of the kind ever carried out of Egypt. It is the entire model of a suite of rooms lately discovered in the tombs of the kings of Thebes, all the walls of which being covered with beautiful carving, fac similes will be taken of them in moulds of wax, and the whole so exactly executed and put into their respective places, that no difference or deficiency will be found in the representation. This work has been commenced about two or three months, and he hopes in another year to accomplish all the models, which will give, when completed, a most correct and distinct idea of the grandeur and magnificence of the Egyptian sepulchres. His attachment to the British nation has been, he says, the principal spur to his endeavours. I am convinced, if Mr. Salt and himself are properly supported by the trustees of the British Museum out of their yearly parliamentary grants, that in the course of a few years every thing worth removing in these parts will have found its way to this great national repository. All that these gentlemen have done has been at their own charge, the former having expended 2000*l.* of his private fortune within the last two years in obtaining what will tend so much to the credit of our country. It behoves us now to attempt surpassing the French nation in their collection of valuable remains of antiquity. We have already, by the taking of Paris, given back to their proper owners the plunder of Europe; and it now only remains for us to enrich our own public collection, so as to uphold its superiority. By the present which Mr. Salt has made to the British Museum in the head of the young Memnon, which, I conceive, from the accounts I have heard, must be the finest thing in Europe, he has made the whole population of Great Britain his debtors.—Belzoni is married to an Englishwoman, who is at this time gone on a pilgrimage to Jerusalem.

In the course of the day I accompanied Mr. Salt to pay some visits to various European ladies. Whilst we were in the house of one of them, I was surprised by the entrance of a Levantine lady in her walking-dress, and who promised but little from her outward appearance, the whole of her person and face, except her eyes, being covered by a brown cloth cloak and hood. I was much astonished to find, on this outer garment being taken off, that there was beneath it a pink satin dress, and still more, when divested of this also, she appeared in a black velvet spencer, not unlike the Spanish bolero dress, richly embroidered in gold, with a silk petticoat, many jewels, and a shawl tied round across the thighs. This last is, I find, the general fashion here. The women throughout Egypt walk in the streets entirely covered, except their eyes: a small piece of cloth not broader than the finger coming from the back of the head down the forehead between the eyes, beneath which is added a cross piece the width of the face, which hangs down the front of the person, and entirely excludes any hope of seeing the fair one's countenance. The dress of the Turks is particularly splendid, as it is only in that, and in their pipes, arms, and horse furniture, that they can shew their wealth; their absurd custom of secluding their women preventing the enjoyments of private society.

This afternoon I rode through the city to the fort, accompanied by Mr. Salt's janissary. In one of the narrow streets I met the Kaiya Bey, preceded by fifty or sixty Turkish soldiers in four ranks. I made way for them, and several, as they passed, with the greatest good humour, patted me or my horse, saying, "Bono, bono cavaliere," without the least appearance of intentional insult.

The fort and well of Joseph, a celebrated governor during the Khalifat, have been often described. The hall of Joseph, which is open at the top, and apparently unfinished, is supported by some splendid Corinthian pillars: the carvings of the capitals have been stuffed with clay or plaster. Here I saw one of the elephants Lord Hastings had sent last year to the pacha, the other having gone as a present to the Grand Seignior. The elephant was much grown, not being three years old when it quitted Calcutta. Within the hall were eighteen light horse artillery guns, with their limbers and tumbrils complete, and in excellent order. Six of the carriages and tumbrils were painted yellow, the same number green, and the rest light blue. There were a few small howitzers amongst them.

On the works were some English twenty-four pounders, several French, one of which had the cap of *Liberté* inscribed with *égalité*, and many other guns with a lion supporting the Gospels; I conceive from the foundery at Venice.

The view was very extensive, and the pyramids distinctly seen. While here, I was driven under shelter by a shower of rain. Considerably more water fell than what we call heat drops in England; but the whole could hardly be considered as an exception to the perpetual drought of this region. I then proceeded to the palace of the pacha, lately finished by him. I paced three of his rooms, one of which was forty-five paces, another thirty-nine, and another twenty-five long, and of good proportions. The smaller rooms were fitted up with carpets, and sofas continued round the walls. They shewed me some cushions covered with Cashmire shawls, with gold borders.

I viewed the outside of the great mosque of Sultan Hassan, which has a very splendid gateway; and on returning through the city noticed several monks of the Propaganda. Of the many curious and interesting things well worth seeing in this city and its neighbourhood, I had only time to visit a few, and consequently did not examine the tombs of the Khaliphs, nor the obelisk on the site of the ancient Heliopolis.

Cairo is built at the foot of the Mokuttum mountain, on an inferior ridge of which is the ancient fort, evidently erected before the introduction of gunpowder, as it is commanded by the main ridge of hills. The present pacha has, however, raised a small fort upon the summit of the latter, which in part remedies this defect. The city is about two miles from the Nile. Its port, if it may be so called, on the river, is the village of Bolac, and beyond this again is a town they call old Cairo. It is possible, from this last circumstance, that the city was originally built upon the banks of the river, and has changed its site, probably with a view to better defence from a situation much preferable to the heated spot under the fort and Mokuttum, the reflection of which increases the warmth to a great degree. Although there are a vast number of ruined houses in Cairo, it is, I think, with the exception of Benares on the Ganges, the best-built city I have seen since I quitted Europe; for Calcutta, which surpasses all that I have ever witnessed, is ranged round the esplanade of Fort William, and consists of a number of insulated palaces so unconnected that it can hardly be called a city. Those parts of Calcutta inhabited by the natives are formed of huts of mats and thatch, intermixed with more solid buildings, as is generally the case in Indian cities.

I can form no decided opinion of the size of Cairo; but it is very large. As to its population, it is exceedingly numerous for its size, speaking comparatively with the cities of Europe, but not by any means equal to those of India. Calcutta, it is supposed, contains, with the villages and bazars in its immediate vicinity, one million two hundred thousand souls; and Benares, six hundred thousand. The population of Mahometan cities is not to be judged from the people seen in the streets; for it should be recollected that, from the almost general custom of secluding their women, nine-tenths of the females do not appear in public.

Cairo is surrounded by stone works of no strength, built by the mamelukes; and there are the remains of several redoubts formed by the French army, and a number of small martello towers erected on the enormous heaps of rubbish and dust, which have been carried out of the city; for the capital of Egypt is absolutely surrounded by its own dirt, and these mounds have accumulated to such a degree and height, that they are only inferior to the Mokuttum. There is an open place in Cairo, round which the best houses are built, which, at the period of my stay, was green with the approaching harvest, but during the time of the inundation of the Nile, having a communication with the Khaliz, it is inundated for several months in the year. One of the houses which overlook it was the residence of Buonaparte, while the French were in Egypt. The streets are not quite so narrow as those of Benares, for in the latter I have known it impossible for a palanquin to pass; but if the streets of Rosetta are similar to these, I am not surprised that our troops did not succeed in forcing that town. In Cairo the windows, consisting of trellised laths, which project from the houses, being formed like the jalousies of the Spaniards, often meet so as almost to touch across the street, though it might be supposed this was perfectly inconsistent with the eastern system of the jealous seclusion of their women. These jalousies render the rooms dark, but in most of the houses I entered they were lighted by pieces of coloured glass let into the wood above the trellis.

The mosques of Cairo are extremely numerous, and from the multitude of minarets, it well deserves, as Thebes of old was called the city of 100 gates, to be designated the city of 100 spires. These minarets or towers are of beautiful workmanship, and possess, in their light and airy form, a great superiority over the steeples of our churches. The mosque of Sultan Hassan is a fine building, with a superb gateway and minaret; but greatly inferior to that of the Jumma Muzjid, at Delhi.

The more eastern sovereigns of the Mahometan faith appear to have been more attached to uniformity than those of Egypt, as the mosque I have spoken of at Delhi, that at Benares (built from a motive of persecution by Aurungzebe on the site of an ancient Hindoo temple), with the generality of those in India, have two minarets. The mausoleum at Agra and that at Arungabad have four, one at each corner of the platform on which the tomb is placed. I believe the mosque of St. Sophia at Constantinople, formerly a christian church, is stated by those who have visited that capital to have had two minarets added to it, rising from the top on each side of the dome. I have, however, always thought, let the minarets be ever so costly, or the workmanship ever so elaborate, that they greatly resemble overgrown chimneys.

The whole city is built in a very confused manner, so much so that it often requires a walk of ten minutes or a quarter of an hour to reach the house you see near you from your windows,—so imperfect is the communication. The houses are of stone, rather high than otherwise, with flat roofs; and in many instances the upper stories project over those below. Most of the bazars are covered in, so as to form agreeable walks; and the entrances to several have iron chains across them, to prevent the intrusion of animals or people on horseback. The police is strict and efficient, and the gates are shut at night. This is equally the custom at Pekin and Timbuctoo. In passing through the streets, I was well satisfied to see vast quantities of English manufactures exposed for sale.

I was present this evening when Mr. Salt received some letters from Alexandria, and Belzoni warned him against thus touching them incautiously, at the same time stating, that as the plague months were fast advancing, every body had, for the last week, to prevent infection, smoked all letters from that city. Mr. Salt informed me that the first year he was in Cairo he was shut up above two months, and continually put in mind of the horrors around him, by the bodies carried before his windows for interment, or the loud lamentations of the hired mourners. The latter I have myself several times heard since I have been here.

Cairo, 11th April, 1818.

A mistake about the dromedaries, which are to carry me to Menouf, has kept me a day longer than I intended, but they will be ready early to-morrow. Both Mr. Salt and Belzoni have been busily employed all the morning in preparing the account of the opening of the pyramid, which I am to take with me. The khamsien or south wind has begun to blow to-day, and is similar to the sirocco of the south of Europe. Every one complained of weariness and a feverish sensation. I found it something like the hot winds at Calcutta; and the period, during the time the khamsien blows, is reckoned very unhealthy.

Mr. Salt and I rode out this evening to the house of Signior Rossi, which I had entered with so much violence on the night of my arrival. This Italian gentleman is mentioned by Bruce. In the yard belonging to the house, being on the side of the river, Mr. Salt had deposited some interesting articles brought from the neighbourhood of Thebes. The first he pointed out to me was the head of Orus. It is ten feet from the top of the mitre to the chin, having a band round the bottom part of it not unlike a turban. It is of red granite, and in very fine preservation. There is an arm 18 feet long of the same statue, with the fist clenched, of excellent proportions. Belzoni thinks he could convey the whole of the figure to England piecemeal, and that it might be placed in any public situation, as one of the greatest and most complete remains of antiquity ever carried out of Egypt. The celebrated French stone has also been removed to this place. It consists of a block of granite about four feet square, and has evidently been an altar. On the sides are figures with draperies, supporting the summit. I hope eventually to see the whole of these in the British Museum.

I have asked Mr. Salt to send, by the first ship from Suez to India, some plants of the date tree. We have the tree throughout that country in great quantities, but from some cause, with which I am unacquainted, the fruit never arrives at perfection. Perhaps, like the apples in the south of England, they may require fresh grafts, or a renewal of the plant. At any rate it is worth trying, as it would be a great addition to the food of the inhabitants: I have offered in return to write for slips of the mangoe trees, which I think would grow in this country.

CHAPTER XXXIII.

Quit Cairo—House belonging to the pacha—Bridge—Delta—Hospitality of the Arabs—Arrive at Menouf—Wells—Mogribee Arabs on their pilgrimage to Mecca—Arrive at Demanhour—A military station—Approach Alexandria—Sleep under the walls—Enter Alexandria—Ruins—Reach the English consul's house—Precaution against the plague—British frigate—Communication with the captain—The princes of Morocco—Plague—The city of Alexandria—Consuls' houses—Pharos—Walls—Dread of the plague—Pillar of Adrian—Plague hospitals—Needles—Bad anchorage—Turtle—Languages—The plague—Force of imagination—Anecdotes—Predestination of the Mahometans—Quarantine—Egypt well worthy of interest—Christians held in good repute—Anecdotes—Visit to the princes of Morocco—Receive their women.

Alexandria, April 15th, 1818.

ABOUT twelve o'clock on the morning of the 12th, I took leave of Mr. Salt, and being provided with a janissary and dromedaries, proceeded across the Delta to Menouf. About four miles from Cairo I passed a house belonging to the pacha, to which, during the time of the plague, he retires into a kind of quarantine; having so far overcome the Mahometan feeling of predestination, from seeing the advantages and safety which the Franks insure to themselves by this precaution, as in some degree to cut himself off from indiscriminate communication with the lower class. About eight or nine miles further is a very handsome stone bridge, built across one of the numerous canals that run from the Nile. It is ornamented with a number of lions, and has a broad and deep Arabic inscription. In some instances like this, and in the court of the lions at the Alhambra at Granada, the Mahometans have conquered their absurd dislike to a resemblance to "any thing that is in heaven above, the earth beneath, or the waters under the earth." The pyramids continued visible for above sixteen or eighteen miles, if not more, and it was with regret that I at last lost sight of them.

The Delta was beautifully cultivated, and being perfectly flat, the scenery was only varied by the villages, more or less distant, indicated by the date trees which surrounded them. We continued travelling till dark, our dromedaries being particularly fine, and enabling us to make great progress. When they are kept out of a walk, their motion is very agreeable, being similar to the amble of a gentle trotting horse.

About eight at night, we crossed a branch of the Nile, in a large ferry-boat, at a small village, where I was absolutely obliged to use violence to prevent being carried by its sheik to his house, to partake of his entertainment. This, I am assured, is ever the case; and therefore Europeans, with a knowledge of the language, might travel throughout Egypt, resting every night at the sheiks' houses, and meeting with the most unbounded hospitality. We pursued our route the whole night, and at nine the next morning reached Menouf. Here I procured horses, and proceeded, after resting half an hour. On the sides of the road, I observed a great number of small brick buildings in the vicinity of wells, with little bowls for travellers to drink.

In the course of this day we met some Mogribee Arabs, or people from the west. Mehumed knew them at a distance from their wearing white dresses made of a kind of flannel, with hoods, not unlike the costume of a monk, which they call benouses. They told us they were upon their pilgrimage to Mecca, having been already five months upon their journey. They looked extremely mean, emaciated, and wretched. Many thousands yearly perish in this useless enterprise; and on the desert, between Cossier and Khenné, vast quantities of their bones are strewed on the road. The pilgrimages in India, of the Hindoos, are still more destructive to the human race, and the numbers who die annually at Jaggernauth, and on the road to it, are stated to be almost incredible. About three, we crossed another branch of the Nile, and towards night passed an encampment of the Bedouin Arabs, which caused some alarm to my attendants, who warned me not to rest, as I was anxious to do, in their immediate vicinity. We continued travelling till twelve, and then tying our horses' legs, lay down for three or four hours. We resumed our way till about twelve o'clock on the 14th, when we reached Demanhour. Here there was some difficulty about procuring horses, and they wished me to take a donkey to carry my despatches; but by threatening them with the name of Ali Pacha, I ultimately received all the assistance I desired. This appeared to be a very large military station, and I counted about 40 pieces of cannon in an open space near the town.

About four miles on this side of Demanhour the cultivation began to decrease, and the desert to encroach upon it, until the whole country became steril and inhospitable. Near six o'clock, we arrived at a village at no great distance from Alexandria; but as I had been cautioned by Mr. Salt, for my own safety as well as the peace of mind of Mr. Lee, the consul, and his family, to avoid the touch of people in Alexandria or its vicinity, I determined not to enter the city that night. We continued along the causeway between the sea and the lake Mariotes, which has been repaired by the pacha. It was destroyed or cut through by our army when before Alexandria. After passing a battery which commanded the causeway, and being assured I was within half an hour's ride of that city, I dismounted, and lay down by the side of the road, wrapped up in my cloak, and slept till daylight this morning.

I then mounted, and proceeded onwards; and passed through a large modern gate and wall, with a ditch, drawbridge, and some heavy guns mounted. From hence to the commencement of the town is a small plain, and the place presented nothing but a heap of ruins. I galloped for a quarter of an hour through the remains of the ancient city (bearing in mind the remembrance of Mr. Salt's caution), before I came to that part which is still inhabited.

From its being commercial, and having gradually declined, the inhabitants have naturally constructed their houses near to the port and shipping. I observed amidst the demolition the vestiges of several porticos unroofed, but the pillars of red granite still standing; and the scene brought to my recollection the ruins of Arungabad, though the style of architecture was totally different. These ruins are in a particularly good state of preservation, and you can trace the shape of the houses by the partition walls, from 20 to 30 feet high, still standing. After passing through them for about a mile or little more, I came to a second gate and wall, which led into an open space where the modern town commences.

By the directions I had received from Mr. Salt, I rode immediately to the consul's house, and alighting, proceeded up a flight of steps to the door of his apartments, where I found the first symptoms of precautions against the plague. There was an outer door made of thick bars of wood, with a little trap-door of about a foot square to receive any thing through, and between it and the inner door was a large bucket of water to contain provisions, and admit of their being immersed for a considerable time before they were taken into the house. As it was very early, the inner door was locked, and from all these precautions, I began to fear the plague had made considerable advances within the last few days, and that I should probably not be admitted to communication; but after some efforts to make them acquainted with my arrival, the door was opened by an Italian servant, and I was allowed to enter, although I found my cloak and baggage were to undergo a quarantine upon the top of the house. None of the family were up, except the servants, and I took possession of an European furnished room, with an excellent English bed, and upon the table files of European papers in all the languages, and from almost all the capitals in Europe.

Mr. Lee's house was upon the sea-shore, looking upon the eastern harbour; but neither the excellent bed, nor my anxiety for European news, retarded, for an instant, my approaching the window, where even the view of the celebrated Pharos became a far inferior object to a British frigate lying at anchor two miles from the shore. I felt assured it must be the Tagus, and I was soon put out of all doubt, by one of the partners of Mr. Lee's house coming into the room, who informed me that both Captain Dundas and my brother would be on shore to breakfast. Mr. Lee received me with the greatest kindness, and soon after breakfast, a boat from the ship brought on shore several officers, amongst whom was my brother. I returned with him on board, and found Captain Dundas, who has, though contrary to his orders, been so kind as to promise me a passage to some port in Europe. This appears to me rather extraordinary, after having come from India, where all the different departments and establishments never fail to aid each other for the public service; and I think it is a cruel situation in which to place an officer, that to meet the exigency of a service for the advantage of his country, he is obliged to break through an order allowing of no exceptions. Perhaps some prohibiting clause may be necessary to prevent the unbounded hospitality and kindness of the officers of the navy; yet surely it ought to be left to the discretion of a captain commanding a frigate, to admit on board his ship those he may deem necessary for the good of his Majesty's service. Fortunately, in this instance, I met an officer, like the generality of those in the navy, ever anxious to forward the interests of their country, and to be of assistance to their brethren in arms, as was invariably remarked during the whole of the Peninsular war; and I trust the cordiality and good will which I have always witnessed may exist between the two services, as long as Great Britain remains an empire.

I find there is no chance of our sailing for four or five days, as their imperial highnesses Muly Ali Sahib and Muly Omar Sahib, the princes of Morocco, will not be ready sooner than that period. The plague betrays its existence in the city by occasionally carrying off a victim; and it has of late shewn itself in the quarter of the Franks, and on board a Maltese vessel, having destroyed the captain and several of the crew within the last week. It is not, however, considered of importance enough absolutely to shut up the houses of the merchants; but, unused to those pests since December last, I do not feel quite comfortable, and shall be truly glad when we quit this "city of the plague."

On board his Majesty's ship Tagus, April 20, 1818.

During the few days I spent at Alexandria, I had some opportunities of seeing it, and found Secundra, as it is called in India, here changed by the Turks into Iskanderea or Ischanderea. It is curious I should thus have reached the most eastern and southern limits of Alexander's conquests, in both of which he has left the vestiges of his name. The houses at present inhabited are evidently modern, and those of the consuls, or as they are designated collectively, the quarter of the Franks, consist of large buildings three stories high, built round a court-yard, containing numerous apartments for the merchants, and spacious warehouses beneath. These have only one entrance, in order to be prepared against the plague, should they be obliged to shut up. The quarter of the Franks is situated on the new harbour, being to the west of the pier on which the celebrated Pharos is built; the other, or old port, being to the westward. At the end of this pier, consisting of several arches, stands the castle, which is modernized, and does not possess the appearance of strength, although many heavy cannon are mounted on it. On this flies the Turkish flag, of deep blood colour; and to give, I suppose, the impression of readiness for action, the sponge and rammers of the guns are constantly crossed over their muzzles. However imposing this may seem, if I may judge from what I have seen of the Turkish soldiers in Egypt, the sentries on guard were in all probability employed lethargically with their coffee and pipes. The present wall which surrounds Alexandria has been built by the pacha, and though I walked out of the city to Adrian's pillar, vulgarly called Pompey's, and several times amongst the ruins, yet I did not see any remains of the old wall. But I did not gratify my curiosity to its utmost extent, as it was unsafe, or gave grounds for alarm to Mrs. Lee, lest we should come accidentally in contact with the inhabitants in their long woollen dresses, which are particularly susceptible of carrying the plague. The pillar of Adrian, which has been so often mentioned, is about 800 or 1000 yards from the walls. It stands upon a small height, which renders it very perceptible from the sea, whence it is used as a landmark. It rests on a square pedestal of several large stones. The base is a surprising stone of enormous magnitude. The shaft is one entire piece of granite, and has originally been beautifully polished, which when you stand under the pillar and look up the western side, sheltered from the sand and winds blowing from the desert, is very visible in the glassy surface. The capital is coarsely carved. The admiration felt by all who have looked upon it took possession of my feelings to the greatest degree. I think it, without exception, the finest thing I ever saw. It is difficult to imagine how it was possible to raise so vast a mass, and to place it on its pedestal; and the ancients having succeeded in this effort, gives us an astonishing idea, even beyond what is excited at Dendera, of the pitch to which they had reached in the science of mechanics.

There is a Greek plague hospital building in the city, and I believe another attached to a catholic convent. The needles or obelisks of Cleopatra, which are supposed to have stood at the end of an avenue leading to her palace, are situated within one hundred yards of the sea amidst the ruins: the building or palace to which they led has been long destroyed, as the ruins of houses and foundations are crowded round their vicinity. I regret that I had not time to see the catacombs in the neighbourhood, but it would not have been right to have rendered Mrs. Lee's family more uneasy, since, as it was, upon our returning from a walk, the impression upon our minds of the necessity of avoiding the touch of people in the street remained so strong, that, when we met in a room, to use a sailor's expression, "we gave each other a wide birth."

The anchorage of Alexandria is particularly rocky, and the cables and anchor-stock of the frigate were much chafed while she lay off the port. Alexandria and its approach from the sea have been likened to Madras, but the latter is far superior, having a few hundred yards to the southward a continuation of the most beautiful and luxuriant foliage, whereas at Alexandria all is brown and sterile. Bordeaux has also been reckoned similar to Calcutta, but Garden Reach surpasses every thing I have seen upon the Garonne below that city. The Egyptian turtles are as celebrated as those of the West Indies, being exactly of the same kind; yet this is not the only place where the *finest* turtle are to be had, the islands in the eastern archipelago of India being equally celebrated for them. Italian appears to be the language most used in Alexandria, and, as I am informed, throughout the Levant. I have several times heard Turkish spoken, which is particularly soft, and sounds not unlike Italian.

During our stay at Alexandria, exposed as we were daily to the plague, it is impossible to describe the general alarm. The nerves of the European merchants, who reside in a country of eternal dread, must be of the stoutest texture; and it may be truly said, that every shilling they amass is dearly earned. This horrid disease is stated never to have quitted Alexandria for the last six years, not even during the hottest and coldest months, though extremes of heat and cold in general check its progress, if they do not annihilate it altogether. Within the tropics it was never, that I am aware of, known till within the last three years, when, as I was informed by Captain Blast, it appeared at Juddah on the Red Sea. Of late years it has not visited India, although we learn from Sir Thomas Rowe during the time of his embassy, the imperial court could not go to Agra on acount of it. Whether this was a malignant fever, which resembled the appalling pestilence, it is impossible to say. At present, happily, it is only throughout the Turkish empire and states of Barbary that it exists as a prevailing epidemic. The subjects of the Porte in Constantinople always refer its origin to Alexandria, and those in Alexandria return the compliment to those at Constantinople. The truth is, that it continues smouldering in the great disseminators of the plague, the warehouses for old clothes, so blindly purchased by the Mahometans, who, throwing themselves upon the immutable decrees of fate, fear no exposure to its direful influence. During the time we were at Alexandria, Mrs. Lee one morning entered the room with the evident appearance of extreme apprehension, and, hesitating, seemed to be an unwilling bearer of bad news. She called Captain Dundas out to inform him that a slave belonging to the French consul, with whose house they had daily and intimate intercourse, had been that morning seized with the plague, and it was impossible to say where or on whom it might be about to shew itself. I cherish the hope that I may never again experience the painful sensation of fear respecting this horrid disease being brought so home to us. I am confident that we all suffered more than we chose to admit, though we felt it necessary by forced gaiety to try to raise each other's spirits. It laid hold so strongly on our imaginations that several of us, returning from the shore to the ship, concurred in thinking that we felt the most acute pains in the glandular parts of the body, where swellings afford the worst symptoms of the disease.

In the course of the day the gentleman belonging to Mr. Lee's house, whom I had seen the first morning of my arrival, informed us that he was alarmed, and not without reason, at having the day before, in putting back his dish of coffee at the French consul's, touched by accident this very slave's hand, and that he had particularly remarked it, from its being customary as much as possible to avoid touching them. This was very unpleasant to every one present, as we had been in constant communication with this gentleman for the last forty-eight hours, and were fully persuaded, that in all human probability, if he had caught the infection, we should not have long cause to boast of our exemption. It was also very distressing to observe how fully he was aware of his situation, as he would not enter the house; and we shewed the dread we had of him by keeping at a respectful distance, and by the earnestness with which we watched all his movements. In short, I pray God I shall never again be in a city where this horrid scourge is known to exist. In consequence of this alarm, the woollen carpets were removed, and in this state of suspense we continued until we sailed, leaving all at Alexandria in expectation of its being still worse, as they were then only at the commencement of the plague months.

Some articles are more susceptible than others, and experience has proved that some will not convey infection. For instance, wood, metals, oil-cloth, grain, never communicate it; while wool, linen, paper, and almost every other article, are highly to be dreaded. Hot bread, feathers, and wool, are supposed to be the most dangerous, and it is said that ten years will not eradicate infection from a feather bed. The Mahometans, excepting in the instances I have mentioned, take no precautions whatever against it, their dogma of predestination being one of the great causes of its spreading with such facility. When this scourge ravaged Cairo or Alexandria, none, till lately, thought of securing themselves against contagion; and though the dead are carried through the streets in great numbers, and the hired mourners are engaged in every house, with their cries and lamentations ascending around, still the Mahometans did not frequent them the less, even when the bearers carrying the corpses thrust by and touched them at the corner of every turning. This belief in predestination extends itself to a very great degree, and, amongst their historians, it is not an uncommon thing to introduce the bad success of an individual by sentences similar to the following—"For his destiny was upon its decline," or, "his fortune was not at its meridian." They have also a verse to the following purport, "By no scheme and by no contrivance is one's destiny to be escaped, be it by a hoary old man or an inexperienced youth." The same feeling does not, however, keep them from trusting at times to flight when on the defeated side in war. This is very inconsistent; for though it is not surprising that their instinct of self-preservation should make them attempt to escape the sword of the conqueror, still in the case of the plague, which commits more ravages than its inferior curse, war, they do not endeavour to fly from it.

The quarantine, to which all are liable on returning from any of these countries, must be a great drawback upon Europeans visiting the East; still, however, what I have seen of Egypt has rendered me anxious to see more of it. The astonishing facility of travelling, all the interesting remains being absolutely on the banks of the river, and the attention shewed to Christians, ought to induce more of our idle countrymen to examine this interesting country.

Christians and Franks, who were wont, during the time of the Mamelukes, to be treated with great indignities, are now, under the present government, in perfect safety. This is no doubt from the pacha's finding them of use to him, and proves how much the character and manners of a people partake of those of their government. His liberality and good sense have placed Europeans at the head of his various manufactories; and thus they have gained a footing of respectability without the aid of a knowledge of medicine, which was for time immemorial the only path to favour and toleration. The pacha has within the last two years afforded a strong, and, I believe, unexampled instance of summary justice, where the crime has been perpetrated against a Christian. The daughter of one of the consuls in Cairo (if I remember rightly, the French), was, whilst walking, shot dead by a drunken Turkish soldier: Mr. Salt's janissary seized the assassin, and on its being made known to the pacha, within a few hours afterwards, in one of the most public places of Cairo, was exposed to view the headless corpse of the ruffian, with a paper on its breast stating that the cause of the execution was the murder of a Frank. In the time of the Mamelukes the Christians were not allowed to ride on horses. This degrading distinction is now abolished.

In the cities of the states of Barbary a Christian (as I have understood) is perpetually liable to insult, being even spit at and pelted with stones by the children; but here I never met with any thing of the kind, and when in the most populous streets of Cairo purchasing a pipe, in two instances, the Turkish soldiers from the vicinity brought and offered me coffee. But there have been exceptions; for Belzoni told me that he had been twice ill treated, once by a Turk on horseback riding against him, and with the edge of his sharp shovel-like stirrup cutting him severely in the leg. On the other occasion, at one of the Mahometan religious festivals, a Turkish soldier fired his pistol at him within a few yards, but fortunately missed him. As to myself, during the whole time I was in Egypt, even without passports from the pacha, having only my janissary, excepting my little fracas (which was certainly not intentional) with the Turkish soldiers on the banks of the Nile, and the occasional hooting of the children at my cocked hat, as those of christian parents would probably do at the turban of a Turk in the streets of London, I never met with a single insult. My red jacket was every where sufficient to point me out as an *Inglaz;* and, as Sir Robert Wilson says, in the time of the occupation of the country by our army, "the red coat appeared to me to be as much respected as the turban of Mahomet." Whenever at a loss, in the absence of my interpreter, to find amusement for the bystanders and keep them in good humour, a mutual inspection of each other's arms was my usual resort; and the peculiarity of a spring on the outside of the lock of my pistols, which secured them at half-cock when let down from the full, drew forth many remarks and symptoms of surprise.

I invariably entered into all the coffee-houses with the Turkish soldiers, always treating them as my equals; for an officer, belonging to a disciplined army, will soon see that there is but little or no subordination in that of the Turks, and but little difference either in appearance or respectability between the officers and men. I used often, by attempting to pronounce the Arabic gutturals and difficult words, to keep half a score of ragamuffin savages in high glee, and none of them were contented without giving me a word for trial.

On the morning of the 17th I accompanied Captain Dundas to pay our respects to the princes of Morocco. The eldest, Muly Ali, is about twenty-five, and the youngest, Muly Omar, about seventeen. They are in charge of a man of very large property, of the name of Hadjee Talub Ben Jelow, who commanded the caravan from Fez to Cairo. They were in a wretched hovel, and seemed quite determined to make us wait their conveniency. On the morning of the 19th, however, we received their women and suite on board, and their royal highnesses in the evening; so that, including the princes, we have at present seventeen women and twenty-eight men on board, in consequence of their having hired at Alexandria an English merchant vessel * to take their baggage and three hundred more attendants to Morocco.

* This vessel carried the plague to Tangiers, and the escape we had from this scourge getting on board the frigate can only be fully felt when I state, that we had daily communication with it during the whole time we were at Alexandria, and that many trunks and boxes were removed from it several times.

CHAPTER XXXIV.

Good passage to Malta—Quarantine—Manners of the young princes of Morocco—Muly Ali—Muly Omar—Very devout—Accounts of Ali Bey—Hadjee Talub Ben Jelow—Women—Pilgrimage—Our interest to keep well with the Emperor of Morocco—Route of the young princes to Mecca from Fez—Accounts of Timbuctoo—Its size—The king—Houses—Negroes—Cows—The Nijer—Inland sea of fresh water—Boats—Fish—Cocoa nuts—Beasts of prey—Elephants—Method of hunting these animals—Commerce—Goldin vastquantities—Shullahs—Caravans—Houssa—Massana—Cannibals—Accounts of Mungo Park and Lieutenant Martyn—Possibility and practicability of an Englishman reaching Timbuctoo—The author fails in landing on the coast of Spain or at Gibraltar—Arrives in England.

May 6, 1818. Lat. 37° 50′. Long. 1° 36′ East, bearing ten leagues distant from Cape Pallas.

FROM the period of our quitting Alexandria on the evening of the 19th of last month, we had an extraordinarily fine passage as far as Malta, at which place we arrived on the 26th. The frigate lay to, off the quarantine harbour, and Captain Dundas and I proceeded to the Pratique Office. We were hailed from the shore by the sentries, directing us to lower our sail; for so strict does their dread of contagion make them, that should the yard or sail of another vessel come in contact with a boat belonging to a ship from a suspicious port, it would, with all the boatmen, be liable to quarantine. We landed at the Pratique Office, and met there various officers of the government, including General Layard, who commanded during Sir Thomas Maitland's absence. The Pratique Office consists of an open gallery, with two cross-bars distant about fifteen feet; no one being permitted to advance between them. They gave us a number of French and English newspapers, and cautiously requested me, after receiving them, not to permit the wind, which was high, to blow them out of my hands, for should one sheet, impelled by its violence, touch them, they would have been put into durance vile. However, the good people of Malta were well contented to run the risk of catching the plague from five or six turtles which Captain Dundas left on shore. I found it totally impracticable to avoid undergoing a long quarantine had I remained at this port, and, as it is customary for the king's ships to reckon their quarantine from the time they sail from a suspicious port, I determined to continue in the Tagus to Gibraltar, hoping there to get pratique.

We were at times much amused with the manners of the young princes of Morocco. It was natural to expect that they would betray, in their manner of conducting themselves, some evidences of the despotic humours which they could not fail to have imbibed from their education. Accordingly when they began to suffer, as landsmen generally do, from the effects of rough weather which we met with two or three days after our departure, they sent a message to Captain Dundas requiring him to put into port without loss of time, though we were then far out of reach of any harbour, and even out of sight of land. The interpreter was desired to say, that if this was not immediately granted, they would themselves come and expostulate. I believe this speech was dictated by Muly Ali, the eldest, who is at times sullen and overbearing; while the youngest, Muly Omar, is good-humoured, and very pleasing in his manners. He enters into all the amusements with the midshipmen, and is the general favourite on board. The heads of all the Turks are shaved; they all wear turbans, and the generality of them are dressed in what they call a benous, not unlike the monastic dress with a cowl to it. They have a large stone which they brought with them from Mecca for their ablutions, and salt water being considered impure, they consequently place their hands upon this stone and rub themselves with the palms. The princes are extremely devout, and read the Koraun to their priests for several hours every day:

during their prayers, as they are bound always to turn towards Mecca, they frequently refer to the officer of the watch to point out to them, by the compass, in what direction the holy city lies, and I believe, upon some occasions, have been wilfully led astray, and faced the polar star, rather than the kaaba. It being customary for them to pray five times every day, it has of course several times occurred, that after they had ascertained the direction of Mecca and commenced their prayers, the vessel has been put about, and they have found themselves unavoidably placed in the most absurd predicament, with their backs towards the holy city. They have, however, at times taken two or three glasses of wine at the captain's table, though they dine by themselves, and have much provision on board. They tell me they never use coffee in Morocco, and mix with their tea, which they drink in the evening, various dried herbs, particularly rue, and much sugar. They have a number of basins, &c. of gold, well executed. They are much delighted with books and prints, and Captain Dundas has given the youngest a very beautiful drawing of this frigate lying off Corfu. They recollect Ali Bey, at Morocco, and speak of him in the highest terms, denying that he was a Christian. But they totally confuted the assertion of his boasted continence, and stated he had left proofs to the contrary in Morocco. They were most anxious that Captain Dundas and myself should go to Fez, making me promise to write to them. They have a custom of dying the inside edge of the eyelid of a blue colour, which I was informed was done by blowing pounded antimony into it.

Their governor, of the name of Hadjee Talub Ben Jelow, who had charge of them during the whole time of their pilgrimage, is a good-looking man, of very mild manners, and, according to report, of immense property, being a successful merchant. He dresses in the most costly manner, and has many suits of the finest European cloths of different colours. He has a great number of the women belonging to him on board; one of whom he purchased at Alexandria, where she lately arrived from Constantinople, and gave 1100 dollars for her. They have, of course, all been secluded from our view, and when brought on board in the barge were towed by another boat. When the Constantinopolitan woman was unwell, however, and the surgeon desired to see her tongue, upon her shewing some reluctance at uncovering her face, Hadjee Talub ordered her to do so: she is represented as being very fair. Captain Dundas has had much conversation with them through an excellent interpreter, and has acquired much information respecting their route when on their pilgrimage, and the interior of Africa. At these conversations I have generally been present, and he has been so kind as to allow me to look over his notes.

About six years ago, the eldest son of the Emperor of Morocco went upon the same pilgrimage on board his majesty's ship the Druid. Our civility and attention to the emperor's sons in this as well as the former instance originate in its being our interest to keep well with Morocco, as the garrison at Gibraltar is in great part furnished with bullocks from the African coast; and, during the Spanish war, was wholly dependent on that country for this essential supply. I have reason to believe that a frigate was offered to the Emperor of Morocco to take these two princes to Alexandria, when on their way to Mecca, but his majesty thought it too luxurious, and not fulfilling the commands of their prophet; he, however, accepted of it upon their return. They have now been absent from Fez rather better than thirteen months, and gave us the following itinerary of their journey.

They started with a caravan of 27,000 people, and in general travelled about ten hours a day. The person who led the caravan was the guide, accompanied by men carrying red flags, and twenty-five horsemen to clear the way. The princes rode mules. The first day they went from Fez to the river Soubu, which is represented as being of considerable size. At the distance of ten days' march from Fez they reached Tessa, a town belonging to their father, where they remained three days, receiving visits and presents; and then proceeded in ten days more to Sama, on an excellent road with plenty of water. This part of their route was through a rich country and friendly people. Their next advance was into the Algerine country, the inhabitants of which they describe as particularly inhospitable, and addicted to robbery. To a question asked by Captain Dundas, what they did to them if they caught them plundering, it was answered, with the greatest *sang froid*, "generally hang them." Twenty-one days were spent in travelling through the Algerine country, leaving Algiers ten days' journey to the north. Water was found every second day, but no trees were to be seen except the date. This country was thickly inhabited, and had vast numbers of horsemen, with Turks for their chiefs. As the pilgrims had letters to the government of Algiers, they received every attention.

They next entered the country of the Bey of Tunis, leaving Constantine eight or ten days' journey on their left: here they met water every three or four days, and proceeded by Tebez Rafa to Gabes, being in all thirty days from the country of Algiers to that city, where they again saw the sea, and found the people extremely hospitable. At this port about 4000 of the caravan quitted them to go by sea to Alexandria. They were ten days on their route from Gabes to Tripoli, five days of which along the sea-shore was exceedingly difficult and laborious travelling, and the proportion of water very small. On their quitting Gabes, and being left by the 4000 men who went by sea, the caravan was reduced to 19,000 souls. When within four days' march of Tripoli the pacha sent 100 camels or horses laden with provisions, &c. to meet them, affording a proof of the strong attachment observable among Mahometans to each other when they meet in distant countries; and it is some compensation to human nature that a religion so degradingly pregnant with imposture and absurdity should thus form a mutual bond for the exercise of hospitality and all the kind affections.

They rested at Tripoli ten days, and when they quitted it, the pacha accompanied them half a day's journey from the city, and treated them with a magnificent review of his cavalry. Indeed his civility proceeded still further, for he not only gave them 100 camels laden with provisions, but furnished them with a ship to carry their heavy baggage to Alexandria; and was remunerated by a present from the Emperor of Morocco of twenty horses, a sabre, and a gun set with diamonds. Twenty-five Tripolins convoyed them seven days on their march, which was constantly along the sea-shore, leaving, as they were told, Fezan on their right, and finding water generally every third day. They were twenty-eight days on their route from Tripoli to Bengazy, and passed through various towns. The Pacha of Bengazy shewed them the utmost respect, and came out half a day's journey to meet them, accompanied by 200 black people dressed as soldiers, each with a musquet and two pistols: he brought them two days' provision for the caravan, and also fifty camels. After resting three days at Bengazy, they proceeded towards Cairo; their route was generally along the sea-shore, and they were informed that they left a place called Bomba five days' journey on their left. They found water every three or four days, and passed the ruins of many towns. They then struck across the desert to Cairo, being twenty-nine days from Bengazy to that city. They halted fourteen days at Cairo, and then joined the caravan which was proceeding to Mecca along the eastern coast of the Red Sea. The caravan consisted of 50,000 people, and generally travelled by night, being protected by the troops of the Pacha of Egypt, and furnished with lights at his highness's expense to facilitate their marches during the darkness. They were distressed for water in this part of their route, and were thirty-four days in journeying from Cairo to Mecca, as they usually rested every fourth day. They stopped in Mecca twenty-one days, performing their various duties, and then, in ten days, proceeded to Medina, where they remained four days. The princes travelled in a box slung between two camels, similar to a sedan, and the women, who accompanied the caravan, rode in panniers slung on each side of a camel. From fatigue and other causes, they lost upwards of 900 of these animals. They returned to Cairo in thirty days, and the remainder of the time was expended at Alexandria waiting for the Tagus frigate, after they had been above nine lunar months constantly travelling.

But what has caused most interest amongst us is a discovery we have made that Hadjee Talub Ben Jelow, as well as several others on board, have been several times at Timbuctoo on commercial speculations; and, as the governor is very communicative, he has answered a number of questions put to him by Captain Dundas and myself. As we were well aware of the diversity of opinions respecting the size and situation of that city, it was the first subject to which we drew his attention. Upon inquiring about Tombuctoo, the hadjee laughed at our pronunciation, the name of the city being Timbuctoo: it is situated about two hours' journey from the great river. He says the king of Timbuctoo is a negro, and resides at Kabra, which is the port of Timbuctoo, being upon the Nijer. The houses, he states, are low and mean: the inhabitants have no shops, but there are stalls for selling the necessaries of life under leather tents. The habitations are built of clay and loose stones, though some of them must be two stories high from their having stairs. He says there are mosques at Timbuctoo, which agrees with the evidence of Hadjee Benata, who asserts "that there are Mahometans there," and some of "no religion at all:" while Hadjee Talub's account is that all religions are tolerated: the majority of the inhabitants are, according to his description, negroes. The cow at Timbuctoo has a hump upon its shoulder, and appears rather larger than the Indian cow: these the natives ride on. In 1807 the king's name was Boobkier, that of the queen Fatima: the dress of the latter is represented to be a short blue petticoat with a stripe of lace; his was said to have cost 100 dollars at Timbuctoo. With respect to the Nijer, he states that it runs towards the east, or as he terms it, towards Mecca. He has invariably called it the Nil, but another person on board, of the name of Hadjee Benata (whose bad state of health for a length of time prevented our gaining much information from him), calls it Dan, but confirms the interesting fact which was so long contested, of the river running to the east. The Nijer is reported to be a quarter of a mile broad at Kabra, but in the summer it is much more considerable. Hadjee Talub has understood that the river runs into a large fresh water sea in the interior of the country, which he calls Behur Soldan; that from this sea the Nile of Egypt takes its rise, so that he calls it the same river; and that half-way to Cairo there are great falls and cataracts which prevent boats from passing. This account of the source of the Nile may, however, be reasonably doubted. The boats on the river are of a middling size, flat-bottomed, having no sails, and being constructed without nails. They are formed of the bark of trees, and some of them are as large as a frigate's launch, or about twenty-eight feet long. Our informant Hadjee Talub adds, that crocodiles abound in the river, are very voracious, and are taken by being harpooned with an instrument with five prongs. There are vast quantities of fish in the Nijer, which, from their colour and size, are supposed to be salmon. Hadjee Benata states, that Timbuctoo is three times the size of Alexandria; and Hadjee Talub conceives the population to be about 60,000, and represents their character as being good and friendly, though he has heard of people being shot for theft, and of offenders being beat on the back with the skin of an animal dried and cut into thongs. He says there are cocoa nuts and dates in abundance, and water melons in great plenty, but all grow wild, there being no garden whatever. The woods in the neighbourhood of Timbuctoo are described as being full of game, and lions and beasts of prey are often seen in the neighbourhood of the town. Hares and rabbits are in vast quantities, and the only dog they have is a greyhound, which is trained to catch these animals: cats they have none. The city is well supplied with every kind of provision, and it is customary for the natives to eat elephant's flesh, which animal is stated to exist in immense herds in the vicinity. Their flesh appeared palatable to Hadjee Talub, tasting like beef, but being quite white. They are ferocious animals, and will attack single persons, which obliges men who ride alone to carry a horn to frighten them away. There are two methods of hunting the elephants, one by driving them into the river, where men by swimming get on their backs and cut and destroy them; the other by driving them into pits, and there butchering them: a few are tamed.

As to their commerce, it is carried on between Fez and Timbuctoo generally by caravans, which leave the former place in March and October, as does that of Mecca at the same season. The articles which sell best at Timbuctoo are salt, tobacco, European scarlet cloth, and English printed cottons, besides pistols and guns. This traffic returns elephants' teeth (of which two are so large as to be a load for a camel), slaves, and gold. The gold is generally in small bags, in each of which is an ounce, valued at fifteen dollars: it is extremely pure and fine: they have also pieces of gold weighing about five ounces. This precious article is very common, and comes from the south-west, where it is found in great quantities. The negroes wear bracelets and other ornaments of this metal, and Hadjee has presented Captain Dundas with some gold articles, consisting of part of a necklace, a pair of ear-rings, and some braids for the hair, similar to the filigree work of the archipelago of the Eastern Seas; which he states that the workmen manufactured as they do in Java and Sumatra, in the house of their employer, by whom they are hired like journeymen. The price of a male slave is from sixteen to twenty dollars.

He speaks of a tribe called Shullahs, who are a savage race, living in leather tents, and of a warlike and brave spirit. They dress with the turban, and place it in many folds round their head and face, so as to project a great way, serving as a guard, and leaving only the eye uncovered. They are armed with a long sword, sharp on both sides, though some of them carry a javelin. For defence they have a shield made of leather, about five feet long and four broad, which covers their whole persons. Their dress consists of a blue shirt and white trowsers. He represents the women as being very fat, and having a protuberance behind like the Hottentot women of whom we have heard so much. The Shullahs receive a certain tribute from the negroes of Timbuctoo, and never cross the river. During the summer they remain two days' journey to the east, but in winter come close to the city. Their women perform all the agricultural labours in the field.

We made inquiries respecting the caravans from Fez to Timbuctoo, and from Timbuctoo in various other directions. He says he travelled by the regular caravan in three months and ten days from Fez to Timbuctoo, but the year after he went the same journey with a guide and two guards in twenty-nine days, on a herrie, performing four days' journey in one. There is no want of water during the winter time; but hordes of Arabs attack travellers at that season. The herrie is mentioned as being the fleetest animal that can be conceived; it is like a dromedary, but is as superior in speed to the generality, as a race horse is to a cart horse.

There runs a tradition that there was at one time a regular caravan from Timbuctoo direct to Cairo, but the distracted state of the

A Sketch of some of the GOLD ORNAMENTS worn by the WOMEN of TIMBUCTOO.

Nº 1. Part of a Necklace. Nº 2. An Anclepiece. Nº 3. Earings. Nº 4. Braids for the Hair.

Copied from the originals in the possession of Captⁿ Dundas, H.M.S. Tagus: by C.R.Malden.

country has of late rendered it so unsafe as to prevent it altogether. Indeed, as two Shullahs accompanied the caravan from Fez to Mecca, having come from Timbuctoo for that purpose, Captain Dundas thinks, in which Hadjee Talub agrees with him, that there is now no direct communication between that city and Cairo. With respect to intercourse toward the east and south-east, our traveller speaks of Houssa being a considerable city, but at such a distance from Timbuctoo that the latter city is only half-way between it and Fez. It is described to be a place of great traffic, where the cloth used by the inhabitants of Timbuctoo is manufactured. Neither he nor Hadjee Benata know any thing of Wassana, although they are acquainted with a large place, twenty days' journey south-east from Timbuctoo, called Massana. Indeed the latter states that his mother came from thence. Beyond this place, to the south-east, are a people who eat their prisoners.

During our various conversations, Hadjee Talub mentioned, that eleven years ago, in 1807, when at Timbuctoo, he heard of two white men, who came from the sea, having been near that city. This was the year before he arrived at Timbuctoo, and he understood that the white men sold beads, as they had no money to purchase grain. He adds, that they went down the Nile to the eastward, and that general report stated that they had died of the climate. This appeared to Captain Dundas and myself to allude to, and certainly all circumstances tend to prove that these persons were Mr. Park and Lieutenant Martyn, who would have arrived there about that period. However, the pacific conduct and friendly intercourse mentioned by Hadjee Talub disagrees with the journal of Amadi Fatouma, who speaks of hostility taking place off Timbuctoo, which city is not on the Nijer; and in what regards the fate of these gentlemen, they differ as to the mode of their death.

It was natural that we should attempt to ascertain if it was practicable for a Frank to pass from Fez to Timbuctoo, and if he thought the Emperor of Morocco would assist the views of any Englishmen in reaching that city, which he answered with the greatest confidence in the affirmative. As to any danger with the caravan, he expresses a conviction that there is not the slightest; but singly, he thinks, that great risks would be hazarded. I further asked him whether, if duly rewarded, he would accompany me to Timbuctoo, to which he assented with the utmost readiness; and added, that we could reach that city in forty-seven days from Fez on horseback, and that he would forfeit his life if he did not bring me back safe.

I conceive from this, from the universal renown of our nation, and from the friendly terms on which we stand with all the world, that a British agent properly accredited, and his objects fairly stated, namely, commerce and rational curiosity, could not fail of being not only safe, but well received, and put in a situation to solve the great geographical problem of the *course and termination of the Nijer.*

After a tedious voyage up the Mediterranean, being refused permission to land both on the coast of Spain and at Gibraltar, lest we should have the plague amongst us, I got on board the packet at Gibraltar, arrived on the 14th of June at Falmouth, and on the 16th in London, where I found that Captain M'Ra had outstript me by 14 days.

REMARKS ON THE BONES FOUND IN THE SECOND PYRAMID.

SINCE my arrival in England, the bones supposed to have been those of King Cephrenes, who is, upon the authority of Herodotus, stated to have been the founder of the second pyramid and buried in it, have given rise to much remark.

Belzoni, on opening the pyramid, found them in the sarcophagus, and added the remainder to several he had previously given me, on my mentioning that it was my intention to place them in the British Museum.

I shewed them to Sir Everard Home, who carried them to Mr. Clift, who has charge of the Hunterian Museum, in order to ascertain, through that gentleman's extensive knowledge of comparative anatomy, and means of inquiry offered by the great collection of bones of all animals in the museum, what they really were. After having them in his possession for a few days, he informed me, on returning them, that they were those of an animal of the bos genus, and forwarded to me the accompanying account of them, specifying the distinct portions of bones of which they consisted:—

1. A portion of the body of an *os humeri.*

2. The outer portion of the lower articulation of the right *os humeri.* Its anterior surface.

3. The neck of the right *os femoris,* before the union of the epiphysis. The deep *fossa* at the root of the *trochanter major.*

4. What appears to be a portion of the upper part of the neck of the left *os femoris.*

5. The inner condyle of the right *os femoris.* The latter is affixed to the anterior part of the bone.

N. B. All the specimens have a very pungent salt taste.

The surgeon of the Tagus frigate, in the Mediterranean, had seen them during our voyage, and had expressed his doubts as to their being human; from which opinion originated many and various speculations.

This decision, from such good authority as that of Mr. Clift, naturally suggests the idea that the pyramids may not have been, as generally supposed, the burial-places of the kings; but more probably those of the god Apis, venerated in their immediate vicinity—Memphis being the city of his residence. The authority upon which the notion of their being the tombs of the kings has been often doubted, so as to allow of many theories being formed respecting them, and when it is considered that it rested only on the communications of the priests of Egypt to Herodotus, (to whom they also stated that there were no chambers in the second pyramid, which has now, by being opened, proved the incorrectness of their assertions) it is still more weakened, and may even suggest a suspicion that they had themselves, at that time, but a very imperfect and perhaps only a traditional account of these monuments. Diodorus Siculus does not look upon the authority of Herodotus as conclusive, and gives a narrative differing from that of the father of history. He says that Chemmies built the first pyramid, whereas Herodotus states that Cheops was its founder; and although he must have been well acquainted with the assertion of the last historian, he assigns two distinct eras for their erection, and dissents, considerably, from him respecting the second pyramid. But so uncertain is this point to history, that he mentions several other persons who were reported to have been their founders. He also records as a fact, what Herodotus only notices from hearsay, that neither of the kings, their founders, were buried in them; as they had so incensed their subjects by the cruelty and toil they had undergone in raising these vast structures, that they threatened to drag their corpses out of their burial-places, and it was, therefore, their last wish and command to their servants to bury them in some unknown place. The priests of Egypt having erred in their account of the second pyramid, and many persons having, previously to this discovery, maintained opposite theories on the subject, without having, antecedent to the present period, any data to build upon, perhaps many will agree with me that they are the burial-places of the god Apis, and not of men; but should Belzoni succeed in opening the third pyramid, the point will be ascertained. The contents of the great pyramid, it should also be recollected, are unknown, as it has been open from time immemorial, and its deposit carried off. And the hypothesis I have offered will gather force, when it is further considered, in addition to the circumstances I have mentioned, that it is more probable that superstition should have induced the erection of these buildings than despotic rule, or veneration for an individual. From their size, the sarcophagi, both that in the great pyramid and that in the one lately opened, are capable of containing four dead bodies, and it would appear that they were, in all probability, intended for a larger animal. The former has occasioned many surmises on its large capacity; but if we suppose them to have contained the bull, all these will vanish: and that this was the case the bones must prove, since it cannot for an instant be believed that the Arabs can have placed them there, as, for reasons I have before stated in the body of the work, the second pyramid was in all probability closed in a short time after it was visited by the sovereigns. That the ancient Egyptians used to bury animals in sacred chests we learn from Herodotus, who states that the Thebans, when they annually sacrificed them to Jupiter, concluded the ceremony by enshrining the carcase in a vessel of that kind. He further tells us that the female animals of the canine species, and the ichneumon, were buried at Bubastis in consecrated chests; and that the expense lavished on the burial-places of the god Apis was immense. We learn also, from Diodorus Siculus, speaking of the burial of this god in the reign of Ptolemy Lagus, that the person who had charge of him not only spent a large sum he had collected, but borrowed of the king 50 talents of silver for the same purpose.

In the late discovery amongst the tombs of the kings of Thebes, (here, perhaps, also, too readily pronounced regal mausoleums) Belzoni has reason to believe that the most superb and magnificent was for the reception of the body of Apis; and so confident is he of it, that in a plan of the ruins he has given me, he calls it the tomb of Apis.

THE END.